ORGANIZED

LABOR

AND

THE NEGRO

Organized Labor
and the Negro

HERBERT R. NORTHRUP

*Formerly Instructor in Economics, Cornell University; Economist,
Tool and Die Commission, Regional War Labor Board, Detroit;
Consultant, President's Committee on Fair Employment Practice*

FOREWORD BY

SUMNER H. SLICHTER

Lamont University Professor
Harvard University

HARPER & BROTHERS PUBLISHERS
NEW YORK AND LONDON

KRAUS REPRINT CO.
Millwood, New York
1976

ORGANIZED LABOR AND THE NEGRO

Copyright, 1944, by Harper & Brothers

Printed in the United States of America

*All rights in this book are reserved. No part of the
book may be reproduced in any manner whatsoever without written permission except in the case of brief quotations embodied in critical articles and reviews. For
information address Harper & Brothers*

FIRST EDITION

B - T

Library of Congress Cataloging in Publication Data

Northrup, Herbert Roof, 1918-
   Organized labor and the Negro [by] Herbert R. Northrup.
Foreword by Sumner H. Slichter. [1st ed.] New York,
Harper; New York, Kraus Reprint Co., 1971 [ᶜ1944]

   xviii, 312 p.   23 cm.

   Bibliography: p. 289-302.

   1. Negroes—Employment. 2. Trade-unions—U. S.—Negro
membership. 3. Labor and laboring classes—U. S. I. Title.
E185.8.N65   1971   331.88'0973   74-157520

ISBN 0-527-67640-3

Reprinted with the permission of Herbert R. Northrup
KRAUS REPRINT CO.
A U.S. Division of Kraus-Thomson Organization Limited

Printed in U.S.A.

This Book

is for

My Mother and Father

CONTENTS

FOREWORD
TO REPRINT EDITION

Organized Labor and the Negro was the product of my experiences and research during the latter part of the thirties and the early forties. A native of New Jersey, I made my first trip south when I entered Duke University, Durham, North Carolina, in September 1935. Durham is a manufacturing town, with prominent tobacco and textile industries. The special condition of Negroes in the South was all new to me. At this time also, labor unions were stirring, with John L. Lewis having organized the Committee for Industrial Organization, which was soon to alter the industrial relations status quo in the United States. I was particularly interested as an undergraduate in the organization of the tobacco workers along racial lines, and my interest in this was furthered by Professor Frank T. deVyver, as well as by other members of the Duke faculty, who encouraged me to go on with my studies.

In September 1939, I entered Harvard University for the prime purpose of studying under the late Professor Sumner H. Slichter, who has remained a source of inspiration to me. Professor Slichter immediately encouraged my interest in industrial race relations and obtained for me the position of Research Assistant with the "Negro in America" survey, conducted under the direction of the Swedish economist, Gunnar Myrdal, and sponsored by the Carnegie Corporation of New York. Serving two summers in this capacity, I was able to travel extensively through the South, as well as to do considerable library research. I wrote my dissertation on this subject and it was accepted in October 1942. For the next year I continued the research while serving as an Instructor in Economics at Cornell University, and as special consultant to the new President's Committee on Fair Employment Practice. The manuscript was turned in to Harper's in the late summer of 1943 and published in March 1944, just after my twenty-sixth birthday.

Since the book was published, I have continued my interest in industrial race relations, both as a researcher and a practitioner. Once again, thanks to a Ford Foundation grant, I am engaged, with associates at Wharton and other universities, in a major study of the Negro in industry. It is interesting, therefore, for me to examine what has occurred since the book was published.

Insofar as the general picture is concerned, the AFL and the CIO have now merged, and unions have deleted racial bars from their constitutions. Nevertheless, union racial restrictions are still maintained, and certainly unions in the building construction and railroad industries plus those in several others, including paper, trucking, and tobacco, cannot be classified as furthering the interests of Negroes. The union remains, by and large, the servant of its white majority, and in more cases than not the white majority is reluctant to expand jobs for Negroes for fear that that will mean fewer jobs for whites. Moreover, those unions affiliated with the CIO, to which I give considerable credit for equalitarian policies, have over the years had a rather checkered career insofar as Negro members are concerned. The CIO itself, for example, as early as 1948, in an effort to obtain the affiliation of one of the most racist unions in America, the Brotherhood of Railroad Trainmen, offered to give that organization jurisdiction over all railroad workers, despite the fact that the union at that time had a bar to nonwhite members in its constitution, and had worked for years to eliminate Negro railroad employees from their jobs.

Chapter II, which deals with building construction, is remarkably current. The building trades unions remain the most restrictive in the United States. Negro workers have made little progress in opening up the barriers of the plumbing and electrical trades, despite tremendous pressure by law, government, and civil rights bodies, although it now appears that there may be some breakthroughs as a result of massive government pressure. Negroes continue to be far better represented in the trowel trades—bricklaying, plastering, and cement finishing—and in carpentry and painting, than in such trades as electrical, plumbing, and sheet metal, which grew out of the technical developments of the latter part of the 19th and early 20th century, a time in which Jim Crow laws were enacted and opportunities for Negroes were much more restricted than they were even during days of slavery. The relatively superior hold which Negroes have in the trowel trades dates from their use in these occupations during slavery days in the South. Moreover, they are stronger in these trades even today in the South, than they are in other geographical locations with supposedly more liberal outlooks.

The decline in railroad fortunes has obscured the near elimination of the Negro in the railroad industry. What the unions began, technology and competitive modes of transportation have largely accomplished. Unions have revoked their color bars and Negroes are now being employed in occupations from which they had heretofore been excluded. But the Pullman porter, the train porter, thousands of other service jobs and the laboring jobs on the maintenance of way and in the shops, have all been drastically reduced. Employment in the railroad industry has declined substantially from a high of nearly one and one-half million during World War II to less than 700,000 now, and proportionately Negroes have suffered even more. If equal opportunity comes to the railroads, it will come thirty years too late.

The tobacco industry has continued to follow the trends set forth in Chapter IV. The racial occupational segregation pattern remained unaltered until the 1960's. The Tobacco Workers International Union institutionalized it and helped to maintain it. Since mechanization affected largely the jobs in which Negroes were employed, and since Negroes were largely excluded from the cigarette manufacturing industry which expanded during this period, the proportion of Negroes has declined from nearly 100 percent in colonial times to about 20 percent now. The left-wing union which organized the Reynolds Company was ousted in a strike in 1948. Reynolds has remained non-union, and lacking any union restrictions was able to integrate its personnel at an earlier date and more thoroughly than any other of the tobacco companies.

The cotton textile industry described in Chapter V, along with clothing and laundries, has undergone a virtual employment revolution. Unions are still a very minor factor in the industry, but first because of labor needs and then because of government pressure, the industry has become a significant employer of Negroes since 1960. The clothing industry unions have not prospered, and their relations with the Negroes have not lived up to their earlier reputation. In an effort to keep training from the non-union plants of the South, which they apparently cannot unionize, they have persuaded the government to deny training funds to the industry. Since the location of much of this industry in central cities makes it potentially a very valuable employment factor for Negroes, this action has been distinctly anti-Negro in effect. These unions are still managed by the same "establishment" which ran them in the early days, and which has grown old in age and outlook. Laundries, also covered in this chapter, have in the large cities almost a 100 percent Negro complement and great difficulty in obtaining employees. The home laundry and the self-service laundry have eaten heavily into their business.

Chapter VI discusses the longshore work in which the Negroes have had no great problem in obtaining ordinary jobs. Indeed there has probably been some expansion in the percentage of Negroes in this trade. But where there are both Negro and white locals, the white locals still get a disproportionate share of the work, and Negroes have instituted numerous lawsuits in vain efforts to work up into the checker classification, a bastion of lily-white employment. Despite the large numbers of black longshoremen in the dominant union, the status quo largely remains and the union does little about it.

The saddest story since 1944 has occurred in the coal mines (Chapter VII). The United Mine Workers once proudly noted that it had an equalitarian policy exceeded by no other union, and that it set the pace for the CIO's unionization on an equal basis. My research in the early forties, however, revealed that mechanization was disproportionately affecting Negroes in the mines, and that the union was doing little about it. Since then coal industry employment has declined dramatically and membership in the United Mine Workers has fallen from a high of 600,000 to an acknowledged low of 120,000, and a probable accurate low of 75,000. Negro coal miners have been all but eliminated. Pushed by the union's wage and welfare fund policy, the bituminous coal industry dramatically mechanized its operations, substituting machines for men. Meanwhile, competitive fuels—oil and gas—took over much of coal's business. Even the coal carrying railroads converted to oil burning Diesels from coal burning steam locomotives. Negroes were not given an opportunity to work on the machines and gradually left the mines. The United Mine Workers did little or nothing to effectuate equal employment opportunity. Negroes once held nearly one-quarter of the jobs in the Southern Appalachian region but are now becoming extinct as coal miners in many of the states in this area.

The steel industry (Chapter VIII) remains somewhat of a paradox. Negroes continue to hold a high percentage of the skilled jobs, and yet continue to be excluded from others, such as those in the rolling mills. The industry's stagnation in recent years has made it difficult for it to advance the cause of Negro employment. The Steelworkers, which adopted the Mine Workers' equal membership policies, has countenanced discriminatory seniority systems and has looked the other way when some of its locals discriminated. Nevertheless Negroes do play an important role both in the union and the industry and are likely to continue to do so for some time. The shift from blast furnaces to the oxygen system may disproportionately affect Negroes because they are heavily concentrated in blast furnace departments.

The auto industry, discussed in Chapter IX, remains the big success story for Negro employment and Negro union relations. While earlier only Henry Ford admitted Negroes to better jobs, they now comprise a large proportion of the industry's total employment and work in all classifications. Moreover, the United Automobile Workers remains in practice one of the most effective practitioners of equal treatment in the labor movement. Today the industry is beset by radical groups of both whites and Negroes desiring to change its policies and to alter the power relationships within the union. It remains to be seen whether in the stress and strain and as a result of the second riot in Detroit in twenty-five years, the relationships within the union and within the industry can stand.

Since Chapter IX of this book was written, the aircraft industry, now the aerospace industry, has become committed to equal employment opportunity. Its problems are extremely difficult, in view of the disadvantaged educational status of the Negro and the high qualifications necessary for work in the aerospace industry. Nevertheless, this industry, without doubt the most effective trainer of industrial employees in the United States, has made impressive progress.

The shipbuilding industry, the last of the industries discussed (Chapter X), has fallen on evil days since World War II. Very few yards are now open, but Negroes have obtained a substantial proportion of jobs in these yards. The old CIO union has virtually disappeared as an effective force, with the Boilermakers and Shipbuilders taking over. The craft set-up and the demarcation of jobs leads one to believe that upward movement of Negroes will continue to be difficult until the industry is reorganized on a modern production basis.

In the final chapter the following factors were listed as determinants of trade union racial policies:

1. Union racial policies are to a large extent the product of their environment.
2. The philosophy of a union and its leadership exert an important influence on union racial policies.
3. In times of labor shortages, union policies are likely to be more equalitarian than in times of labor surpluses.
4. National union control of such policies as admission and promotion is likely to prove of more benefit to Negroes than local control.
5. The policies of rival unions may induce a more liberal union racial policy, or a relaxation of an equalitarian policy, depending upon the attendant circumstances.

Twenty-five years later I believe I would list the same factors as being most relevant. Let me emphasize again, however, how unions institutionalize the status quo and therefore make it more difficult to change. Certainly my experience in the paper and tobacco industries in modern times emphasizes this.

Insofar as my public policy discussions are concerned in the remainder of this chapter, I think they are still relevant. We have adopted a Fair Employment Practice Committee and the government is moving in, as I felt it necessarily had to, to insure equality of treatment. The plethora of organizations operating in the field prevents the government from speaking with any reasonably unified voice, and actually serves more often to harass than to heal. Nevertheless, I believe government pressure is essential. Experience with the operations of the National Labor Relations Board and its seemingly infinite capacity to rewrite what appears to have been Congressional intent, however, leads me to oppose powers for the Equal Employment Opportunity Commission similar to those lodged in the NLRB.

I closed the book on an optimistic note, and this seemed to be justified for several years after the war. During the 1950's, however, Negro labor suffered disproportionately because of mechanization, layoffs of unskilled labor and continued denial of opportunity. Nevertheless, the optimism now seems to have been well-founded. Negroes have advanced in industry far beyond my expectations of that date. Unions have remained largely a passive force in this process, but have not been a major hindrance, except in a few industries. Fair employment remains fundamentally a management function except in building construction, where management has abdicated its duties to unions.

When *Organized Labor and the Negro* was written, interest in this subject was relatively high but soon died down. Few scholars chose industrial race relations as a field in which to make their contribution. Now, twenty-five years later, it is very fashionable. The great degree of interest in the subject is all to the good. It is hoped that the republication of this book will continue to stimulate interest in a field that now interests so many but which once interested so few.

> Herbert R. Northrup
> Professor of Industry
> and Director
> Industrial Research Unit
> Wharton School of Finance
> and Commerce
> University of Pennsylvania

Philadelphia
February 1971

FOREWORD

By Sumner H. Slichter
Lamont University Professor,
Harvard University

America has prided itself on being a land of opportunity. The careers of millions of European immigrants and the high business birth rate support this claim. The greatest shortcoming in making America a land of opportunity is represented by the barriers which we have imposed against Negroes. These are indeed a black mark on our record—a black mark which we are now struggling to remove.

Mr. Northrup's book is a searching and comprehensive analysis of the influence of unions upon economic opportunity for Negroes. As Mr. Northrup points out, the attitude of unions toward Negroes varies all the way from downright exclusion to full acceptance. Mr. Northrup examines the circumstances that condition the attitudes and policies of unions toward Negroes. How can the variations in union policy toward Negroes be explained? Have the white workers through their unions excluded the Negro only where the Negro was pretty much excluded to begin with, and have they accepted him where he already had a pretty good foothold? Are the policies of craft unions the same as the policies of industrial unions? Are the policies of unions the same in depression as in prosperity? Are the policies of unions the same today as they were a generation ago? Is there evidence of a long-range change in the policies of unions toward Negroes?

Mr. Northrup points out that unions sometimes take the racial employment pattern of the industry as given, and make no attempt to alter it. In the vast majority of cases, however, unions attempt to change the employment policies of employers. In some instances, fortunately few, unions have attempted to exclude Negroes from the industry or, at least, to narrow the field of their employment. The ground which the Negroes lost in some of the skilled trades in the South is partly explained by the policies of a few unions and their Southern locals. In the great majority of cases, however, unions have attempted to broaden the economic opportunities of Negroes and to help them rise to semiskilled or skilled jobs. This is particularly true of industrial unions—though it is not invariably true as recent experiences in the copper mines indicate. The unions which attempt to foster class cleavage in the community are opponents of racial cleavage.

Mr. Northrup has attempted to classify unions by the policies which they pursued toward the admission of Negroes. Where a specific provision in the constitution or the ritual is involved, such classification is fairly simple—although even in these cases one encounters instances every now and then where Negroes have been admitted contrary to the constitution. Where the policy is a matter of practice rather than of formal authorization, the difficulties of classification are formidable. Many unions give their locals a high degree of autonomy with respect to admission of members. In nearly all instances the influence of the national officers of unions is thrown against discrimination. Indeed, a number of national officers have taken their political lives in their hands to fight discrimination against Negroes. The auxiliary local is a case in point. Admittedly, the auxiliary local is no solution to the problem. It is a stopgap. Honest-minded men will disagree over whether it is a step backward or a step in advance. Nevertheless, the men who have fought for the modification of exclusion policies to permit the establishment of auxiliary locals have displayed political courage and have risked political retaliation.

Is progress being made in removing union discrimination against Negroes? The answer seems to be "yes." It is not spectacular progress, but it seems to be real. The constitutional prohibitions against the admission of Negroes are becoming fewer. Whether or not one likes auxiliary locals, one must admit that they are a step in the direction of full equality of treatment for Negroes. The very fact that a union is collecting dues from Negroes means that sooner or later it must give them full voting rights. Nonetheless, there is a long way still to go. Local autonomy cannot be indefinitely permitted to result in the exclusion of Negroes from the union wherever a local wishes to keep them out. Furthermore, when the barriers to admission are removed, Negroes may or may not have a fair chance to advance to skilled jobs.

Mr. Northrup's book has broader interest than a study of the economic opportunities of Negroes. It raises certain fundamental questions about unions. Unions, being democratic organizations, reflect fairly well the prevalent attitudes of the wage earners in the community. But do unions *merely* reflect existing attitudes? Are they *merely* instruments for implementing existing scales of values? Do not unions *modify* attitudes and scales of values? Does not the fact that wage earners have their own organizations, their own opportunities for discussion, their own opportunities to gather facts, their own leaders, all mean that the attitudes and the scales of values of workers are different from what they would have been if no union had existed? The answer seems to be "Yes," and the history of the attitude of unions toward economic opportunity for Negroes illustrates the point. Unions have been greatly influenced by prevailing attitudes toward Negroes and, to a considerable extent, they have instruments for translating these into policies. More important, however, unions have also been vehicles for appraising and modifying the prevailing attitudes of workers. They have been a creative influence.

Another fundamental question raised by Mr. Northrup's study is whether unions are private clubs or quasi-public institutions. They started out as private clubs or fraternal societies. Many of them still retain the traditions and the point of view of such organizations. The growth of unions in numbers and power, however, is causing them to be clothed with a public interest. More and more they are in a position to determine who is permitted to make a living in a particular trade, industry, or locality. Consequently, their admission requirements are becoming a matter of public interest as the laws of New York, Kansas, and Nebraska make plain. Likewise, the manner in which they exercise discipline over their members and deprive men of membership is increasingly becoming a matter of public concern.

PREFACE

The unprecedented growth of organized labor during the past decade and the increasing importance of utilizing the nation's manpower without regard to race, so forcibly demonstrated by the present emergency, call for an impartial study of the effect of the policies of labor unions on the welfare of our country's most important racial minority, the Negro. This book seeks to fill, at least partially, that need. After a discussion of the general picture, which is a rough outline of the entire work, the relation of Negroes to unions in eleven American industries is analyzed. The approach is to examine, first, the position of the Negro in the industry, and then to ascertain how the union's policies affect the welfare of the Negro workers. The concluding chapter summarizes the book's findings and discusses some relevant questions of public policy.

The industries studied are for the most part those in which the proportion of Negroes is significant, and in which labor unions are an important factor in determining personnel policies. Had the time and funds been available, the book would have included chapters on the meat-packing industry, in which Negroes have long been an important part of the labor force, and the electrical products industry, in which Negroes have just recently obtained an important foothold. Such industries as domestic service, southern lumber, and fertilizer, in which large numbers of Negroes are employed, were purposely excluded because of their small degree of unionization. It is felt, however, that the industries chosen for investigation are sufficiently varied so that general conclusions can be reached.

Throughout the book, the South is defined to include the states of Alabama, Arkansas, Florida, Georgia, Louisiana, Mississippi, North Carolina, South Carolina, Tennessee, and Virginia; the border states, to include the states of Kentucky, Maryland, Missouri, Texas, and West Virginia, and the District of Columbia. These definitions have proved serviceable, if arbitrary—and they are no more arbitrary than any others would be.

The basic material for this book was gathered in the field during the summers of 1940-1943. Scores of individuals gave me valuable assistance. It would be impossible to mention all their names. Officials of almost all the unions whose policies are examined were most generous in giving me their time or sending me materials. The fact that I am critical of some of their policies makes my debt to them all the greater. I particularly want to mention Miss Cornelia Anderson, research director, United Cannery and Agricultural Workers; and Messrs. Noel R. Beddow, director, southern region, United Steelworkers; William Blizzard, vice-president District 17, and William Mitch, president, District 20, United Mine Workers; E. J. Brown, president, International Brotherhood of Electrical Workers; George Googe, southeastern director, American Federation of Labor, F. C. Pieper, New Orleans regional director, Congress of Industrial Organizations; Mark Starr, educational director, International Ladies Garment Workers Union; Richard Rohman, publicity director, Amalgamated Clothing Workers; George Kleinman, educational director, International Fur & Leather Workers; George Millner, vice-president, International Longshoremen's Association; R. J. Petree, secretary-treasurer, Tobacco Workers International Union; A. Philip Randolph, president, Brotherhood of Sleeping Car Porters; Williard S. Townsend, president, United Transport Service Employees; and Charles Houston, general counsel, and Joseph Watty, general chairman, Association of Colored Railway Trainmen and Locomotive Firemen, Inc.

The National Urban League placed its facilities at my disposal. Those who were most helpful include Messrs. Lester B. Granger, executive secretary, Julius Thomas and Franklin Nichols, of the national office; and A. J. Allen, Clarence Laws, Edward S. Lewis, Wiley A. Hall, George E. DeMar, Thomas A. Webster, Clifford E. Minton, L. J. Searcy, and John T. Clark of various local offices.

The National Association for the Advancement of Colored People was also of material assistance.

Governmental agencies gave aid on numerable questions. Particular assistance was rendered by Messrs. N. Arnold Tolles and

E. K. Frazier of the Bureau of Labor Statistics; Drs. J. J. Joseph and Robert C. Weaver, of the War Manpower Commission; Father Francis J. Haas and members of the staff of the Fair Employment Practice Committee; and Louis G. Silverberg, director of information, National Labor Relations Board.

The 1940 field trip was undertaken while I was a member of the staff of the "Negro in America" study, sponsored by the Carnegie Corporation of New York. Mr. Charles Dollard, assistant to the president, and Professor Samuel A. Stouffer, acting director of the study, gave valuable time to help me, in addition to providing financial assistance.

To Dr. Paul H. Norgren I owe an especially heavy debt of gratitude. As chief of the labor division of the Carnegie study, he taught me much. If he had not accepted a position in a war agency, he would have by now completed what would undoubtedly have been the most comprehensive book on Negro labor ever published. Unpublished manuscripts written principally by him were of material aid to me in writing Chapters I, II, VII, and VIII.

The original plans for the book called for Dr. Lloyd H. Bailer to write Chapter IX. After agreeing to do the job, however, pressure of other work forced him to give up the attempt. That left me with the choice of either omitting one of the most vital chapters, or writing it myself. I chose the latter. The fact that Dr. Bailer let me use manuscripts prior to publication saved me many weeks of field work. To these manuscripts must go the credit for much of whatever merit several sections of that chapter have.

Others who kindly lent valuable unpublished manuscripts were Professors B. R. Brazeal, J. Douglas Brown, Alvin H. Jones, and John P. Troxell. Several manuscripts were obtained through the courtesy of members of the staffs of the Cornell University and Harvard College libraries.

Much of the material in this book was originally presented in my doctoral dissertation, deposited in the Harvard College library. Professor Sumner H. Slichter, under whom the dissertation was written, exhibited a keen interest in the subject throughout and contributed many valuable suggestions, besides writing the Foreword. Others who read parts of the manuscript to my advantage were Professor W. H. McPherson, Drs. John T. Dunlop and Joseph

Shister, and Mr. Henry Epstein. Mr. Epstein was helpful in many other ways, as well, as was Mr. Bartley C. Crum.

The editors and publishers of the journals listed below have kindly permitted me to reproduce some of the material which I originally published in the following articles: "The Tobacco Workers International Union," *Quarterly Journal of Economics,* August 1942; "The New Orleans Longshoremen," *Political Science Quarterly,* December 1942; "The Negro and the United Mine Workers of America," *Southern Economic Journal,* April 1943; "The Negro and Unionism in the Birmingham, Ala., Iron and Steel Industry," *Southern Economic Journal,* July 1943; "Organized Labor and Negro Workers," *Journal of Political Economy,* June 1943; "Negroes in a War Industry: the Case of Shipbuilding," *Journal of Business,* July 1943; "Unions, Restricted Clientele," *The Nation,* August 14, 1943; and "Unionization of Foremen," *Harvard Business Review,* Summer 1943. In addition, parts of Chapter III were first presented in my testimony before the Fair Employment Practice Committee's hearings on discrimination in the railroad industry, September 1943.

The published works from which I have drawn material have been cited in both the footnotes and the bibliography. Special mention, however, should be made here of my debt to the path-breaking book, *The Black Worker,* by Professors Sterling D. Spero and Abram L. Harris. Any study of Negro labor must lean heavily for background material upon this book. In addition, the works of Dr. G. S. Mitchell and Mr. H. R. Cayton, Professor Charles S. Johnson, Professor Slichter, and the Twentieth Century Fund study of collective bargaining under the editorship of Dr. Harry A. Millis were of very great assistance to me.

Finally, I want to record gratitude and thanks to my parents. Because of their faith and sacrifice, I was able to spend the greater part of seven years in study and research, the necessary preludes to the writing of this work. It is to them that I gratefully dedicate the book.

HERBERT R. NORTHRUP

Detroit, Mich.
December 1943

ORGANIZED

LABOR

AND

THE NEGRO

CHAPTER I

THE GENERAL PICTURE[1]

The racial[2] policies of American trade unions vary from outright exclusion of Negroes by some organizations to the full acceptance of them with all privileges of membership by others. Moreover, union policies toward Negroes are somewhat fluid and subject to change if the circumstances so warrant. For example, the appearance of a rival union with a liberal racial policy may result in a reversal of the policies of its competitor which had up to that time discriminated against colored workers. On the other hand, the presence of an exclusionist union in the same jurisdiction with one which usually tolerates no discrimination may cause the latter to relax its principles for fear that it will alienate its predominately white membership.

The attitude of unions toward Negroes also often varies within the same organization from region to region, depending upon local customs and the type of leadership that is selected. It sometimes happens that Negroes are refused membership in an organization in one part of the county while received freely by it in another. In one local union a sympathetic president or business agent may play an important role in cementing good feeling between the white and colored workers; in a neighboring local of the same national union, a prejudiced leader may cause the whites to exclude the Negroes.

Dynamic elements such as these prevent any clear-cut classification of American labor unions according to their racial policies. This fact should be borne in mind for the discussion that follows, in which (1) union racial policies will be classified and analyzed; (2) the position of the American Federation of Labor; and (3) that of the Congress of Industrial Organizations will be set forth.

[1] All numbered notes appear at end of book, pp. 259-88.

Union Racial Policies Classified

At least[3] fourteen American unions specifically exclude Negroes
from membership by provisions to that effect in either their constitutions or their rituals. Of these, six—the Airline Pilots, the
Masters, Mates, and Pilots, and the Wire Weavers,[4] all AFL affiliates, and the Train Dispatchers, the Railroad Yardmasters of
America, and the Railroad Yardmasters of North America, which
are unaffiliated—are of no appreciable importance in barring
Negroes from jobs since none of them has a membership exceeding
3,000. Quite different, however, is the effect of the remaining eight
exclusionist unions on job opportunities for colored workers, for
they include some of the larger and more influential organizations
in the American labor movement, namely: the International Asso-
ciation of Machinists, the Railroad Telegraphers, the Railway Mail
Association, the Switchmen, all AFL affiliates, and the Locomotive
Engineers, the Locomotive Firemen and Enginemen, the Railroad
Trainmen, and the Railway Conductors, the independent railway
brotherhoods.* In addition,[5] eight unions—six AFL affiliates, the
Flint Glass Workers, the Brotherhood of Electrical Workers, the
Plumbers and Steamfitters, the Asbestos Workers, Heat and Frost
Insulators, the Granite Cutters, and the Seafarers, and two inde-
pendent unions, the Marine Firemen, and the Brotherhood of Rail-
road Shop Crafts—usually refuse admittance to Negroes by tacit
consent. Nine others—the Boilermakers, Iron Shipbuilders, Welders,
and Helpers, the Railway and Steamship Clerks, Freight Handlers,
Express and Station Employes, the Railway Carmen, the Maintenance of Way Employes, the Blacksmiths, Drop Forgers and
Helpers, the Sheet Metal Workers, the Federation of Rural Letter
Carriers, the Rural Letter Carriers' Association, and the American
Federation of Railroad Workers—permit Negroes to join and give
them the privilege of paying dues, but limit their participation to
"Jim Crow" auxiliary bodies which in one way or another prohibit
them from having a voice in the affairs of the union, from negotiating
their own agreements, or from having an opportunity to advance in

* Typical is the constitution of the Locomotive Firemen, which limits membership to "white born, of good moral character . . ."

the occupational hierarchy.* All but the last two of these organizations are likewise AFL affiliates.

To summarize the above in tabular form:

I. Union which excludes Negroes by provision in ritual:
Machinists, International Association of (AFL)

II. Unions which exclude Negroes by provision in constitution:
  A. AFL Affiliates
    Airline Pilots' Association
    Masters, Mates and Pilots, National Organization
    Railroad Telegraphers, Order of
    Railway Mail Association
    Switchmen's Union of North America
    Wire Weavers' Protective Association, American

---

* These restrictive rules are summarized as follows:

Before 1938, the Boilermakers excluded Negroes and the "white" clause is still retained in the ritual. The 1937 convention amended the union's rules to permit the chartering of Negro auxiliary locals. The auxiliaries are limited to localities where a white local exists and where there are sufficient Negroes employed to maintain a local. Negroes have no voice in national union affairs, but must obey all union rules. They cannot transfer except to other auxiliary locals. They are dependent upon the business agent of the "supervising" white local for job assignments. Their opportunities for promotion are severely restricted. And although they pay the same dues as white members, they receive only half as much in death and disability benefits and are not eligible for voluntary insurance plans to which white members may subscribe. (Cf. Brotherhood of Boilermakers, etc., *Subordinate Lodge Constitution*, ed. 1938, with *idem., By-laws Governing Auxiliary Lodges*, ed. 1942.)

Before 1939, the Railway Clerks excluded Negroes, and the "white" clause is still retained in the union constitution. The 1939 convention empowered the Executive Council to establish an auxiliary for Negroes. Auxiliary members must abide by all union rules and pay the same dues as the white members, but they have no voice in the governing bodies of the union. (See Brotherhood of Railway Clerks, etc., *Regulations for the Government of Lodges of the Auxiliary*, ed. 1940.)

"On railroads where the employment of colored persons has become a permanent institution they shall be admitted to membership in separate lodges. Where these separate lodges of negroes are organized they shall be under the jurisdiction of and represented by the delegate of the nearest white local in any meeting of the Joint Protective Board Federation or convention where delegates may be seated." (Brotherhood Railway Carmen, *Subordinate Lodge Constitution*, ed. 1941, sec. 6, clause C.)

"Rights of membership of the colored Maintenance of Way Employes . . . shall be under the direct control of the System Division . . . They shall be entitled to all the benefits and protection guaranteed by the Constitution to its members and shall be represented in the Grand Lodge by delegates of their own choice selected from any white Lodge on the System Division . . .

B. Unaffiliated Organizations
    Locomotive Engineers, Brotherhood of
    Locomotive Firemen and Enginemen, Brotherhood of
    Railroad Trainmen, Brotherhood of
    Railroad Yardmasters of America
    Railroad Yardmasters of North America
    Railway Conductors, Order of
    Train Dispatchers' Association, American
III. Unions which habitually exclude Negroes by tacit consent:
    A. AFL Affiliates
        Asbestos Workers, Heat and Frost Insulators
        Electrical Workers, International Brotherhood of[6]
        Flint Glass Workers' Union, American
        Granite Cutters' International Association
        Plumbers and Steamfitters, United Association of
        Journeymen
        Seafarers' International Union
    B. Unaffiliated Organizations
        Marine Firemen, Oilers, Watertenders, and Wipers'
        Association, Pacific Coast
        Railroad Shop Crafts, Brotherhood of

---

where employed. Nothing in this section operates to prevent the colored employes from maintaining a separate Lodge for social purposes and to receive official communications and information from the Grand Lodge and the System Division . . ." (Brotherhood of Maintenance of Way Employes, *Constitution,* ed. 1940, Art. XIII, sec. 1.)

"Where there are a sufficient number of colored helpers, they may be organized as an auxiliary local and shall be under the jurisdiction of the white local having jurisdiction over that territory . . . Colored helpers shall not transfer except to another auxiliary local composed of colored members, and colored members shall not be promoted to blacksmiths or helper apprentices and will not be admitted to shops where white helpers are now employed." (Brotherhood of Blacksmiths, etc., *Constitution,* quoted in E. M. Stewart, "Handbook of American Trade Unions," *Bulletin No. 618,* U. S. Bureau of Labor Statistics, Washington, 1936, p. 175.)

Negro sheet metal workers may be organized in separate locals "with the consent of the white local" of the locality or else in "auxiliary locals" if consent of the white local is not obtained. Negro locals are under the supervision of the white locals. (See Stewart, *op. cit.,* p. 110.)

Both of the rural letter carriers' unions prohibit Negroes from holding office or from acting as delegates to conventions. (*See ibid.,* p. 309.)

The American Federation of Railroad Workers bars Negroes from membership by constitutional provision, but it does admit them to an auxiliary which denies them any voice in union affairs.

IV. Unions which afford Negroes only segregated auxiliary
status:
A. AFL Affiliates
Blacksmiths, Drop Forgers and Helpers, Brother-
hood of
Boilermakers, Iron Shipbuilders, Welders, and Help-
ers, Brotherhood of
Maintenance of Way Employes, Brotherhood of
Railway Carmen of America, Brotherhood
Railway and Steamship Clerks, Freight Handlers,
Express and Station Employes, Brotherhood of
Rural Letter Carriers, Federation of
Sheet Metal Workers' International Association
B. Unaffiliated Organizations
Railroad Workers, American Federation of
Rural Letter Carriers' Association

In most instances the exclusionist and discriminatory practices
of these unions have been in effect for many years, and there is no
doubt but that they have the support of the majority of the membership of the unions. For despite the efforts of a number of
members in several of these organizations to have the anti-Negro
provisions erased, only two unions, the Commercial Telegraphers
and the Hotel and Restaurant Workers, both AFL, which once
adopted racial restrictions, later completely removed them from
their laws. Nor does it seem necessary to discuss at great length the
underlying motives which bring them into being. Undoubtedly
racial prejudice plays a part and particularly so on the railroads,
where a majority of the exclusionist unions are found. Most of the
railroad unions came into being as fraternal and beneficial societies.
To admit Negroes to their ranks on an equal footing would be, in
the minds of many white members, tantamount to admitting that
the colored man is a social equal, and this the majority of white
railroad workers has always refused to countenance.

But it is much more important to note that nearly all the unions
practicing discrimination—and railway labor organizations are no
exception—are organizations of skilled craft workers. In view of the
well-known work scarcity consciousness of most craft unionists, it
seems likely that economic interest, or, as Spero and Harris so well
put it, "the desire to restrict competition so as to safeguard job

monopoly,"[7] is the major contributing factor. To exclude Negroes, these craft unionists have found, is a convenient and effective method of limiting the number of sellers of a particular type of labor or skill, and that, in turn, enables the white craftsmen to obtain a larger share of the available work for themselves and/or higher wages.

A few other craft unions which do not exclude Negroes or confine them to inferior status do, nonetheless, tolerate, if not sanction, discrimination by their local bodies. Thus the Carpenters and the Joiners and the Painters, Decorators, and Paperhangers, both AFL affiliates, which have no rules or stipulations providing for exclusion or segregation of colored artisans, follow a policy of organizing Negro workers into separate local unions. While it is true that these separate Negro locals have equal status with the white locals, and while it is also correct that in certain instances, notably among longshoremen, Negroes seem to prefer a separate setup, it is an undeniable fact that in the building trades, as in most other industries, the Negro workers segregated into separate local bodies are at a distinct disadvantage. Unless, as is infrequently the case, the white and Negro locals co-operate in the allocation of union jobs, the members of the two local groups will be competing for work. Since the white local is usually the larger and more powerful, the result is usually that the colored unionists are unable to obtain a proportionate share of the employment. Moreover, discrimination resulting from separate local unions as featured by the Carpenters and the Painters is, although effective in eliminating Negro workers from job opportunities, quite difficult to prove to have taken place. Once a national trade union adopts a policy of segregation, the way is open to white locals to deal with the situation as they wish, however much the national officers may deplore the results.

In some industries, notably textile manufacturing, the printing trades, and clerical and white-collar pursuits, Negroes are largely excluded from employment by the decisions of management. Undoubtedly, however, such decisions meet with the approval, if not the assistance, of the majority of the white workers in these fields. Yet in some of the comparatively rare instances in which Negroes have obtained employment in these industries, they have been admitted to the unions.

There are, it should be pointed out, also craft unions which have on a number of occasions endeavored to enforce economic equalitarianism upon their locals, and which officially condemn discrimination in all its forms. Foremost among these organizations are the Bricklayers, Masons, and Plasterers and the Operative Plasterers and Cement Finishers. Both of these AFL unions have constitutional stipulations providing for $100 fines to be assessed against members who discriminate against fellow members because of race, creed, or nationality; and both permit the national officers discretionary power to grant a local charter to a body of craftsmen if the objection of the subordinate union to the establishment of a second local is based on race or national origin. It is worthy of note that in the South nearly 50 per cent of the tradesmen over which these two organizations have jurisdiction are Negroes. Had the Bricklayers and Masons and the Plasterers and Cement Finishers not offered an equalitarian program to Negroes, they would have had considerably more difficulty in organizing the workers in their crafts in the South.

Besides these "liberal" craft unions, those organizations having jurisdiction over workers engaged primarily in unskilled or semi-skilled labor, e.g., the Hod Carriers, Building and Common Laborers, and the International Longshoremen's Association, and the unions organized mainly on an industrial basis, e.g., the Ladies' Garment Workers and the Hat, Cap, and Millinery Workers, all of which are AFL affiliates, and the unions which are members of the CIO, usually afford colored workers equal treatment.

The fact that some trade unions use a color bar to restrict the competition for jobs should not be regarded as too extraordinary. A great many barriers against economic opportunity are sought by a wide variety of organized groups—farmers, business and professional men, and consumers, as well as by labor organizations —this is only one of several. That is not to say that the writer wishes to condone any of these attempts to create barriers. Each must be considered on its merits, and the use of a color bar by workers' organizations to limit the job opportunities of a minority race is one of the most difficult of all to justify.

But whatever one may think of the ethics of trade union discrimination, there is a fundamental inconsistency between the racial policies of most of the organizations in question [8] and the oft-repeated principles of their parent body, the American Federation of Labor, the spokesmen for which never tire of "reiterating, re-endorsing, and reaffirming" the fact that the AFL has no color bar, and of proclaiming that the "workers must organize and unite under its banner, without regard to race, color, creed, or national origin."

THE AMERICAN FEDERATION OF LABOR

For the first few years after its formation, the leaders of the AFL apparently made a real effort to adhere to their expressed policies of racial equality. Candidates for affiliation were forced to pledge "never to discriminate against a fellow worker on account of color, creed, or nationality," and the 1890 convention refused to sanction the admittance of a machinists' union because the organization excluded Negroes from membership by constitutional provision.

These sentiments, however, were of short duration. The Knights of Labor with its ideal of solidarity irrespective of race was rapidly disappearing as a rival of the AFL, and the Federation heads soon came to realize that their ideals were standing in the way of expansion. Hence, when in 1895 this same machinists' union removed its color bar from its constitution and transferred it to its ritual, it was allowed to affiliate, and became the International Association of Machinists. So the AFL's policy of racial equality came to an abrupt end. One year after the Machinists affiliated, the Boilermakers and Iron Shipbuilders were welcomed despite a similar method of excluding Negroes. Since then, AFL officials have not troubled to insist on this questionable ruse, but have admitted as affiliates without question organizations which exclude Negroes by constitutional provision.[9]

After 1900 the Federation adopted the explicit policy of organizing Negroes into separate locals or directly affiliated "federal" unions when they were refused admission to an affiliated national union because of their color. The AFL constitution was further amended to permit the Executive Council to charter separate Negro central labor unions "if the situation warranted" —meaning, if a local central body refused to seat colored delegates.[10]

This method of compromise has proved quite unsatisfactory to Negro workers. The AFL Executive Council is supposed to act as the "international" for federal locals, but as a matter of fact it is rarely in a position to do so. Usually it refers matters pertaining to these locals to the national union which has jurisdiction in the field. Since, however, the rules of the national union to which the affairs of the federal locals are referred exclude Negroes, it is not surprising that colored workers organized in federal locals have lacked competent assistance in settling grievances and in negotiating contracts, and have failed to receive adequate support in preventing the encroachment of white workers on their job opportunities. Moreover, when, as in the cases of the Railway Clerks and the Railway Carmen, the exclusionist unions have amended their rules so as to permit the affiliation of Negroes in a subordinate, Jim Crow status, the AFL Executive Council has not hesitated to revoke the federal charters despite the opposition of the affected colored workers, and to transfer the locals to national unions under rules which deny to Negroes even the autonomy which they enjoy under federal local charters.

The Negro migration into northern industry during the first World War brought the color question to the fore in several AFL conventions. Most important for our purposes was the discussion at the 1920 meeting. Federal locals of railway coach cleaners introduced a resolution demanding that the Railway Carmen, which had jurisdiction over that group of workers, either remove its color bar or permit the coach cleaners to establish a national union of their own. The same resolution demanded that the AFL take action on the refusal of the Machinists, the Boilermakers and Iron Shipbuilders, and the Blacksmiths and Drop Forgers to admit Negroes. A resolution, similar in content to the one introduced by the coach cleaners, was offered by federal locals of Negro freight handlers who asked that the AFL act on the refusal of the Railway Clerks to admit Negroes.

Reporting on the resolution of the coach cleaners, the resolutions committee found that the Machinists and the Boilermakers had "no law in their constitution prohibiting the admission of colored workers following the trade," and that the "Blacksmiths issue charters to colored workers of the trade and have no law denying admission to colored workers." The committee did find that the Railway Carmen excluded Negroes, and therefore, it could "only recommend" that the Carmen "eliminate from their

constitution all reference to the admission of colored workers."
The resolution of the freight handlers was referred to the committee on organization. It "non-concurred" on the ground that the
AFL could not interfere with the autonomy of an affiliate, but
after one of the most vigorous debates on the race question in
the history of the Federation, an amendment was carried recommending that the Railway Clerks remove the color bar.[11]

The report of the resolutions committee on the resolution of
the coach cleaners contained a significant number of factual
omissions. It is true that neither the Machinists nor the Boilermakers have clauses denying Negroes admission in their *constitutions*. But both at that time excluded Negroes by provisions
to that effect in their *rituals*.[12] It is inconceivable that the members of the resolutions committee did not know this. It is also
true that the Blacksmiths issue charters to Negroes. But the committee must have known that the purposes of these auxiliary
charters are to control the competition of Negroes and to prevent
them from advancing in the occupational hierarchy, without at the
same time permitting them a voice in the affairs of the union.

The action taken by the conventions of the Railway Carmen
and the Railway Clerks on the 1920 AFL convention's recommendation that they remove the color bars from their constitutions is also revealing. Meeting in 1921, the Railway Carmen
amended their constitution so as to permit the chartering of Negro
auxiliary locals with rules not unlike those imposed on colored
workers by the Blacksmiths. This the AFL Executive Council
found quite satisfactory. It revoked the charters of the federal
locals of Negro coach cleaners and turned them over to the
Carmen's union. Thus the Negro coach cleaners lost the right to
run their own unions and to attend AFL conventions without being
granted anything worthy of mention in return.[13]

The Railway Clerks convention of 1922 did not even go as far
as the Carmen's conclave of the previous year. When a resolution urging the elimination of the "white only clause" was introduced, it created such an uproar that it was declared out of order.[14]
No action was taken on the question, but the AFL exacted no
penalty on the Clerks' union for ignoring its recommendation.
Having once admitted as an autonomous affiliate an organization
excluding Negroes, the AFL was powerless to force equality upon

it except by expulsion from the Federation, and this has never been done.

As membership in AFL unions declined in the twenties, interest in organizing Negroes also died down. The Federation did not trouble to give serious heed to proposals of Negro leaders or other socially minded individuals interested in achieving a greater organization of colored workers.[15] It was not until the resurgence of trade unionism during the decade of the thirties was coupled with the presence of a recognized spokesman of Negro labor at AFL conventions in the person of A. Philip Randolph, president of the Brotherhood of Sleeping Car Porters, that the debate on the minority race question again became a feature of AFL conventions. Yet the results continue to be disappointing.

At the 1934 convention, for example, Mr. Randolph demanded expulsion from the AFL for "any union maintaining the color bar." The resolutions committee voted adversely on the grounds that the "American Federation of Labor . . . cannot interfere with the autonomy of National and International unions." However, an amendment to the committee report was adopted, which authorized the appointment of a five-man committee "to investigate the conditions of the colored workers of this country and report to the next convention." [16]

The committee, composed of John E. Rooney of the Operative Plasterers and Cement Finishers, John Brophy of the United Mine Workers, John Garvey of the Hod Carriers and Common Laborers, Jerry L. Hanks of the Journeymen Barbers, and T. C. Carroll of the Maintenance of Way Employes, held open hearings in Washington and recommended a threefold plan: (1) that all international unions which in any way bar Negroes or afford them only inferior status take up the "Negro question at their next convention for the purpose of harmonizing constitution rules and practices to conform with the oft-repeated declarations of AFL conventions on equality of treatment of all races within the trade union movement"; (2) that the AFL issue no more charters to unions practicing discrimination; and (3) that the AFL inaugurate a campaign of education "to get the white worker to see more completely the weakness of division and the necessity of unity between white and black workers to the end that all workers may be organized." [17]

Although this report would by no means have solved the AFL's race problem, it might have provided a workable method whereby significant reform could have been accomplished had not the Executive Council effectively sabotaged the whole thing. Instead of allowing this committee to report its findings to the 1935 convention, as it had been directed by the resolution which created it, William Green, president of the AFL, handed over the report to George M. Harrison, an AFL vice-president, and president of the exclusionist Railway Clerks. In so doing, Mr. Green followed an unusual and, without doubt, unconstitutional procedure.* The committee had been ordered by a convention, the AFL's highest governing body, to report to it the following year. Yet Mr. Green permitted a member of the Executive Council to substitute a document more pleasing to himself. In fact, one wonders whether *any* report would have been presented to the delegates had it not been for the continual prodding of A. Philip Randolph. As it was, Mr. Harrison delayed action until about 10 P.M. on the eleventh and last day of the convention. By then the delegates had already become exhausted and divided by the craft-industrial union controversy.[18] And so when President Green submitted a totally innocuous document, which Mr. Harrison had substituted for the original committee report, advocating no action except "education," it was adopted by the tired delegates over Mr. Randolph's protests.[19]

Despite the fact that the suspension of the CIO unions by the AFL Executive Council provided Randolph and his supporters with an excellent argument with which to demand the expulsion of unions violating the AFL constitution by excluding workers because of race, they have been unable to convince that body that it is guilty of any inconsistency.[20] Moreover, the departure of the more liberal industrial unions into the CIO renders it unlikely that either the AFL or its constituent unions will take any action on their own initiative to remove color bars. On the other hand, however, is the fact that increased publicity has been given both union affairs and the rights of minority peoples by the war, and

* "The Annual Convention is the supreme authority of the American Federation of Labor . . . When the majority will of labor is expressed in the convention it becomes law by which the whole of the American Federation is bound." (William Green, *Labor and Democracy*, Princeton, N. J., 1939, p. 175.)

this has supplied new ammunition to those who are demanding the end of union exclusion. Bolstered by the appointment of the Fair Employment Practice Committee, a development for which he was in no small way responsible, Mr. Randolph introduced two resolutions at the 1941 AFL convention. The first called for the appointment of a seven-man committee to investigate discrimination by affiliated unions and to report back to the next convention. When the resolutions committee reported adversely, Randolph rose to cite case after case in which AFL unions were preventing Negro workers from obtaining employment on defense projects. The Boilermakers and Shipbuilders and the Machinists drew his heaviest fire for preventing the employment of Negroes in shipyards and airplane plants, but the building trades—the Carpenters, the Painters, and even the Bricklayers and the Plasterers and Cement Finishers—were also prominent on his list. Some of the presidents of the unions mentioned in his report attempted to answer his charges, but none of them was able to refute his facts. The official AFL attitude was clearly stated once more in the speeches of three Federation spokesmen—John P. Frey, president of the Metal Trades Department, Matthew Woll, a vice-president, and President William Green. In brief they stated that: (1) discrimination existed before the AFL was born and human nature cannot be altered; (2) such a committee as proposed by Randolph would violate the sacred doctrine of autonomy of the Federation's affiliates; (3) the AFL, per se, does not discriminate because it gladly accepts Negro workers into its directly affiliated federal locals. Besides, the AFL hopes that "if there is any barrier" in the way of organizing Negroes, it will ultimately be broken down; and (4) that Negroes should be grateful for what the AFL has done for them.

To which Mr. Randolph and his supporters replied (1) that condoning existing discrimination, the AFL had nurtured its growth; (2) that Randolph's proposal would not violate trade union autonomy, but would only investigate a means of ending discrimination (Mr. Woll's claim that it would do otherwise was merely an appeal to the delegates to vote against the proposal by misstating the intents and purposes of the resolution); (3) that not only does the policy of organizing Negroes into federal locals give tacit approval of discrimination, but the AFL only recently had itself committed an act of discrimination against Negro freight handlers and station porters who had been so organized. The exclusionists Brotherhood of Railway Clerks had amended its rules so as to permit the organization of Negroes in separate Jim Crow auxiliaries, the members of which have no voice in the affairs of the Brotherhood. Over the protests of the leaders of these Negro workers, the AFL Executive Council revoked the federal local charters of these workers and allowed the Railway Clerks to assume jurisdiction over them (an action on the part of the Executive Council which duplicated the one twenty years before in the case of the Negro coach cleaners and the Railway Carmen); and (4) that Negro workers are grateful for what the AFL has accomplished, but they feel it could and should do far more.[21]

Defeated in this attempt to force at least a study of AFL discrimination, Randolph attempted to have the AFL convention go on record as opposed to Jim Crow auxiliaries. But John P. Frey declared that if the resolution was passed it would forbid unions to establish ladies' auxiliaries, composed of the wives and daughters of union men. On this pretext, the resolution was defeated.[22]

Similar resolutions introduced at the 1942 convention met a like fate.[23] The tenor of the debates at both 1941 and 1942 conventions offers little hope to Negroes that the offending unions will relax their discriminatory rules and practices. Fortunately, the racial policies of the CIO and its affiliates are, in general, much more liberal.

The Congress of Industrial Organizations

One of the main objectives of the Congress of Industrial Organizations, according to its constitution, is to ". . . bring about the effective organization of the working men and women of America regardless of race, color, creed, or nationality . . ." Thus far there can be little doubt that both the CIO and its constituent unions have sedulously adhered to this nondiscrimination policy in organizing Negroes. Of course, this is not to say that colored workers have never been accorded unfair treatment by either CIO members or local unions; but in so far as this writer has been able to determine, no national CIO union excludes Negro workers from membership nor segregates its colored members into Jim Crow local unions.

Moreover, the national officers of the CIO unions have, by and large, a consistent record of practicing what they preach in regard to the treatment of Negroes.

It is not difficult to comprehend why the CIO has pursued its liberal racial policy. Unlike craft unions, which are organized on an exclusive and narrow basis, and which depend upon their control of a few highly skilled and strategically situated jobs to obtain their bargaining power, industrial unions acquire their strength by opening their ranks to all the workers in an industry.[24] The United Mine Workers, the Amalgamated Clothing Workers, and the Ladies' Garment Workers [25] had been organized on an industrial basis for many years prior to 1935 when their leaders founded the CIO. Few, if any, labor unions had better records for fair treatment of Negroes than did these three. Besides, their officers saw the projected campaigns to organize the workers of the iron and steel, the automobile, and the other mass production industries doomed to failure unless the unions in these fields opened their doors to workers of all creeds and colors. Finally, the CIO contains within its ranks most of the left-wing elements in the American labor movement. These groups have always most vociferously opposed racial discrimination in all its forms. For these reasons, then, the CIO has attempted to enroll workers regardless of race, creed, color, or nationality.

True, economic equality, however, involves more than organizing workers into one union regardless of race. It entails also the establishment of some standard by which jobs may be allocated without prejudice. The general principle adhered to by most unions in this respect is that seniority of tenure, with certain qualifications for ability, should be the governing criterion. But it makes little difference, for the purposes of this discussion, what the standard is, so long as it is applied without discrimination. The question is whether this standard has been applied fairly (a) with respect to layoffs and rehirings and (b) with respect to promotions.

The application of racial equality to seniority in layoffs and rehirings has not caused serious difficulties. The fairness of such action is too obvious for either management or white workers to protest, and the principle now has fairly general acceptance in a large segment of American industry.

On the other hand, however, the question of literal application of the equalitarian policy to seniority in promotions has caused no end of trouble. "Because few Negroes have been promoted to the better paying jobs in the past, white workers have come to regard white priority as the established order of things. At the same time the Negro workers have justly pointed out that if the principle of equal treatment is to have real meaning, it must be applied to this, as well as to other, aspects of the collective bargaining agreement." [26]

The manner in which this issue has been resolved has varied considerably from union to union, and from region to region. Probably nowhere has promotion seniority been applied with no discrimination whatsoever. Yet it may be said that the national officers of such unions of the Steelworkers, the Automobile Workers, and the Marine and Shipbuilding Workers have made praiseworthy attempts to enforce a literal application of the principle regardless of race. As a result of their efforts, they have been able to open up a sizable number of new employment opportunities to Negroes in the North, despite the opposition of some white members. In the South, however, these same union leaders have felt it necessary to act more slowly. For there they have encountered a much more determined opposition from their white membership. Consequently, they have felt that to force the issue would either result in wrecking their southern locals by internal dissension or in inducing the predominately white membership to transfer its allegiance to a rival union whose leaders are not committed to a policy of racial equalitarianism.

The seniority promotion problem is, without doubt, one of the most important and most difficult problems which must be solved if unions are to be truly equalitarian. Detailed examination of this and other questions here raised is, however, best postponed for discussion in the chapters on conditions in particular industries.

CHAPTER II

THE BUILDING TRADES

More than one-half of all skilled Negro workers in the United States are building craftsmen. Sixty per cent of them dwell in the South; yet in that area, the proportion of skilled building work done by Negroes has steadily declined since the Civil War. In other parts of the country, however, Negroes have recently been receiving an increased share of such work.

This chapter examines the position of the Negro mechanic with particular reference to the racial policies of six building trades unions: the Plumbers and Steamfitters, the Electrical Workers, the Carpenters, the Painters, the Bricklayers, and the Plasterers and Cement Finishers, all of which are AFL affiliates. The attempts of the federal government to ensure Negroes a proportionate share of jobs on public construction work and the efforts of colored artisans to protect their interests by forming pressure groups also are given attention. A final section discusses the unskilled Negro building worker.

THE NEGRO'S SHARE OF SKILLED BUILDING WORK

The bulk of the building work in the ante-bellum South was performed by Negroes. The shortage of skilled mechanics forced the slaveholders to train their chattels for these tasks. This, in turn, discouraged the migration of free labor to the South, undercut the wages of white mechanics, and aroused much antagonism on the part of white craftsmen, who attempted, usually unsuccessfully, to restrain the use of slave labor by licensing laws and other such measures.

The social upheaval which followed the Civil War resulted in a drastic weakening of the Negro's position in the skilled building trades. Former slaves found difficulty in plying their trade for wages instead of at the direction of a master; "emancipation engendered among many freedmen an aversion for manual labor,

17

TABLE Ia

Total Workers, Number and Proportion of Negroes in Selected Occupations of the Building Trades in the United States and in the South,[1] 1890-1910

	1890			1900			1910		
	All Workers	Negroes	% Negro	All Workers	Negroes	% Negro	All Workers	Negroes	% Negro
Carpenters									
U. S.	611,482	22,318	3.6	602,741	22,435	3.7	682,490	29,039	4.3
South	70,327	18,017	25.6	78,728	17,241	22.5	104,606	24,624	23.2
Painters									
U. S.	219,912	4,386	2.0	277,990	5,934	2.1	273,441	8,035	2.9
South	13,105	2,911	22.2	17,763	3,821	21.5	22,212	5,628	25.3
Bricklayers									
U. S.	158,518	9,647	6.1	161,048	14,457	9.0	160,151	12,014	7.5
South	14,628	6,857	47.0	14,855	7,933	53.4	16,125	8,817	54.7
Plasters and cement finishers									
U. S.	39,002	4,006	10.3	35,706	3,754	10.5	47,682	6,175	13.0
South	2,408	1,261	52.5	2,964	1,841	62.1	3,329	2,213	66.5
Plumbers									
U. S.	56,607	616	1.1	97,884	1,197	1.2	119,596	1,990	1.7
South	(2)	(2)	(2)	4,375	781	17.9	8,822	1,368	15.5
Electricians									
U. S.	(2)	(2)	(2)	(2)	(2)	(2)	47,024	293	0.6
South	(2)	(2)	(2)	(2)	(2)	(2)	8,056	250	2.9
Total Seven Crafts									
U. S.	(2)	(2)	(2)	(2)	(2)	(2)	1,330,384	57,546	4.3
South	(2)	(2)	(2)	(2)	(2)	(2)	163,150	42,900	26.3

Source: U. S. Census of Occupations, 1890-1910.
[1] Includes states of Alabama, Arkansas, Florida, Georgia, Louisiana, Mississippi, North Carolina, South Carolina, Tennessee, and Virginia.
[2] Not available.

TABLE Ib

TOTAL WORKERS, NUMBER AND PROPORTION OF NEGROES IN SELECTED OCCUPATIONS OF THE BUILDING TRADES, IN THE UNITED STATES AND IN THE SOUTH, 1920-1940

	1920			1930			1940[4]		
	All Workers	Negroes	% Negro	All Workers	Negroes	% Negro	All Workers	Negroes	% Negro
Carpenters									
U. S.	887,379	34,217	3.9	929,426	32,413	3.5	690,526	25,427	3.9
South	125,913	25,774	20.5	125,714	20,699	16.5	129,779	17,785	13.7
Painters									
U. S.	248,497	8,026	3.2	430,105	15,677	3.6	439,472	16,841	3.8
South	23,067	5,228	22.6	40,184	6,830	17.0	52,194	7,578	14.5
Bricklayers[3]									
U. S.	131,264	10,606	8.1	170,903	11,701	6.9	135,013	8,159	6.0
South	13,634	7,317	53.6	17,386	7,716	44.4	19,228	6,050	31.5
Plasterers and cement finishers									
U. S.	45,876	7,079	15.4	85,480	13,465	15.8	68,750	10,431	15.2
South	4,105	2,619	63.8	10,325	6,317	61.2	10,515	5,729	54.5
Plumbers									
U. S.	206,718	3,516	1.7	237,814	4,729	2.0	198,477	4,299	2.2
South	15,287	2,002	13.1	20,340	2,445	12.0	22,210	2,461	11.1
Electricians									
U. S.	212,964	1,342	0.6	280,317	1,913	0.7	217,075	1,555	0.7
South	15,393	393	2.6	23,659	391	1.7	29,119	443	1.5
Total Seven Crafts									
U. S.	1,732,698	64,786	3.7	2,134,045	79,898	3.7	1,749,312	66,712	3.8
South	197,399	43,333	22.0	237,608	44,398	18.7	263,045	40,046	15.2

[3] Includes stone cutters in 1940.
[4] Includes totals of "employed" and "experienced workers seeking work" groups, which are roughly comparable to "gainful worker" definition of previous enumerations.

springing, no doubt, from the psychological association of such work with their former chattel status"; slave training ceased; and the unsuccessful substitutes devised to take its place were regarded by the freedmen, often with ample justification, as slavery thinly disguised; but most important in the post-Civil War displacement of Negro mechanics was the intense race feeling of the reconstruction period. The Negro building mechanic was faced with the same antagonism and competition from white craftsmen as in prewar days, but now he lacked the protection of the white plantation oligarchy. The latter group allied itself with the poorer white classes, and gave them preferences on jobs in return for support against the reconstruction governments. By 1890, the year of the first federal census of occupations, the proportion of Negroes to all building tradesmen in the South had shrunk to less than one-third.[1]

Prior to the Civil War, Negro artisans did not occupy a position in the border states of Kentucky, Maryland, Missouri, Texas, what is now West Virginia, and the District of Columbia comparable to that in the South, but their number was not inconsiderable. The course of events in these states after the Civil War seems to have followed much the same pattern as in other slave states, so that by 1890 only 4.5 per cent of the workers in seven crafts there were colored.[2] This proportion remained quite constant during the ensuing fifty years.

Few Negro mechanics were found in the North before World War I. Their numbers have increased substantially since then, especially in the states of New York, New Jersey, Pennsylvania, Ohio, Indiana, Illinois, and Michigan. Yet in 1940, the 15,693 Negroes in seven crafts in these states were only 2.1 per cent of the total there.

Table I shows the number and proportion of Negroes in selected occupations of the building trades for the United States, and for the South, 1890-1940.

Taking first the figures for the South, it appears that Negroes continued to lose ground in the nineties in carpentry and painting, but more than held their own in bricklaying and plastering and cement finishing—the "trowel trades." Between 1900 and 1910, there is evidence of a general gain, but during the past thirty years, the trend has been indisputably downward, even for the trowel trades.

A further examination of these data reveals that there was no actual displacement during the years 1890-1920, for the number of Negro mechanics increased. The decreased proportion resulted from the failure of the colored craftsmen to obtain a proportionate share of the increased employment opportunities. This was especially noteworthy in the newly developed electrical trade, in which Negroes have never been able to secure more than a slight foothold.

Although the total number of southern Negro craftsmen increased slightly during the twenties, the gain was ascribable almost solely to the plastering and cement finishing trades. The number of Negro carpenters decreased by almost 5,000, and colored painters, bricklayers, and plumbers barely increased.

During the thirties, Negroes in the South suffered disproportionately from the depression in the building industry. In each of the six crafts, the proportion of Negroes declined. The especially heavy loss in bricklaying may be partially attributable to the inclusion of stone cutters with bricklayers in the 1940 census. But even though the proportion of Negroes in the former occupation is considerably lower than that in the latter, the number of stone cutters is not enough to make the difference significant.

The trend in the United States followed closely that in the South up to 1920. But thereafter a decided difference is noticeable. In sharp contrast to the situation in the South, the proportion of Negro craftsmen has remained quite constant since 1920 for the country as a whole. Thus the decline in the South since then has been offset by an increase elsewhere. In 1910, 75 per cent of all Negro building mechanics were found in the South; but in 1940, only 60 per cent were located there.

The decreasing share of skilled building work is a serious loss to southern Negroes although it is partially attributable to migration northward. For in the South, this is almost the only industry which employs large numbers of Negroes in skilled positions. Even the new war industries in the area have generally either excluded Negroes entirely or confined them to unskilled work. Unless the trend is reversed, this already disadvantaged minority group will suffer a serious setback.

THE EARLY POSITION OF THE UNIONS

The decline in importance of Negro building mechanics in the South in recent years has much in common with the similar occurrence which followed the Civil War in that it seems to have derived its main impetus from the pressure of the white workers. That is not to say that other forces were not at work. Migration northward has already been noted; industrial education in the South continues to be woefully lacking for Negroes;[3] and employers' independent decisions have undoubtedly been a factor. In the building industry, however, the competition for jobs is keen, and the necessity for the contractor to meet a deadline makes speed the essence of his effort. He is, therefore, unlikely to oppose "reasonable" demands of the dominant labor faction, whether those demands are for higher wages or for an increased share of jobs formerly performed by Negroes.

It is improbable that southern white workers were able to use unions as a means of displacing Negro craftsmen before 1900, for it was not until after then that the building unions became established strongly in the South. From its inception, however, organization was accompanied by discrimination against colored workers, as an early study clearly showed. Yet exclusion was not universal and racially mixed unions were found in many communities.[4]

In the border states, however, Negro mechanics found themselves in an environment which was socially and politically southern, but which lacked the advantages of the southern labor market —a high percentage of Negro mechanics and a group of employers used to hiring them. Consequently, white mechanics were able to exclude Negroes from their unions, and did so almost without exception until recent years.[5]

The few Negro mechanics who came North before World War I were not accorded a warm welcome. Although some who carried union cards were granted reciprocal privileges, exclusion was far more prevalent. Before World War I, investigators generally agreed that employment opportunities for colored building mechanics were superior in the South.[6] In each region, however, even at this early date, there were decided differences as to the treatment of Negroes among the various crafts.

THE UNITED ASSOCIATION OF JOURNEYMEN PLUMBERS AND STEAMFITTERS

Most exclusionist of the larger building trades unions is the Plumbers and Steamfitters. To it must go a major portion of the blame for the failure of Negroes to obtain a better representation in this craft. For although it has no rules prohibiting the admission of Negroes, its locals have always practiced exclusion by tacit consent. There may have been Negro union plumbers, but this writer has failed to locate them after a diligent search.

In Chicago, for example, Negro plumbers have been vainly trying to gain admission to the Plumbers' union for twenty years. They were offered membership on condition that they work only for colored contractors in colored sections of the city. When they refused to accept such stipulations, they were barred by the union from work on all the housing projects and war jobs in the area. Then, in June 1942, the Fair Employment Practice Committee forced the union to give them working permits, but no Negroes have been admitted to the union.[7]

The reasons for the exclusionist policies of the Plumbers' union are not difficult to find. It was founded by craftsmen who, highly conscious of their skill, attempted to exclude helpers from both the union and the job before finding it imperative to admit them.[8] Its policies toward Negroes reflect the work scarcity consciousness typical of craft unionists, as well as race prejudice. The fact that plumbing is a relatively new trade, with no pre-Civil War tradition of Negro employment, has facilitated a general acceptance of this policy. But it has been most successfully enforced by means of state and municipal licensing and inspection laws.

Many states and municipalities have enacted legislation requiring that all those desirous of practicing the plumbing trade must obtain a license from boards or commissions, which may determine the fitness of candidates by examination. The Plumbers' union is the leading advocate of these laws ostensibly for reasons of public health and safety. Probably its basic reason for urging their enactment is that they tend to raise wages by limiting entrance to the trade and by making the employment of strikebreakers difficult.

Competent Negroes have found it difficult, and sometimes impossible, to pass examinations given by these boards. The Plumbers' union usually is represented on the boards. Since officials of this union have frankly advocated licensing laws as a means of eliminating Negroes from the trade, it is not surprising that color has often been made a practical test of competence.[9]

State and municipal inspection ordinances work in much the same manner. Many inspectors are recruited from the Plumbers' union. By refusing to approve work done by Negroes, they have forced contractors to hire whites instead.[10]

Recently, the constitutionality of the Maryland law, a typical plumbers' licensing law, was challenged. Like most such legislation, it permitted the examination boards wide latitude in promulgating rules of procedure. Among its requirements was that all candidates must obtain recommendations from two master plumbers before they could be examined. No Negro had ever been able to meet this condition. In May 1941, Attorney Harold Buchman, in behalf of the Baltimore Urban League, presented the assistant attorney general of Maryland with a brief in which he maintained that the law creating the board and the rules promulgated by it were unconstitutional because: (1) unrestrained discretion was granted the board; (2) the law was administered so as to make illegal discriminations between persons in similar circumstances; (3) the endorsement requirement was a "burdensome and unreasonable restriction on an ordinary occupation totally unrelated to the real issue, that is the competency of the workman and the consequent welfare of the public"; and (4) the endorsement requirement gave to members of a trade the powers of exclusion and monopoly.[11]

Following receipt of Mr. Buchman's communication, the Maryland Plumbing Board agreed to waive the endorsement requirement. Two Negroes have since taken the examination, but both failed primarily because of deficiencies in theoretical physics. At present six Negroes are studying nights in the hope of being Maryland's first licensed plumbers of their race. They may soon reach this goal. It would seem that an examination of state and municipal licensing laws in the light of the Constitution would be worth while.

The Plumbers' union and the national association of contractors in the trade have agreed on national apprenticeship standards for plumbers. The evidence presented here scarcely permits one to suggest that as a result Negroes will be encouraged to learn the trade. Instead, one must conclude that future employment opportunities for Negro plumbers are likely to be at least as small as they have been in the past.

THE INTERNATIONAL BROTHERHOOD OF ELECTRICAL WORKERS

The electrical trade has been dominated by white workers since its beginnings at the end of the last century, and they have used their union to maintain their position. Like the Plumbers' union, the IBEW practices exclusion by the tacit consent of its locals rather than by formal rule. On several occasions since 1899 the color question has been debated in the union journal or in conventions, but each time the exclusionist stand has been reaffirmed.[12]

The exclusion of the IBEW, however, is not so all-pervasive as is that of the Plumbers. Negro union electricians are known to have existed in Boston and Chicago. In the latter city Negroes received an IBEW charter, but they are confined to working for colored contractors in the Negro districts.[13] Moreover, some IBEW locals in other industries, particularly electrical power and electric products, have recently admitted Negroes.

On the other hand, most attempts of Negroes to join IBEW locals in the building industry have been unsuccessful. Vain efforts have been made, for example, in New York City, Newark, N. J., Cleveland, Columbus, Ohio, Pittsburgh, and Philadelphia. In Baltimore, a Negro was given a work permit, and began payment on his initiation fee. Unfortunately, he never completed his payments, and so the question of admitting him never came before the local. A licensed electrician applied for membership in a Savannah local, but was informed that "no preparations" had been made for Negroes and that he could not join. The business agent of this local declared that it "has always been strictly a white organization." [14]

In May, 1941, twelve Negro electricians applied for membership in Local No. 80, Norfolk. The secretary of Local No. 80 referred the matter to the IBEW's newly elected president, Ed. J. Brown. Replying, Mr. Brown pointed out that there was no color bar in the union constitution, and he expressed the hope that the "local union would not vote against an American citizen applicant for membership" because of his race, but would decide "solely on the basis of competency." He further urged the secretary of Local No. 80 to put the question of admitting the Negroes up to the local's membership as soon as possible. However, he also noted that local unions of the IBEW had the right to admit or reject whomsoever they desired.

After further consultation, Local No. 80 agreed to a separate local for the Negroes, but this the latter rejected because "both the union fee and the standards of qualifications were exceedingly higher and beyond those for white electricians." Proof of the ability of these colored electricians, most of whom were trained at Hampton Institute, is afforded by the fact that, by the end of 1942, they were able to form an electrical company and obtain contracts for war construction projects to an amount exceeding $45,000.[15]

So long as the IBEW leaves local unions complete freedom to reject competent workers, its present policy described by President Brown, as one of "nondiscrimination because of race, color, or creed,"[16] will have little effect in altering the almost universal rule that IBEW locals do not admit Negro building mechanics.

The IBEW, like the Plumbers, sponsors state and municipal licensing and inspection laws. The result is the same for Negro electricians as it is for Negro plumbers. However, ordinances affecting the former are not so numerous as those affecting the latter.[17]

Also like the Plumbers, the IBEW has agreed upon national apprenticeship standards with the national association of contractors in its field. Negroes are likely to find instruction in this trade as closed to them in the future as it has been in the past. Because the use of electrical tools, equipment, and machinery is increasing, however, the consequences in this case are more serious.

The United Brotherhood of Carpenters and Joiners

From the standpoint of the number of workers involved, carpentry is by far the most important of the skilled building trades. Moreover, it is the occupation in which southern Negroes suffered their largest absolute and relative displacement, and one in which these losses have not been quite counterbalanced by gains elsewhere. It is, therefore, altogether fitting to examine the racial policies of the Carpenters' union at some length.

The Carpenters' union has never made exclusion of Negroes a national policy, nor has it confined them to an inferior "auxiliary" status. In 1886, only five years after its founding, it claimed fourteen locals composed exclusively of Negroes in the South. By 1900, it was able to report a Negro membership of 1,000, again mostly in the South. During the next decade, twenty-five additional Negro locals were added, principally, it appears, through the efforts of a colored organizer employed by the national office.[18]

An explicit feature of the Carpenters' policy, however, has always been the segregation of white and colored carpenters into separate local bodies. In fact, with the Negro question in mind, the union's rules were modified in 1886 "so that more than one chapter might be issued in the same locality provided the existing local union offered no reasonable objection."[19] Segregation of the races subsequently developed into a fixed policy of the union, rigidly adhered to throughout the South, and practiced occasionally in the North as well.

During the two decades following 1910, the Carpenters' national officials seem, for reasons which are not clear, to have lost interest in encouraging organization of colored carpenters. During this period, southern white carpenters made use of their superior numbers and favored political status to obtain control over an ever-increasing share of union work. In accomplishing this task, the white carpenters found their union's separate local policy of substantial aid.

When two branches of the same national union exist in the same locality, friction is likely to develop over wages, working conditions, division of work, etc. The result may be a constant struggle for supremacy and much ill-feeling between the local unions.

These problems arise even where the separate locals are all composed of white mechanics, but they are aggravated when the locals are divided on the basis of race. Ordinarily, the Negro local is severely handicapped. It is usually smaller and, therefore, less powerful. The white business agent has, by reason of his race, easier access to employers' offices. He is thus likely to be better informed on future building plans than his colored rival. Out-of-town contractors, unused to dealing with Negro craftsmen, are easily misled into believing that the white local is the only local of the craft in the vicinity. If a Negro local does secure a contract to construct a large building, it frequently does not have enough members to supply the full need for a job, and consequently must call on the white local to furnish some men. On the other hand, white locals are usually large enough to furnish a full quota. If not, they find it easier to import white workers than do the colored locals; for Jim Crow restrictions make travel in the South difficult and unpleasant for Negroes. By refusing to work on the same section or building with Negroes, white locals can sometimes exclude them.

On occasions, white locals have been able to restrict Negro craftsmen to the colored section of the community. This method of discrimination is especially popular in newer southern cities where the Negro neighborhoods are most clearly defined. The restriction is enforced either by a building trades council ruling or by municipal ordinance, which the disenfranchised Negroes have been powerless to oppose. It has served not only to exclude Negro carpenters from the most lucrative projects, but also to prevent them from learning new techniques which have developed with the use of concrete, steel, and plywood. When a large construction project has been put up in a Negro neighborhood, however, prohibitions on the free movement of artisans have been hastily waived.[20]

That is not to imply that Negroes in mixed locals are never discriminated against. Unless they are in the majority and can control the business agent—a situation which probably does not exist in the carpentry trade—they frequently do not receive a proportionate share of jobs, especially in slack times. Nevertheless, most Negro mechanics prefer mixed locals. For then they can make their protests heard and have a better opportunity to obtain redress. By their presence at meetings, they are likely to know when jobs are available. And it is much more difficult to confine members of a mixed local to work in the colored community.

The difficulties encountered in obtaining work induced many Negroes to give up their union membership in order to take jobs at sub-union wages. By 1926, a survey could locate but fourteen local unions of Negro carpenters as compared with an estimated thirty-nine in 1912.[21]

Other Negro carpenters migrated to the North. Perhaps because by this time the colored mechanic was not such a rare phenomenon, discrimination was not so intense there, although it was by no means absent. In Chicago, a number of Negroes entered the industry through employment on open-shop jobs, and later were admitted to the local unions.[22]

In Philadelphia and New York, separate locals of Negro carpenters existed during the twenties. Negroes organized their local in the former city because they "were not justly treated in mixed locals." But their venture was not a success, and they have now returned to mixed locals. Local No. 1888 was organized in the latter city in 1916 as a mixed local, but the white members soon withdrew. Although other locals of the Carpenters in New York have had a few colored members for many years, Negroes applying for admission in that area are usually referred to No. 1888, whose members now work principally in the Harlem area where they are virtually confined by rulings of the New York Carpenters District Council, to which all New York locals of the Brotherhood must belong.[23]

The depression of the 1930's caused a serious shrinkage in the membership of the Carpenters' union, and nearly all of the already weakened colored carpenters' locals passed out of the existence. Consequently, when the building industry was partially revived by the New Deal public works program, which at the same time gave official recognition to the building unions, Negro carpenters, as well as many other Negro mechanics, were virtually excluded from participation.

This situation induced the PWA Housing Division to attempt to guarantee Negroes a proportionate share of work on its projects. A clause was inserted into all contracts let for cities with an appreciable Negro population, stipulating that the failure to pay colored workers a certain percentage of the skilled and unskilled payroll—the exact amount to be determined by the figures of the 1930 occupational census—"would constitute *prima facie* evidence of discrimination," for which, if proved, certain penalties were set. Efforts were also made to facilitate union affiliation for Negro craftsmen. Like provisions have been inserted in contracts let by the United States Housing Authority, the Federal Works Agency, and later, the various war agencies.[24]

This program has resulted in real material gains for Negro carpenters which would not have been possible without the assistance of the federal government even though all sorts of ruses were practiced by local unions and contractors to circumvent the racial clause. In a number of instances, the quota of Negroes were hired, only to be dismissed shortly on charges of incompetency. Often such dismissals were justified. Having been confined to small housing jobs by union practices, many Negro carpenters had never had the opportunity to learn the specialized techniques and operations developed for large-scale wood construction work in recent years.* Nevertheless, many competent Negro carpenters were summarily discharged or, as in Chattanooga and Birmingham, confined to rough work, which is first finished, and hence, means an early layoff.

Some white local unions of the Carpenters granted Negroes temporary work permits, in order to ensure that their union affiliation would not be permanent. In the South, several separate Negro locals were organized. In Birmingham, Augusta, Ga., and Louisville, Ky., Negroes were admitted to the Carpenters' locals for the first time. The first Negro Carpenters' locals in the history of Baltimore and Kansas City were founded. In the North, white unionists were forced either to admit Negroes for the first time or to increase their numbers if some were already members.

That Negroes did not obtain their proportionate share of carpentry work is indicated by the fact that, of the 3,641 skilled Negro workers employed on 277 projects sponsored by the USHA, up to January 1, 1941, only 634, or 9.9 per cent, were carpenters.[25] Yet carpenters comprise approximately 38 per cent of all Negro craftsmen.

The new federal nondiscrimination policy has been of material assistance to Negroes in obtaining jobs on war projects. Because many Negro locals had already been organized, Negroes were in a favorable position to exert pressure for their share of work. A

---

* In a letter to the writer, May 24, 1940, President W. L. Hutcheson of the Carpenters stated that he is "of the opinion, although we have no figures to show, that the negro carpenter would be less competent than the white on what you might term large jobs, particularly where concrete forms are used to a large extent." But the real reason for any lack of competency on the Negro's part has been discrimination which has prevented him from learning new techniques. In this, locals of the Carpenters' union have played a prominent role.

colored local of the Carpenters, founded in New Orleans in 1936, has been able, by astute leadership and federal assistance, to increase its membership to 700, most of whom have been continually employed. It is probably the largest and strongest Negro local of the Carpenters' union in the country. A small Negro local was organized in Chattanooga in 1939 to work on a housing project. At first excluded from war work, it has succeeded in placing over 100 men on various jobs at one time, thanks to federal assistance. The course of events at Columbia, S. C., followed a similar pattern. The Baltimore and Kansas City colored locals, established in 1940 and 1941, respectively, have prospered since their inception. The fact that Negroes had already been admitted to the previous all-white locals in Birmingham, Louisville, and in several northern cities facilitated the use of additional colored carpenters on war jobs in these areas.[26]

But Negro carpenters have not found jobs in war work with ease. The business agent of the Jackson, Tenn., local declared he would "recognize no Negro as a union man" and prevented qualified colored union carpenters from working on a huge army ordnance plant construction. The Washington, D. C., local has accepted Negro unionists' transfer cards only for a job being done by a colored contractor. The St. Louis local still bars Negroes. The white Baton Rouge local kept Negro carpenters of the colored local from working on a near-by Air Corps Cantonment until the job was almost completed. The Negro carpenters of Atlanta have had considerable difficulty in obtaining war work.[27]

Attempting to refute charges of discrimination leveled at his organization at the 1941 AFL convention, President W. L. Hutcheson, of the Carpenters, referred to a large colored local in Savannah. Yet that local had been virtually excluded from work between August 1941 and April 1942. The Savannah Building Trades Council had signed a closed-shop contract with a wooden ship construction company and excluded the Negroes from participation. On December 8, 1942, the Fair Employment Practice Committee ordered the Council to permit the Negro local to become a party to the contract.[28]

Although the white and colored locals in Mobile have both been in existence for over fifty years, there has been no co-operation between them since 1921. In March 1941, the business agent of the white local called a strike to prevent Negroes from working on a local bakery. In July 1941, the Federal Works Administration was forced to intervene to obtain work for the colored local on a war housing project. By refusing to work with Negroes, the white local has prevented their employment at the Brookley Field Air Base. The business agent of the white local has publicly stated on several occasions that his members are "strictly white and only seek employment where white carpenters are employed and do not mix." [29]

In Virginia, Negro carpenters were unorganized and virtually excluded from war work until April 1941, when they obtained charters for locals in Norfolk and Richmond, the first in the history of the state. This occurred only after a state-wide press campaign had been inaugurated in their behalf by Virginius Dabney, editor of the *Richmond Times-Dispatch*. After receiving their charters, however, the Negro carpenters were able to obtain work with relatively little effort, although for a time the Richmond group experienced some difficulty.[30]

The credit for the organization of large numbers of Negroes in recent years cannot go to the Carpenters' union. In many instances, the Negroes were accepted by local unions because of government pressure. Nearly all the members of separate locals organized recently have been brought together by secretaries of branches of the Urban League, a Negro social agency, or by other interested individuals desirous of assisting the Negroes to obtain their quota of federal construction jobs. Moreover, the national officers of the Carpenters' union have refused to intervene on behalf of colored unionists who have been denied work because of their race. Usually they have been willing to issue charters once a Negro group has been formed. In at least two instances, however, they had to be prodded by federal agencies. In Little Rock, a Negro local was scheduled to be set up on February 1, 1941, but was not done so when President Hutcheson intervened in behalf of the protesting white local there. He explained that to install a Negro local would "disrupt matters in Little Rock." After the USHA applied pressure, however, a charter was granted.[31]

The other case occurred in Birmingham. In 1936, Negro carpenters there applied for admission to the white local. They were advised to seek a separate charter. They did so, but their charter fees were returned with the explanation that an investigation had found it inadvisable to issue the charter. The next year, however, the PWA intervened on their behalf, and they received a charter.

Whether the gains which have accrued to colored carpenters as a result of federal government intervention will be permanent will depend, to a considerable extent, upon whether the present policy is continued. Of the twenty colored locals which now exist in thirty-five southern and border cities, not more than six or eight could obtain reasonably steady work for their members without federal aid. This is well-illustrated by the course of events in Birmingham and Atlanta. The colored local established in the former city in 1937 went defunct immediately after the completion of the PWA Housing Project. When a USHA project was inaugurated two years later, Negroes were able to obtain membership in the white local.

A colored Carpenters' local existed in Atlanta as early as 1898, but it went defunct during the twenties. A second local was formed in 1938, but following the completion of a housing project, its members could get no work, and it folded up. In 1940, a third local was organized for work on new housing projects. Today, nearly all of its jobs are on government construction.[32]

Federal racial policy in public construction has encountered much opposition in Congress. It has been alleged that Nathan Straus, former USHA administrator, and John M. Carmody, former Federal Works Agency head, were both forced to resign because they attempted to enforce strict compliance with racial quotas.[33] If this is correct, one cannot be too sanguine as to the permanency of the Negro carpenters' gains in the southern and border cities, where most separate locals exist.

On the other hand, the future seems brighter for colored carpenters in the North. Their presence is now taken more as a matter of course than twenty years ago, and the separate local, with its attendant evils, is found far less frequently. During recent years, union membership in Carpenters' locals in the North has been greatly increased, principally because of the federal government's racial policies. This increase appears less dependent for its maintenance upon federal policy than does the one in the South which is mainly confined to separate locals. Certainly, it no longer seems true that employment opportunities for Negro carpenters are superior in the South than in the North.

It is likely, however, that most Negro carpenters will continue, as they appear to have done in the past, to work on residential housing construction, in small towns, and on repair and maintenance jobs. These sections of the industry have never been thoroughly organized, partly at least because the unions have not found it worth while to devote their energies to it.[34] The wages are lower and the jobs of shorter duration than in large-scale construction. The ability of southern Negro carpenters to maintain their control over these jobs is sometimes attributable to their acceptance of a wage differential, which places their rate below the white non-union rate, and considerably below the union scale.[35] If the Carpenters' union enters this field after the war and equalizes wages, Negro carpenters may have difficulty in maintaining their present share of even this work.

The Brotherhood of Painters, Decorators, and Paperhangers

Second in importance only to carpentry as a source of employment for building craftsmen is painting. A glance at Table I reveals that, despite sizable losses in the South, the proportion of Negro painters in the country has been increasing slightly since 1890. The present section will indicate that this gain has occurred in spite of certain policies of the Brotherhood of Painters.

The policies of the Painters resemble in many ways those of the Carpenters. Negro membership was encouraged before 1910, and colored organizers were used for that purpose.[36] Interest in fostering Negro membership then fell off, and by 1926 a survey could find only 718 Negro union painters—less than 0.5 per cent of the Brotherhood's membership at that time.[37]

Again, like the Carpenters, the Painters at an early date adopted the policy of segregating Negroes into separate locals. In the North, it has adhered to this policy much more frequently than has the Carpenters. Moreover, because of certain peculiarities in the structure of their organization, white union painters have been able to use separate locals as an even more effective means of excluding Negroes from union jobs than have white carpenters. This President Lindelof virtually admitted when he told the 1941 convention of the Brotherhood that he "was almost daily in receipt of communications from National Negro Welfare Organizations"[38] protesting against discrimination.*

The peculiarities of the Painters' constitution which have aided race discrimination are the high degree of autonomy allowed locals (till quite recently), the district council, and the exclusive local contract. Even today, a local may reject by majority vote the membership application of a qualified mechanic. Before January 1, 1943, no second local could be chartered in the same jurisdiction in which another local union existed, except by permission of a majority of the members of that local. When, therefore, locals of the Brotherhood, such as those in Baltimore, Little Rock, and Omaha, refused either to admit Negroes to membership or to permit the establishment of a colored local in their jurisdiction, the national union could do nothing.[39]

The 1941 convention of the Painters thoroughly overhauled its constitution. Included in the revisions was an amendment which gives the general executive board the authority to grant a charter to any group of workers which a local union or district council refuses to organize for reasons which "are not sound or satisfactory." The Baltimore Negro painters have recently been admitted to the local there, not so much, however, because of pressure from the national union as because of the political power of Negroes on the Baltimore Central Trades Council.[40]

The district council is much more important in the Painters' union than in the Carpenters'. This has proved detrimental to Negroes. Before the recent amendments to the constitution, every local within the jurisdiction limits of the district council had to be represented in the council and be subject to its rules or be expelled from the Brotherhood.[41] The councils usually elect a busi-

---

* Later Mr. Lindelof denied Negroes were discriminated against by his Brotherhood and declared that the President's executive order, which created the Fair Employment Practice Committee unnecessarily cast aspersions. Said he: "I fail to see the reason for such an order. Our Brotherhood is a liberal Brotherhood, the members of our Brotherhood are liberal men . . . We do not at any time discriminate against color, creed, or nationality. We have [four] Negro representatives sitting in the hall today . . . I felt hurt when I read this order as it inferred that we, the Brotherhood of Painters and Decorators, were discriminating against anyone . . ." (Brotherhood of Painters, *Proceedings of Sixteenth General Assembly*, 1941, p. 115.)

ness agent or secretary who acts in that capacity for all the council's affiliates.

The district council system thus removes control of its affairs from a local, and by so doing can reduce a Negro local to the status of a Jim Crow auxiliary, which is dominated by the numerically superior white membership of the council. In Atlanta, for example, the Negro painters, after fighting for the privilege for nearly four years, were chartered as Local No. 102 on January 15, 1937. Then they had to wait for almost as long a period before they were given their first big job. In St. Louis, seven Negroes, the minimum necessary to receive a charter, managed to secure permission from the white painters to establish a separate local in November 1937. But the district council has refused to seat their delegate, although it forces them to pay per capita tax; prior to November 1940, it prohibited them from working on city or federal financed projects; and it still restricts the membership of the local to the original seven.[42]

Some district councils do treat Negroes more fairly. Those in New York, Chicago, and Kansas City are cases in point, but the last only recently permitted Negroes to organize after thirty-five years of exclusion. Although District Council No. 9 in New York has a permanent Negro organizer, a Negro delegate from one of its largest locals, and has taken a firm stand against discrimination, a large group of Negro painters in Manhattan have refused to affiliate with the Brotherhood unless they are exempted from the rule requiring that they join this district council. Perhaps it was to placate such groups that the 1941 convention of the Painters amended its constitution permitting the general executive board to penalize "as it deems proper" the refusal of a local union to affiliate with a district council. Formerly, expulsion of such a local was mandatory.[43]

Probably the most effective method of preventing Negroes from competing for union work is by means of the form contract which all unions and district councils of the Painters use in their dealings with employers. These contracts bind the employer to obtain all his painters from a *particular* local or district council. In areas where just a white and colored local and no district council exist, the white unionists can legally exclude the Negroes by signing up all the contractors. In both Mobile and New Orleans,

Negro painters have been organized in separate locals with the assistance of the white unionists desirous of preventing them from undercutting union wage scales. In both cities, the white locals were able to sign closed-shop contracts with nearly all the employers before the colored painters received their charters. Then, after the Negroes were organized and prohibited from working at sub-union wages, the white locals signed up most of the contractors for whom the Negroes had formerly worked. Since these contractors were now forced to pay union wage rates, they lost any special preference which they might have had for colored painters. Local No. 621, the colored local in New Orleans, went defunct in 1940, after less than two years of existence. The Negro painters of that city secured a new charter (No. 1353) in June 1941, and since then it and Local No. 1319, its Mobile contemporary, had fared better because of the war boom, but neither can be counted upon to survive a slack period of employment.

Negro painters have been able to make some gains as a result of the federal government's racial quotas on public construction. The Brotherhood now has sixteen Negro locals, ten of which have been chartered since 1937. Negroes have been admitted to local unions in Louisville, Norfolk, Baltimore, and Cleveland for the first time in recent years, and additional numbers have gained entrance in cities which have had a few colored members for a long time. However, exclusion continues in Newark, New Jersey, Columbus, Ohio, and in several cities in the South. And only 90, or 2.5 per cent, of the 2,641 Negro craftsmen employed on 277 U. S. Housing Authority projects prior to January 1, 1941, were painters.[44] Yet approximately 25 per cent of all Negro craftsmen are painters.

The fact that the proportion of Negroes in the painting trade has increased in spite of the policies of the Brotherhood of Painters can be attributed to the disinclination or the failure of the latter to organize workers on residential construction, maintenance, and alteration work. It is in this sector of the industry that most Negro painters have found employment to an even greater extent than have Negro carpenters. Recently, however, after the CIO entered the field, the Painters' union commenced chartering locals of these workers.[45] Whether organization of this sector of the industry will be accompanied by the same discrimination observable elsewhere in the trade remains to be seen.

The Bricklayers, Masons, and Plasterers' International Union

A larger proportion of Negroes are found in the trowel trades than in the other building crafts. This is primarily the result of conditions surrounding the entrance to these trades. Negroes find little difficulty in obtaining employment as hod carriers or as tenders to bricklayers and plasterers. In due course, many "pick up" enough of a particular trade to become "graduated artisans."

In recent years, however, semiskilled workers have found informal instruction in the trowel trades more difficult to acquire. Increased specialization and subcontracting have limited opportunities for instruction. With the development of large construction companies, employers no longer worked with their men, but left training in the hands of workers, with haphazard results. To a lesser extent, union restrictions have been a factor. Apprentice training has thus had to become more formalized.[46]

The substitution of formal training for "picking up" the trade has limited the opportunities of Negroes. White employers and workmen prefer white apprentices as a matter of course. Negro craftsmen are frequently hard enough put to maintain their own employment opportunities without insisting upon the use of colored apprentices. In the South, vocational training is often not available to Negroes. The consequences are indicated by the data in Table I, which show a decline in the proportion of Negro bricklayers between 1920 and 1940 from 8.1 per cent in the country and 53.6 per cent in the South to 6.0 per cent and 31.5 per cent, respectively.

It is not likely that the policies of the Bricklayers' union contributed materially to this decline. As early as 1870, the national officers of this union began a campaign to achieve equal status for Negroes. Affiliated locals which had color bars were forced to delete them from their rules, and independent locals excluding Negroes were denied admittance. Finally, in 1903, the national officers were strong enough to induce their constituents to amend the union constitution to give the executive board power to grant a charter to a local group if the objection of the subordinate union to the establishment of a second local was based on race, nationality, or religion. This provision was supplemented by a second one providing that a "fine of one hundred dollars shall be imposed on any member or union who shall be guilty of discrimination against any member of the B.M. & P.I.U. of A. by reason of race or color." A third section of the constitution prohibits the "black-balling" of an applicant for union membership except on grounds of incompetency as a mechanic.[47]

Unlike the Carpenters and the Painters, the Bricklayers did not adopt the separate Negro local as a national policy, but have only used it as a last resort. This policy was made easier by the fact that, in many southern cities, Negroes controlled the trowel trades and received the first charters there. The national union, however, has uniformly opposed the chartering of two locals in one jurisdiction, especially if the proposed locals were divided on the basis of race or nationality, because of the friction which almost inevitably results. Moreover, on a number of occasions, it has either fined locals for discriminating against Negroes, or forced them to honor the traveling cards of colored members. In northern cities, Brick-layers' locals were usually the first, and before World War I, often the only, locals of building craftsmen to admit Negroes. In the border cities, however, the familiar pattern of exclusion extended even to this union till recent years.[48]

In the writer's field survey of 1940-41, separate locals of Negroes were found in only three cities—Charleston, S. C., Atlanta, and Richmond. The Charleston local was organized about forty years ago as a mixed local, and still has a few white members. Its officers and most of its members have always been colored. In 1937, both they and the national union gave the white artisans permission to found a second local.[49] Work has been plentiful since then, but the Charleston Negro bricklayers may regret their decision if the experience of Negroes with separate locals in other crafts is repeated there.

The Atlanta bricklayers first organized as a mixed local in 1899. In 1921, the Negroes, who controlled the local, permitted the whites to establish a separate local. The white local succeeded in obtaining most of the jobs, the Negroes then undercut the union scale and by 1927 both locals were defunct. In 1928, a new mixed local was chartered, this time with the whites in control. The Negroes complained about job allocations, withdrew, and in 1934 secured a separate charter despite the objections of the whites. Relations between the two locals are poor, and the Negroes have not been able to obtain steady employment. This has induced about twenty colored bricklayers to form an independent association, the members of which work principally on residential construction at a wage below the union scale.[50]

The white Bricklayers' local of Richmond is decidedly exclusionist. By control of the largest block of stock in the holding company which owns the Richmond Labor Temple, it has been able to exclude Negroes from the Central Trades Council. It allegedly refuses to affiliate with the local building trades council because that body seats Negro delegates. The Negro bricklayers of Richmond were organized by the Urban League there in the summer of 1941. On August 6, 1941, the business agent of the white local agreed not to oppose a separate local, but an application addressed to him was not answered. Thereupon, the Negroes applied directly to the national union, and on November 25, 1941, received a charter. Because of the large amount of war construction in the area, work has been plentiful for them since then.

In ten cities, all in the South, mixed locals were found in which Negroes were in a majority. In all of these, the business agent was colored, an assurance that Negroes receive a proportionate share of work. The strongest is the Louisiana Local No. 1, New Orleans, which was founded in the 1890's. Approximately 60 per cent of its 300 members are colored. It was the first local in Louisiana to adopt apprenticeship standards. In September 1941, it had twenty-three apprentices, including seventeen Negroes, indentured for four-year terms. Either because New Orleans has a vocational school for whites but none for Negroes or because "bricklayers can only be made on the job," Local No. 1 has refused to accept any vocational school graduates as apprentices.

Negro bricklayers, as a rule, have had comparatively little trouble in obtaining their quota share of jobs on federal construction work. In fact, frequently when the quota could not be met in the carpentry or painting trades, a blanket percentage was substituted, and an attempt was made to make up the difference in the trowel trades. Of the 3,641 Negroes employed on 277 USHA projects up to January 1, 1941, 1,054, approximately 30 per cent, were bricklayers.[51] Yet less than 13 per cent of all Negro craftsmen are brick-layers.

The racial quota clauses in federal construction contracts have also resulted in an increase in Negro membership in the Bricklayers' union. Locals in Louisville, Ky., Norfolk, and Kansas City admitted them for the first time. The colored locals of Atlanta and Richmond were formed because of their influence. And many mixed locals admitted numbers of Negroes to enable them to meet the racial quota.

Sometimes, however, the Negro bricklayers have encountered difficulty. The national union executive board forced the St. Louis local to admit two Negroes who had joined the union elsewhere. Although this local has given work permits to colored unionists from other cities, it had admitted no others. Similarly, pressure from the national union forced the Baltimore local to give working permits to visiting Negro unionists, but this local has admitted no Negroes. The failure of the Negroes to make an issue of local membership is largely responsible in this instance.

In the spring of 1941, colored members of mixed locals in Birmingham and Mobile, who had been sent to Columbus, Ga., in response to an appeal by R. J. Gray, secretary of the Bricklayers, were allegedly discharged after a few hours' work by the local business agent because of their race. The Mobile local, a majority of whose members are white, filed a protest with Mr. Gray, and demanded that the Columbus local be fined $100 in accordance with the union constitution. Mr. Gray promptly informed the Mobile local of the proper manner to take up the grievance, and requested the secretary of Columbus local to explain his actions. The latter denied the discrimination, and claimed that the Negroes' workmanship was unsatisfactory. Although members of the Mobile local claim to have followed up their protest, Mr. Gray has received no communication from them since the original one. Hence the case has not been brought before the national executive board.[52]

On the whole, Negro bricklayers have fared well in their union relationship. Their experience indicates that more than a relatively liberal union policy is necessary if they are to maintain their position in a skilled occupation. Unless members of their race are afforded an opportunity to learn the trade in the future, as they once "picked it up" in the past, their share of the work will continue to decline.

The Operative Plasterers' and Cement Finishers' International Association

An even larger proportion of Negroes are plasterers and cement finishers than are bricklayers. In 1940, 15.2 per cent of the plasterers and cement finishers in the country and 54.5 per cent of those in the South were colored. Although Negroes have lost some ground in the South since 1920, this has been largely counterbalanced by gains elsewhere.

The high proportion of colored plasterers and cement finishers is, of course, to a large extent, attributable to the ability of Negro laborers, hod carriers, and plaster tenders to become "graduated artisans." There are also other factors. The plastering trade is made relatively unpleasant by the necessity of standing in uncomfortable positions in order to apply plaster to walls and ceilings. Until attracted by the high wages of recent years, southern whites were often content to leave this work to Negroes. In addition, many workers, who are classified as cement finishers are actually paid laborers' wages. This is especially common among nonbuilding construction cement workers in the South, most of whom are colored and unorganized.

The policies of the Operative Plasterers and Cement Finishers are somewhat similar to those of the Bricklayers. Founded in 1864 by plasterers, it absorbed the American Brotherhood of Cement Workers in 1915. This was decidedly to the advantage of Negroes. For, whereas the American Brotherhood not only organized Negroes in separate locals but also permitted them to transfer only to other colored locals, the Plasterers makes mixed locals, regardless of race, its general policy. Moreover, the constitution of the latter provides that discrimination against a member because of race which results in loss of a job shall be punished by a $100 fine.[53]

Only two separate locals were found in the writer's 1940-41 field survey. One, in Birmingham, came into existence in the twenties when the Negroes, who were in the majority in a mixed local, gave the whites permission to establish a second local. The other, in St. Louis, was chartered recently. Before that non-union Negroes were permitted to work on union jobs by a "gentlemen's agreement."

Twelve mixed locals were found in which Negroes were in a majority and had elected Negro business agents. The ones in Atlanta and New Orleans were especially strong.

No Negro craftsmen have had less trouble in obtaining work on federal construction projects than have plasterers and cement finishers. Of the 3,641 skilled Negroes employed on USHA projects prior to January 1, 1941, 1,643, about 45 per cent, were plasterers or cement finishers.[54] Yet colored plasterers and cement finishers comprise only 16 per cent of all Negro craftsmen.

Like the Painters, the government of the Plasterers' union requires membership in a district council, and before 1937 permitted the local unions considerable autonomy. No second local could be chartered in an area if the existing local protested, and union members from other locals could be excluded. In the South, these provisions were not detrimental to Negroes. They usually secured the first charter, and the number of workers in the trade is only large enough to support more than one local, and hence a district council, in the larger cities.

In the northern and border states, however, discrimination was not infrequent. But in 1937 the union constitution was amended giving the national officers discretionary power to charter locals and prohibiting discrimination against traveling members. These provisions, coupled with the quota clauses in federal construction contracts, and pressure from the national union when locals, for example the one in Kansas City, refused admission to Negroes, have usually resulted in the granting of full rights to the affected colored craftsmen.[55]

In so far as race discrimination is concerned, Negro plasterers and cement finishers have less difficulty than do other colored building craftsmen. But the employment opportunities of all plasterers, Negro and white, are likely to be diminished in the future by the use of prefabricated plaster board, which is becoming increasingly more popular in building construction.

THE FUTURE OF NEGRO BUILDING CRAFTSMEN

Two conclusions may be drawn from the material presented in this chapter. First, it is obvious that the racial policies of the building trades unions vary considerably. This seems primarily attributable to the differences in the bargaining strength of Negroes in the various crafts. The large proportion of Negroes in the trowel trades forced the Bricklayers' and Plasterers' unions to offer them equal status in order to organize the South. Negro carpenters and painters, being in a minority, have not been able to command that price, and have been forced to accept segregation. Negroes have never been able to gain entrance to the plumbing and electrical trades in large numbers, and therefore the unions have found that they can be effectively excluded.

The other conclusion is that one can scarcely be sanguine as to the future of Negro building mechanics. Even in the trowel trades, where union policies are favorable, new techniques threaten their position. The one bright spot has been the efforts of the federal government to guarantee Negroes their proportionate share of work on federal financed projects. Yet at best, this only freezes a none too favorable *status quo*. Besides, it may be discontinued with a change in administration.

There is another hopeful sign. The Negro community has awakened to the seriousness of the situation, and efforts have been made to establish pressure groups to assist Negro mechanics both within and without unions. Many of these groups were started by the efforts of the National Urban League, a Negro social agency with branches in cities throughout the country. The influence of the League was an important factor in persuading the federal government to insert nondiscrimination clauses in its construction contracts. To help make this policy a success, local League secretaries organized Negro building tradesmen into "mechanics' associations," and then assisted the Negroes either to gain admission to their respective unions or to obtain a charter for separate locals. Even after Negroes were admitted to unions, the local Urban Leagues have continued in many instances to handle their grievances with both unions and employers.

Most of the newly organized colored locals of the Carpenters and Painters were founded in this manner, and a considerable portion of the increased membership in the Bricklayers and the Plasterers is also attributable to Urban League activity. Local Leagues in Baltimore, Kansas City, Richmond, and Louisville, Ky., brought the benefits of union affiliation to Negro mechanics for the first time. But in Memphis, the AFL Central Trades Council branded the mechanics' association as "communistic" and the local League was threatened with being cut off from the community chest unless it ceased such activities and dismissed its industrial secretary. Being the only social agency for Negroes in Memphis, it was forced to comply. Likewise in St. Louis, not much progress was made by the League's mechanics' association in breaking down the barriers of the local craft unions. The St. Louis League requested an injunction from a state court prohibiting the St. Louis Housing Authority from paying out more funds until the nondiscrimination clauses of their contracts were complied with. Although this request was accompanied by a supporting affidavit from Nathan Straus, then USHA administrator, the case was continually postponed till the project was completed.

In the Norfolk-Newport News area, Negro mechanics found themselves excluded from unions and from jobs despite a shortage of workers. Assisted by Hampton Institute faculty members, they formed the Peninsula Trade and Labor Union in December 1940, which soon enrolled 250 members. The activities of this group, which received wide publicity in the Virginia press, resulted in a charter for the first Negro local of carpenters in Virginia and in the admission of Negroes to locals of the Painters, the Bricklayers, and the Plasterers. Negro electricians, being unable to gain admission to the union of their craft, formed a successful co-operative company. The Peninsula Union has now ceased to function, a fact which these Negroes may regret when work is not so plentiful as now and when an intercraft pressure would again be useful.

A successful mechanics' association was formed in Birmingham in 1939, under the leadership of L. S. Gaillard, one of Alabama's few Negro licensed master plumbers. It is still in existence. It maintains an office which acts as an employment bureau for colored mechanics, many of whom formerly missed jobs because employers were unable to contact them when they were needed. It has encouraged youths to serve apprenticeships and has sought to improve the business methods of its members. It induced the Carpenters' local to admit Negroes for the first time and the Bricklayers to increase its colored membership. The Painters refused to admit Negroes, but finally permitted non-union Negro painters to work on a USHA project without charge even though it was a closed-shop job.

In a few cities, Negroes are strongly enough situated to exert pressure within the established AFL organizations. They control the Bricklayers', the Plasterers', and the Hod Carriers' unions in New Orleans, and the colored Carpenters' local there is almost as large as the white. Consequently, they have an important voice in the Building Trades Council. Several times, the president of the Council, who is white, has intervened with contractors who have discriminated against Negroes. In Baltimore, Negroes held the balance of power in a recent election of officers of the Central Trades Council. In return for their votes, they were given representation on all the Council's committees, and because they supported the business agent of the Painters for an office, he was able to persuade his union to admit Negroes for the first time.

A Union Mechanics' Association for Negroes existed in New York City from 1909 to 1937. It was later absorbed by the New York Negro Labor Committee, an organization composed of AFL, CIO, and independent Negro unionists. It operates throughout industry, rather than just in the building trades. Similar organizations have been formed in Chicago, Washington, and Baltimore. Even more ambitious plans have been inaugurated in Indiana and the San Francisco Bay region. There management, labor, and Negroes are represented on committees which attempt to integrate Negroes in industries, including the building trades.[56]

If these various pressure groups can survive the dislocations of the war, they may open up new opportunities to Negroes in the building industry, which seems certain to boom after the war. In that case, the previous conclusion would be too pessimistic.

The Unskilled Negro Building Laborer

No analysis of the position of Negroes in the building industry could be complete without mention of their favored status in unskilled work. In 1940, 19 per cent of the 435,808 "construction laborers" in the country and 45 per cent of the 87,060 in the South were Negroes.[57] While the census classifications for this type of work are not comparable from one enumeration to another, there seems to have been some racial displacement in the South during the thirties, but this was counterbalanced by gains elsewhere. Generally, Negroes have had little trouble obtaining work as building laborers. White workers are frequently loath to accept these jobs, for which neither the pay nor the working conditions are good. Moreover, employers appear to favor Negroes. Since the contractors' profits usually depend upon the speed with which the work is completed, and since Negroes, because of their disadvantaged socio-economic status, are likely to be more amenable to "slave-driving," this employer preference is quite understandable.[58]

Prior to 1936, unskilled building workers were organized only in the larger cities. Since then, the International Hod Carriers', Building & Common Laborers' Union, AFL, has made great strides. In 1941, it claimed 250,000 members, including 70,000 Negroes, and has since continued to prosper.

This union has always organized workers without regard to race. In view of the racial character of the laboring force in the building industry, it could do nothing else if it wished to succeed. A Negro is a member of the national executive board, and 250 Negroes were among the delegates to the 1941 convention.[59] Union discrimination is not a problem for the Negro building laborer.

CHAPTER III

THE RAILROADS

The Negro railroad worker is in an anomalous position. He is denied a voice in the affairs of nearly all railway labor organizations; yet collective bargaining on the railroads has received wider acceptance than in almost any other American industry. He is, for the most part, ineligible to promotion although promotion in the industry is based almost exclusively upon seniority. And he frequently receives lower pay than white men when doing the same work, a fact which is often disguised by separate occupational classifications for white and colored workers who perform identical tasks.

The result has been that the Negro has become a pawn in industrial relations: employers have used him to fight unions and to depress wages; unions have retaliated by attempting either to limit the employment of Negroes or to drive those already employed from the roads. The material here presented shows that, as a consequence of the spread of collective bargaining, the proportion of Negroes in railroad industry has steadily declined since 1900 and especially since World War I; that certain agencies of the federal government and some state legislatures have aided the discrimination against Negroes; and that Negroes may soon be virtually eliminated from some departments of the industry at a time when every competent person is needed. The first two sections will analyze the position of Negroes in the operating department; the third will discuss the efforts of Negroes to prevent their complete extinction from this department; the fourth will discuss the Pullman porters; the fifth will describe the racial picture in the railway shops; the sixth, that in the clerical, freight handling, and station employee group; the seventh, that in the maintenance of way department; the eighth, that in the dining car service. The final section will be devoted to some conclusions about collective bargaining on the railroads and public policy.

THE OPERATING DEPARTMENT TO 1930

The "Big Four" railroad transportation unions, the Brotherhood of Locomotive Engineers, the Order of Railway Conductors, the Brotherhood of Locomotive Firemen and Enginemen, and the Brotherhood of Railroad Trainmen, have always limited their membership to white persons.[1] Nearly all other railroad unions have adopted racial restrictions similar in character. For example, the Switchmen's Union, a small AFL affiliate whose jurisdiction lies wholly within that of the Trainmen, has occasionally outdone its larger rival in its opposition to Negroes. Even insurgent industrial organizations, such as Eugene Debs' short-lived American Railway Union or the American Federation of Railroad Workers, have not granted Negroes equal status.[2]

The employment of Negroes in the train and engine services has always been confined almost exclusively to the southern and border states. Until World War I, it was usual for railroads in these areas to use Negro firemen and trainmen (brakemen, switchmen, or flagmen) on from 25 to 90 per cent of their runs. Contrary to general custom, however, Negro firemen and trainmen have almost never been promoted to engineer and conductor. Consequently, the racial restrictions of the Engineers' and Conductors' unions usually, although certainly not always, have served merely to institutionalize the *status quo*.

Before World War I, Negro railroad workers received lower wages than whites for performing the same work. Thus southern railway management found in the Negro a convenient tool with which to fight unionism and to depress wages. The Locomotive Firemen's and the Railroad Trainmen's unions dared not press for wages too high above those paid to Negroes lest their members be entirely replaced by black crews. Wages in the South for these occupations were thus considerably below those in other areas.

During the last two decades of the nineteenth century a vigorous debate on the "Negro question" was waged in the journals of the Firemen and the Trainmen. These Brotherhoods had two possible methods of meeting the competition of the unorganized Negroes. The first, as some northern member suggested, was to admit the Negroes into their union and to "teach him and educate him" to present a solid front against the employer. The second was to force the railroads to eliminate the Negro from train and engine service. The social origins of the Big Four made it almost inevitable that the second alternative would be chosen.

Except for the Trainmen, the Brotherhoods were founded as fraternal and beneficial societies rather than as trade unions. Much emphasis is still placed on these social features. To admit Negroes, the southern members declared, would be tantamount to admitting that the Negro is the "social equal" of the white man. This they refused to countenance. In 1899, the convention of the Trainmen adopted a resolution calling on the four Brotherhoods to "give their support toward clearing our lines" of Negroes. The Firemen had already espoused this policy. Since then, officials of these two unions have made zealous efforts to carry out the mandates of that resolution.

The issues between the black and white railwaymen were first brought before the public during the decade preceding World War I. Protesting against the increased use of Negroes, white firemen struck on some southern railroads, and threatened walkouts on several others. They failed to dislodge the black workers, but they were able to force a number of railroads to agree not to increase the percentage of colored firemen, and not to use Negroes on certain runs or in certain territories. Similar provisions were included in the 1910 agreement signed by the Trainmen and the Southern Railroad Association, which, in addition, barred Negroes from being employed henceforth as baggagemen, flagmen, or yard foremen.

It was not until World War I, however, when the federal government took over the roads, that a fundamental change in the position of Negro railwaymen was effected. Large numbers of them left the industry for more remunerative employment elsewhere. To halt this exodus of skilled labor, and as "an act of simple justice," William G. McAdoo, director-general of the railroads, issued an order providing that after June 1, 1918, "colored men employed as firemen, trainmen, and switchmen shall be paid the same rates as are paid white men in the same capacities."

Immediately after the war, the white railroad unions renewed their attack on the Negro. The federal government's World War I labor policy had greatly strengthened the railroad unions, and the equalization of pay order reduced the incentive of employers to hire Negroes. In addition, the decline in railroad employment from 2 million in 1920 to 1.6 million in 1921, (where it remained fairly constant till 1930) [3] made the white workers all the more anxious to displace the Negroes. These new factors worked very much to the advantage of the Brotherhoods.

Early in 1919, the Trainmen forced the U. S. Railroad Administration, by a threat to tie up all southern lines, to agree to a new set of rules, which stipulated that when vacancies occurred or new runs were created, the senior man would have preference in choice of runs or vacancy either as baggageman, brakeman, or switchman, except that Negroes were not to be used as conductors, flagmen, baggagemen, or yard conductors. Since Negroes could not work as flagmen, many of the older white trainmen followed instructions of their union president and exercised their seniority on brakemen's jobs, "bumping" junior Negroes; the younger whites then chose jobs as flagmen where they could not be bumped by senior Negroes. Hence many colored men who had been in train service for a considerable length of time were displaced.

Negro train porters also suffered heavy losses of jobs in the period immediately after World War I. These workers perform services similar to those rendered by Pullman and chair car porters, but they are often required to act as brakemen as well. Thus Negroes often fill two jobs at a wage lower than that paid a white worker for doing one.

Attempting to abolish wage inequalities, the Railroad Administration classified porters handling brakemen's duties as "porter-brakemen" and gave them brakemen's pay. In many instances, the wages of these workers were more than doubled. But because Negro porter-brakemen's wages were raised to the same level as those of white trainmen, the seniority lists for porters and brakemen on many roads were consolidated.[4] Whites were, therefore, made eligible to the post of porter-brakemen without at the same time opening to Negroes any of the jobs from which they had been barred, and more displacement of Negroes resulted.

This same agreement also provided that "porters shall have no rights as trainmen except where such rights may have been established by three months continuously in freight service." Since Negro porters have always been hired for passenger, and never for freight service, this clause has had the effect of preventing Negro porters from ever achieving a trainman's status. In addition, many contracts of the Trainmen's union stipulate that only "promotable" (i.e., white) men may be hired for freight service.[5] Taken with the first clause, it effectively bars Negroes from both freight *and* passenger service.

The hostility of the white trainmen toward the Negro has also been a major reason for the passage of many state "full crew" laws. Legislation of this type usually provides that a train crew shall consist of five persons: an engineer, a fireman, a conductor, a brakeman, and a flagman. While usually disguised as a safety measure, it is in fact a make-work, or "featherbed," rule written into law.[6]

By 1939, full crew laws were in effect in twenty-four states.[7] Most of them have been enacted in the North and obviously are not aimed at Negroes. In the southern states, however, the Trainmen's union has sponsored full crew legislation, not only as an ordinary make-work measure, but also as a means of displacing Negroes. For state enforcement officials usually rule that the Negro porter is not a brakemen even though he performs brakeman's duties. The U. S. Supreme Court has not actually endorsed such an interpretation, but it has refused to issue an order prohibiting prosecution of a railroad under a state full crew law for using Negro porter-brakemen instead of white brakemen.[8] The Big Four have attempted to induce Congress to pass a national full crew law, but without success.

Like the Railroad Trainmen, the Locomotive Firemen continued its drive against the Negro with renewed vigor after World War I. Contracts were continually altered with each new stipulation further reducing both the percentage of Negro firemen and the type of service and the territory in which Negroes could be employed. Before World War I, 80 per cent of the firing force on the Southern Railway were colored; by 1929 it had been reduced to $33\frac{1}{3}$ per cent. On the Atlantic Coast Line and the Seaboard Air Line the percentages were reduced from 90 to 50 and 90 to 25, respectively; and so on.[9]

In a number of instances, however, the Firemen's and Trainmen's unions were able to go much further. They induced several roads, including the huge San Francisco and St. Louis System, to agree to

TABLE IIa

ALL LOCOMOTIVE FIREMEN, NUMBER AND PROPORTION OF NEGROES IN THE UNITED STATES, AND IN THE SOUTH, 1910-1940

Year	UNITED STATES			THE SOUTH[1]		
	All Workers	Negroes	Per Cent Negro	All Workers	Negroes	Per Cent Negro
1910	76,381	5,188	6.8	11,782	4,897	41.6
1920	91,345	6,505	7.1	13,621	5,636	41.4
1930	67,096	4,642	6.9	11,534	3,818	33.1
1940[2]	47,410	2,356	5.0	7,215	2,128	29.5

SOURCE: U. S. Census of Occupations, 1910-1940.
[1] Includes Alabama, Arkansas, Florida, Georgia, Louisiana, Mississippi, North Carolina, South Carolina, Tennessee, and Virginia.
[2] Includes total of "employed" and "Experienced Workers Seeking Work" groups, which is roughly equivalent to "gainful workers" (workers attached to industry) as used in previous enumerations.

TABLE IIb

ALL RAILWAY TRAINMEN,[3] NUMBER AND PROPORTION OF NEGROES IN THE UNITED STATES, AND IN THE SOUTH, 1910-1940

Year	UNITED STATES			THE SOUTH		
	All Workers	Negroes	Per Cent Negro	All Workers	Negroes	Per Cent Negro
1910	165,530	6,839	4.1	16,381[4]	4,886	29.8
1920	216,024	7,609	3.5	22,944[5]	5,083	22.2
1930	180,414	5,918	3.3	22,929	3,745	16.3
1940	113,736	2,857	2.5	13,604	2,060	15.1

SOURCE: U. S. Census of Occupations, 1910-1940.
[3] Includes brakemen, switchmen, and flagmen.
[4] Data for eight states only.
[5] Data for nine states only.

fill all vacancies with white men, thus pointing to the eventual elimination of Negroes from the firing and train services.

A comparison of the census figures for the years 1910-1930, as shown in Table II, indicates clearly the effects of the activities of the Brotherhoods. In the ten southern states in which more than 90 per cent of the Negro firemen and trainmen are found, 41.3 per cent of the firemen and 29.8 per cent of the trainmen were colored in 1910; twenty years later, these percentages had dropped to 33.1 and 16.3, respectively. The number of train porters declined from 7,000 in 1920 to less than one-half that figure in 1930.[10] Although this decline was probably primarily attributable to the general decrease in employment on the railroads, undoubtedly it was also influenced by the activities of the Trainmen's union.

THE OPERATING DEPARTMENT, 1930-1943

During the 1930's, Negro firemen and trainmen also lost ground, but at a slower rate than during the previous decade as the data in Table II indicate. There was, however, no letup in the strenuous opposition of the Brotherhoods to their employment. An examination of their activities shows that they were preparing for an offensive which would drive the Negro entirely from the railroads. Before describing this offensive, which was launched *after* the 1940 census was taken, it is appropriate to discuss the events of the 1930's which led to the present crisis.

After remaining relatively stable at 1.6 million between 1921 and 1929, employment in the railway industry began a further decline in 1930. It fell below a million in 1933 and fluctuated around that figure for the rest of the decade.[11] Because of the strict seniority which prevails in the railroad industry white trainmen and firemen were displaced in large numbers by conductors and engineers senior in service, whose jobs had been abolished by technological progress or business depression.[12] Since most Negro firemen and trainmen were hired before World War I, they had been able to accumulate more seniority than whites and were therefore entitled to good jobs while whites were either assigned to inferior work or displaced altogether.

This situation resulted in intense racial antagonism which culminated in a reign of terror in the lower Mississippi Valley. A careful investigation revealed that at least ten Negro firemen and trainmen were killed and twenty-one wounded in this area between September 7, 1931 and July 10, 1934.[13] Nor was this the first time that such violence had occurred there. A decade previously, a similar outbreak resulted in the death of at least five Negro firemen and injuries to eight others.

Yet it must be emphasized that not violence, but the peaceful methods employed by the Brotherhoods have been primarily responsible for the present plight of Negro railwaymen. Since 1934, they have found federal agencies useful in accomplishing their purpose.

Collective bargaining on the railroads has been carried on since 1926 within the framework of the Railway Labor Act. As initially written, this Act guaranteed workers the right to choose their bargaining representatives. As interpreted by the Supreme Court, however, it did not force that carrier to deal *only* with the representatives chosen by the majority of employees.[14] In 1934, the Railway Labor Act was amended to provide that: "The majority of any craft or class of employees shall have the right to determine who shall be the representative of the class or craft. . . ." In addition, the 1934 amendments outlawed yellow-dog and closed-shop contracts and established the National Meditation Board and the National Railroad Adjustment Board. The functions of the latter will be discussed at a later point.[15]

Under the Amended Act, the Meditation Board determines, by vote if necessary, which union shall act as sole bargaining agent of any class or craft. The Firemen's and the Trainmen's unions have been so designated for their respective classes, on 99 per cent of the total mileage covered by Class I* railways.[16] If, for example, 51 per cent of the firemen on a particular railroad are white, the former can obtain exclusive bargaining rights and thus become the duly accredited representative of 49 per cent of the firemen who are barred from joining it. This provision, which, under ordinary circumstances, would ensure effective union management relations, makes collective bargaining a mockery for the black minority on the roads when considered in the light of the almost universal exclusion practiced against them. The writer

* Class I railways are those having an annual operating revenue of $1 million. They employ about 90 per cent of all railway workers.

does not wish to argue for minority representation under the Railway Labor Act. Experiences with it have shown that it merely disrupts collective bargaining without effectively protecting the interests of the minority.[17] But there is a serious question of public policy involved when an agency of the federal government designates an organization as sole bargaining representative of a group of workers, and yet a minority of these workers are forbidden, solely because of their color, to join and to participate in the activities of this organization. Moreover, the attitude of the Mediation Board toward Negroes, particularly in jurisdictional disputes between Big Four unions, has not been above criticism, as will be shown presently.

As the Big Four are unaffiliated organizations, there is no central governing body to settle disputes as to seniority, jurisdiction, etc., which frequently rise amongst them. During the twenty years preceding 1925, relations between the Conductors and the Trainmen and between the Engineers and the Firemen were governed by agreements. Soon thereafter, however, these compacts were abrogated, and since then jurisdictional disputes have been frequent as each has attempted to take over members of the other. Ever since its inception in 1934, the Mediation Board has been compelled to spend a considerable portion of its time attempting to resolve these interunion squabbles. In the South, the Engineers and Firemen have made the Negro a pawn in their disputes. An examination of a few of these cases will reveal how representation under the Amended Railway Labor Act can work to the disadvantages of Negroes.

In November 1933, the Firemen's union chartered a local union of engineers on the Florida East Coast Railway. In a series of hotly contested elections conducted by the Mediation Board during the ensuing seven years, it won sole bargaining rights for engineers, who up to that time had been represented by the Brotherhood of Locomotive Engineers. On March 6, 1941, however, the latter regained bargaining rights in still another election.

The Firemen's union has had no contract for firemen on the Florida East Coast since 1912, when the management broke a strike by hiring Negroes. Since then, it has used an all-black firing force, allegedly at wages below those paid on other roads.

At present, this is the only Class I railroad which employs Negro firemen exclusively.

Also since 1912, the Engineers' union had been unable to secure seniority rights for engineers in firemen's jobs in case of layoffs. Hence, when the working force was reduced, senior engineers could not displace junior firemen, as is the custom on almost every other American railroad.

The dissatisfaction of the Florida East Coast engineers over this fact was further increased when, during more recent years, the general chairman of the Engineers' union acted as representative for the Negro firemen in return for monetary compensation. Thus he helped to protect the jobs of the unorganized Negroes while demoted engineers were unemployed. After his death, his wife took over the allegedly lucrative job.

The Firemen's union persuaded the Florida East Coast engineers to transfer their allegiance to it by promising to alter this situation. When it failed to fulfill this promise, they transferred back to the Engineers' union. On February 19, 1942, the latter induced the trustees of the railroad to agree that engineers in their employ should be credited with seniority rights in firing jobs as of January 1, 1942, and that newly employed engineers shall have such rights as of their hiring date. This contract also stated:

Engineers accredited with seniority rights as firemen as of January 1, 1942, will not be permitted to exercise such rights in firing service until all of the colored firemen having seniority rights prior to January 1, 1942, have fully exercised their seniority rights to positions of firemen. When all of the colored firemen, with seniority rights prior to January 1, 1942, have fully exercised such rights, promotable [i.e. white] firemen will be used in firing positions until fifty-five per cent of the firing positions are filled by promotable men.

This contract means that Negro firemen are about to lose their last stronghold.[18]

In an endeavor to gain the right to represent firemen in the South, the Brotherhood of Locomotive Engineers has attempted to persuade Negro firemen to vote for it in return for promises to mitigate the percentage quotas imposed by its rival. If, for example, the Engineers could persuade all the Negro and one or two white firemen to vote for it on roads where approximately 50 per cent of the firemen are colored, it could secure bargaining rights.

As early as October 1930, the Engineers sought the aid of the Negro employees of the Jacksonville (Fla.) Terminal to take over the contract for firemen and hostlers. On April 17, 1935, it won a Mediation Board election conducted among that company's firemen, 19 to 0. Accordingly, it was certified as the bargaining agent for the then all-colored firing force. Hostlers, who were all white, and hostler helpers, who were all colored, were put in a separate bargaining class.* As they split their votes evenly between the two unions, no certification was possible.

Immediately, the president of the Firemen's union filed a protest with the Board, which induced the latter to suspend its certification on November 26, 1935, less than one month after it had been issued. He denounced the bargaining units which the Board had defined, maintaining, among other things, that Negroes should not have been placed in the same class as whites because they were not eligible to membership in either his union or in the Engineers, and hence their interests "are frequently in conflict with the interests of the members of the applicant organization," and also because it was usual to place firemen, hostlers, and hostler helpers in the same bargaining unit.

On June 8, 1936, after a mediator of the Board had investigated the situation, Dr. Wm. L. Leiserson, then, as now, chairman of the Board, addressed a joint communication to the heads of the Engineers and the Firemen in which he stated that the bargaining units in this case were unusual, but had been adopted because white employees had interchangeable seniority rights in the three occupations, and Negroes had seniority rights only among hostlers and their helpers. He admitted such a grouping was questionable, but he warned the Brotherhoods that no matter what bargaining units were deemed appropriate, the colored employees would control the result. Besides, the Negroes had informed the Board of their intention to choose a union of their own as bargaining agent rather than vote for either Brotherhood. Hence he advised the Brotherhoods to withdraw the case from the Board, which they did after a long delay.[19]

Exactly on what grounds the Board's chairman deemed it his responsibility to suggest to the heads of the two Brotherhoods that they withdraw their requests for representation elections because

* Hostlers handle engines in and around roundhouses.

Negroes would control the results, or why he warned them of the Negroes' determination to choose a union of their own, is not clear. Undoubtedly, the Negroes would not have informed the Board of their intentions if they expected that it would be communicated to the white union chiefs. Sound public policy does not recognize such behind-the-scenes arrangements.

Even less praiseworthy were the sentiments expressed by the late James W. Carmalt, member of the Board, in a letter to the heads of the Engineers' and Firemen's unions on January 4, 1936. In it he reviewed the history of the dispute between the unions and offered his services to help bring peace. Among other things, he noted that in "the southeastern region the Negro question interjects itself in that the B. of L. E. are [sic] soliciting the votes of Negro firemen so as to align them with a small minority of whites in the craft so as to control the representation of the craft." This "demonstrates the unhealthy condition that has grown in the relation between the two Organizations *when the votes of the colored employees are used to determine white representation.* From an organization standpoint it would seem more objectionable than anything that has preceded it." Mr. Carmalt then questioned the wisdom of these tactics "because of the degrading effect in the immediate locale where applied, because of the internal dissension in the B. of L. E. Organization that is inevitable, and *because of the ultimate menace to the present set-up of railway labor organizations in the impetus that will be given to the general movement toward organization of a vertical union among colored railway employees.*"[20]

At the time Mr. Carmalt wrote this letter, a group of Negro railroad workers were attempting to form an industrial union.[21] Had this movement been successful (as it was not), it might indeed have been a "menace to the present setup of railway labor organizations." In fact, it might even have been able to counteract the activities of the Firemen's and Trainmen's unions enough to preserve some of the employment opportunities which Negroes have since lost. After reading Mr. Carmalt's letter, and the similar one written by Dr. Leiserson in the Jacksonville Terminal case, one cannot avoid receiving the impression that the Board regards collective bargaining in the train and engine services as strictly a white man's affair. Accordingly, any attempt on the part of

Negro firemen or trainmen to avail themselves of the provisions of the Railway Labor Act by organizing unions for their own protection is looked upon as disruptive and is to be avoided. This impression appears to be substantiated by the actions of the Board in an Atlanta, Birmingham, and Coast (A.B. & C.) Railroad case.

On April 30, 1940, the Board certified the Locomotive Firemen as the exclusive bargaining agent of the engineers and the firemen, hostlers, and outside hostler helpers employed by the A.B. & C. According to the Board's records, the Brotherhood defeated "other organizations or individuals" in the election, 43 to 2 in the engineers class, and 47 to 41 in the firemen, etc., class.

At the time of this election, the A.B. & C. employed ninety-four firemen, hostlers, and outside hostler helpers, of whom not more than twenty-five were white. The engineers and the white firemen were represented by a local organization, the Railway Employes' Co-operative Association; the Negro firemen and hostlers by a similar union, the Colored Hostler Helpers and Locomotive Firemen, Inc. Whereas the white organization had a collective contract, the Negro union had only an "understanding."

Although the Mediation Board's policies permit a union on the ballot if it "holds an agreement covering the employees whose representation is in dispute," it refused to give either the colored or the white organization a place on this ballot. The election was held with no member of the colored union acting as observer at the polling booths, and the ballots were counted in a hotel room to which no colored union member was admitted. The Negro union protested the results to the Board, claiming that nearly all the colored firemen had written the names of their union on the ballot, but the protest was not allowed.[22]

In view of the fact that approximately seventy of the ninety-four firemen, hostlers, and hostler helpers on the A.B. & C. were colored, it is difficult to understand how the Locomotive Firemen could have obtained a majority of the votes. Uneducated as these Negro firemen may have been, they certainly must have been aware of the policies of the Brotherhood and, if so, could not have been expected to vote for it as their bargaining agent. Had the Board thoroughly investigated the results of this election, as circumstantial evidence alone clearly warranted, perhaps the reasons for the strange outcome would have been unearthed. Nor is this the only time that a discriminating union has won or retained bargaining rights for a class, the majority of whom were Negroes who protested the results in vain. Similar cases involve trainmen on the A.B. & C., trackmen on the Florida East Coast, coach cleaners on the Texas and Pacific, firemen on the Central of Georgia, and redcaps in the St. Paul terminal, among others.

The appropriate bargaining unit question, which was raised in the Jacksonville Terminal case, was definitely settled by the Board as early as 1936. Since then, it has "definitely ruled that a craft or class of employees may not be divided into two or more on the basis of race or color for the purpose of choosing representatives." Instead, it has decided that "all those employed in the craft or class must be given the opportunity to vote for the representatives of the whole craft or class." [23] This policy has been upheld by the courts.[24]

Whether Negroes would benefit by a reversal of this ruling is not at all clear. True, most colored firemen would prefer to be represented by an organization of their own rather than by the BLF & E. But bargaining units set up on the basis of race would not hinder that union from demanding more of the work performed by the "Negro craft." On the other hand, when two crafts such as firemen and hostlers can be separated, and when, as at the Jacksonville Terminal, the majority in the one craft is ineligible to membership because of race in the organization claiming jurisdiction over both crafts, there appears good reason for taking race into account in determining the appropriate unit.

The Board, however, has decided against such an interpretation of the appropriate unit on other grounds. After a year's experience, it was "impressed that the tendency to divide and further subdivide established and recognized crafts and classes of employees" had already gone so far that it threatened "to defeat the main purposes of the Railway Labor Act, namely, the making and maintaining of agreements covering rates of pay, rules, and working conditions and the avoidance of labor disputes." Accordingly, it has attempted to establish as the appropriate unit, "the customary grouping of employees into crafts and classes as it has been established by accepted practice over a period of years in the making of wage and rule agreements." [25] Since, however, crafts and classes have been "established" principally as a result of the activities of the so-called "standard" railway labor organizations, what the Mediation Board usually does in actual practice is to place in one craft or class all the workers within the jurisdiction of a standard railway union.* In view of the fact that nearly all these unions either exclude Negroes, or afford them only inferior status, it is not surprising that the units deemed appropriate by the Board should not be the ones best suited to advance the welfare of colored railwaymen. The discussion of the position of Negro freight handlers, track laborers, and dining car workers in succeeding sections of this chapter will shed further light on this question.[26]

At the 1931 convention of the Locomotive Firemen, a plan for a "concerted movement"—i.e., a regional bargaining conference— to achieve the complete elimination of Negroes was decided upon. Subsequently, it was reaffirmed by its 1937 convention, which passed a resolution authorizing such a campaign in the interest of "safety." [27]

The decision of the Firemen's union to raise the "safety" angle derived from two technological developments—the mechanical stoker and the Diesel engine. The former was used as early as 1900 to offset the difficulties encountered by handfiring the larger and more powerful engines, but many engines continued to be fired by hand. As a result of a petition filed by the Engineers' and the Firemen's unions, the Interstate Commerce Commission ruled in September 1937 that by July 1, 1943 all engines for use in fast passenger or freight service, with certain exceptions, must be equipped with mechanical stokers.[28] Soon thereafter, the Firemen entered into a secret agreement with the Gulf, Mobile, & Ohio Railroad, whereby in return for preference given members of its organization on stokerized engines, it waived its right to request and to obtain a higher wage scale.[29] Such agreements are, of course, aimed at displacing Negroes.

Diesel engines, which are a comparatively recent development, reduce the need for firemen. On February 28, 1937, however, the

---

* It is interesting to note that the National Labor Relations Board has deemed it advisable on many occasions to designate appropriate bargaining units much smaller in size than those found suitable by the Mediation Board, despite the fact that the Wagner Act, unlike the Railway Labor Act, does not require that the appropriate unit be a "craft or class."

Firemen's union induced the Association of American Railroads to sign an agreement to place a "fireman" (helper) on all Diesel locomotives, which were being operated at that time with only an engineer and a mechanic.[30] In order to restrict the assignment to this "featherbed" job to white (or promotable) men, separate agreements were reached during the ensuing three years with the Atlantic Coast Line Railroad, Seaboard Air Line Railway, and the Gulf, Mobile & Ohio Railroad, which "specifically provide that the employment and assignment of firemen (helpers) under the terms of the Diesel-electric agreement shall be confined to those firemen duly qualified for service on such locomotives; and that only firemen in line for promotion shall be accepted as duly qualified for such service."[31]

By 1940, the Firemen's union was ready for a concerted movement to extend the principles of these two agreements to nearly all railroads which then employed Negro firemen. It asked for contracts with these railroads,[32] stipulating that only promotable men be employed on Diesels, and that all vacancies and new runs be staffed by promotable men.[33] With the assistance of two members of the National Mediation Board,[34] an agreement was reached on February 18, 1941, which provided, in effect, that the percentage of Negroes on nonsteam-power engines shall not exceed 50 per cent; that in seniority districts where said percentage is above 50 per cent, only whites shall be hired, and all new runs and vacancies shall be filled with whites; and that "on any road having, in the opinion of its BLF & E Committee, more favorable rules or conditions than that above stipulated, such rules and conditions may at the opinion of such committee be retained in lieu of the above provisions." But the provision of the agreement which has proved most disastrous to Negro firemen is the following one:

It is expressly understood that in making this agreement representatives of the employees do not waive and are in no way prejudiced in the right to request agreement on the individual carriers here represented which will restrict the employment of helpers on other than steam power to promotable men; and it is agreed that this question is to be negotiated to a conclusion with the individual carriers.[35]

There is, of course, no way of knowing how many secret agreements have been negotiated pursuant to this last provision, with the exception of those already mentioned in connection with the earlier Diesel agreement. The latter refers only to road service, and the Atlantic Coast Line and the Southern Railway use Negroes on Diesel switch engines. The Central of Georgia signed a supplementary agreement with the Locomotive Firemen since the date of the February 18, 1941, "nonpromotable" agreement, which specifically provides that white firemen shall receive first priority on vacancies in all classes of service; the Norfolk Southern has agreed to a similar arrangement. So far as this writer has been able to determine, only two railroads, the Florida East Coast, where all firemen are colored, and the Louisville & Nashville, employ Negro firemen on Diesels in road service.[36]

Whatever the number of secret agreements, scores of cases and dozens of affidavits have been brought to the writer's attention, which show beyond the shadow of a doubt that the net result of the nonpromotable agreement has been a wholesale displacement of Negro firemen. Should the present trend continue, it is not unlikely that colored firemen will have been virtually eliminated by 1950. A few illustrations will show why this may be expected.

A colored fireman may be displaced on the grounds that by his presence the 50 per cent Negro percentage is exceeded. But he has no way of checking whether this is so, for only the management and the sole bargaining agent, the BLF & E, know just what percentage of Negro firemen is currently employed. Actually, Negroes may have only 25 per cent of the jobs, but they have no redress.

Under the nonpromotable agreement, all new runs must go to whites until the percentage of Negroes is reduced to 50. On December 6, 1942, freight operations were slowed up by government orders. Hence "new runs" were created. "New runs" are likewise created if the mileage is changed by at least twenty miles per day, if a terminal is changed, or if the number of trains in a "pool" is changed. Thus "new runs" have resulted in a tremendous displacement of senior Negroes by junior whites since the signing of the nonpromotable agreement.

Likewise all vacancies must be filled by white men until the 50 per cent quota is reached. White firemen have exercised their seniority on junior Negroes. They remain in these jobs only a day, or even a few hours, and than take a better position. This creates a "vacancy," which can be filled only by white men.

Some railroads are co-operating with the BLF & E by posting

notices of vacancies in places where only whites can see them, such as white waiting rooms or rest rooms in the South so that Negroes have no opportunity to apply for openings. Others, such as the Seaboard, are announcing new positions as open to whites only. There is evidence that some railroads are hiring inexperienced white workers instead of recalling furloughed Negroes. Added to all this is the already mentioned fact that Negroes are about to lose out on their last stronghold, the Florida East Coast Railway.[37]

The nonpromotable agreement was signed at a time when employment on the railroads had begun to increase as a result of the defense program. Since then it has continued to rise until, by October 1942, a figure of 1.4 million was reached, the highest in ten years.[38] For the first time in a quarter of a century, the demand for railroad labor exceeds the supply. Since the summer of 1942, an average of between 500 and 1,000 vacancies have been reported for firemen.[39] Yet Negro firemen are either unemployed or working in positions of less value than those to which their skill and seniority entitle them. Moreover, the Locomotive Firemen has consistently refused to sanction any changes in its agreements which would permit the employment of Negroes to mitigate the labor shortage. On the Atlantic Coast Line, for example, where the Brotherhood and the railroad agreed in 1925 that no more Negro firemen would be employed, the former conducted a strike vote in December 1942, in protest against the railroad's plan to employ a few Negroes in order to meet the labor shortage. Thus the nonpromotable agreement has acted to impede the efficiency of a vital war industry.

In 1926, President D. B. Robertson, of the BLF & E, stated that he hoped Negro firemen would soon be eliminated.[40] Largely through the efforts of himself and his coworkers, his wish may soon come true. After the war, employment in the railway industry is likely to decline. The BLF & E will probably demand a further reduction in the quotas of Negro firemen. Unless prompt action is resorted to, Negro firemen, who are among the highest paid colored workers in America, are doomed—a terrific blow to a racial minority whose employment opportunities are already severely limited.

The Railroad Trainmen also continued its active opposition to Negroes during the 1930's. Its 1931 convention resolved to have

Negro porter-brakemen removed.[41] To accomplish this, officials of the Trainmen availed themselves of the National Railroad Adjustment Board.[42]

The Adjustment Board has jurisdiction over disputes arising out of the interpretation of collective agreements in the railway industry. A bipartisan organization, it is composed of thirty-six members, one-half of whom are chosen and compensated by carriers, the other half by unions. The Board is divided into four divisions.[43] If a division deadlocks (except on a question of procedure), the members choose a neutral referee, or if they cannot agree on one, he is chosen by the Mediation Board.[44]

The unions which are eligible to participate in the selection of labor members are those which are free from employer interference and which are *national in scope*. The Secretary of Labor has the final decision as to whether unions possess these qualifications. Actually, except in cases of the Pullman porters and the dining car employees, no organization composed mainly of Negroes has been found qualified to participate on the Board, although one, the United Transport Service Employees, appears more fitted than do some which have been declared eligible. This union represents redcaps on at least 35 per cent of the nation's Class I railway mileage, as well as a substantial proportion of the train porters and dining car employees, and all Pullman laundry workers. On the other hand, the Switchmen's Union, which represents yard foremen, helpers, and switchtenders on 7 per cent, and yardmasters on 1 per cent of the Class I railway mileage, has been deemed national in scope and participates in the selection of employee representatives for the First Division.[45] Apparently the definition of "national in scope" is elastic in scope and can be stretched or slackened, depending upon the organization involved.

The Adjustment Board has refused to permit individuals to petition it for relief although this seems contrary to both the language and the intent of the Amended Railway Labor Act. Sec. 3 (i), after referring to "disputes between an employee or group of employees and a carrier or carriers," states that "the dispute may be referred by petition of the parties or by either party to the . . . Adjustment Board." [46] When, however, attempts have been made by individuals to bring cases before a division, it deadlocks as to whether to hear it, the employer members voting "Yes," the employee members voting "No." Since referees are not used to break deadlocks, the case is not heard.[47] The same thing occurs on the question as to whether notice and opportunity to be heard should be given to those whose welfare may be affected by an award of the Board, although Section 3 (j) of the Act states that divisions "shall give due notice of all hearings to the employee or employees and the carrier or carriers involved in any disputes submitted to them." Obviously, a person whose earning power would be adversely affected by an award is "involved" in a dispute within the meaning of the Act. The latter practice has continued although the federal courts have not only refused to enforce awards handed down under such circumstances, but have also granted injunctions preventing their enforcement on the ground that failure to give notice is a denial of due process.[48]

Since an award may adversely affect the earning power of a worker, the refusal to permit interested parties to be heard is clearly a denial of due process. Neither the carrier nor the union can adequately represent certain individuals. The carrier and an individual may both oppose the union's claim, but the former may only slightly resist in a matter vital to the latter. Even to a lesser extent can the union represent the interests of an employee if the claim it is seeking injures that employee's economic status. And when an employee not eligible to equal membership because of race is adversely affected by an award, it is still more obvious that the setup of the Adjustment Board can lay no claim to fair treatment.

Recently a United States District Court ordered the Adjustment Board to hear a case brought by an individual who was not a union member. The court ruled that the benefits of the Railway Labor Act are not confined to organized employees, and that the Board erred in refusing to hear cases brought by individuals who had exhausted their remedies under the Act before coming to the Board. This decision is a significant step in the right direction. But even if Negroes could present their case before the Board it is doubtful if they would obtain justice. For the case would be judged by representatives of the railroad and the union which were responsible for their grievances in the first place.[49]

There are other features of the Adjustment Board which mark

it as the most questionable administrative agency ever created by Congress. It operates in secrecy, admitting neither the public nor reporters. Its published awards are often too brief for one to determine upon what evidence decisions are reached. Precedents are slavishly adhered to, but equities are virtually ignored. The right of appeal is reserved to the winning party. Congress apparently thought that when the losing party refused to obey an unjust award, the winning party would apply to the courts for enforcement, and thus judicial review would be observed. Instead, however, unions have enforced questionable awards by direct action, i.e., a threat to strike, and so in practice the Board's awards are usually final.

The climax of this unique agency's operations is the character of its awards, which have been described by an outstanding authority as "amongst the strangest in the annals of industrial relations." Of particular interest here is the doctrine established by the Board (with referee sitting in and employer members dissenting) "that each and every piece of work in the operation of the railroad no matter how minute, belongs to some particular class of employee and, in effect, is *owned* by that class." The basis for the Board's interpretation is the seniority district. All those in one district are entitled to do certain work. Should the Board's interpretation of property rights differ from those of management, the latter must conform and is, in addition, liable for back pay even though no bad faith was evident. Moreover, under this doctrine railroads are often prevented from abolishing switching yards which no longer are needed, and frequently are forced to pay for work which no longer exists.[50]

Now if the right to do certain work is the property of a particular class, and if Negroes perform that task, but are not classified by the same title, they really have no "right" to such work. This is the sophistry which the Trainmen's union has put forward to displace Negro porter-brakemen. On April 20, 1942, the First Division of the Adjustment Board handed down a decision which accepted such extraordinary reasoning.

The case rose on the Sante Fe Railroad, which since March 1, 1899, has hired Negroes to perform the duties of both porters and brakemen. The wages of these Negroes were raised to the level of those of white brakemen during World War I and kept there since then, but contrary to general practice, the seniority lists of porters and brakemen were not consolidated.

Beginning in September 20, 1920, the Trainmen's union made several attempts to obtain the work done by the Negroes for its members. The Sante Fe refused because the whites declined to do porters' work. Both in 1926 and 1927, an arbitration board *on which the Trainmen's union was represented refused* its claim to take over the Negroes' jobs and each time the union agreed that the award would be final and binding. Since 1926, the Trainmen-Sante Fe agreement has defined "trainmen" to mean "freight and passenger Brakemen and Baggagemen, *with the further understanding that this definition does not change, alter or extend present application of these rules to baggagemen or train porters.*" [51]

In spite of these uncontested facts, the Trainmen's union again laid claim to the work of the Negro porter-brakemen, and upon being refused, took their case to the Adjustment Board. Moreover, it attached considerable importance to the case and requested the Board to understand that this case constituted "just one of many cases of a like character." Accordingly, it contended "that the award covering this particular case shall also be applicable to all other instances of a like character."

The majority of the First Division, consisting of the employee members and Referee James B. Riley, upheld in full the claim of the Trainmen in these words:

The use of porters or other employes, who do not hold seniority as brakemen, is in violation of claimants' [white brakemen] seniority rights. It follows that protest and specific claim should be sustained. *Claim that like settlement shall be made in all instances of similar nature now on file is likewise sustained.* As to claim based on subsequent dates this division has no evidence before it and therefore does not pass upon said claims. [52]

In other words, the majority of the First Division declares that brakemen *own* certain jobs. Negroes, who do the same work, and in addition, perform other duties, are *porter-brakemen*, not brakemen. Consequently, they have no *right* to perform brakemen's work, and the management has no *right* to hire them to perform brakemen's work. Whether porter-brakemen have done brakemen's work since March 1, 1943, or since March 1, 1899, or whether a carrier *always* used porter-brakemen and *never* used brakemen to perform what the First Division now defines as "brakemen's work" is immaterial. All that is pertinent is that certain work *belongs* to brakemen, and all that they must do to obtain it is to claim it before the First Division of the National Railroad Adjustment Board! The classification of porter-brakemen, established by order of the director-general of the railroads in 1918, is thus declared a mistake which has no right to exist! Professor Slichter's claim that the Board's decisions "are among the strangest in the annals of industrial relations" appears to have been an understatement.

A vigorous dissent was filed by the employer members in this case. They declared:

This award seriously transgresses our authority and duty. The lesson of this award is that contracts may be altered, changed or amended, in plain violation of the Railway Labor Act, merely by the assertion of a claim which has no foundation for support in the agreement. That these are the correct conclusions to be drawn from the wanton usurpation of power by the majority which voted for the award, is adequately fortified by the undisputed facts of record which were before us.

After reviewing the facts of the case, the dissenters stated:

In the teeth of these facts, the majority simply cannot defend its position that the claim involved only agreement interpretation, which is our only function. Therefore, it is perfectly clear that the majority has deliberately, in plain violation of the Railway Labor Act, granted the Trainmen's request for a change in the collective agreement. *Whatever controlled the majority is purely speculative, but a continuation of such wrongs may some day be the subject of Federal investigation and perhaps then the reasons for such an unwarranted award to which the majority subscribed will be unearthed.*[53]

Rather than put this award into effect, the Sante Fe Railroad has applied for a rehearing before the Adjustment Board. Moreover, the affected porter-brakemen have made known their intention to institute court proceedings on the basis of denial of due process. Since they, as affected parties, were not heard, they are likely to obtain favorable judgment.[54] At least one other railroad, however, the Texas & Pacific Branch of the Missouri Pacific System, has already complied with this award and demoted approximately forty Negro porter-brakemen to the classification of train porter, with wage reductions from \$3.25 to \$2.68 per 100 miles. It is likely that the Trainmen will force other roads to comply with this decision, regardless of the outcome of the case in the courts. If past practice is any guide, it and possibly other members of the Big Four will probably threaten to strike unless the award is put into effect. Most railroads may then be expected to acquiesce. Unless a federal agency takes speedy action, Negro brakemen, who, like Negro firemen, are among the highest paid colored workers in the country, also are doomed. That they are threatened with removal from jobs at a time when an average of more than 1,500 vacancies for brakemen is being reported monthly, appears immaterial to both the Trainmen's Union and the majority of the First Division of the Adjustment Board.[55]

ATTEMPTS OF NEGROES TO PROTECT THEIR JOBS

With the scales so heavily weighted against them, what have the Negro firemen and trainmen attempted to do to protect their jobs? To a considerable extent, especially in the past, they have felt that the extreme racial antipathy of the white Brotherhoods placed them on the side of the employer. They have, therefore, appealed to stockholders and executives of the railroads, relying upon the rich white man's sense of justice.[56] This attitude was long typified by the Florida East Coast Railway firemen, the last all-black firing force.[57] They refused to organize and to avail themselves of the Railway Labor Act for fear of offending their employer and endangering their jobs, until after the latter had signed the already noted agreement with the Locomotive Engineers, which provides that 55 per cent of the firing jobs will eventually go to white men. Then they formed the Florida East Coast Association of Colored Locomotive Firemen, Inc., and won bargaining rights for their new union in September 1943. Whether they have acted in time to save their jobs is debatable.

Negro railwaymen have also attempted to preserve their jobs by resorting to court action. This method has proved singularly unsuccessful. Nor is this surprising. Usually their grievance involves an injury to their seniority status. After examining fifty-seven seniority cases which came before the courts prior to 1940, Dr. D. H. Mater found that only eight had been decided favorably for the plantiff. Declaratory judgment was granted once; injunction solely, three times; damages solely, three times; and injunction and damages, once.[58] He concluded:

In the first place, damages are not adequate for a continuing injury; but, in addition, it is extremely difficult to make the computation thereof sufficiently exact to satisfy a court. In the second place, the courts rarely recognize a seniority injury as deserving of equity proceedings and, therefore, almost invariably will refuse to issue an injunction—the only appropriate remedy for a continuing injury such as a seniority injury or loss. And, finally, in addition to the fact that the courts almost invariably remind the complainant employee that the union is his representative in all matters pertaining to his working contract with the employer, they also point out that the union's settlement of all disputes of the members with the union or among themselves is final. In other words, the courts practically wash their hands of seniority disputes.[59]

Although all but four of the fifty-seven cases examined by Dr. Mater involved the railway industry, in none was a Negro the complainant. The courts, however, have not felt that exclusion of Negroes from unions alters the situation. State courts have dismissed cases brought by Negro firemen on the grounds that, by working under a Firemen's union agreement, they had ratified it and were bound by its modifications; or that discrimination is not shown merely because one contract is less favorable to a group of employees than a preceding agreement.[60] Federal courts have refused relief to Negroes displaced by secret contracts of the same organization on the grounds of no jurisdiction.[61] Moreover, since the legal process is so costly and time-consuming, even a favorable judgment is likely to come too late to save many jobs.

Negro firemen and trainmen have also made numerous efforts to organize unions of their own in order to counteract the attempts of the Firemen's and Trainmen's unions to force them out of the industry. The first of these organizations was founded in 1902 during a period of heated discussion of the Negro question in the *Locomotive Firemen's Magazine*. But although nearly every attack upon the Negro's position on the railroads has been accompanied by the formation of a new organization, few have had any success. The Railwaymen's International Benevolent and Industrial Association was, during World War I, an exception to this rule, and successfully represented Negro railwaymen before government boards then. However, it was destroyed by internal dissension after the war when a united front was needed most.[62]

Several other Negro unions were founded between 1917 and 1934, when an attempt was made to unite them in an organization known as the International Association of Railway Employees. After the formation of the International, however, most of the participating unions either continued their own way or went defunct. The net result was that not only no federation of organization or unity of purpose was secured, but in addition, the International became a separate union in itself, competing with the others in the field.[63]

The only union of Negro firemen and trainmen other than the Florida East Coast organization, which has collective agreements is the Association of Colored Railway Trainmen and Locomotive Firemen, Inc. Founded in 1912, the Association reached a peak membership of 3,500 in 1926, but today it claims only 1,000 members. Two of its agreements cover "car riders" in Virginia railroad yards. Car riders are really yard brakemen, and are so classified in yards near by to those under contract to the Association where the majority of the workers are white and the Railroad Trainmen is the bargaining agent. Whereas the "yard brakemen" in the Norfolk yards of the Norfolk & Western and the Chesapeake & Ohio receive $7.82 per eight-hour day, the "car riders" in the neighboring yard of the Virginian Railway receive but $6 for identical work in the same period. Thus by classifying Negroes as car riders instead of yard brakemen, railway management disguises what is in fact a race wage differential.

The Association's other agreement covers the Negro firemen and brakemen employed on the Louisiana & Arkansas Railway. The Firemen's and Trainmen's unions represent, respectively, the white firemen and brakemen on this road. It is probably the last instance of dual representation, once a fairly common phenomenon on southern railroads. The *status quo* is maintained because Negroes are in a majority as brakemen, and whites, as firemen. Should, for example, the Firemen's union ask the Mediation Board to certify it as sole bargaining agent for firemen of both races, the Association would do likewise for brakemen and freeze out the Trainmen.*

---

* Recent consolidations of the L. & A., however, threaten the existence of the Association on its lines. For the Mediation Board has ruled that an entire

The L. & A. management has been quite hostile to organized labor regardless of race. The consequence has been some co-operation between the black and white unions on its lines, including joint participation in a two months' strike in 1936. Big Four representatives technically kept their promise not to return to work until both the white and colored unions were satisfied. But whereas the Big Four obtained contracts when the strike was settled by the intervention of the governor of Louisiana, the Association had to be satisfied with a promise to negotiate and did not secure an agreement till May 2, 1941.[64]

Negro firemen and brakemen employed by the L. & A. are paid from two to three dollars less than whites for performing the same work.[65] It is one of the few roads that reverted to the undisguised race wage differential after World War I. On several occasions, leaders of the Association have asked the management to equalize the wages of Negroes with those of whites, only to be told: "If we have to pay white man's wages, we might as well hire whites." [66]

The price of such limited job security as the L. & A. Negro firemen and brakemen possess appears to be the race wage differential. Yet they are continuing their fight to overcome this inequality and to apply the principle of equal pay for equal work. Their plight illustrates clearly the weakness of independent Negro unions in the train and engine services. They have almost no political or economic influence. They cannot affect railway labor legislation, and as a minority group in a craft they are powerless under the Railway Labor Act. Should they strike, their members would be eliminated from their jobs. Their position is analogous to that of a company union; for what few concessions they do obtain are likely to be attributable to the railroads' generosity or sense of justice. Consequently, they cannot be counted upon to protect Negroes from further job deprivation except perhaps in isolated instances, and then only at the cost of the race wage differential.

Having failed to obtain redress in any other manner, Negro railwaymen brought their case before the Fair Employment Practice Committee. Hearings were scheduled in January 1943, but were

---

carrier is the only proper employer unit for collective bargaining. The Railroad Trainmen may, therefore, request an election involving the L. & A. and its newly acquired lines as one unit, which, if granted, would easily permit the Trainmen to win sole bargaining rights.

suddenly canceled by War Manpower Commissioner McNutt, into whose agency the Committee had been placed. After much delay, a new Committee was formed outside of the jurisdiction of the Manpower Commission, and the hearings were held in September 1943. Most of the railroads admitted the charges; the unions ignored the hearings. On November 18, 1943, the Committee issued "findings and directions," declaring the February 18, 1941, "nonpromotable" agreement and all supplements thereto null and void, and ordering the various railroads and unions to cease their discriminatory practices. The unions were further instructed to confer with the Negroes for whom they held bargaining rights and to give heed to their wishes.

No statement was forthcoming from the unions. But the railroads who signed the nonpromotable agreement have announced their intention of defying the Committee. If the latter cannot enforce its orders, Negro railroad workers will have lost what apparently is their last hope for justice.

THE PULLMAN PORTERS

Nearly all of the 8,500 Pullman attendants are Negroes.[67] Yet the competition of other races is not absent. Filipinos have been employed, allegedly to weaken the Negro porters' union, and white conductors have attempted to impose limitations on the scope of the porters' work. Moreover, advancing technology and decreased business have cost 3,500 porters their jobs since 1927.[68] And porters are not "promotable" to conductors' jobs.

To the Pullman porters belongs the distinction of building the most successful union managed by Negroes. Prior to 1925, they made several unsuccessful attempts to organize. Then, in that year the Brotherhood of Sleeping Car Porters was founded under the leadership of A. Philip Randolph, a Negro intellectual. Two years later, the Brotherhood claimed a majority of the Pullman porters as members but the Pullman Company refused to recognize it instead of an employee representation plan. In 1928, after the company called the Brotherhood's bluff and a threatened strike was canceled, membership in the union declined rapidly. However, it came back strongly after 1933. In a Mediation Board election, conducted during May and June 1935, it won sole bargaining rights for Pullman porters, maids, and attendants and two years later signed its first contract with the Pullman Company.

The Sleeping Car Porters was established as an independent union, but early in its career it received the support of both the American Federation of Labor and, interestingly enough, the Big Four railway brotherhoods. In 1928, it applied to the AFL Executive Council for an international charter, but its application was blocked by the claims of the Hotel and Restaurant Employees' union, which had been granted jurisdiction over sleeping car porters and dining car employees. As a compromise, the AFL Executive Council chartered the Brotherhood's locals as "federal," or directly affiliated, local unions.

Randolph continued to press for an international charter, making a second application in 1930, which was refused because of the then weak condition of the Brotherhood. In 1934, a third was made, but while it was still pending, the AFL granted jurisdiction over the Pullman porters to one of its affiliates, the Order of Sleeping Car Conductors.

The Sleeping Car Conductors' union was founded in 1918, and has had contractual relationships with the Pullman Company since 1922. Its membership never exceeded 3,000, and for the most part was less than half that. Its constitution restricted membership to the white race. In June 1942, it left the AFL and amalgamated with the Order of Railway Conductors.[69]

The Sleeping Car Conductors based its claim for jurisdiction over the porters on what is really another aspect of the white trainman-Negro porter controversy. Almost since the inception of Pullman services, porters-in-charge, who act as both conductor and porter, have been used. They receive extra compensation, but despite the fact that they are handling two jobs, they receive considerably less pay than do the white conductors for performing one job. For example, in June 1941, in standard Pullmans, porters with five to fifteen years' experience received $97 per month, porters-in-charge, $117.25 per month, and conductors, $197-$200 per month.[70] According to M. S. Warfield, the head of the Sleeping Car Conductors, this practice had increased since 1929, and so it was necessary for his union to have jurisdiction over the porters in order to protect the conductors from porters running in-charge.

Mr. Randolph, however, informed the AFL that, rather than

submit to the Sleeping Car Conductors' jurisdiction, the Porters would leave the AFL. In the face of this threat, which the Mediation Board election had shown could be backed up, the AFL Executive Council rescinded its decision and on August 17, 1935, granted the BSCP's application for an international charter.

Mr. Warfield has continued his fight against the porter-in-charge. In the southern states, propaganda has developed a racial angle. For example, leaflets have been distributed implying that it is not safe to ride on a Pullman with a (Negro) porter-in-charge. By 1940, the railroad commissions in the states of South Carolina, Florida, Kentucky, and Texas had issued orders forbidding the Pullman Company to operate without conductors within their borders. Bills to that effect, similar in nature to full crew legislation, have been introduced in several southern state legislatures, and one was also introduced in Congress, but it died in committee.[71]

Since it began contractual relations with the Pullman Company, the Sleeping Car Conductors' union has attempted without success to secure by negotiation a clause limiting the use of porters-in-charge. Such a rule has, however, been read into the Conductors' agreement by the Adjustment Board. Unless the Pullman Company can show that porters-in-charge have customarily been used on a run, or that conditions have materially changed, the Third Division has ruled that the use of porters-in-charge is a violation of the Conductors' agreement. Here again it appears that the Adjustment Board has gone beyond its statutory limits of interpretation and has actually altered collective agreements.[72]

The Sleeping Car Porters has been designated as a union "national in scope," and therefore eligible to participate in the selection of employee representatives to the Third Division of the Adjustment Board. Because, however, more than five unions are involved, the Brotherhood has been unable to place one of its own members on the board.[73] It has, however, used the Board to good advantage to settle grievances with its employers.

Since winning their first Pullman contract, officials of the Sleeping Car Porters have devoted much effort to assisting other Negro railroad workers. Dining car employees and redcaps have been aided in forming unions.[74] The AFL has given the Brotherhood jurisdiction over train porters, including porter-brakemen, and sleeping car porters employed by railroads which own their own sleeping cars. By June 30, 1942, these workers on 34 per cent of the Class I mileage were covered by BSCP contracts.[75] But it is doubtful if the Brotherhood can save the jobs of the porter-brakemen in view of the Adjustment Board's decision that such work "belongs to" white trainmen. Yet, if these workers are to have any chance whatsoever to survive, they must be organized, and the BSCP is their best hope.

Recently, the Brotherhood has attempted to alleviate the plight of colored firemen. A Provisional Committee to Organize Colored Locomotive Firemen was set up and soon claimed 1,000 members.[76] Since the Committee, as a minority within a craft, cannot win bargaining rights, emphasis was laid on publicity and appeal to the government, especially to the Fair Employment Practice Committee.

RAILWAY SHOPS

Negroes have never been employed in large numbers in railway shops. They have been used, however, for many years as laborers and mechanics' helpers in the South, and to a lesser extent as laborers in the North.[77]

Ordinarily, railway managements have not seen fit to employ Negroes as skilled shop mechanics, but during strikes they have often done so. The first Negroes to hold such jobs in St. Louis were hired during the Knights of Labor strike on the Gould Lines in 1886.[78] In 1911, a strike of shopmen began on the entire Illinois Central railroad, which lasted officially for three years. It was defeated principally by the use of Negro strikebreakers.[79]

The greatest gains of Negroes in the shops were made during the nation-wide stoppage of the shopmen in 1922. Negro helpers and laborers, who had been organized, went out with the white mechanics, and Negroes generally were not a significant factor in the final result. For although colored workers were able to obtain permanent jobs as skilled mechanics in a few cities, there were not enough of them to meet the demands. Consequently, the railroads employed mostly whites as strikebreakers.

The Pullman Company was, however, an exception. It offered jobs to the approximately 600 extra porters which it habitually employed during the peak summer months and, through them, other Negroes. Thousands responded and were given permanent positions.

Following the strike, the Pullman management made employment of Negroes a permanent policy, which is still adhered to. Today more than 50 per cent of its shop workers are colored. Negroes are used in all skilled capacities, but few are employed in supervisory positions.[80]

The use of Negroes as strikebreakers was undoubtedly the principal reason for the fact that they more than doubled their share of jobs in railroad shops between 1910 and 1930. Yet only 7.1 per cent of the 225,638 shop workers were colored in 1930.

Negroes also advanced in the occupational hierarchy during this period. In 1910, approximately 83 per cent of the colored shop employees were classified as unskilled, and most of the remainder as semiskilled. In 1930, approximately 58 per cent were classified as unskilled, 30 per cent as semiskilled, and 12 per cent as skilled.[81]

Comparable data for 1940 are not available, but field studies by Dr. G. S. Mitchell and the present writer indicate that Negro shopmen lost many of their gains of the 1920's during the following decade. Several reasons may be adduced to support this contention.[82]

Most informants agreed that Negroes had been unfairly dealt with during the layoffs and rehirings incident to the depression. Senior Negroes were layed off, while junior whites were retained; junior whites were recalled before senior Negroes. Jobs of Negroes were abolished, re-created, and whites hired, thus causing permanent displacement.

Even if the seniority system in the shops had been adhered to without discrimination, it would have worked a hardship on Negroes. Helpers are not usually promoted to mechanics; instead, promotion goes from apprentice to mechanic. Since Negroes are almost never employed as apprentices, promotion is effectively closed to them. In layoffs, a senior mechanic may displace a helper if the latter is his junior, but of course, a senior helper is not qualified to displace a junior mechanic. Since few Negroes are mechanics, they suffer in layoffs.[83]

The disadvantageous status of the shop helper is only partially attributable to the tendencies of employers to use Negroes for the work. The shop craft unions were founded by skilled mechanics who tried "in every conceivable manner to check the encroachment of the helpers, both in work and in numbers, before reaching the conclusion that it is a good policy to have the helpers connected with their respective organizations." In the South, however, at least the Blacksmiths have also exerted special efforts to prevent Negro helpers from being promoted.[84]

Technical change also has been an important factor in the losses of employment opportunities for Negroes in the shops. The substitution of a machine for heavy work often means, in the South especially but in the North as well, the displacement of Negro handworkers by white machine operators. This happened to a considerable extent in the shops during the thirties.

The movement for the displacement of Negro shop workers derived its principal impetus from the white workers. To racial antipathy was added the fact that many Negroes first entered the shops as strikebreakers. Yet the racial policies of the shop unions can scarcely be said to discourage strikebreaking. The standard unions having jurisdiction over shop workers are the Machinists, the Boilermakers and Shipbuilders, the Blacksmiths and Drop Forgers, the Sheet Metal Workers, the Electrical Workers, and the Railway Carmen, which are known as the Six Federated Crafts, and the Firemen and Oilers. These unions are all AFL affiliates, and together comprise its Railway Employes Department. On June 30, 1942, they represented their respective classes on from 79 to 89 per cent of the Class I railway mileage.[85]

Only the Firemen and Oilers, which organizes powerhouse employees and shop laborers, admits Negroes on a basis of full equality. The Machinists excludes Negroes by a provision in its ritual; the Electrical Workers does likewise by tacit consent. The railroad locals of the Sheet Metal Workers refuse to admit Negroes even to Jim Crow auxiliaries which their rules permit them to establish. Prior to 1937, the Boilermakers completely excluded Negroes. Since then, they have admitted them to Jim Crow auxiliaries under rules which deny them any voice in union affairs, compel them to pay the same dues as are charged white workers, but pay them only one-half as much as whites receive in death and disability benefits, and *virtually forbid their promotion*. Similar regulations have been imposed upon Negroes since World War I by the Blacksmiths, the rules of which confine colored workers to auxiliaries, forbid them to handle their own grievances, deny them representation in conventions, and *forbid their promotion or use in shops where white helpers are employed.*

By far the largest number of shopmen come under the jurisdiction of the Railway Carmen, which excluded Negroes till 1921, when auxiliaries were established "on railroads where the employment of colored persons has become a permanent institution." Auxiliary locals are under the jurisdiction of, and represented in conventions by, the nearest white local. Attempts since then (as before) of a large minority within the Carmen's union to obtain equal rights for Negroes have been unsuccessful.[86]

The 1922 strike taught the shop unions the necessity of controlling the competition of Negroes. The auxiliaries of the Carmen, Boilermakers, and Blacksmiths are obviously designed for that purpose. In 1924, the Machinists, Boilermakers, Sheet Metal Workers, and Electrical Workers made an agreement with the Fireman and Oilers whereby the latter admits colored mechanics and helpers coming under the jurisdiction of the three crafts.* Negroes so organized work under the rules of their respective crafts, and their grievances are handled by the committee of that craft. Thus, although these Negroes are granted full privileges in the Firemen and Oilers, they have no voice in the organization which determines the conditions under which they work. This has left the white workers free to use their unions as a means of displacing Negroes, and they have done so.[87] Moreover, the same unions which have given jurisdiction over colored mechanics and helpers to the Firemen and Oilers, have consistently opposed the upgrading of Negroes and have entered into agreements with the railroads which stipulate that "none but white, English-speaking helpers shall be employed." [88]

In the Pullman shops, however, Negroes appear to have maintained their position and comprise a majority of the working force. The shop craft unions have made little headway in these plants because of their racial policies. Most Pullman shops now deal with an alleged company union, the Independent Pullman Workers Federation. Recently two CIO affiliates, the Utility Workers and the United Transport Workers, have begun organizing campaigns in these shops. The former admits Negroes without discrimination;

* Since 1937 the Boilermakers has not been a party to this contract but has placed Negroes in its auxiliary which was created at that time.

the latter is run by colored redcaps and is discussed in the next section.[89]

CLERICAL, FREIGHT HANDLING, AND STATION EMPLOYEE GROUP

In the clerical, freight handling, and station employee group, Negroes are employed almost exclusively in common labor and service occupations. Thus they have never been used to an important extent as telegraphers, towermen, or agents. Such employees come under the jurisdiction of the Railroad Telegraphers, an AFL affiliate, which since its inception in 1886 has limited membership to the white race. As its contracts cover its class on 99 per cent of the country's Class I railway mileage, employment opportunities for Negroes in the field are not likely to expand.[90]

Even fewer Negroes have ever been used as train dispatchers. Most of the workers in this class have been organized by the Train Dispatchers' Association, an independent union. It also excludes nonwhites.[91]

The majority of workers in this group come under the jurisdiction of the Brotherhood of Railway and Steamship Clerks, an AFL affiliate. The largest of the standard labor organizations, its membership now exceeds 200,000. It was founded in 1899 by clerks, a white-color worker group, virtually all of whom were then, as now, white, and only white workers were made eligible to membership.[92]

During World War I, the Railway Clerks not only grew rapidly, but also assumed jurisdiction over related groups of workers, including freight handlers and station, express and store employees. In so doing, it was for the first time faced with the problem posed by large numbers of Negroes coming under its jurisdiction.

Negroes have been employed as freight handlers, particularly in the South, and as station workers (janitors, attendants, and redcaps) ever since railroads hired such workers. Today, perhaps 25,000 of the estimated 290,000 workers coming under the jurisdiction of the Railway Clerks are colored. About 4,500 of these Negroes are redcaps. Most of the remainder are freight handlers, whose principal task is the loading and unloading of freight cars.[93]

A majority of the Negro freight handlers and station employees, who joined unions during World War I, were organized into AFL

federal locals. At the 1920 AFL convention, their delegates secured
the passage of a resolution recommending that the Clerks remove
its color bar. When this was proposed at the 1922 Clerks' convention, it was howled down, and no mention of the subject was
made at the ensuing three conclaves. The AFL exacted no penalty
from the Clerks for ignoring its recommendation, but instead attempted to work out a plan whereby the Clerks would assist
Negro federal locals under its jurisdiction. The officials of the
Clerks showed little interest in the idea at this time, with the
result that by 1930 most of these federal locals had gone defunct.[94]

Beginning in 1934, however, the officers of the Railway Clerks
began to assist Negroes under its jurisdiction to organize into AFL
federal locals. This policy, which was endorsed by the Brotherhood's 1935 convention, resulted in the enrollment of 6,000
Negroes by May 1939. Admittedly, it was undertaken because of
the realization that the wages of white workers could not be substantially increased so long as those of the Negroes remained
depressed.[95]

By agreement with the AFL and the Clerks, members of Negro
federal locals paid per capita tax to the system committees of the
Brotherhood, which in turn represented them and handled their
grievances. Negroes contributed no tax to the Clerks' national office,
but instead paid it to the AFL directly. Under this arrangement,
many colored workers received substantial wage increases and improved working conditions.[96]

Neither the affected Negroes nor the Brotherhood were, however, satisfied. The union objected to the fact that the Negroes
received its service, but paid per capita tax directly to the AFL;
the Negroes objected because they had no voice in the affairs of
the Brotherhood. In his report to the 1939 convention, President
George M. Harrison urged the delegates to work out "a more satisfactory arrangement." He appealed particularly to delegates from
the Southeast for assistance. A resolution was accordingly passed
giving the Clerks' Executive Council the authority to arrange "for
the proper representation and a more immediate contact with
colored employees." [97]

The plan adopted by the Executive Council met the main objection of the Brotherhood, but did less than nothing about that of
the Negroes, for it deprived them of any voice whatsoever in the

conduct of their affairs. On July 1, 1940, the Railway Clerks launched a Negro auxiliary, the members of which pay the same dues and receive the same insurance benefits as do white members of the union, but are denied the right to handle their own grievances or to send delegates to system or national conventions. Clerks' spokesmen announced that the AFL "is in complete accord with the creation of the Auxiliary and no difficulty is expected in promptly transferring the membership of existing Federal unions to the new Auxiliary."[98]

But the affected Negro workers objected vigorously. Twenty-one of their locals petitioned the AFL Executive Council to rescind the order transferring them to the Clerks Auxiliary. When the Council could find "no justified reason" for these protests the fight was carried to the 1940 AFL convention floor. The spokesman for the federal locals pointed out that they were not consulted before they were told to transfer to auxiliary locals of the Clerks, and that they were willing to join the Brotherhood, but were not permitted to do so. Hence it was not their fault if the Clerks did not receive their dues. The Negroes then offered to pay per capita tax to both the AFL and the Clerks during a trial period in which they would determine if the Clerks were as interested in their welfare as in their dues.

William Green, president of the AFL, assured the Negro delegates that President Harrison of the Clerks had promised them a letter, which would set forth clearly that they "will be members of the Brotherhood of Railway Clerks and fully entitled to enjoy the rights and privileges of the Brotherhood of Railway Clerks." There the matter rested.[99]

Mr. Green did not explain just how President Harrison's letter could accomplish its purpose and yet be in harmony with the Brotherhood's constitution, which lists as eligible to membership only white persons. Apparently, however, his conception of what is meant by being "fully entitled to enjoy the rights and privileges of the Brotherhood of Railway Clerks" differs somewhat from that which one might ordinarily expect. For just two months before, he had written the secretaries of these federal locals ordering them to exchange their federal charters for ones in the Clerks' auxiliary. Those that did not comply had their federal charters revoked on March 1, 1941.[100]

Protesting against this arbitrary action, a large number of Negro freight handlers sought to establish an organization of their own, the National Council of Freight Handlers, Express and Station Employees. But their venture was doomed from the start. For unless they could induce the National Mediation Board to establish a separate class for freight handlers and/or station employees, they would be outvoted by white workers in any employee representation election. This the Board has refused to do. From the first, it has ruled that clerks, freight handlers, station and store employees should be considered one class because they are customarily so grouped by collected agreements (i.e., by the Clerks); because their work is similar; and because there was just as much reason to split them into a dozen classes as into two classes, and this would make collective bargaining impossible, and defeat the purposes of the Railway Labor Act. Profiting from this ruling, the Clerks have won bargaining rights for workers under their jurisdiction on 98 per cent of the Class I railroad mileage.[101]

The failure of the National Council to win bargaining rights on any railroad led to its gradual disintegration. In August 1942, it disestablished its national organization and affiliated with the CIO Utility Workers' Organizing Committee.[102] Yet it is difficult to see what the UWOC can do for these Negro workers so long as the Clerks remain their legal bargaining agent.

In terms of membership, the auxiliary of the Railway Clerks has prospered since its inception. By the time it was one year old it claimed 10,000 members, and today that figure has risen to 12,000.[103] Moreover, the officers of the Clerks have continued to improve the wages and working conditions of the Negroes under their jurisdiction. On a number of occasions, however, the Clerks has opposed the upgrading of Negroes. This, together with their reluctance to agree to the Jim Crow Auxiliary, has induced a sizable portion of the nation's redcaps to set up their own organization, for which they have been quite successful in winning recognition.

The employment of station porters to assist passengers with baggage seems to have begun in the 1890's, and to have become general custom at railroad terminals soon thereafter. From the first, Negroes were employed almost exclusively. Today, nearly all of the nation's 4,500 redcaps are colored, the exceptions being whites at a few midwestern cities, and before their eviction from the west coast, some Japanese there. Although the work is essentially unskilled, employment is fairly regular and the labor force steady. Because of their limited employment opportunities elsewhere, redcapping attracts intelligent and surprisingly well-educated Negroes. Yet Negro redcaps, like most other colored workers in the railroad industry, are "nonpromotable." For them, redcapping is a blind alley job. A white man employed as a redcap, however, may advance through a whole hierarchy of occupations up to the position of stationmaster.[104]

Unions of redcaps are known to have existed as early as 1921, and after 1933 local or system-wide organizations were founded in most terminals. Many of those in the West and Midwest affiliated with the AFL as federal locals; a majority in the East remained independent. They often succeeded in settling grievances and in obtaining general adherence to the principle of seniority. But they were nearly all confronted with the same problem—their status as employees in view of the tipping system of remuneration.

About 70 per cent of the country's redcaps worked exclusively for tips prior to October 24, 1938, when the Fair Labor Standards Act went into effect. The remaining 30 per cent who received wages plus tips, were mainly found on the west coast. Because of the long hauls required from train to street there, trucks and carts have been in use for many years. Most railroads in this area conceded the employee status of redcaps and signed collective agreements with their unions beginning in 1937.

Elsewhere, however, railroads preferred to regard them as "independent contractors" although they were subject to discipline and discharge like other workers. The purpose of this fiction was to deny redcaps the coverage of social and labor legislation.[105]

To consider this situation, delegates from AFL federal locals of redcaps met in Chicago in 1937 and founded the International Brotherhood of Redcaps, since 1940 known as the United Transport Service Employees of America. Because the federal local setup kept them isolated, they withdrew from the AFL, and with the aid of A. P. Randolph, president of the Sleeping Car Porters, brought several eastern and midwestern groups of redcaps into their new union.[106] Those on the west coast joined in March 1941 instead of taking out auxiliary charters in the Clerks, as ordered by the AFL.

Soon after their national union had been founded, the leaders of the redcaps petitioned the Interstate Commerce Commission to determine their employment status. Sometime thereafter, the Railway Clerks filed an intervening petition. On September 29, 1938, the ICC ruled that redcaps were employees within the meaning of the Railway Labor Act.[107] Henceforth redcaps working under the provisions of collective agreements were to be the rule, rather than the exception.

A month after the ICC had decided that they were "employees," the Fair Labor Standards Act went into effect, and the redcaps were faced with another serious problem: were tips wages within the meaning of the Act?

The railroads answered the question in the affirmative. Redcaps were ordered to report all tips to the management, and were to be compensated only with the difference between their tips and the legal minimum wage. Actually the "accounting and guarantee plan" proved no guarantee. For when redcaps reported less than the legal minimum, they were subject to discharge either for "inefficiency" or for "dishonesty." Under these circumstances, a redcap who earned less than the minimum usually reported the minimum anyway so as to preserve his job.[108]

Both the UTSEA and the Railway Clerks made the abolition of the accounting and guarantee plan a leading issue of their organizing campaigns. Both took the issue to the courts, the cases initiated by the Clerks reaching the Supreme Court first.

On March 2, 1942, the Court ruled, by a 5-to-3 vote, that tips can be counted as wages. It found that the Act neither specifically included nor specifically excluded tips from wages; that railroads could, and had under the accounting and guarantee plan, taken title to tips; and that such an arrangement did not constitute an unreasonable condition of employment. Said Justice Black for the minority: "The tip paying public is entitled to know whom it tips, the redcap or the railroad."[109]

By the time that the Supreme Court reached its decision, the railroads had largely abandoned the accounting and guarantee plan in favor of the ten-cents-a-bag scheme. The reporting of tips was dropped, and redcaps were placed on the payroll at the minimum rate. The public, however, was charged ten cents per bag, which went to the railroads. Checks attached to bags permitted an accounting of the baggage handled.[110]

The validity of this plan was challenged by the UTSEA with the assistance of a customer of the Cincinnati Terminal, but the ICC ruled that it was legal.[111] The grievances of the redcaps against this plan were mainly the result of managements' attempts to make the plan pay for the cost of the service by speed-ups, introduction of hand trucks, etc. Gradually these problems have been worked out by collective bargaining. Redcaps' wages had risen well above 40 cents per hour by 1941, as compared with less than 30 cents in 1938; weekly earnings rose faster than the cost of living; hours of work were cut from an average of 56 to 48, and the seven-day week was all but eliminated. "Rationalization" did, however, reduce employment by about 200 persons at a time of increased railway business, except in the Far West, where the work had already been mechanized. The ICC decision in 1938 gave redcaps the benefits of railroad retirement and unemployment compensation as well as minimum wage legislation.[112] But now the redcaps are faced with still another problem: will they be transferred to more essential work by the War Manpower Commission?

The rivalry between the Railway Clerks and the UTSEA has not diminished in intensity. On June 30, 1942, the UTSEA represented the redcaps on 33 per cent of the mileage covered by Class I railroads; most of the rest come within the scope of the Clerks' agreements. Actually, however, a majority of the redcaps are members of the UTSEA. For it has agreements with most of the large terminal companies in eastern, midwestern, and farwestern cities. There the bulk of the redcaps are employed. It is the weakest in the South and Southwest, where because of their disadvantaged social and political status, Negroes are more likely to accept without overt protest the Jim Crow regulations of the Clerks. Although the amount of railroad mileage in this area is great, the number of redcaps employed is relatively small.[113]

On several occasions, the Railway Clerks has been able to block the efforts of its rival to win bargaining rights for redcaps merely by extending the "scope" of its already existing agreement. Such a case occurred at the St. Paul (Minn.) Union Terminal Company. Early in 1938, a majority of redcaps employed by this company designated the UTSEA as their bargaining agent. The company refused to deal with the UTSEA on the ground that the redcaps were within the scope of the agreement which it had had with the Railway Clerks for twenty years. Although the evidence showed that the Clerks had never bargained for these redcaps, the National Mediation Board ruled that they were part of the clerical, freight handling, station and store employee class, and dismissed the UTSEA's petition for a representation election. The UTSEA then filed injunctive proceedings against the Mediation Board, the company, and the Clerks in the United States District Court, Washington, D. C.

In July 1942, Judge Daniel W. O'Donoghue found that these redcaps were a separate class within the meaning of the Railway Labor Act; that they "did not and could not belong to" the Brotherhood of Railway Clerks; and that "they had not designated the said Brotherhood as their bargaining agent, nor was the said Brotherhood as a matter of fact their bargaining agent." Whereupon, the court ruled that the Mediation Board's order dismissing the case was void and ineffective, and ordered the Mediation Board to certify the UTSEA as the redcaps' sole bargaining agent in accordance with their desires.[114]

The Clerks appealed Justice O'Donoghue's decision to the Federal Circuit Court of Appeals, District of Columbia. On August 2, 1943, this court handed down an opinion unanimously upholding the lower court.[115] Chief Justice Eicher, speaking for the court, noted that the Amended Railway Labor Act grants railway employees "the right to organize *and* bargain collectively through representatives of their own choosing, which carries the corollary that the right to organize is essential to the right to bargain collectively. And yet the employees in the case . . . are ineligible to organize with the only labor union that their employer will recognize as their bargaining agent." Moreover, the Act gives each employee the right to participate in the selection of his bargaining agent, but the St. Paul redcaps had not been allowed to make any choice. Therefore, the National Mediation Board "was called upon to do more than to reach a decision on a mere issue of fact. . . . To say in a vacuum that the Saint Paul 'Red-Caps,' historically or by definition or both, belong to the same craft or class as station laborers, even tho' less than one half of their time is devoted to janitorial or custodial work, is one thing. To say it in the light of the resultant deprivation of rights preserved to them by statute, is quite another thing."

Said Justice Groner in a concurring opinion:

> . . . I think that . . . the question of the precise meaning of the words "craft or class" and of whom they shall be composed, needs [not] to be decided in this case. And this for the reason that here is admitted to exist a totally different situation from any contemplated by the Act . . . this grows out of the fact . . . that the Brotherhood, designated by the Board as the bargaining agent of the porters, is a white organization which does not permit membership by the colored employees . . . As a result, the effect of the action of the Board is to force this particular group of employees to accept representation by an organization in which it has no right to membership, nor right to speak or be heard in its own behalf. This is obviously wrong, and if assented to, would create an intolerable situation . . . that the Brotherhood, in combination with the employer, should force on these men this proscription and at the same time insist that the Brotherhood alone is entitled to speak for them in the regulation of their hours of work, rates of pay, and the redress of their grievances is so inadmissable, so palpably unjust and so opposed to the primary principles of the Act as to make the Board's decision upholding it wholly untenable and arbitrary . . . nothing in the Act nor in its construction by the courts can be found to justify such coercive action as to force upon any class of employees representation through an agency with whom it has no affiliation nor right of association . . . to enforce the Board's decision would be contrary to both the word and spirit of our laws.

To the writer's knowledge, this is the first time that the courts have taken full account of a union's racial policies in determining whether an administrative agency has acted correctly in designating the appropriate bargaining unit. Justice Groner's statement that "nothing in the Act nor in its construction by the courts can be found to justify such coercive action as to force upon any class of employees representation through an agency with whom it has no affiliation nor right of Association" is a clear condemnation of the National Mediation Board's practice of ignoring the restrictive racial rules of the railroad unions in determining the "craft or class." That such facts should not be ignored seems incontestable if "representation by unions of their own choosing" is not to be a mockery for Negro workers.* Unfortunately, the Supreme Court overturned

* It might be maintained that despite the Jim Crow setup, the Clerks in a

the Circuit Court's decision on December 6, 1943, without going into the merits of the case. The Supreme Court has consistently ruled that the courts should not review an administrative agency's determination of the appropriate bargaining unit except when the employer refuses to bargain. (In the St. Paul case the employer was quite willing to bargain with the Clerks.) In general this is sound, liberal law, for it protects collective bargaining from the continual delay which would result if an employer could challenge every administrative decision in regard to the bargaining unit. In this instance, however, it ignores the special situation created by the refusal of the Clerks to admit Negroes to equal membership. Unless the Supreme Court reviews its own decision and examines the case on its merits, not only will a grave injustice result, but in addition the purposes of the Railway Labor Act will be thwarted.

When the members of the UTSEA adopted the present name for their union in 1940, they did so with the object of organizing other classes of Negro railroad workers as well as redcaps. An unsuccessful attempt was made to win bargaining rights for maintenance of way workers on the Florida East Coast Railway,[116] but a drive among train porters of the same road succeeded. The Brotherhood of Dining Car Workers merged with it in 1942, bringing contracts covering two railroads. Two more agreements covering dining car employees have since been signed.[117] In June 1942, the UTSEA affiliated with the CIO, and since then it has won bargaining rights for the 800 Pullman laundry workers, most of whom are Negro women, and for the 300 train porters employed on the Southern Railroad and four of its subsidiary lines. More recently, it has begun an organizing drive among Pullman shop workers.[118]

At one time UTSEA's leaders considered an organizing campaign among Negro firemen, and that, together with its activities among

case similar to this one would, by reason of their superior bargaining power, be able to do more for the Negroes than the UTSEA. But this ignores the fact that only since the rise of the UTSEA have the Clerks shown any interest in Negro redcaps. Had it admitted Negroes or given jurisdiction over redcaps to the Sleeping Car Porters, which requested it three times, there would have been no UTSEA. Moreover, as the wages of redcaps are increased, their jobs may become more attractive to whites. A Jim Crow auxiliary would afford Negroes no protection against racial displacement. Should anyone think this argument is farfetched, let him remember that whites have already invaded the field and that they displaced Negroes in scores of service occupations during the Great Depression.

train porters, has brought it into conflict with the Sleeping Car Porters. In the case of firemen, the UTSEA canceled its plans so as not to interfere with the Provisional Committee of the Brotherhood. No such generous action has been forthcoming in so far as train porters are concerned. The two organizations have already clashed on the Louisville & Nashville Railroad, where the Brotherhood defeated the UTSEA 52 to 43, in a Mediation Board election conducted among train porters.[119] Such dual unionism can serve no good purpose. It is hoped that these organizations will not continue to weaken each other in this manner.[120]

MAINTENANCE OF WAY DEPARTMENT

The maintenance of way department may be divided into three general groups: signal, bridge and building, and roadbed. Generally, only whites are employed as signalmen. The Brotherhood of Railroad Signalmen has contracts covering this class on 83 per cent of the Class I railroad mileage.[121] It has no color bar in its bylaws, but managements' hiring policy makes the question purely theoretical.

Likewise mainly white workers are employed as bridge and building mechanics and as foremen of road section gangs, although in the South it is not uncommon for a few Negroes to be used in these capacities. Large numbers of Negroes, however, have always been employed as track laborers, not only in the South, but in other parts of the country as well. Nor is this surprising, for the work requires strong muscles and great physical endurance, but practically no skill or training, typically the work consigned to Negroes.

Track laborers may be divided into two classes: section men and extra gang men. The former usually are permanent employees who perform the day-to-day repair work; the latter are essentially casual workers who are hired for a specific job only and are not necessarily attached to the railway industry. The proportion of Negroes in these two classes in 1940 was approximately the same.[122]

In 1910, 15.4 per cent of the 453,925 "steam railroad laborers" in the country and 73.0 per cent of the 77,882 in the South were

Negroes; twenty years later, 22.5 per cent of the 435,058 such workers in the country and 72.7 per cent of the 82,972 in the South were colored. While other than trackmen are included in this classification, the latter so predominate that an accurate picture of the racial setup among maintenance of way laborers is given.[123]

The fact that Negroes increased their number during these two decades by 28 per cent in the face of a 4 per cent decrease in the total number of railroad laborers is ascribable to the increased use of Negroes outside of the South, and to the fact that there was little change either in the number of railroad laborers or in the proportion of Negroes in that area. The latter, in turn, can be attributed mainly to the failure of trucking to cut into the railroads' business in the South, as elsewhere, because of the lack of good roads; and to the deterrent to mechanization caused by the presence of Negroes, who were available in the South at wages of 15 to 25 cents per hour.[124]

After 1930, employment in the railroad industry declined rapidly and this time the South joined the rest of the country in the downtrend. The 1940 census lists 20.9 per cent of the "railroad and railroad shop laborers" in the country as colored, as compared with 22.5 per cent for "steam railroad laborers" in 1930. Were shop laborers not included in the 1940 data, the proportion of Negroes would probably have been lower, for in 1940, the Railroad Retirement Board reported that only 15.4 per cent of the track laborers employed by Class I railways were Negroes, whereas 22.8 per cent of the shop laborers so employed were colored.[125]

The available data indicate that there was no decline in the proportion of Negroes in the South, but that the force reductions in this area were unusually heavy.[126] This was to be expected, for the South suffered not only from business depression, but for the first time from mechanization and truck competition. Since approximately two-thirds of the Negro track laborers are found in the South, an extra heavy force reduction there would account for the decrease in the proportion of Negroes in the entire country.

After the war ends, declining employment as a result of both decreased traffic and increased mechanization is again likely to plague track laborers. Negroes will probably be especially hard hit. The new 40 cents per hour minimum wage in the railroad industry has been felt almost only in the South and will tend to accelerate mechanization there.[127] Most of the machines replace laborers, the occupation in which Negroes predominate, and besides, employers have a decided preference for whites rather than displaced Negroes, as machine operators.[128] The brief examination of unionism in this department will reveal nothing to alter the conclusion that further reductions in the proportion of Negroes may be expected.

Unionism in the maintenance of way department was inaugurated by the track foremen, who founded organizations in Iowa and Alabama in 1886 and 1887, respectively, and amalgamated in 1892. Later the union assumed jurisdiction over all trackmen and changed its name to the Brotherhood of Maintenance of Way Employees, which since 1900 has been an AFL affiliate.[129]

From its inception till 1917, membership in the Brotherhood was limited to the white race. The convention of that year gave Negroes the right to join "allied lodges," which are under the control of the system division and are represented in conventions by delegates "selected from any white lodge." [130]

Until quite recently, many southern locals of the Brotherhood have refused to organize Negroes, even under this Jim Crow setup. This attitude has been opposed by Vice-president T. C. Carroll, chief southeastern representative, who has repeatedly stressed that the wages of Negroes must be increased if those of whites are to rise, and that "on roads which have organized the colored employes and properly represented them in building up their wages, they have long ceased to predominate, their places being taken by white men," but elsewhere "the colored man predominates." [131]

Mr. Carroll's arguments have prevailed, for the Brotherhood's contracts now cover Negroes as well as whites on virtually every southern railroad with which it has contracts. On June 30, 1942, it had agreements on 94 per cent of the country's Class I railroad mileage.[132]

Although the Maintenance of Way Employes has long ceased to be an organization composed only of foremen, the latter are still the key men in the union. This is to be expected because gang foremen are frequently the only permanent employees, all the others being casual workers who have no permanent interest either in their jobs or in the union. The foremen are also the most difficult to replace in case of a strike; hence the success of the organization depends to a much larger extent upon its ability to control them than upon its success in enrolling the more numerous laborers.

Besides being essential to the union, however, foremen are also representatives of management, with power of hire and discharge. This places them in a strategic position to "encourage" organization. Wrote a correspondent of the union journal recently: "The best organizer we have is the foreman of any crew regardless of classification. If the foreman asks a man to join the Brotherhood, you can be sure that in most every case this man will join. . ."[133]

It might be argued that instead of foremen controlling laborers, the reverse will be true because the latter outnumber the former by a considerable margin, and through the union can limit their power. This might occur so long as both foreman and laborers are accorded equal privileges of membership within the same local, as they are *provided both are white*. In the South, however, where frequently the foreman is white and the laborers are Negroes, the latter are consigned to "allied lodges" and have no voice in their union's affairs. This places foremen in a unique position to control the laborers both as management and as union representatives.[134] A recent case which arose on the Florida East Coast Railway is illustrative.

During World War I, and since 1936, the Brotherhood has represented the white foremen and bridge and building men on the Florida East Coast, but it never made any serious attempt to enroll Negro laborers till the spring of 1941 when a campaign among them was initiated by the then independent redcaps' union, the United Transport Service Employees of America. Soon thereafter, both petitioned the Mediation Board for a representation election.

The UTSEA urged that foremen and laborers be placed in separate classes on the grounds that the former were really the employers of the latter.* The Board rejected this contention, however, as it has almost always done in the past, and ruled that both

---

* The UTSEA's contention rested on good historical grounds. Consider the following communication sent to the union journal in 1906 by a foreman-member on the Florida East Coast: 'All my laborers [colored] have struck on me, and since my last payday, two weeks ago, I have had no one on my section but myself, and I don't see any prospects of getting other laborers very soon." (*Advance Advocate*, XV [1906], 400-01.)

foremen and other trackmen should be considered one class because that has been general custom in the past (i.e., by the Brotherhood) and because too great a subdivision of workers makes collective bargaining difficult and thus tends to defeat the purpose of the Railway Labor Act.

The election among the Florida East Coast maintenance workers resulted in a 418 to 339 victory for the Brotherhood. The UTSEA filed a protest charging misconduct by the Board's mediator, coercion by foremen-members of the Brotherhood, and collusion among the mediator, foremen, and county police which prevented the UTSEA's observers from being present. The Board denied the first, noted that the Department of Justice and not it had jurisdiction over the latter two, and certified the Brotherhood as sole bargaining agent. Whereupon the UTSEA sought an injunction in federal court to compel a new election.

The Brotherhood's representative admitted that foremen had discharged several UTSEA members with long service records prior to the election, but stated that it was for "insubordination," not pro-UTSEA activities. In March 1943, this view was sustained in the District Court of the District of Columbia. The court also absolved the Board of misconduct, and both the Board and the Brotherhood of implication in the arrest of UTSEA observers. Hence it denied the injunction.[135]

The distinction between discharge for "insubordination" and for "rival unionism" is likely to be a tenuous one, difficult to distinguish. So long as foremen and laborers are placed in the same bargaining units, and so long as the Maintenance of Way Employes' union maintains its present racial policies, this writer finds it hard to believe that an election can be held in circumstances similar to those on the Florida East Coast without coercion of Negro laborers by white foremen playing an important role in the result.

DINING CAR EMPLOYEES

Negroes have been employed as dining car waiters and cooks ever since such services became an integral part of railroading. In 1940, approximately 70 per cent of both the 5,124 "chefs and cooks," and the 15,512 "waiters, camp cooks, kitchen helpers, etc.," employed on Class I railways were colored.[136]

On the other hand, Negroes are universally denied employment as "stewards and dining car supervisors." In 1940, there were 1,639 workers of this class employed on Class I railways.[137] Negro waiters and cooks, however, are frequently run in-charge at a small differential in pay. Thus like the Pullman porter-in-charge, Negro dining car workers often handle two jobs at a wage that is considerably less than that paid to a white steward for performing one. This has prompted the Railroad Trainmen, which now organizes stewards, to agitate for state laws, particularly in the South, requiring that "white stewards should be placed in charge of all lounge, parlor, club or café cars where drinks or food is [sic] served on trains"—a sort of full crew law aimed at Negro waiters-in-charge.[138] The Trainmen have also made an unsuccessful attempt to have the National Railroad Adjustment Board rule out the cook or waiter-in-charge.[139]

Recently, however, the waiters themselves began a successful attack on waiter-in-charge pay. Their union, the Hotel & Restaurant Workers, AFL, demanded that waiters so employed be paid stewards' wages. When the Pennsylvania Railroad refused to comply, the case was taken before the Third Division of the Adjustment Board as a violation of their agreement. Before an award could be made, the railroad agreed to settle and to pay waiters-in-charge stewards' wages henceforth.[140] So long as Negro waiters are not "promotable" to stewards' jobs, however, and so long as Negroes perform two jobs for the wages of one, inequalities based on race are present. The Pennsylvania did not classify these Negroes as stewards and hence they were not able to obtain any seniority as stewards or permanent claim to that occupation. Moreover, in 1942 when the Missouri-Kansas-Texas Railroad substituted standard dining cars for its café and lounge cars, experienced Negro waiters-in-charge were demoted to waiters and inexperienced white stewards were employed. It now seems likely, however, that the Fair Employment Practice Committee will be able to break down the barriers to the employment of Negroes as stewards, for on November 18, 1943, it ordered several railroads to employ *and classify* Negro waiters-in-charge as stewards, and compliance with this order is expected.

Successful organization of dining car employees dates from World War I. Several unions were founded then, most important of which was the Brotherhood of Dining Car Employees, which won contracts on most of the important lines in the East and Southeast.[141]

In 1920, the AFL gave jurisdiction over dining car employees to the Hotel & Restaurant Workers' union. It achieved little success till after the passage of the Amended Railway Labor Act in 1934. Then an organizational campaign was begun which brought the cooks and waiters on 73 per cent of the Class I railway mileage into the fold. Only the Boston & Maine and the Southern Railroad remained with the Brotherhood of Dining Car Employees.[142]

The Hotel Workers has set up a railroad department known as the Joint Council of Dining Car Employes, which has the status of a district council within the national union. One national vice-president is allotted to the Joint Council. As a union "national in scope," the Joint Council has been declared eligible to participate in the selection of employee members to the Third Division of the Adjustment Board. A vice-president of the international union has served on the Third Division, but the Hotel Workers has not been able as yet to place a Negro in this position.[143]

Prior to 1936, the rules of the Hotel Workers' union restricted Negroes to separate locals or compelled them to join as members-at-large, in either case with full privileges except for these provisions. In actual practice, the national union permitted its locals to accept Negroes if they so desired. At the 1936 convention, these restrictions were removed, and two years later the constitution was further amended to provide: "Any local law prohibiting the admission of any competent person, male or female, 'because of race, religion or color' is contrary to our laws and is, therefore, null and void."[144] The writer knows of only one other union which once adopted discriminatory laws, and then completely eliminated them.

Although most of the Joint Council's members and all of its officers are colored, it does have white cooks and stewards among its membership. This has resulted in jurisdictional conflicts with the Railroad Trainmen and the Railway Conductors. Both organize stewards, and the latter, white cooks as well. The Trainmen's interest in stewards began in 1935, when the independent Brotherhood of Dining Car Conductors amalgamated with it. This union was organized in 1918, but its attempts to affiliate with the AFL were blocked by the Hotel Workers. It restricted membership to

the Caucasian race. On June 30, 1942, the Trainmen's contracts
covered stewards on 70 per cent of the Class I railway mileage,
as compared with 4 per cent covered by the Conductors, and less
than 1 per cent by those of the Joint Council.[145]

The Railway Conductors has attempted to induce the Mediation
Board to declare cooks a separate class from waiters, but the Board
has usually refused to rule that way, following its principle of
relying upon past practice in determining the appropriate unit. It
might be argued that, in this instance, the Board's rulings favor
Negroes by denying white cooks separate representation, and thus
it tends to balance the scales. Such reasoning, however, ignores
the fact that white cooks are accepted without discrimination into
the Joint Council, whereas Negroes are denied equal rights in
most of the cases where the Board's rulings have hurt them. Besides,
on several occasions the Board has placed cooks and waiters into
separate classes "by agreement of the parties to the dispute" so
that on June 30, 1942, the Railway Conductors represented cooks
on 10 per cent of the Class I railway mileage.[146]

In the summer of 1941, a revolt within the Brotherhood of Dining
Car Employees deposed Rienzi B. Lemus, president since its inception, and amalgamated the Brotherhood with the United Transport Service Employees. At that time, the Brotherhood had contracts with the Boston & Maine, the Southern, and the Atlantic
Coast Line, but soon thereafter, the last-named was lost to the
Joint Council in a representation election.[147]

Following its affiliation with the CIO in June 1942, the UTSEA
opened a drive among dining car employees. It soon won bargaining rights on the previously unorganized Colorado and Southern,
and the Bangor and Aroostook, but it had no success in winning
over the Joint Council's members until September 1943. Then it
defeated the latter in a representation election conducted on the
Chicago, Rock Island and Pacific. Whether Negro dining car employees are being benefited by this union rivalry is doubtful.

CONCLUSION

The Negro railroad worker suffers from serious discrimination by
employers and unions—discrimination that is assisted by the policies of government agencies. The refusal of employers to promote

qualified Negroes or to pay them equal wages for equal work and the secular decline in railway employment has encouraged the white labor unions to attempt to eliminate Negroes from the industry. As a result, Negro firemen and trainmen, among the highest paid workers of their race, appear to be doomed at a time when railway employment has increased to a point where an actual shortage exists.

In no other industry has collective bargaining had such disastrous results for Negroes. The racial policies of railroad unions are far from typical of those of organized labor in general. Of the thirty-one national unions which exclude Negroes either by explicit provision or by general practice, or which confine them to inferior status, nineteen are found in the railroad industry. This is in sharp contrast to the situation in many other industries, as succeeding chapters will reveal.

The Amended Railway Labor Act has been characterized "a model labor policy based on equal rights and equitable relations." [148] Because industrial peace has prevailed in the railroad industry when strikes and industrial unrest were prevalent elsewhere, some have urged that laws similar to the Railway Labor Act be passed to govern industrial relations in other industries.

To such reasoning, this writer dissents. Industrial peace has been preserved in the railroad industry, and due credit should be accorded to the Railway Labor Act and its administrators for this laudable accomplishment. But peace on the rails has had its price. One price, as many observers have pointed out, is the acceptance by employers of obsolete make-work, or "featherbed," working rules. Another has been the toleration of intense discrimination against Negroes. This, nearly all observers have ignored.[149] It is high time that it was brought to the public's attention.

No labor law can provide "a model labor policy, based on equal rights and equitable relations" if it is used as a means of economically disenfranchising a minority race. Yet the Amended Railway Labor Act has served such a purpose. Under it, the National Mediation Board often designates as exclusive bargaining agent for Negroes a union which excludes Negroes, or affords them only inferior status. It assists parties to reach agreements which result in the displacement of colored workers. It has refused to take the racial policies of unions into consideration in determining appropriate bargaining units, thus consigning smaller groups of Negroes to the domination of discriminatory unions. And finally, evidence has been presented which seriously questions the impartiality of the Mediation Board, especially in disputes involving Negro workers and the Big Four Brotherhoods.

The record of the National Railroad Adjustment Board is even more open to criticism. Composed of partisans, appointed, for the most part, by organizations which do not afford Negroes equal status, it has denied aggrieved Negro workers even a hearing, let alone justice. Its ruling that a craft of workers "own" a particular type of work, whether or not such workers ever performed that work in the past, threatens to eliminate Negro trainmen from the industry. Since judicial review of the Adjustment Board's decisions is available only to the winning, and never to the losing party, the Board is virtually a labor court which can enforce its decisions, however inequitable.

The discussion of the Negro in the railroad industry thus reveals serious injustice occasioned primarily by the racial policies of railway labor organizations and by the provisions and administration of the Railway Labor Act. Sound public policy demands that this law be drastically amended rather than serve as a model for future labor legislation.*

* We shall return, in the final chapter, to some of the questions of public policy which have been raised here.

CHAPTER IV

THE TOBACCO INDUSTRY

Although the jobs in the tobacco industry are almost evenly
divided between whites and Negroes, contacts between the races
are limited because of an unique racial-occupational segregation
pattern. In addition, more than one-half of the workers of each
race are women, a fact which, when coupled with the racial division and the southern location of the industry, makes labor organization difficult. This chapter will analyze the position of the
Negro in the industry, and then discuss his relation to the Tobacco
Workers International Union (AFL) and the United Cannery and
Agricultural Workers (CIO).*

The Racial-Occupational Segregation Pattern

Nearly all the labor in the tobacco factories of pre-Civil War
Virginia and North Carolina, which made principally smoking
tobacco, was performed by Negro slaves hired out to the manufacturers by their owners. By 1860, these factories employed
12,843 hands, more than one-half of whom were found in the three
Virginia towns of Richmond, Petersburg, and Lynchburg. In the
last years of the 1850's, however, the high rates asked by the slave
owners, and to a lesser extent, the difficulties of controlling the
chattel labor, induced a few Virginia manufacturers to employ
white girls for some of the lighter operations.[1]

During the remainder of the nineteenth century, Negroes continued to perform the bulk of the work in southern tobacco factories, but the introduction of cigarettes in America and the development of machinery led to the employment of large numbers of

* The tobacco industry is defined here to include the manufacture of smoking and chewing tobacco and snuff (commonly referred to as "manufactured
tobacco") and of cigarettes, and the processing, or rehandling operations incident to their manufacture. The cigar industry is excluded as it presents quite
different problems and as its proportion of Negroes is much smaller.

102

white workers as well, until the number of the latter was equal to that of the former.

Cigarettes were first introduced into this country in 1867, and were soon being hand-rolled in southern factories, first by Jewish immigrants imported for that purpose, and later by Negroes taught by them. By 1884, however, a cigarette-making machine was perfected enough to turn out 120,000 per day (expert hand rollers could hardly exceed 2,500). Likewise in the 1880's, machines were invented to perform many of the operations in manufactured tobacco factories. Following the practice established in the textile industry (which is adhered to by most southern industries today),[2] the machine-tending jobs were reserved for white workers, in this case mostly women. By 1900, the tobacco industry had developed the unique racial-occupational segregation pattern which characterizes it today.[3] It may be roughly described as follows:[4]

The leaf is first removed by Negro men from the auction room, where it has been purchased from farmers, to the redrying plant. The redrying machine is operated by white men, and the tobacco is fed into it by Negro men. Going into a cooling chamber, it is packed into hogsheads and stored in the warehouses by Negro men. After aging, the tobacco goes to the factory for the first stages of preparation. Negro women perform the operations preparatory to stemming, and remove the stems, either by hand or, more recently, by machinery. They also handle the other processing operations. The leaves are then blended and flavored by Negro men and shredded by a machine operated by white men and fed by Negro men. The shredded tobacco goes to the cigarette-making machine operated by white women. Foremen, inspectors, mechanics, and other skilled maintenance workers are white. White women do the weighing and counting; Negro men, the sweeping and cleaning. White men and women perform the various operations of packing and boxing; Negro men make the box containers and remove them for shipment.

For manufactured tobacco, the operations vary after stemming, but the general pattern is the same. Negroes do the blending; whites operate the machines and weigh and pack the final product. Negroes make the box containers and remove them for shipment. There is, however, a somewhat higher proportion of "Negro jobs" in these establishments than in cigarette factories.

The racial-occupational segregation pattern is made practical because the stemming and blending and shredding departments, where the majority of Negroes are employed, have to be housed in separate buildings or at least separate floors, for these operations require special atmospheric conditions. Thus the separation is very real, with little contact between the races.

The Negro jobs in the tobacco industry are generally the less desirable. For example, a study conducted by the United States Bureau of Labor Statistics in 1940 found that female cigarette-making machine operators and cigarette catchers, practically all of whom are white, had average hourly earnings of 54 and 57 cents per hour, respectively; female machine stemmers and hand stemmers averaged but 44 and 42 cents per hour. These are typical Negro jobs. The comparable figures for male machine packers and cutting machine feeders, typical white and Negro jobs, were 68 and 53 cents per hour, respectively.[5] The differences, if any, in the comparative degree of skill or responsibility required by these white and Negro jobs scarcely seem enough to justify the racial-occupational wage differentials.

From a nonmonetary standpoint, the work performed by Negroes is made unpleasant by the tobacco dust particles which fill the air in the stemming and shredding departments, and by the humid atmosphere which is often necessary for proper processing and blending. Although modern ventilating systems have done much to improve these conditions in recent years, the departments of the industry in which the bulk of the white workers are employed are still decidedly more pleasant places in which to work.

The Trend of Employment

Table III gives the total laborers and operatives, and the number and proportion of Negroes in the three principal tobacco manufacturing states, 1910-1930. More than 90 per cent of all Negroes in the tobacco industry (excluding cigar manufacturing) are found in these three states. The inclusion of cigar workers in these data is of little consequence since few cigars are produced in North Carolina, Virginia, or Kentucky. On the other hand, the proportion of Negroes in the industry is somewhat less than is indicated by the figures in Table III. The term "operative" as defined by the census

TABLE III

TOTAL LABORERS AND OPERATIVES, NUMBER AND PROPORTION OF NEGROES, IN CIGAR AND TOBACCO FACTORIES OF THE THREE MAJOR TOBACCO MANUFACTURING STATES, 1910-1930

	1910			1920			1930		
	Total	Negroes	% Negro	Total	Negroes	% Negro	Total	Negroes	% Negro
Total N. C., Va., and Ky.	31,028	18,780	61.3	50,265	33,830	68.0	37,956	25,725	68.4
North Carolina	7,735	5,716	73.9	20,006	14,852	74.3	19,856	15,049	76.2
Virginia	14,397	9,018	64.3	15,520	10,457	62.5	11,104	7,142	64.4
Kentucky	8,896	4,046	45.8	14,739	8,521	57.9	7,006	3,534	50.5

SOURCE: U. S. Census of Occupations, 1910-1930.

does not include skilled production or maintenance workers, or supervisors, nearly all of whom are white. Thus in 1930, when 68.4 per cent of the laborers and operatives in these states were colored, only 58.7 per cent of all gainful workers there were so classified. Nevertheless, the data in Table III do present a fair picture of the trend of employment during the two decades following 1910.

Between 1910 and 1920, the number of laborers and operatives in the tobacco industry in the three states increased by 38 per cent, the number of Negroes, by 44 per cent. The increase in employment is attributable to the tremendous rise in the number of cigarettes produced from 8.6 billion in 1910 to 47.4 billion in 1920. The increase in cigarette production was thus able to offset the factors making for a decrease in employment: namely, the improvement in machinery and the slight decline in the production of manufactured tobacco from 447 to 412 million pounds.[6]

Negroes secured a larger proportion of the employment gains in this decade than did whites because of the rise in importance as a tobacco manufacturing state of North Carolina, the state in which the largest percentage of tobacco workers are colored, and because the incidence of mechanization fell principally on jobs manned by white workers.

The decade of the twenties saw a sharp decline in employment in the industry. The number of operatives and laborers in the three states declined by 24.4 per cent; the number of Negroes by an almost equal amount—23.5 per cent. This was caused, first, by a decline in the production of manufactured tobacco from 412 million pounds in 1920 to 371 million in 1930; second, by the extraordinarily rapid rate at which mechanization increased labor productivity in cigarette factories. Using 1929 as a base of 100, the index of output per wage earner per year in the cigarette branch rose from 32.8 in 1920 to 112.8 in 1930 and that of output per man-hour, from 28.7 to 105.3[7] Although the production of cigarettes increased from 47.4 billion in 1920 to 123.8 billion in 1930, the percentage increase in production was less than that in labor productivity. Thus the rate of mechanization not only prevented the cigarette branch from compensating for the decline in employment due to the decrease in the production of manufactured tobacco, but it was also so rapid that it caused unemployment within the cigarette branch itself.

Employment in the tobacco industry of North Carolina, Virginia, and Kentucky would have declined still further during the 1920's had there not occurred a major shift in the location of the industry. The major tobacco companies abandoned their New York and Philadelphia plants and transferred the bulk of their operation to these three southern states. Although an important reason for this migration was the desire to be near the source of raw materials, the principal motive seems to have been a desire to take advantage of a labor supply which was both cheaper and less likely to catch the union contagion than that found in northern centers.[8]

Since 1930, the tobacco industry has remained concentrated not only in the three states of North Carolina, Virginia, and Kentucky, which in 1939 produced 88.6 per cent of the country's cigarettes and 56.9 per cent of the manufactured tobacco, but also within these states in five cities: Winston-Salem, Durham, and Reidsville, N. C., Richmond, Va., and Louisville, Ky.[9]

Mechanization continued at a rapid rate during the 1930's, but this time it was counterbalanced by a reduction in the hours of labor. Thus, while the cigarette branch's index of output per man-hour increased from 105.3 in 1930 to 127.3 in 1939, the index of output per wage earner declined slightly from 112.8 to 112.1 for the same period. A similar trend was observable in the manufactured branch.[10]

After a slight slump in 1931-1933, cigarette production resumed its expansion, increasing from 123.6 billion in 1930 to 180.6 billion in 1939. The output of manufactured tobacco declined from 371 million to 343 million pounds in the same period. Although data comparable to those presented in Table III are not available, it is quite clear that the net effect has been an increase in employment in the industry. Moreover, the major portion of the increased jobs appears to have gone to white workers. Thus, whereas between 1930 and 1940 total operatives in tobacco factories in North Carolina, Virginia, and Kentucky increased by 14 per cent, Negro operatives increased by only 4 per cent. In 1930, the census reported that 58.7 per cent of all tobacco workers in these states were colored; in 1940, a sample survey conducted by the U. S. Bureau of Labor

Statistics found that only 48.7 per cent of the tobacco workers there were Negroes.[11]

The principal reason for the decline in the proportion of Negro tobacco workers since 1930 has been the introduction of machinery into the stemming department where the bulk of the Negro women are employed. Prior to 1933, the low wages of these employees discouraged mechanization. As a result of the NRA, however, the average hourly earnings of hand stemmers employed by tobacco manufacturing companies increased from 19.4 cents in March 1933 to 32.5 cents two years later.[12] Many of the larger companies thereupon installed stemming machines, which displaced a considerable number of Negro workers. For example, at the R. J. Reynolds plant in Winston-Salem, 1,000 were reported to have lost their jobs; and local union officials claim that the former labor force of 3,500 at the Liggett & Myers stemmery in Durham has been more than halved since 1933.[13]

Because of the impact of the NRA, the cigarette and manufactured tobacco companies were largely unaffected by the Fair Labor Standards Act of 1938. This law, however, did have important repercussions on the labor force of a sector of the industry about which nothing has been said up to now—namely, the independent stemmeries or rehandling plants.

Stemmeries may be divided into two classes—manufacturers and independents. The former are operated as departments in conjunction with tobacco manufacturing companies. Manufacturers carry on their stemming operations throughout the year according to their needs in the manufacture of their own products. In 1939, approximately 15,000 workers were employed in manufacturers' stemmeries, and most of them received employment the year around.[14]

Independent stemmeries, on the other hand, are operated by leaf tobacco dealers, the middlemen who are engaged principally in buying "green" leaf tobacco from farmers and selling it to manufacturers. These leaf dealers also stem much of this tobacco for smaller companies and for foreign concerns. Some of the independents have large storage facilities and can operate all year around, but most of them confine their operations to the late summer and fall months after the tobacco crop has been harvested.

The several hundred independent stemmeries are located in

dozens of small towns through the tobacco-growing region. Thus their employees have to be selected from a limited labor market, but usually the Negro women who comprise nearly all their workers have little else but domestic service for alternative employment. Approximately 40,000 workers received employment in these establishments in 1939 at the peak of the season, but the average number employed during the year was less than 19,000. Ninety per cent were employed in North Carolina, Virginia, and Kentucky.[15]

Unlike the employees of manufacturers' stemmeries, those employed by the independents were not covered by NRA codes. Thus, whereas the wages of the former increased by 40 per cent, those of the latter remained very low. In May 1934, the median hourly earnings of workers in independent stemmeries were 12.3 cents; of workers in cigarette companies' stemmeries, 25 cents. In September 1935, stemmery employees were still among the lowest paid in American industry, with average earnings of 16 cents per hour and $6.92 per week.[16]

Following the passage of the Fair Labor Standards Act, many of the independents mechanized their stemming operations. For example, in 1935 ten such stemmeries surveyed by the Bureau of Labor Statistics employed no machine stemmers; in 1940-41, the identical ten plants reported that 54 per cent of their employees were working on machine stemmers.[17] Hence it was the adjustments to the NRA and the Wage and Hour law which caused a decline in the proportion of Negroes in the tobacco industry during the 1930's.

On the other hand, in eleven independent stemmeries surveyed by the Bureau of Labor Statistics in both 1935 and 1940-41, average earnings rose from 16 cents to 32.5 cents per hour, and from $6.92 to $12.44 per week. During the same five years, the earnings of stemmers employed by manufacturers also increased materially.[18] Moreover, the substitution of machinery for hand labor has not meant in the stemmeries, as it has so often in the past, the substitution of white labor for Negroes. Only in Louisville, Ky., are white women employed in any numbers as hand stemmers, and that development began before 1933.[19]

Thus a mitigating feature of the decline in the proportion of Negroes in the tobacco industry since 1933 was the substantial increase in earnings won by those still employed. Since 1940, cigarette production has continued to increase and that of manufactured tobacco has not declined. It would appear, therefore, that the future of Negroes in the industry will depend largely on the extent to which mechanization goes forward in those departments which are allotted to them under the racial-occupational segregation pattern. This, of course, assumes that trade union policies, to a study of which we now turn, will do little to alter the *status quo* in the employment pattern.

The Tobacco Workers International Union

Prior to 1933, the Tobacco Workers International Union, an AFL affiliate which was founded in 1895, existed with few exceptions, only on the outer fringes of the industry. Its policies were shaped from the beginning by the opposition to collective bargaining on the part of the American Tobacco Company, which then controlled 85 per cent of the country's cigarette production and approximately 75 per cent of that of manufactured tobacco. The TWIU retaliated by placing an ineffectual boycott on the products of the trust and by allying itself with the smaller concerns. In exchange for a closed shop and minor wage concessions, it gave the union label, symbol of opposition to the trust. The result was that most of the TWIU locals were organized by the employers and remained weak and company-dominated. The dissolution of the American Tobacco Company by the Supreme Court in 1911 made no immediate difference to the TWIU, as the Big Four successor companies—Reynolds ("Camel"), Liggett & Myers ("Chesterfield"), American ("Lucky Strike"), and Lorillard ("Old Gold")—continued the labor policies of the parent.

During World War I, the TWIU was able to organize the 12,000 tobacco workers in Winston-Salem, including those of the Reynolds Company. Its membership in 1920 reached 15,000 almost three times the highest previous figure. The next year, however, the Reynolds Company broke with the union without an overt protest from the latter, and in 1927 a second drive in Winston-Salem failed, again because the union leaders would not fight to hold early gains. By 1933, the Axton-Fisher Company was the only important concern under contract with the TWIU.

A revival occurred after the NRA became law, and a two-year, closed-shop, union label contract was signed covering the three plants of the Brown & Williamson Company. Most of the plants of Liggett & Myers, American, Lorillard, and Philip Morris signed agreements soon after the Supreme Court declared the National Labor Relations Act constitutional in April 1937. The union label is not included in these later agreements. Reynolds remains outside the TWIU's fold. Further organizational gains were made after the veteran officials had been deposed by the 1940 convention, which was called only after a rank-and-file committee had won a two-year court fight to force a convention. In January 1943, the membership in the TWIU exceeded 20,000, the highest in its history. Progress, however, was halted by a resurgence of internal dissension. Even so, the TWIU has definitely been transformed from an organization whose principal interest was the sale of the union label to the familiar type "business union." [20]

The TWIU constitution has always forbidden discrimination because of race or color, and between 1897 and 1900, Negroes served on the national executive board. In the convention of the latter year, an all-white board was elected, and although a resolution was passed recommending the appointment of a Negro organizer, it was not acted upon till thirteen years later. In the enrollment drives in Winston-Salem, however, Negro organizers were used with excellent results, and Negroes flocked into the union. During the attempts of organization under NRA, the efforts of the TWIU to enroll Negroes, and the success it had, varied considerably from place to place. In Durham, the union, assisted by the Central Trades Council, made strenuous attempts to organize the colored tobacco workers, but had little permanent success. In Reidsville, and at the Brown & Williamson plant in Winston-Salem, it was able to organize large numbers of Negroes as permanent members. In Richmond, the union organizers made little effort to unionize the Negroes. They considered the white workers difficult enough to organize, and besides, they were convinced that Negroes would not join unions. In addition, they felt that they could afford to neglect Negroes because the racial-occupational pattern precluded the use of Negroes as strikebreakers.[21]

The TWIU has generally organized Negroes in the South into separate locals. This policy has been facilitated by the racial-occupational segregation pattern, and undoubtedly the majority of white workers, as well as many Negroes, prefer such a system. It is also in conformance with southern mores, and eliminates the possibility of tense situations which may arise in a southern community as a consequence of the presence of large numbers of both races and both sexes in the same meeting hall.

On the other hand, the separate local system limits interracial co-operation to the leaders. White workers remain ignorant, if not contemptuous, of the colored locals, and Negroes are more likely to regard the union as solely a "white man's organization." Separate locals also tend to institutionalize the *status quo*, and to place still another obstacle in the path of those who would award employment on the basis of skill and capacity rather than on race and custom. Finally, such a setup increases the feeling on the part of white workers that they can ignore the Negroes because the rigidity of the segregation pattern prevents the use of colored strikebreakers.

In recent years, the TWIU's racial policies have been somewhat liberalized. White and colored workers in the Durham and Richmond plants of Liggett & Myers struck together in 1939, and jointly worked out an agreement with management to end the walkout. After that, these locals formed an "allied shop committee" which now not only handles negotiations with management, but which meets once a month to discuss common problems. The new administration, which took office following the 1940 convention, brought the five Brown & Williamson locals (three white, two colored) under a similar arrangement. It has also sponsored an allied shop committee for all local unions in the North Carolina-Virginia tobacco region, which meets at frequent intervals to discuss policies, but which does not handle negotiations. In 1940, a Negro, George Benjamin, became the first of his race to be elected to a vice-presidency in forty years.

The new TWIU administration has also adopted a policy of mixed unionism "whenever possible." All locals in northern and border cities are so organized, as is the local at the Memphis, Tenn., plant of the American Snuff Company, where approximately 30 per cent of the 300 workers are Negroes. On the other hand, an unsuccessful organizing campaign amongst the Reynolds workers in Winston-Salem was conducted on a separate local basis, and the TWIU representatives there attacked a rival union for advocating racially mixed unions.

Much, moreover, remains to be done. Thus far the TWIU has placed only two full-time Negro organizers in the field. The evidence indicates that more could be used to advantage. Both the Liggett & Myers and the American Tobacco companies have refused to sign closed-shop agreements covering their North Carolina and Virginia plants on the ground that the Negro workers are not well-organized. The white organizers charged with altering this condition have not shown the persistence or the understanding that is required for a successful campaign. It has been the experience of many unions that colored organizers are the best qualified to bring the union's message to members of their race. They can visit the Negroes' homes without arousing their fears or suspicions, and their presence on the union staff is convincing evidence that it is not exclusively a "white man's organization." The success of Vice-President Benjamin in organizing members of his race is further proof of this fact. If a higher proportion of Negroes are to be brought into the TWIU, more Negro organizers must be used to solicit their membership.

Since 1937, the three white locals in the American Tobacco Company's Durham, Reidsville, and Richmond plants have jointly negotiated a contract with the management. The three Negro locals in these plants, however, make separate agreements. The white leaders usually assist the Negroes in their negotiations, and now all the contracts are renewed at the same time. Still, the co-operation between the white and colored locals in the American Tobacco plants is decidedly limited in scope. A consequence is that neither in Durham nor in Richmond are the Negroes as well-organized in American Tobacco plants as they are in those of the Liggett & Myers Company.

There is likewise no joint contract committee for the white and colored locals in the Richmond factory of Philip Morris. In fact, Richmond continues to be a center of disunity between white and colored workers. The AFL Central Trades Council there refuses to seat Negro delegates.[22] The TWIU has acquiesced to this discriminatory practice by permitting its white locals to affiliate with the Council. The new union officers have attempted to mitigate the effects of this exclusion by furnishing a central meeting for colored tobacco workers at the national union's expense. But so long as its white locals pay per capita tax to an exclusionist organization, the TWIU is, in fact, condoning discrimination. And it was the failure of TWIU representatives to assist Negro women strikers in Richmond that led to the formation of a rival union.

THE UNITED CANNERY AND AGRICULTURAL WORKERS

In May 1937, 400 Negro women employees of the rehandling plant of the I. N. Vaughan Company in Richmond walked out. There was no outside agitation; it seems to have been a spontaneous protest against wages of $3 per week and working conditions equally bad. They contacted the local TWIU representative, only to have their case rejected as hopeless; but they soon obtained counsel from leaders of the Southern Negro Youth Congress, who helped them to organize an independent union. Within forty-eight hours, the strikers had obtained wage increases, a forty-hour week, and union recognition. A similar walkout occurred at the Carringington-Michaux plant a few days later, with like results. According to press reports, these strikes were the first in the Richmond tobacco industry since 1905.[23] What is even more remarkable is that the strikers were considered absolutely unorganizable before they walked out. Yet this all-Negro union continued to make gains, thanks to powerful assistance.

About this time, the newly former CIO sent a representative to Richmond. The independent union affiliated with it, and the Youth Congress leaders were employed as organizers. Three other tobacco stemmeries were brought into the fold within a year. But when the CIO attempted to wrest control of other branches of the industry from the TWIU, it had little success, for the latter pushed organization among Richmond's Negro tobacco workers for the first time in twenty years. Undoubtedly the appearance of a rival union was an important factor in stimulating the efforts of the TWIU organizers to obtain their contracts with the Richmond factories of Philip Morris, Liggett & Myers, and American Tobacco. At the smoking tobacco plant of the last named, the CIO was able to challenge the TWIU to a National Labor Relations Board election, but the latter was victorious by eight votes out of 700. That most of the whites supported the TWIU and the Negroes the CIO is indicated by the fact that the former proposed a bargaining unit which segregated Negroes and whites, whereas the latter favored one unit for both races, the unit decided upon by the Board.[24]

The recession of 1937-38 and the defeat in the "Little Steel" strike of 1937 so weakened the revenues of the CIO that it was forced to abandon a proposed drive to organize the tobacco industry. In 1941, however, after the CIO Executive Board had given jurisdiction over tobacco workers to its affiliate, the United Cannery and Agricultural Workers (UCAPAWA), an additional Richmond local was organized. Here again, however, the workers divided by race. In separate NLRB elections, the white workers employed by the Larus Bros. company's manufacturing plant selected the TWIU; the Negro employees of the same company's stemmery chose the UCAPAWA.[26]

In 1942, the UCAPAWA began an organizing drive amongst the 12,000 employees of the Reynolds Company in Winston-Salem. The TWIU had begun a similar campaign during the previous year. Neither union made any substantial progress until June 1943. Then a series of spontaneous sit-down strikes occurred, apparently as a result of unsettled grievances over increased work loads. UCAPAWA representatives took charge, and a settlement was arranged. The UCAPAWA soon enrolled a majority of the workers and petitioned for a NLRB election. The company and the TWIU, which intervened in the case, requested that stemmery workers (mostly Negroes) and manufacturing plant employees (mostly white) be placed in separate bargaining units. The UCAPAWA, which had conducted its organizing campaign on a mixed local basis, in contrast to the separate local drive of the TWIU, at first demanded a single unit, but later acceded to the demands of the other parties in order to expedite the election. This proved a costly concession, for whereas the election, which was held on August 3-4, 1943, resulted in an easy victory for the UCAPAWA in the stemmery unit, where it received 3,598 votes to 236 for "no union" and 20 for the TWIU, it proved indecisive in the manufacturing unit, where "no union" received 2,856, the UCAPAWA 2,826, and the TWIU 115.[26]

The UCAPAWA's victory in the stemmery unit was a tribute to its equalitarian racial policies, as well as its effective settlement of the June strike wave. Its representatives made special efforts to organize Negroes and to ensure them equal treatment within the union. But this very fact played into the hands of its opponents, including both company and TWIU partisans. Both accused the UCAPAWA of advocating "social equality." Such propaganda alienated a large number of white workers and undoubtedly was the chief cause of the UCAPAWA's defeat in the manufacturing unit.

The complete repudiation of the TWIU by the Reynolds workers was not so surprising. Whereas UCAPAWA's representatives were on the spot at the right time and played a major role in settling the strikes in June, those of the TWIU were rendered almost totally inactive by the internal dissension within their union. Moreover, the latter had two previous failures to live down in Winston-Salem. This was especially important for Negro workers. They had joined the TWIU in large numbers in both 1919 and 1927, but when mass firings for union activity occurred, the TWIU took no countermeasures. The latter never had much appeal for Negro employees of Reynolds thereafter; and what following it did have among them prior to the NLRB election it alienated by playing up the race issue. Moreover, these tactics did not win it any substantial following among white workers, but instead helped to induce them to vote "no union."

Following the August election, all parties protested the results for one reason or another. Whereupon, the NLRB found that the purposes of the consent election had failed and voided it. The UCAPAWA then filed a new petition for an election, which the Board ordered after ruling that *one* unit was appropriate, and that the UCAPAWA did not prejudice its right to ask for a new election by agreeing to the earlier compromise consent election.

The TWIU declined a place on the ballot in the new election, but a new "independent," the Employees Association, Inc., appeared. The UCAPAWA waived any objection to its request for a place on the ballot in order to expedite matters. Apparently, however, the Association did not want an election, for it obtained injunctions, first from a U. S. District Court, and then from a state court, which postponed the balloting. Meantime, a vigorous anti-CIO campaign was launched by business interests in Winston-Salem in which the race issue was played up as much as possible. Nevertheless, when the election was held on December 16-17, 1943, the UCAPAWA won easily, receiving 6,882 votes, to 3,175 for the Association, and

301 for neither. Again, as before, the UCAPAWA had the overwhelming support of the colored employees.[27]

CONCLUSION

The TWIU has accepted the racial-occupational pattern as a fact and, therefore, has made no attempt to alter it. Moreover, little effort has been made by the union leaders to educate the rank and file in order to improve race relations. As a purely "business union," educational and social activities are, for the most part, absent from its program.

Prior to August 1943, the UCAPAWA's contracts in the tobacco industry covered locals composed almost solely of one race—those in Richmond, Va., having an all colored membership, and one in Middletown, Ohio, having an almost all-white membership.* Since then, it has won bargaining rights for the 12,000 white and Negro workers employed by the R. J. Reynolds Company in Winston-Salem, N. C., as well as for the all-colored labor force employed by two independent stemmeries in that city. Its experience will provide an important test of the workability of mixed unionism in the South, where not only large numbers of both races are involved, but also large numbers of both sexes as well.

Also, if the UCAPAWA is able to build a strong union in Winston-Salem, it will be important to note whether its program of equal treatment results in the breakdown of the racial-occupational segregation pattern and the opening of new employment opportunities to Negroes. Such a revolutionary move is not likely to occur for many years. Already on the defensive because of its left-wing leadership and its advocacy of equalitarian unionism, the UCAPAWA has been forced to make numerous public denials in Winston-Salem of stories to the effect that it sponsors "social equality." Moreover, any attempt to alter the racial employment pattern in the industry would undoubtedly meet with considerable opposition from the majority of the white workers. Unless they are able to obtain some form of a closed shop, which would permit them to act decisively without fear of losing a large portion of their membership, the UCAPAWA leaders cannot be expected to

* The UCAPAWA has, however, had locals composed of both races in the cigar industry, and in other industries under its jurisdiction, for several years.

press for any drastic changes. Even under that circumstance, they would have to move cautiously and would need the wholehearted support and co-operation of employers in order to ensure success.

There is still another factor to be considered. Because of the increased wages and the introduction of machinery, stemmeries are becoming more desirable places in which to work. If a union were instrumental in opening up to Negroes jobs which are now reserved to whites, would not turnabout be fair play? There are without doubt large numbers of southern white women who would be delighted to work in tobacco stemmeries. In Louisville, Ky., a considerale portion of the rehandling work is already being done by white women. Negro tobacco union members in North Carolina and Virginia would be certain to protest if white workers were introduced into stemmeries there, even though Negroes were at the same time being advanced to the better paying jobs now held exclusively by whites. For in the colored community the fear is all-pervasive that the introduction of white workers to what has been a "Negro job" means the gradual displacement of colored workers. This is natural enough in view of the Negro's limited employment opportunities, as well as, in view of past experiences. Negroes have too often found gains in the occupational hierarchy to be temporary, but losses permanent. To them, it is certainly as important to protect the job opportunities which they have as it is to gain new ones. It, therefore, does not seem probable that unionism will alter the racial-occupational segregation pattern in the tobacco industry in the near future.

CHAPTER V

TEXTILES, CLOTHING, AND LAUNDRIES

Although the textile, clothing, and laundry industries are in many ways quite different, they do have much in common. All three are concerned with the manufacture and care of wearing apparel; a majority of the labor force in the three industries is composed of women; and the unions in each industry are closely related. For these reasons, the Negro-union relationships in all three industries will be discussed in this chapter.

THE COTTON TEXTILE INDUSTRY

Few Negroes have ever been employed in any capacity in northern textile mills; nor has the rise of the cotton textile industry in the South meant much to them in terms of employment opportunities. The industry developed in the South in the post-Civil War reconstruction period. During its early growth, it served almost as a crusade to rehabilitate the South and to provide work for the poverty-stricken poor whites. Negroes were denied employment in all but menial jobs, such as outside labor, cleaning and sweeping, or the hot, dirty, heavy work in the picking room, where the bales are opened and the cotton dumped into machines. Although cotton textile manufacturing has become the South's most prominent industry, the racial employment pattern remains intact. Legislation demanding the complete segregation of workers of the two races by imposing extra financial burdens incident to dual accommodations, has not only helped to institutionalize the exclusion of Negroes from the cotton textile industry, but has also assisted white workers to pre-empt most of the desirable work opportunities in more recently developed southern industries. In 1940, only 3.1 per cent of the 300,880 workers in the cotton textile industry were colored; yet the bulk of the industry is now located in the South.[1]

The Textile Workers Union of America, CIO, the leading union in the field, now claims approximately 400,000 members in the various branches of textile manufacturing. Less than 10 per cent of its membership is found in the South, where most of the mills remain non-union. The much smaller United Textile Workers of America, AFL, claims 10,000 workers in the South. Its policies are similar to those of the CIO affiliate.[2]

Negroes employed in and around textile mills are admitted to the Textile Workers Union on equal terms with whites. In the South, Negroes and whites are placed in the same locals except where the number of workers is very large; then a separate Negro local is sometimes organized. Thus at the Dan River Mills, Danville, Va., there are two white locals and one colored local. The locals are brought together by a joint board on which Negroes are fully represented. A similar setup exists among the workers of the Marshall Field Mills in North Carolina. To the writer's knowledge, no other CIO affiliate has adopted the separate Negro local as union policy.

The adoption of the separate local for Negroes means that the Textile Workers Union has accepted the racial employment pattern in the industry. It is difficult to understand how it could do otherwise. It has under contract only a small portion of the industry, and it would probably lose most of that if it advocated the use of Negroes as machine operators. The cotton mill workers, who are recruited mainly from the low-income rural South, are, as a group, most emphatically opposed to the employment of Negroes in mills except in the traditional "Negro jobs." To advocate an alteration in the *status quo* at this time would ensure the Textile Workers Union, or any other labor organization, complete defeat in the southern textile mills.

The Negro in the Clothing Industry

The labor force in the clothing industry includes almost every nationality and race in America. Twenty-two races and nationalities are found in single union locals; others are composed solely of one nationality. Although late arrivals in the industry, Negroes have been accorded treatment by the unions which has not been exceeded in fairness elsewhere.

The manufacture of ready-made apparel is really not one but several related industries, known as the "needle trades." It includes the manufacture of men's and boys' coats, pants, and vests, cotton garments for both sexes, women's cloaks, dresses, undergarments, nightwear, infants' wear, millinery, furs, and a host of related articles. Negroes first entered these trades in New York about 1900 through the women's waist industry, but it was not until World War I that large numbers of Negroes found employment even there. Then the labor shortage induced manufacturers in New York, Chicago, Philadelphia, and other clothing centers to give employment to Negroes. In Chicago and Philadelphia, additional colored workers were recruited as strikebreakers in the early twenties. By 1930, the census reported 18,405 Negro men and 17,001 Negro women out of a total working force of 789,846— 4.5 per cent of those employed in the "clothing industries." [3]

Since 1930, and especially since the United States entered World War II, both the number and proportion of Negroes in the needle trades has increased. For one thing, the cotton garment industry has continued the migration to the South, which commenced during the twenties. Although most of the jobs in these factories have been assigned to whites, a higher proportion of Negroes are found in southern factories than in those elsewhere. More important, however, has been the labor shortage which the needle trades began to feel during the summer of 1942. White workers left clothing factories in large numbers for jobs in war industries, and once again employers turned to Negroes to fill their places or to man shops which had expanded in order to fulfill army contracts. The greatest increase appears to have occurred in New York City where, on the basis of a field survey conducted in June 1943, the writer estimates that 4,000 new Negro employees were hired during the preceding eighteen months, an increase of more than 60 per cent.[4] A large influx of Negroes was also reported in the other principal garment centers and, to a lesser extent, in the southern cotton garment industry. However, many cotton garment factories in the South still employ no Negroes except for menial labor.

The largest percentage of Negro clothing workers are employed in the women's dress industry, particularly in New York City. Nearly all of these workers are women. As has been the case with other racial groups, Negroes came into the industry in shops manufacturing the cheaper grades of dresses, which require less skill than do the more expensive brands. Gradually, as they have acquired more skill, they have found employment in the better grade shops.

Until the present labor shortage, some branches of the industry employed scarcely any Negroes. Corset and brassière factories were a conspicuous example. But in New York, at least, these factories are now employing a few hundred colored workers.

Few Negroes are found even now in the women's cloak and suit industry, which has been declining since World War I. Negroes as latecomers in the trades, found little opportunity or incentive to enter an already overcrowded industry. Likewise, men's clothing employs few Negroes in New York, Philadelphia, or Chicago. Even in Baltimore and Cincinnati, where the proportion of Negroes is greater, the number of Negroes is not large. The failure of Negroes to enter this industry is attributable to the fact that employment has not increased since World War I, the period in which Negroes first entered the needle trades in large numbers.

Next to the New York women's dress industry, the largest number of Negro needle trades workers are found in the Chicago cotton garment industry. Negroes are also found in cotton garment factories in Philadelphia, Baltimore, and in many small southern towns.

Negroes entered the hat and millinery industry during World War I, but not in large numbers. Union offiicials estimate that not more than 2 per cent of their membership of 32,000 is colored. Probably even fewer Negroes are found in the fur industry, although the proportion has increased recently. It is noteworthy that both these industries have been suffering from declining employment and hence many new workers have not been recruited for some years.

In both the men's and women's clothing industry, there is a decided tendency for Negroes to be concentrated as pressers. Men operate the heavy machine presses; women, the lighter hand irons. In the southern cotton garment industry, frequently the pressing room is all-colored, the stitching room, all-white. Occasionally, a large plant will have two pressing rooms, one manned by Negroes, the other by whites. In New York, Chicago, or Philadelphia, no such segregation exists, but a larger proportion of Negroes are pressers than are found in any other occupation.

The concentration of Negroes in pressing jobs is undoubtedly attributable to the hot, unpleasant character of the work. In the unionized shops, this is offset by the fact that pressers receive higher wages than do operators. In the unorganized southern cotton garment industry, however, it is usual for colored pressers to be paid lower wages than white operators.

Few Negroes are employed as cutters, the most skilled and highest paid occupation in the needle trades. Most cutters learn the trade from friends, and it is difficult for an outsider to break in. There is no formal promotion system in the industry. Once a worker becomes proficient in a job, he tends to remain there, especially since earnings in the stitching and pressing departments are usually paid on a piecework basis and thus increase with experience. Since the cutting, stitching, and pressing operations are quite distinct, and frequently are handled in different rooms, there is little opportunity or incentive for workers to shift from one occupation to another.

During the last year, however, Negroes have increased their share of operating jobs in nearly all centers. In Baltimore, St. Louis, and Kansas City, Negro operators are now being used for the first time. Most companies in these cities adhered to a segregated pattern in introducing Negroes into the stitching room. Some set up separate colored shops in Negro districts; others used different floors or rooms in the same building. Usually, however, segregation has been handled by placing Negro operators on a row of machines at one end of a room, or putting all Negro finishers around one table or group of tables in one corner of the shop.

Thus in the clothing industry, there is a racial-occupational segregation pattern, which in some ways is not unlike that in the tobacco industry. It is, however, not nearly so rigid, and in the North often shows a tendency to break down completely.

THE INTERNATIONAL LADIES' GARMENT WORKERS' UNION

By far the largest number of Negroes in the clothing industry come under the jurisdiction of the International Ladies' Garment Workers' Union, AFL. In 1936, a field survey counted 6,260 Negroes among its 128,275 New York City members.[5] Most of the Negroes had been organized during the ILGWU's great drive in 1933-34 which, with more recent gains, brought its membership to 300,000. Since 1936, its total New York membership has declined, and its Negro membership has probably risen past the 10,000 mark. In Chicago, union officials estimate that 1,300 Negroes, or 30 per cent of the total membership, are found in the cotton garment industry, which has been unionized since 1937.[6] Moreover, the bulk of the increase of Negroes in the garment trades in recent months in other cities has been in women's clothing.

The official policy of the ILGWU has always been to accept workers of any race or color without question. As an industrial union, it is pledged to organize all the workers in its industry. It is composed largely of immigrant workers, many of whom have themselves been the subject of discrimination. They have little sympathy for the advocates of race prejudice. It is noteworthy that when Negroes have been discriminated against by ILGWU members, it has usually occurred in areas where the native American element is predominant. Finally, the outlook of the ILGWU is not limited to the narrow concept of business unionism which dominates the typical AFL organization. It is moved instead by a broad social philosophy which emphasizes the solidarity of labor and supports progressive movements and worthy causes of all kinds. Race prejudice and craft snobbery have little place in the union's thinking.[7]

In some instances, language difficulties induced certain ILGWU groups to organize locals of their own. Thus the business of the early New York locals was carried on in Yiddish and, to a lesser extent, in English. Italian immigrants could understand neither, and so they established two locals of their own, which still exist. But there is probably only one separate local for Negroes, and none for the multitude of other racial groups which are found in many locals in the larger clothing centers. In the New York locals, Negroes have long been accepted as a matter of course. Negro chairladies—the equivalent of shop stewards—are found in nearly all locals where the colored membership is significant, and Negroes are well-represented in other offices and activities.

The recent increase in the number of Negroes in the New York locals has been achieved with little difficulty. In the case of the corset and brassière industry, a small minority did express disapproval over the introduction of Negroes, but a firm stand by local officials overrode their objections.

Negro labor was introduced into the Chicago women's garment

industry during World War I, and was used thereafter, at first because it was cheap and non-union. Some employers located in the Negro districts and employed all-Negro labor. When the ILGWU organized these shops, Negro labor lost its attractiveness to the employers, but the ILGWU forced them to retain their colored help, and on several occasions called strikes "in order to carry out its policy of full racial equality . . . against employers who persisted in discriminating against Negro workers." [8]

During more recent years, the ILGWU has been faced with a recurrence of the attempt of manufacturers of cotton garments to escape unionization by locating in Negro districts and employing Negro labor. One large firm, which moved there, fled to a small New England town after its colored help was organized. The ILGWU pursued it and finally unionized it. In June 1937, the union called a strike at the Nellie Ann Dress Company, whose 300 employees were nearly all Negro girls. The strike was won after a sixteen-week struggle. At present, one large shop in the colored district is still unorganized. [9]

In Philadelphia, where large numbers of Negroes gained entrance to the industry as strikebreakers, the ILGWU has gradually won over the Negro community to its side by the fairness of its action. Today only about 10 per cent of the workers under the jurisdiction of the Philadelphia locals are non-union. Although some Negroes are employed in the non-union shops, they are not found there in disproportionate numbers. [10]

As might be expected, the race problem causes more complications for the ILGWU in the border cities of St. Louis, Kansas City, and Baltimore than in New York or Chicago. Yet Negroes were recently introduced in St. Louis shops and admitted to the union without incident. Most of the shops employing Negroes there do, however, segregate them.

In Kansas City, progress has not been without trouble. Negro pressers and floor help have been used for many years, but only recently have colored workers been employed as operators, and here, again, they are usually segregated. In May 1943, two Negro women pressers employed by the Brand and Purvitz Company and a newly employed Negro woman were placed on operating machines. Although all workers in the plant are members of the same local, and although picnics and parties have long been conducted by this local without segregation, the white workers immediately walked out until the Negroes were removed from the machines.

The regional director and other ILGWU officials made strenuous efforts to secure the co-operation of its white members but failed. Their task was made difficult by a number of factors. The employer did not notify the union in advance of the proposed change in the racial employment pattern, and then made the mistake of yielding to the strikers before ILGWU officials could halt the walkout. Perhaps more important was the fact that, a few years previous to this strike, a neighboring plant was experiencing difficulty in obtaining Negro pressers. It hired a few whites as pressers and the Negroes promptly struck till they were removed. Hence, there was an element of retaliation in this move.[11]

The situation in Baltimore is somewhat similar to that in Kansas City. Negroes have long been used as pressers, but only recently as operators and finishers. At least one walkout occurred when Negroes were introduced although they were segregated. But in this case the employer sent for the union officials, and they succeeded in getting the workers back to their jobs in a few hours without having to remove the Negroes.[12]

The ILGWU has had considerable trouble with the race question in Atlanta. A separate local was organized for Negro pressers and sweepers there, but for a time representatives of a white local would not meet with the colored delegate on the joint executive board. In addition, the Negro pressers complained that they were not receiving their proportionate share of work. More recently, these difficulties appear to have been overcome.[13]

In general, ILGWU locals do not directly open up new employment opportunities to Negroes. Most Negroes have entered the industry in times of labor shortages. They are accepted by the union, and union officials do their utmost to see that they are treated fairly both in the union and on the job. Local agreements usually contain a closed-shop provision, stipulating that the employer must hire from the union if it can supply workers. Some locals forbid employers to request any specific nationality or race, but the agreements generally provide for a short trial period during which a worker may be discharged without recourse on his part. An employer who does not wish to use Negroes can thus often avoid doing so even though the local union assigns them to jobs without discrimination.

Some locals send workers to jobs where they feel that they will be accepted. In some cases this is done to spare the feelings of the workers involved. Other locals attempt to break down color bars only when they feel confident of succeeding, such as in times of labor shortages. Others, however, actively try to prevent discrimination in placements. One New York local will send an employer only workers of one race or nationality if it believes that discrimination is being exercised against that group. Thus the employer must recede from his position in order to obtain workers. Another local forced an employer to discontinue advertising for "white help wanted" by a threat of a strike. Long before the United States Employment Office in New York ceased accepting race or nationality tags on employment requests, the ILGWU put pressure on the needle trades branch of that organization to adopt such a policy.

Seniority is not used to determine promotions, layoffs, or rehirings in the women's garment industry. Promotion is limited and almost completely informal. A person picks up an operation, and if she can prove that she is capable of performing it, she obtains the job. Local union agreements provide a trial period of from five days to four weeks during which a worker may be discharged for almost any reason. After the trial period has been served, a worker is entitled to the same privileges as one who has worked in that shop for twenty years. When business slackens, division of work is instituted under the direction of the shop chairlady, who attempts to equalize earnings. Although there have been some instances of discrimination against Negroes in the "fight for the bundle," they are not common. For the most part, the intra-union squabbles are between the slow workers and the fast ones, with workers of all races and nationalities represented in both groups.

In the postwar period, the new segregated colored units promise to test severely the ILGWU's equalitarian policies. If, as expected, employment in the industry declines somewhat, many companies will probably abolish their segregated units. ILGWU locals in St. Louis, Kansas City, and Baltimore will then be duty bound to find Negroes employment in plants using an all-white labor force. Many white union members are certain to protest if Negroes come into shops where they are employed at a time when work is not too plentiful. It will then be up to the regional and national officials to enforce their equalitarian program.

Whatever is the outcome in the border cities, Negroes may be expected to hold many of their gains in the women's garment industry. For most of the new colored recruits in the industry are in New York, Chicago, and other northern cities where segregation is not found. There the division of work policy of the ILGWU should permit these new workers in the industry to obtain their proportionate share of employment in the postwar period.

In its efforts to educate its membership, the ILGWU ranks first among American unions. "No other union in the American labor movement can come near matching its annual expenditures of $200,000 for education, recreation, and cultural activities, the participation of as many as 22,000 members annually in its program, or its two dozen full-time educational directors serving locals and joint boards throughout the country, in addition to the national staff."[14]

A wide variety of programs are sponsored by the ILGWU educational department: classes in art, music, dramatics, and the social sciences, sports, concerts, shows, and workers' scholarships. "Activities were organized on three levels—popular lectures, dramatics, and recreation for the masses, systematic class work for the more serious students, and advanced training for those who aspired to union office." [15] The ILGWU also maintains an excellent health center in New York, which provides competent medical attention at low rates, and a summer resort in the Pocono Mountains in Pennsylvania which enables its members and friends to enjoy vacations at a low cost.[16]

In all these programs, each union member is encouraged to participate. Negro members of the ILGWU have the opportunity to obtain an excellent education or to develop whatever artistic talents they may possess. All educational and cultural activities are conducted without segregation, and social affairs are carried on separately for whites and Negroes only in the South where local custom demands conformance. The ILGWU has done its utmost to raise the cultural, as well as the material, level of its membership. In so doing, it has made a substantial contribution to the well-being of the Negro in America.

THE AMALGAMATED CLOTHING WORKERS

The number of Negro clothing workers who are included within the jurisdiction of the Amalgamated Clothing Workers, CIO, the dominant organization in the men's clothing industry, is considerably less than that under the ILGWU's jurisdiction. In men's and boys' suits, the number of Negroes is small, especially in New York, the leading center.[17] In men's cotton garments, however, the proportion of colored workers is larger.

In structure, composition, and philosophy, the Amalgamated is very similar to the ILGWU. In 1919, when the problem of organizing Negroes in any number first arose, a colored organizer was appointed and special efforts were made to reach Negroes who had recently come into the industry.[18] Later, when Baltimore, Cincinnati and Richmond were organized, the Negroes, mainly pressers, were taken in as a matter of course. The same policy has been followed in the organization of cotton garment factories in recent years. A sizable portion of the southern cotton garment industry remains unorganized, as do the summer goods houses in New Orleans, where a fairly large proportion of Negroes are employed.

During recent months, many cotton garment factories have converted to the manufacture of mattress and parachute covers, knapsacks, and a host of related articles for the armed forces. In such shops, in Philadelphia particularly, but in other areas as well, there has been an influx of Negro women who have been employed both as operators and as pressers. Following the war, employment in these factories will very likely fall off sharply. The Amalgamated, like the ILGWU, uses division of work rather than seniority. When, however, the available work is so small that division of work becomes division of poverty, seniority is resorted to by some locals in order to reduce the labor force. This is likely to occur in the Philadelphia area. Since Negroes were the most recently employed, they are likely to lose many of their gains after the war.

Negroes have made gains recently in the men's garment industry which they may be expected to retain. In Baltimore, for example, they have broken in as operators in pants factories. In other areas, there has been a noticeable increase in cotton garment factories which are not working exclusively on army contracts.[19]

The gains of the Negroes, in the men's garment industry, again like the situation in women's garments, are attributable to the labor shortage. The Amalgamated makes little attempt to alter the racial composition of the industry. Once a Negro gains entrance to the trade, however, he is treated like any other union member.

The Amalgamated also engages in educational and recreational activities, although on a smaller scale than does the ILGWU. The national office and the locals and joint boards sponsor a wide variety of activities, including classes, lectures, concerts, sports, dances, and various group activities for children and adults.[20] Negroes, as other union members, are urged to participate freely in the cultural programs.

THE SMALLER NEEDLE TRADES UNIONS

Probably not more than 600 Negroes are found in factories under the jurisdiction of the United Hatters, Cap, and Millinery Workers, AFL. Most of these Negroes are employed in New York, where they first entered the industry in 1920. They are concentrated in the millinery branch of the industry, especially as trimmers, the least skilled workers. A sizable number are, also employed as millinery blockers.[21]

The union in this trade is an amalgamation of two organizations, the United Hatters, and the Cloth Hat, Cap, and Millinery Workers. The former was the second oldest labor union in America, typically AFL in philosophy; the latter was composed mainly of Jewish immigrants, whose outlook and philosophy is identical with those of the ILGWU and the Amalgamated. Since most of the Negroes in the industry are found in the millinery branch, their experience has been similar to that of Negroes in the other sectors of the needle trades. From the time that they came into the industry, every effort was made to organize them and make them an integral part of the organization. Like the larger clothing unions, the Millinery Workers sponsors a comprehensive educational program in which Negroes participate as a matter of course.[22]

Negroes have never found employment in large numbers in the fur industry, which is heavily concentrated in New York City. Most of the workers are Jewish immigrants or their sons, but there are also a sizable number of Greeks brought to this country by Greek employers. A few Negroes are now employed as nailers, one of the four skilled occupations in fur manufacturing. They learned the trade as "floor boys"—youngsters employed to run errands and do odd jobs about fur shops. The fact that a large number of floor boys are now colored may mean an increase in the proportion of Negroes in the industry in the future, for floor boys are usually given prior consideration as learners. Since, however, the industry is both seasonal and overcrowded, it will be some time before many new workers are needed.

In the dress and dyeing branch of the fur industry, where the skins are tanned and colored, a higher proportion of Negroes is found, but the number is still small.[23]

The entire fur industry in New York, as well as most of that in the rest of the country, operates under a closed-shop agreement with the International Fur & Leather Workers Union, CIO. The Fur Workers' leaders are nearly all members of the Communist party. Their policies toward Negroes reflect the program of this organization. Every effort is made to push Negroes forward and to give them a prominent role in the union. In addition, the Fur Workers Union has been instrumental in opening up new opportunities to Negroes in the dress and dyeing branch and as floor boys in the manufacturing shops. In its educational program, special attention is paid to problems of Negroes and to antidiscrimination activities.[24] The union's official publication, the *Fur & Leather Worker,* has in recent issues devoted an entire page to Negro problems.[25]

The United Garment Workers, AFL, is quite different from the other needle trades unions in philosophy and structure. Most of its 40,000 members are employed in shops manufacturing men's working clothes. The United owes its pre-eminence in this field to the power of the union label. Primarily because its leaders were content to organize almost solely by selling labels, the founders of the Amalgamated Clothing Workers split away from it in 1914 and built their union's membership to seven and one-half times that of the older organization.[26]

The United never has made any special efforts to organize Negroes.[27] It has had a few Negro members, but not many are found in work clothing factories. Overalls require little pressing; thus the principal occupation in which Negroes are employed in the industry is frequently of little importance in factories with which the United has agreements.

The laundry industry employs approximately 200,000 persons, who relieve several million housewives of much of the heavy task of washing and ironing household linen and family wearing apparel. The bulk of these employees are found in power laundries, in which clothes are laundered on a mass production basis in large shops employing as many as 100 or more persons. Hand laundries, including those run by Orientals, often send most of their work to a power laundry, but they do the hand pressing of shirts and other garments on their own premises. Finally, there are linen supply houses, which supply uniforms and linen to hotels, restaurants, hospitals, and barber shops. The linen is usually owned by the laundry, and sometimes manufactured by it as well.[28]

Approximately two-thirds of all laundry workers, and a higher proportion of the production workers, are women. In 1934, a study made by the United States Women's Bureau among power laundry workers in twenty-two cities in the North, Midwest, and South, found that white men comprised 11.8 per cent of the production workers; Negro men 5.6 per cent; white women 46.5 per cent; and Negro women 36.1 per cent. Routemen (truck drivers) and mechanics were nearly all white men, and office help, white women.[29] Undoubtedly, the proportion of Negroes would have been smaller if the Rocky Mountain and Pacific regions had been included in the Bureau's survey.

The occupational distributions found by the Women's Bureau still holds true today. Except for a few colored wholesale drivers, laundries rarely employ Negroes as routemen on the grounds that white women object to their presence at the door. Office work remains white women's work. And Negroes are concentrated in production jobs, especially in the ironing department.[30]

Work in power laundries is not only hot and disagreeable, it is also poorly paid. Women operatives have been paid as low as $266.86 per year, and wages in excess of $750 per year were almost unheard-of till the recent rise of unionism. The high proportion of Negroes in laundries reflects the unwillingness of whites, with their greater opportunities for employment elsewhere, to accept the low pay and unpleasant working conditions of the industry.

At present the laundry industry is suffering from a serious labor shortage as thousands of its former workers have sought more remunerative employment elsewhere. Because Negroes have more difficulty in obtaining jobs in war factories, they have not left laundry work to the extent which whites have. Moreover, many more Negroes than whites have entered the industry during recent years. The result has been a substantial increase in the proportion of Negroes in laundry work.

Unionism in the laundry industry dates back to 1900 when the Laundry Workers International Union, AFL, was founded in Troy, N. Y. For the next thirty-five years this union had little success in organizing the laundry workers. Its total membership rarely exceeded 5,000, and it held no convention between 1909 and 1939.[31]

Beginning in 1936, however, local organizations sprang up in many of the larger cities of the country, including Chicago, Philadelphia, and San Francisco, as well as in many smaller communities. Today the Laundry Workers Union has a membership of 45,000.

Negroes are admitted to the Laundry Workers Union without discrimination. Separate colored and white locals were established in Miami, Fla., but their charters were recently revoked, and a new charter for a mixed local granted instead. In most of the local organizations, Negroes are well-integrated, holding various offices and being well-represented as shop stewards.

Contracts of the Laundry Workers Union usually include the closed shop. In Philadelphia, for example, employers must hire from the union if it can supply workers. Members wishing employment register in the morning and are sent to jobs in the order of registration. Each morning a new list is established. The burden of proof is on the employer in case he rejects any person sent by the union, and he must prove his case before an impartial chairman. Nevertheless, it was not until the current labor shortage that three Philadelphia laundries employed Negroes for the first time; yet they have been under contract to the Laundry Workers Union since 1937.[32]

The larger locals of the Laundry Workers, such as those in Philadelphia and Chicago, have developed educational and recreational programs. The Philadelphia local has acquired a large serviceable building for its headquarters, and has included therein recreation rooms and a large auditorium in which lectures on disease prevention and care and current topics of interest are given. It also pays a $100 death benefit without charge to its membership in excess of the regular dues, which are nominal.

In the South, where the highest proportion of Negroes in the laundry industry are found, the Laundry Workers Union has not made much progress. A few locals in Galveston, Birmingham, Miami, and Tampa account for most of its membership in that region. New Orleans, however, and New York, Detroit, and several other cities have been unionized by the Laundry Workers Union's CIO rival, the Amalgamated Clothing Workers.

The Amalgamated's interest in laundry workers developed in New York in 1937. In March of that year, a strike of 1,000 laundry workers in the Brownsville section of Brooklyn was won by the laundry workers with the assistance of the Women's Trade Union League, the United Hebrew Trades, the New York Negro Labor Committee and the AFL Central Trades Council. A majority of these workers were colored, and they were led by a Negro, Noah A. C. Walter. A charter had already been issued to them by the Laundry Workers Union, but the national union was either unable or unwilling to assist with further organization. Yet the strike victory had made a majority of New York City's laundry employees anxious to join a union, and the employers were willing to negotiate rather than risk an expensive struggle. The Brownsville laundry workers thereupon joined with the city's laundry drivers, who had become dissatisfied with the leadership furnished by the Teamsters' union, AFL, and together they formed the United Laundry Workers, CIO.

The New York employers, however, insisted that their employees would have to obtain responsible and experienced leadership if they wished to negotiate terms. Through the medium of the United Hebrew Trades, the Amalgamated was persuaded to establish a laundry workers unit with which this group affiliated.

Once under the Amalgamated's banner, unionization of New York laundry workers went forward at a rapid rate. Within a year, 30,000 workers there were under contract. A single local union became unsatisfactory after the movement spread to include nearly all the workers in the industry in Greater New York. Nine separate locals were then established for the various sections and location of the industry, and these were united under the Laundry Workers Joint Board. Organization later spread to other cities, particularly those where the CIO is strong.[33]

The New York laundry industry operates under the closed-shop. The Laundry Workers Joint Board maintains five employment offices throughout the city from which workers are referred on a rotary basis. Workers are sent out without regard to race. For a time, this aroused resentment among a minority of the white workers, who felt that they rated priority in certain laundries. When, however, they were laid off, they demanded an equal chance to work in laundries where large numbers of Negroes are ordinarily employed. The unfairness of such an attitude was so obvious that it was ignored by the union leaders.

Although workers are referred to employers without bias, there can still be discrimination in the actual selection. Employers have the right to refuse to accept a person or to discharge him within three weeks, with or without cause. Union officials claim that, if an employer refused to accept Negroes "too persistently," the union would take up the matter as a grievance.[34] Prior to the current labor shortage, however, at least two laundries in New York employed only white workers, and presumably they would have maintained that policy if white labor had continued to be available.

Besides greatly improving the wages and working conditions of the laundry workers in its organization, the Amalgamated has sponsored for its New York locals a comprehensive educational and recreational program, under the direction of Mrs. Sidney Hillman, wife of the president of the Amalgamated. It includes classes in English, the social sciences, physical education, drama, and music. Sports, games, and a summer camp, where seminars are conducted for union members, also are featured. Activities are carried on in four union centers located in various parts of the city. Since the outbreak of war, emphasis has been shifted to mobilizing the membership behind the Civilian Defense Volunteer Organization and its work.

All these activities are conducted without any discrimination. Negroes participate at least as well as whites. To the laundry workers, which it has organized, the Amalgamated has thus brought much more than material improvement. And the Negroes, because of their limited opportunities for cultural and recreational participation elsewhere, have undoubtedly derived great benefits from these activities of their union.

CHAPTER VI

THE LONGSHOREMEN

The loading and unloading of ships, commonly called long-shore work, has always been an important source of employment for Negroes. This chapter discusses the relations of Negroes with the longshore unions in several ports, after first analyzing the position of the Negro in the industry.

THE NEGRO'S SHARE OF LONGSHORE WORK

Negroes have performed the bulk of the longshore work in the South since slavery days. Even before the Civil War a few found work in northern ports. This infiltration continued throughout the nineteenth century, with Negroes being used to break strikes on several occasions. Their greatest gains, however, came during World War I, as is shown by the data in Table IV, which gives the number and relative position of Negro longshoremen for the United States, and for selected states, 1910-1940. During the war period, in both the North and the South, Negroes took the places of white longshoremen who found more desirable employment else-where. Following the war, they not only held their gains, but con-tinued to increase their share of the work. Although they suffered some losses during the thirties, they comprised 30.1 per cent of all longshoremen in 1940—almost three times the proportion of Negroes to the total population. Approximately 75 per cent of the colored longshoremen are located in eight southern and border states, and most of the rest are employed in the New York and Philadelphia metropolitan areas.

The fact that Negroes have so little trouble in obtaining long-shore work is not difficult to understand. While certain of the jobs do require more than a modicum of skill, the essential qualifica-tion for most of the operations is physical strength and endurance. Under such conditions, it is not surprising that white workers take advantage of the broader economic opportunities available to them and seek employment elsewhere.

TABLE IV

TOTAL LONGSHOREMEN, NUMBER AND PROPORTION OF NEGROES FOR THE UNITED STATES, AND FOR SELECTED STATES, 1910-1940

	1910			1920			1930			1940[2]		
	Total	Negroes	% Negro	Total	Negroes	% Negro	Total	Negroes	% Negro	Total	Negroes	% Negro
Total United States	51,841	15,000[1]	28.9	85,928	27,206	31.6	73,954	25,434	34.3	73,611	22,855	31.0
Total Eight States	16,390	12,074	73.6	22,394	17,519	78.2	20,790	16,775	80.6	22,298	17,223	77.3
Alabama	888	715	80.5	1,117	1,010	90.5	1,433	1,383	95.8	1,410	1,319	93.5
Florida	1,709	1,530	89.5	1,470	1,312	89.2	2,028	1,882	92.8	3,150	2,923	92.7
Georgia	1,762	1,683	95.5	1,799	1,680	92.8	1,608	1,554	96.6	1,527	1,479	96.8
Louisiana	2,654	1,587	59.9	4,320	2,862	65.2	5,322	3,953	74.2	4,217	2,949	69.9
Maryland	2,975	1,933	64.9	4,394	3,179	72.3	3,400	2,334	68.6	3,546	2,150	60.6
South Carolina	560	513	91.6	762	733	96.2	(³)	(³)	(³)	803	783	97.5
Texas	2,386	843	35.2	3,601	2,052	54.2	3,926	2,739	69.8	4,890	3,072	62.8
Virginia	3,456	3,279	90.5	4,931	4,691	95.1	3,073	2,930	95.3	2,755	2,548	92.4
New York	18,545	1,119	6.0	37,526	5,429	14.4	22,119	3,357	15.1	20,072	1,916	9.6
New Jersey	4,984	136	2.7	4,977	383	7.7	4,437	542	12.2	4,594	515	11.2
Pennsylvania	3,552	1,428	40.2	4,224	2,409	57.1	4,345	2,252	51.8	4,209	2,738	65.0
Massachusetts	3,341	154	4.6	2,843	275	9.7	3,045	255	8.4	2,527	193	7.6
California	2,593	38	1.5	3,728	44	1.2	6,346	91	1.4	7,243	96	1.3

SOURCE: U. S. Census of Occupations, 1910-1940.
[1] Estimate. Census figure an obvious misprint.
[2] Total of "employed" and "experienced workers seeking work" categories, which is roughly comparable to "gainful worker" classification used in previous enumerations.
[3] Unavailable.

There is also a strong probability that employers prefer Negroes to whites. Longshore work is conducted almost entirely on a contract basis. Hence one finds in this type of work the same emphasis on speed and continuous effort that exists in the building industry.[1] In view of the greater tractability of Negroes in submitting to continual prodding—a result of their inferior socio-economic status —it is not difficult to imagine that many employers hire them even when white workers are available at the same pay.

<h3 style="text-align:center">THE DECASUALIZATION PROBLEM</h3>

In addition to severe physical strains, there are two other aspects of dockwork which make for a high over-all undesirability and which tend to reduce the number of white workers who might otherwise seek employment as longshoremen. The first of these is risk—that is, the high accident hazard which prevails in almost all heavy loading and unloading work. The other is intermittency of employment. The volume of longshore work available in any port at a given time is bound to be highly uncertain since it depends almost wholly on the timing of the arrival and departure of vessels, which in turn depend to a large extent on weather conditions and on chance. As one might expect, the existence of a large number of job opportunities for short intervals tends to keep many more people attached to the industry than can find reasonably steady employment in it.

Both the casual nature of longshore work and the high accident rate of the industry are aggravated by the method of hiring, known as the "shape-up," which prevails in most ports between New York and New Orleans. Under this system, longshoremen line up, or "shape," at least once a day at certain designated places, where representatives of the steamship or stevedoring companies pick whomsoever they wish to work for them. Usually the men are chosen by gangs. This method of employment results in an inequitable distribution of work. It increases the accident rate because men, once hired, work as long as possible, since they do not know when next they will be employed, and once overfatigued, lose their agility. Worst of all, it gives the stevedore or hiring foreman tremendous power over the employment opportunities of longshoremen, with the consequence that job-selling and bribery and corruption of all sorts become quite common.[2]

Neither the employers nor the national officers of the International Longshoremen's Association, an AFL affiliate which has agreements covering nearly all the longshoremen on the Atlantic and Gulf coasts, appear to be interested in plans to "decasualize," or somewhat regularize, longshore work. Indeed, the latter are emphatically opposed to such a move, although plans instituted by their locals in Texas and by the west coast longshoremen are operated to the undoubted advantage of the workers there. Nor has any governmental agency been accorded the responsibility for improving port labor conditions, despite the many studies, public and private, which have condemned the present setup.[3]

The failure of the ILA leadership to work for decasualization seriously limits the effectiveness of that organization as a means of improving the well-being of its membership, white or colored. This will be made amply clear in the ensuing discussion of conditions in the various ports. The attitude of the ILA leaders is apparently attributable, first of all, to the lack of a strong rank-and-file demand for decasualization. This is the result of apathy and ignorance to a considerable extent, but it is also a consequence of the fear on the part of union members of being blacklisted or "roughed-up" for opposing the wishes of those in power. And secondly, the present leadership allegedly holds power principally because of its control of the unions in New York, the largest and most racket-ridden port in the country.[*] Should this port be decasualized, the ILA would have to cease encouraging the continuous entrance of new men into the field and would have to reduce the membership of its New York locals, which have from two to three times more members that can earn a decent livelihood. The consequent decline in the voting strength of the New York locals might endanger the tenure of the present officers. In addition, decasualization would probably substantially reduce the income of the members of the "machine," who seem to profit con-

---

[*] "Assistant District Attorney Gurfein, head of the [New York] Rackets Bureau, . . . after a lengthy investigation of racketeering along the city's waterfront, told the court the waterfront of Manhattan, because of a reign of terror by racketeers, has developed into 'a Western outlaw frontier'. He added that four 'mobs' dominate the waterfront. . ." (New York Times, January 17, 1942.)

siderably from the initiation fees and dues payments of the in-
flated membership.[4]

For these reasons, then, the ILA leaders have opposed decasualization, and concentrated on obtaining the closed shop and higher
wages. Agreements of the former type now cover nearly all the
workers in Atlantic and Gulf ports, and wages vary from $1.25 per
hour in the North Atlantic ports to 75 cents per hour in the South
Atlantic. Since high wages attract more workers to the ports,
however, they tend to defeat their purpose in the absence of any
control over the labor supply.

BOSTON, NEW YORK, AND PHILADELPHIA

From its inception in 1892, the ILA has officially opposed racial
discrimination. Negroes compose a large portion of its membership,
and today four of its fifteen vice-presidents are colored. No less
an authority than William Green, president of the AFL, has declared that the ILA applies the Federation's "cardinal principle"
of nondiscrimination "more religiously" than any of its other
affiliates.[5] Actually, however, Negro-union relations vary considerably from port to port. In many instances, strong local unions
had been in existence for years before they affiliated with the ILA,
and their racial policies were developed without regard to those
of the national union.[6] Nevertheless, the discussion in the remainder
of this chapter will reveal that relations of Negro and white union
longshoremen are often amicable.

Unionism on Boston's waterfront dates back to 1847, and by
1912, when the locals there affiliated with the ILA, their rules had
long since been formulated. The port is kept at least partially decasualized by strict limits on union membership. Negroes and immigrants from southern or eastern Europe have never been
welcomed into the old Irish-controlled locals. The few Negroes
who have entered longshore work in Boston are employed in the
coastwise locals, which were not completely organized till after
1935.* A survey conducted in 1941 revealed that 12 per cent of

---

* Longshore work is generally divided into two groups—"deep-sea," or
foreign trade, and coastwise. A third, intercoastal, is sometimes recognized.
Coastwise work is much less intermittent than deep-sea, but the amount of
cargo handled and the number of workers involved is far less. Except on the
west coast, coastwise workers receive lower hourly wage rates, and in the larger

the membership of the ILA locals in Massachusetts were colored—the largest proportion of Negroes in any union in the state.[7]

Longshore unions appeared in New York soon after their formation in Boston, but unlike the case in the New England port, they lacked staying power. The port was plagued by dual unionism (until 1920, when the ILA won complete control) and by a diversity of races and nationalities which made organization difficult. Today, New York port conditions are featured by the archaic shape-up on nearly every important pier, which results in an oversupply of labor on one dock and a shortage on another. This has been aggravated since the outbreak of war because newspapers no longer are permitted to announce the arrival and departure of ships. There is more evidence of racketeering and job-selling in New York than in any other port, with Negroes and whites victimized alike. Generally, conditions for longshoremen in this, the country's largest and most important port, are worse than in any other port.[8]

Negroes entered longshore work in New York as early as 1855 in the role of strikebreakers. Although colored workers were used in this capacity several times during the next forty years, with resulting riots and bloodshed, it was not till 1895 that they won a permanent place on the waterfront. Then they broke a strike on the Ward Line docks, and for some time were used exclusively by this company. Strikes in 1899 and 1907 brought more Negroes into the port, and the labor shortage incident to World War I made them a factor of major importance. Since 1920, however, there has been a steady decline in the number of longshoremen in the port because of declining traffic and mechanization, and during the 1930's, Negroes suffered more heavily than whites from the loss of jobs.

In New York, there is no institutionalized racial segregation. A large number of the colored longshoremen are found in one Brooklyn local, which also has a few white members. The rest of the Negroes are scattered throughout the port. It is quite common for most of one local to be composed of one nationality, for example, Italians or Hungarians; for working in gangs demands close com-

---

ports their weekly earnings are generally lower than deep-sea workers. In small ports, however, where few vessels in the foreign trade call, the earnings of the former exceed those of the latter.

radeship and understanding, which appears to be more easily obtainable among homogeneous groups.

Although Negroes have long been accepted both on the job and in the union in New York, they do not feel that they are regarded as equals. Even colored union officials have declared that they were admitted to the union only to prevent their "scabbing." This feeling has been strengthened by the fact that many lines hire no Negroes. In several instances when companies planned to alter this hiring policy, white longshoremen protested and the *status quo* was maintained. On other occasions, informal committees representing white longshoremen visited stevedores on the various piers requesting that preference be given to whites. Although the officials of the ILA oppose such activities, there is no evidence that any forceful measures have been taken to prevent its recurrence. Yet the ILA prides itself on its equalitarian policies.

Often Negroes in New York complain of discrimination if they are unable to obtain work, when actually whites are being victimized in the same manner by the shape-up system. Nevertheless, it is quite clear that discrimination does exist and that it adds to the difficulties of the Negroes in the port.[9]

Conditions in the port of Philadelphia in many ways resemble those in New York, but the position of the Negro is different. The waterfront stretches for many miles and is badly in need of decasualization. No system of division of work is in effect, and only a few employers give steady work to "permanent gangs." The men are required to shape three times a day at each pier. In actual practice, however, most Philadelphia longshoremen line up in one area and those who are picked for work are given transportation to the various piers.

Since World War I, a majority of Philadelphia's longshoremen have been colored. Perhaps for this reason, and probably also because of the unique origin of the unions, discrimination is largely absent from the Philadelphia waterfront. White and colored workers work together, often in the same gangs, and are members of the same locals. One hears few complaints among Negroes that they are denied work because of their race, or that they are used more exclusively for dirty work, such as unloading fertilizer, as is the case in New York.

Longshore unions, which had existed in Philadelphia during the

nineteenth century, were destroyed before 1900. The present organizations date from a strike in 1913, which was conducted without outside assistance. After the walkout was won, the strikers
voted to affiliate with the Marine Transport Workers of the Industrial Workers of the World (IWW), rather than the ILA. A
majority of the strikers were Negroes.

For seven years, the IWW controlled this port despite favoritism
shown the ILA by governmental agencies. Although affiliated with
an avowed revolutionary organization, this local was run as a practical business union. After 1920, the Communists won control of
the Philadelphia longshoremen and destroyed their union by a
series of ill-timed strikes. The ILA fell heir to the remnants and
has since completed the organization of the port.

The IWW in this case, as elsewhere, made strenuous efforts to
eliminate discrimination from its ranks. It managed to "bring
white men and black men into one organization in which race dis-
tinctions were obliterated in both the leadership and the rank and
file." After the ILA took over, this policy of labor solidarity and
equalitarianism was maintained.[10]

BALTIMORE AND HAMPTON ROADS

As early as 1871 a union of Negro longshoremen existed in the
port of Baltimore, but during the ensuing thirty years immigrant
labor, particularly German, displaced most of the Negroes. Then
in 1900, Baltimore's German longshoremen struck against Sunday
work. Their strike was broken by Negroes imported from Norfolk,
and for the next two decades the number of Negro longshoremen
in Baltimore steadily increased. Today approximately 60 per cent
of the longshoremen there are colored.

The ILA first appeared in Baltimore in 1900, but it was not
until twelve years later that any real progress was made. At first
Negroes and whites were organized into the same local union;
however, a disagreement between the white and colored members
soon arose and the Negroes withdrew to form their own local.
Today the ILA locals have signed closed-shop contracts with
nearly all the waterfront employers.

Longshore work in Baltimore is conducted under a system similar to that in Boston. By means of a high initiation fee and exact-

ing port regulations, the supply of labor is kept within fairly strict limits. Although there is a "shape" at the local unions' headquarters, the usual practice is for the stevedores to notify the union business agent how many gangs are needed, and the men are dispatched from the union office. Generally, the men know sometime beforehand whether there is work.

In Baltimore, gangs are divided into two general classes: regular and casual. Each company has certain regular gangs for which it generally asks the union business agent when work is available. The casual gangs fill in the extra work. When a new man is admitted to the union, he must "make his own job"—that is, he must associate himself with a gang. If he is fortunate, he may be able to join a regular gang and thus enjoy relatively stable employment. The present business agent of the colored local is attempting to bring about a more even distribution of work, and in this he has received the co-operation of several employers. However, there has not developed as yet any comprehensive scheme for rotating the gangs on the basis of earnings or shifting them from one employer to another. Since in Baltimore, unlike the ports where no effort has been made to limit union membership, the members of regular gangs are in the majority, it is unlikely that the local unions would favor such a move.

The relations between the white and colored longshoremen in Baltimore have not always been too cordial. For many years prior to the World War I only white longshoremen could obtain work on the railroad piers. Rightly or not, the colored longshoremen blamed the white locals for this. When a strike occurred on these piers in 1916, Negroes broke it. Since then colored longshoremen have been employed there in force, but for many years they refused to join the ILA. After 1933, however, they came into the union.

The work in the port of Baltimore is divided between the white and colored locals. But, until quite recently, it has been the custom to give the Negroes a disproportionate share of the disagreeable or difficult cargoes. By militant opposition to such tactics on the part of either employers or white unionists, the colored longshoremen have been able to curtail substantially this practice. However, colored local union officials state that stevedores are still more inclined to attempt to speed up Negro gangs than the less pliable white workers.[11]

At Hampton Roads, Negro labor has always been in the majority, and today about 90 per cent of the longshoremen there are colored. Unions organized by the Knights of Labor existed in the 1890's, and before 1900 the ILA had a few locals at Newport News composed entirely of Negroes. White longshoremen refused to join them, and the colored longshoremen were finally persuaded to consent to the issuance of a separate charter for white men.

It was not until the World War I that the ILA became a real force in Hampton Roads. Then several independent groups of Negroes affiliated with it and during the war it had nearly 9,000 members in the port, of which two-thirds were Negroes. During the 1920's most of the coastwise longshoremen and several other groups were lost to the union following unsuccessful strikes, so that by 1930 only 2,200 longshoremen remained in the ILA, 2,000 of whom were colored.

Also after World War I, mechanization of operations went forward at a rapid rate, and substantially reduced the number of available jobs. The coal trimmers' local has been particularly hard hit, losing all but 200 of its former 1,500 members. In addition, many concerns have substituted factory common labor for longshoremen in unloading bulk cargoes. The loss of this work for fertilizer factories alone has cost Norfolk's longshoremen an estimated 1,000 jobs. Thus, even though the ILA has made considerable progress in reorganizing the port, it claimed but 2,500 Negro and 200 white members in August 1941.

In Hampton Roads and Baltimore, as well as in all southern ports, Negroes and whites are organized in separate locals. There is good reason to believe that most Negroes, as well as whites, prefer this system. By concentrating their membership into separate local unions, the Negro longshoremen are able to obtain a larger voice in the district councils and conventions of their union than they otherwise would. In Hampton Roads, Negroes control the district council to which all locals of the ILA must belong. Thus, because of the Negroes' numerical preponderance, the district council cannot be used to facilitate discrimination as it frequently is in the building trades. In addition, there is the fact that the gang system of work requires a foreman for each fifteen to twenty-five men. These foremen are members of the local unions. Under the separate local setup, Negro longshoremen work under foremen of their own race. If the local unions and the gangs were mixed in the South, it is likely that most foremen there would be white.

Probably no port in the country except New York City is more in need of decasualization than Hampton Roads. Union officials estimate that 35 per cent of the men do 65 per cent of the work. Nor is the unfair division of employment the only evil that decasualization could help to correct.

Because of the size of the port, the longshoremen at Hampton Roads shape at the various local union headquarters. Theoretically, the stevedoring companies get their workers by telephoning the union business agent. Buses are provided to take the men to the piers at the city fare rate.

In actual practice, the hiring of longshoremen often works out quite differently. The stevedoring companies usually delegate the task of hiring to gang foremen who are also members of the local unions. By their authority over hiring, the foremen have gained control over most of the local unions. It is alleged that a local of 500 men is run by the sixty foremen-members. And this in turn has helped rackets of all sorts to flourish. For example, many longshoremen claim that all the foremen and petty bosses have cars. To secure job preference, one must ride to work in an automobile instead of a bus—and contribute generously to the upkeep of that car. One has but to loiter on the docks of Hampton Roads for a few days to hear of "kickbacks," usury rackets, etc.—all of which are evidence of the need of decasualization.[12]

THE SOUTH ATLANTIC PORTS AND MOBILE

In the South Atlantic ports of Charleston, Savannah, and Jacksonville, the longshore labor force is, and presumably always has been, all-Negro. In Charleston, there existed one of the first all-Negro labor unions, the Longshoremen's Protective Union Association, which in 1867 was called "the most powerful organization of the colored laboring class in South Carolina." For at least eight more years, it continued to function.

In Savannah, recorded strikes of Negro longshoremen occurred as early as September 19, 1881. Some ten years later the Knights of Labor established assemblies in the South Atlantic ports, and in the 1890's the ILA entered the region. The latter organized most of the workers there during World War I, but was driven out soon thereafter. In 1936, unionism was revived, and today most of the stevedoring companies are under contract.

In addition to tripling wages from 25 to 75 cents per hour, the ILA has improved the conditions of the South Atlantic Negro longshoremen by limiting the loads per worker and halting the stevedore's right to speed up the work at will. However, the ports are not decasualized, and the work is not divided. The result is that a minority of the local union members receive a major share of the work and that rumors of the abuse of power by hiring foremen are current on the docks, although neither of these evils appear to be as prevalent as at Hampton Roads.[13]

Today Negroes comprise the entire longshore labor force of the port of Mobile, but formerly a substantial minority of the dockworkers were white. Both white and colored longshoremen succeeded in forming local unions in the late nineteenth century, which later affiliated with the ILA. In 1923, they struck in sympathy with the New Orleans longshoremen and were completely defeated. Non-union Negroes replaced black and white unionists and the ILA ceased to exist in the port.

During the NRA period, an attempt was made to revive the ILA local, but a strike was defeated by the use of white strikebreakers, and an "independent" union was established instead. When unrest continued on the docks, an international ILA representative came to Mobile and engineered a deal whereby the charter of the existing local was revoked and a new charter was granted to the "independent," which immediately signed a closed-shop contract with the employers' association. Dues in the new local were raised to 4 per cent of total earnings. The white strikebreakers were then driven from the docks and again only Negroes were employed.

Capitalizing on the resultant dissatisfaction, the International Longshoremen's and Warehousemen's Union (CIO), composed of west coast workers who had seceded from the ILA, sent organizers to Mobile. The IL&WU representatives, however, were not especially qualified for the difficult job entrusted to them. They failed to counter the fears of the local Negroes that the decasualization plan which they espoused would cause unemployment; or that it would result in the displacement of local Negroes by unemployed west coast whites. The Mobile longshoremen also feared that ILA locals in other ports would boycott them out of jobs if the IL&WU won the election. In addition, the local police and employers made it plain that they preferred the ILA. As a result, the latter won the National Labor Relations Board election by a narrow margin.

Thus the shape-up, dues of 4 per cent of total earnings, the lack of division of work plan, and the usual rumors of bribery and racketeering, which are always present in an unregulated port, remain problems which confront Mobile's all-black longshoremen.[14]

New Orleans and the Texas Ports

About 50 per cent of the New Orleans longshoremen were colored prior to 1900. During the ensuing years, the proportion of Negroes steadily increased till by 1930 the whites were almost driven off the docks. After 1933, however, the whites regained some of their lost ground.

Each shift in the racial composition of the New Orleans dockworkers has resulted directly from the struggles of organized employers and workers. Unionism in the port dates back to 1850, when the white workers, who "screwed" the cotton with hand screws and stowed it aboard ships, founded the Screwmen's Benevolent Association. In 1865, white and black longshoremen struck side by side for wage increases, but were defeated. During the following twenty years, Negro longshoremen and screwmen formed unions to co-operate with the existing white locals. In 1873 and again in 1894, however, strikes accompanied by serious race riots occurred, as the white and black dockworkers fought over the division of work. In 1902, this matter was settled when it was agreed to divide all work on a fifty-fifty basis between the races. All longshore locals and teamsters of both races joined forces to form the Dock and Cotton Council, and most of the locals affiliated with the ILA.[15]

The invention of the high-powered cotton press which made obsolete the screwmen's skill and the large numbers of new workers who were attracted to the docks during World War I upset the *status quo.* The screwmen's unions were able to force employers to continue to pay them high rates for handling cotton for some time. In 1923, however, they led the Dock and Cotton Council, which they controlled, on strike, and all the unions were completely defeated. Strikebreakers were easily obtained. The white locals had kept their doors closed to the newcomers, but the Negro unions had admitted a large number of new workers. The result was that the colored longshore local had a membership of 4,400, the white, but 1,400, and the even division of work between the two was no longer equitable. White "casuals" and dissatisfied Negroes broke the strike.

For the next ten years, the New Orleans Steamship Association did not deal with organized labor. White longshoremen were gradually driven off the docks, although large numbers of the strikebreakers in 1923 were white. Hiring was placed in the hands of a Negro, Alvin E. Harris, and local politicians charged that the waterfront had been "Africanized." In 1925, Dr. Boris Stern found more evidence of the abuse of hiring foremen and racketeering in New Orleans than in any other large port, with Negroes being especially victimized.[16]

With the NRA, the New Orleans Steamship Association turned to company unionism. Whites were again employed, and white and colored "independent" unions were founded. In 1936, following the failure of the old ILA locals in the port to gain any important following, the national union revoked their charters for "insubordination" and chartered the "independents" which ILA spokesmen had assailed for three years as company-dominated.

As in Mobile, the International Longshoremen's and Warehousemen's Union attempted to capitalize on the longshoremen's unrest with an organizing campaign, but it was decisively defeated in a NRLB election. The failure of the New Orleans longshoremen to repudiate the ILA is attributable to the same reasons as in Mobile, plus a comprehensive intimidation campaign by state and city officials and the expenditure of $63,825.14 for "direct and indirect" education by the ILA colored local.

The IL&WU did, however, have a salutary effect on the New Orleans longshoremen. A rank-and-file revolt upset the leader of the white local, and the new head instituted a division of work program. In 1940, a "discrepancy" of more than $200,000 was discovered in the books of the Negro local, which charges its members dues of 5 per cent of their earnings. The officials were ousted, but unfortunately the new leaders have not shown interest in anything but maintaining their own positions.

Today the 700 members of Local No. 1418 (white) work quite regularly, and the available employment is divided among them in a reasonably equitable manner. The same cannot be said for the 2,100 Negro members of Local No. 1419. Their leaders have instituted no division of work, their dues remain amazingly high, and their leaders have given no indication that they intend to remedy either of these evils. Moreover, the shape-up seems to be especially hard on Negroes, for charges of corruption and graft at the expense of the colored longshoremen are persistent on the docks. Nor is there likely to be any change for the better so long as the vast majority of the New Orleans Negro longshoremen maintain their present attitude of indifference concerning the kind of officials who manage the affairs of their local union.

As in New Orleans, Negroes steadily increased in numbers in the Texas ports after 1900. Today, approximately 60 per cent of the longshoremen there are colored. Again, as in New Orleans, unionism in the Texas ports dates quite far back in the nineteenth century, but the subsequent history has been quite different, for the locals remained intact throughout the 1920's.

The ILA entered Galveston in 1900, and by 1912 had all the locals in the port under its banner. Before the port of Houston was opened to oceangoing vessels during World War I, a Negro local of the ILA already existed. It not only permitted the organization of a white local, but signed a ninety-nine year contract for an even division of work between the two locals. When the stevedore for the Southern Steamship Company refused to permit white longshoremen to work, the Negro local struck in sympathy and stayed out for more than three years. The Texas State Federation of Labor indorsed "the fight that the colored men have made for the white men . . ."

In all the Texas ports, the work is divided between the white and colored workers by agreements between their locals. When there are just two locals, as in Houston, the division is on a fifty-fifty basis. In Galveston, where there are two Negro locals and one white, a portion of the work is set aside for one Negro local, and the balance is divided evenly between the other colored and the white local. When loading the same ship, Negroes and whites usually work on opposite sides.

Although this seems at first sight perfectly fair, actually the white longshoremen receive more than their proportional share of work because their local unions have less members. For example, in February 1942, there were approximately 500 Negro longshoremen in Houston, but only 400 whites. Moreover, Negroes are usually assigned to work on the far side of ships. Nevertheless, Negro longshoremen in Texas do have better working conditions and more regular work than in any other port on the Atlantic or the Gulf coast. The reason for this is the decasualization scheme which has been developed there.

The total membership of each Texas local is kept within specified limits. There is no shape-up. Instead, the companies notify the local's business agent of their needs and he dispatches the required number of gangs. The business agent keeps account of the number of hours that each gang works, and rotates the gangs in order to keep their earnings as evenly distributed as possible. Each local employs "pagers" whose job it is to round up workers when they are needed and inform them where to report. The success of this system is a living refutation of the arguments of top ILA officials against decasualization.[17]

San Francisco

The struggles of the Pacific coast longshore unions date back to the 1850's, but their organizations were mostly destroyed soon after World War I. Commencing in 1934, however, they engaged in two spectacular strikes which have gained them the best conditions of longshore workers in the country. In 1937, they seceded from the ILA and formed the International Longshoremen's and Warehousemen's Union, CIO. A few Puget Sound ports did, however, remain with the ILA.

Until recently Negroes were not welcomed in west coast longshore locals, but they did enter the port of San Francisco in 1901, 1916, and 1919 in the role of strikebreakers. Only the last time did they obtain a permanent foothold, and even then they soon lost most of their gains. Before the great 1934 strike, only twenty-three Negroes were ILA members. Once again several hundred were used as strikebreakers.

Immediately after the 1934 strike, Harry Bridges, leader of the west coast longshoremen, announced that "Negro labor will never again find the doors of the San Francisco" longshore locals closed. Special interracial antidiscrimination committees were organized to see that no worker would be discharged or intimidated because of race or color. Segregated gangs are not permitted, and the union's no-discrimination policy is strictly enforced despite the small number of Negroes involved.

The west coats ports have been effectively decasualized since 1934. In each port, all hiring is done through a central hiring hall, run jointly by the employers and the union. The dispatcher is, however, a union member and that permits union control to be somewhat dominant. Work is effectively divided, with the result that variations in the earnings of union members, white or black, are small. The ILA would do well to espouse the decasualization scheme of the west coast longshoremen.[18]

CONCLUSION

Negro longshoremen are among the most completely unionized group of workers of their race. As a result their wages have increased substantially in the last decade. But it must be emphasized once again that until longshore work is decasualized, high wages cannot be transplanted into comparably high earnings. The west coast longshoremen and the local unions in the Texas ports have demonstrated that it is possible for the ports to regularize employment to a considerable extent and to divide it equitably between the white and colored workers. Until similar schemes are worked out for other ports, the colored longshoremen there will not obtain the maximum benefits possible from their organizations.

CHAPTER VII

THE COAL MINES

The bituminous coal industry has served as a laboratory for the development of many trade union policies. Of considerable importance is the manner in which the United Mine Workers has met the problem posed by the presence of large numbers of both white and Negro workers in the coal industry. The "miners' formula" for resolving this question has been adopted by many of the CIO unions, which it helped to bring into existence, and in which the influence of the experiences of collective bargaining in the coal industry is still strong, although the UMW has now dissociated itself from the CIO.

This chapter discusses the effects of the UMW's racial policies on the welfare of Negro miners. Before turning to the main topic, however, it will be necessary to examine briefly the trend of employment and the racial-occupational pattern in the industry.[1]

The Trend of Employment

Table V shows the number of workers attached to the industry, and the proportional strength of colored miners, in the country as a whole, and in the coal-producing states of the Southern Appalachian region, for the years 1890-1940. The data for 1890 and 1900 cannot, of course, be strictly compared with those of the four succeeding census years, as they include metal miners and, in the case of 1900, quarrymen as well. But since coal is the predominant mineral produced in all these states, these figures do convey the idea of the rapid increase in the number of coal miners employed during the two decades before 1910.

Taking first the figures for the entire country, both the absolute number of miners and the proportion of Negroes showed marked increases during the first decade after 1910. Most striking, however, is the fact that between 1920 and 1930 the number of Negro miners rose by 5 per cent in the face of a 14 per cent decrease in total employment in the industry; and then, in the next ten years, the Negroes' gains were more than wiped out: the total number of coal miners decreased by 16 per cent, whereas the number of Negroes decreased by 33 per cent. The circumstances under which these gains and losses of colored miners took place will be described in detail below.[2]

Turning next to the data for the individual states, we find that in 1940 approximately 90 per cent of all the Negroes in the industry were located in the five southern and border states of Alabama, Kentucky, Tennessee, Virginia, and West Virginia, the so-called Southern Appalachian region, where 16 per cent of the workers were colored. In no other state did Negroes comprise as much as 3 per cent of the total number of coal miners.

In three Southern Appalachian states—Kentucky, Tennessee, and Virginia—the percentage of Negroes declined by approximately one-half between 1910 and 1930. In Alabama, during this period, the proportion of Negro miners remained quite stable. In West Virginia, however, the proportion of Negroes remained constant from 1910 to 1920, but during the next ten years almost one-half of the new job opportunities created by the expansion of the industry went to Negro miners despite the fact that they comprised but one-fifth of the labor force in the state in 1920. It was in West Virginia, then, that the aforementioned rise in Negro employment was concentrated, a gain which was large enough to outweigh significant losses in three other southern states.

Between 1930 and 1940, the proportion of Negro miners in each Southern Appalachian state declined sharply, despite the fact that employment in that region, although not in the total industry, took a turn for the better. The downward trend, observed since 1910 in Kentucky, Tennessee, and Virginia, continued at an accelerated rate; for the first time since 1890, the proportion of Negroes in Alabama mines fell below 50 per cent; and in West Virginia, the gains of the Negroes during the 1920's were more than swept away.

The Development of the Southern Appalachian Region

The causes of these shifts in the racial-employment pattern are found, first, in the comparatively late exploitation of the south-

TABLE Va

TOTAL WORKERS, NUMBER AND PROPORTION OF NEGROES IN THE COAL INDUSTRY FOR THE UNITED STATES AND FOR THE PRINCIPAL COAL PRODUCING STATES OF THE SOUTHERN APPALACHIAN REGION 1890-1910

	1890[1]			1900[2]			1910		
	All Workers	Negroes	% Negro	All Workers	Negroes	% Negro	All Workers	Negroes	% Negro
Total United States	(3)	(3)	(3)	(3)	(3)	(3)	644,500	40,584	6.3
Total So. Appalachian	31,475	9,148	29.1	66,253	22,304	33.7	112,358	29,642	26.4
Alabama	7,966	3,687	46.3	17,898	9,735	54.3	20,779	11,189	53.8
Kentucky	5,091	976	19.2	9,299	2,206	23.7	18,310	3,888	21.3
Tennessee	4,889	769	15.7	10,890	3,092	28.4	11,094	1,609	14.5
Virginia	3,924	1,700	43.3	7,369	2,651	35.9	7,291	1,719	23.6
West Virginia	9,605	2,016	21.0	20,797	4,620	22.2	54,884	11,237	20.5

[1] Includes all miners.
[2] Includes all miners and quarrymen.
[3] Total U. S. figures would be without meaning because of inclusion of metal miners and quarrymen. U. S. totals in subsequent years include 100,000 to 150,000 anthracite miners.

TABLE Vb

Total Workers, Number and Proportion of Negroes in the Coal Industry for the United States and for the Principal Coal Producing States of the Southern Appalachian Region, 1920-1940

	1920			1930			1940[4]		
	All Workers	Negroes	% Negro	All Workers	Negroes	% Negro	All Workers	Negroes	% Negro
Total United States	733,936	54,597	7.5	621,661	57,291	9.2	519,420	38,560	7.4
Total So. Appalachian	182,845	42,666	23.3	197,162	44,266	22.5	214,253	34,793	16.0
Alabama	26,204	14,097	53.8	23,956	12,742	53.2	23,022	9,605	41.8
Kentucky	44,269	7,407	16.7	54,307	7,346	13.3	54,676	5,474	10.0
Tennessee	12,226	913	7.5	8,765	578	6.6	9,534	168	1.8
Virginia	12,418	2,450	19.8	12,629	1,511	12.0	20,086	1,190	5.9
West Virginia	87,728	17,799	20.3	97,505	22,089	22.7	106,935	18,356	17.2

Source: U. S. Census of Occupations, 1890-1940.
[4] Before 1940, the figures are those "gainfully occupied,"; i.e., attached to the industry. The 1940 figures are those actually employed. But the difference between these terms is not substantial. It is highly probable that most people in 1930 reported not their *usual* status, but their *actual* status at the time of enumeration, and the latter is just the point stressed by the 1940 census.

ern coal fields and their subsequent rapid development and, second, in the displacement of men by machines. Both are inextricably entwined with the story of collective bargaining in the industry.

Because of their greater distance from the centers of coal consumption, and because of inferior transportation facilities, the rich coal deposits of West Virginia and Kentucky were not exploited on a large scale before 1900. Since then, however, they have been developed at a rapid rate; nor is this difficult to explain. "The coal seams of these states are unusually thick and contain an exceptionally high grade coal." But, most important, "the southern coal industry was from its inception, and with a few years excepted, for nearly forty years thereafter, strictly non-union; whereas the central competitive field, composed of the mine fields of Illinois, Indiana, Ohio, and Pennsylvania, was to a large extent organized as early as 1900. Since labor costs constitute the principal element in total costs of production, the non-union coal operators in the southern fields were able to encroach steadily on the markets of the union employers in the North by paying lower wages than the union scale."[3]

The gradual infringement of the southern coal industry upon that of the North was noticeable even before World War I, but because of the expanding market and a still favorable freight rate structure[4] the northern operators were able to market increased quantities of coal until 1920. After that date, however, both these favorable factors were lost to them. In addition, they became involved in a series of costly strikes and lockouts with the United Mine Workers, mainly over the issue of whether wage rates should be reduced. Although the UMW was able to maintain the wage structure, one group of operators after another went non-union until 1927 when the entire collective bargaining system in the central competitive field collapsed.

The consequences of these events were that production in the Southern Appalachian region increased as fast as that in the North fell off, until in 1927 the former area was producing as much as the latter. After the collapse of collective bargaining in that year, the northern operators succeeded in regaining a slight supremacy by drastic wage and price reductions, and since then they have been able to maintain their top position, either by further wage slashes or, since 1933, because of government stabilization of the industry.

The sharp gain of the Southern Appalachian field, particularly West Virginia, at the expense of the northern coal-producing states during the twenties accounts for the already observed fact that Negro coal miners were able to increase their share of employment between 1920 and 1930 despite the fact that the number of white workers decreased by nearly one-sixth. Of special interest is the fact that in West Virginia, the state in which all the employment gains of colored miners were made during this decade, the coal operators imported Negro labor primarily for strike-breaking and anti-union purposes. But in Kentucky, Tennessee, and Virginia, the coal operators found the white "mountaineers" and recent immigrants from southeastern Europe less likely to catch the union contagion, and consequently the number of white employees was increased at the expense of the Negroes in these three states.[5]

THE RACIAL-OCCUPATIONAL PATTERN

The decline in importance of Negroes in the coal industry since 1930 is attributable primarily to the displacement of men by machines. To understand this clearly, it is necessary to discuss briefly the racial-occupational pattern of the industry.

The range of occupations in coal mining is comparatively narrow. Except for a few maintenance men, there are in the average coal mine no jobs which require more than a modicum of skill. Over 50 per cent of the personnel "consist of hand coal loaders, and most of the other workers are machine operators of one sort or another. While the former are paid by the piece, and the latter by the day, there is seldom any great difference in the earnings of the two groups."[*]

Segregation either by occupation or by place of work, unlike most factory industries in the South, is conspicuous by its absence in the coal mines. In mines where the two races are employed, they invariably work side by side and at the same occupations. Negroes are used in all capacities, but their share of work varies from oc-

* The discussion in this section owes much to an unpublished manuscript by Dr. P. H. Norgren.

cupation to occupation. Thus, in a sample study of some twenty southern West Virginia mines in 1932, it was found that only 2 per cent of the Negroes were undercutting-machine operators as against 6 per cent of the white. In all the "indirect labor" jobs, except that of brakemen (one of the most dangerous jobs in a coal mine), and in all jobs carrying a supervisory function, the whites were more heavily represented than the Negroes. On the other hand, however, 77 per cent of the colored miners were found to be hand loaders, but only 60 per cent of the whites were engaged in this occupation.[6] The field work of the present writer, carried on in southern West Virginia and Alabama during the summers of 1940 and 1941, confirms the general tenor of these findings.*

Despite this uneven distribution of jobs between the two races, the fact remains that the outstanding characteristic of the southern coal industry from a racial-occupational standpoint is the comparatively high degree of mixing of the races. Besides, since the earnings of piece- and day-workers are usually about equal, no wage differential based on race is present in the industry.[7]

On the other hand, the relatively heavy concentration of Negroes in hand loading jobs has made them especially vulnerable to technological displacement. Since World War I, mechanical loaders of various types have been put on the market, which perform these operations and in so doing displace a substantial number of hand loaders. Before 1933, mechanization of loading operations was confined almost without exception to the high-wage North. Together with the competition of other fuels, and the introduction of more efficient methods of fuel utilization, it contributed to the

* The author of this study maintains that the relatively heavy concentration of Negroes in hand loading jobs is, to a large extent, a matter of choice. Negro miners, he claims, prefer piecework jobs because such work allows them a relatively high degree of freedom from supervision and permits them to take an occasional day off if they so desire. A like conclusion was reached by the author of another study, which was based on a survey of some fifty mining communities in Kentucky and West Virginia, conducted at approximately the same time as the former's investigation.

It should also be emphasized, however, that hand loading requires the greatest amount of physical effort of any of the occupations in coal mining. When one considers that it is a general custom to assign such tasks to Negroes, it seems likely that other factors besides the desires of the colored workers are involved. E.g., it has long been customary to assign machine jobs to whites, and leave the hand loading for Negroes, and usually the preferences considered, have been those of the white workers, and not of the Negroes.

already noted 14 per cent decline in employment in the industry.[8] With the advent of collective bargaining and high wages after 1933, the introduction of loading machines went forward at a rapid rate in the South. It is to this fact that the sharp decline of Negro miners in the industry is mainly attributable. For Negroes not only suffered heavily by reason of being concentrated in the occupation which the machines eliminated, but they also failed to receive a proportionate share of employment as machine operators. Since the causes of this last event are explicable only if one understands the Negro-union relationships in the industry, further discussion of the subject will be postponed until we have examined the racial policies of the United Mine Workers.[9]

THE NEGRO AND THE DEVELOPMENT OF COLLECTIVE BARGAINING

The United Mine Workers of America was founded in 1890 by a merger of the Progressive Miners' Union with Knights of Labor District Assembly No. 135. From its beginning the UMW was organized on an industrial basis, taking into membership all those who worked "in and around the mines," regardless of race, color, creed, or nationality. To what was left of the Knights of Labor's "take in anybody" philosophy was added the special feeling of unity among all mine workers engendered by the isolation of the mining towns. Usually cut off from direct communication with the outside world, these communities rarely developed more than two classes: the "company" with its manager, mine guards, and all-pervasive authority, on the one hand, and the workers, whether machinists, coal loaders, or what not, on the other.[10] The workers' solidarity was also strengthened by the narrow wage differential between the highest and lowest paid. Race and nationality differences remained the primary disturbing element, and this, as we shall see, the UMW leaders strenuously combated.

In the early years of its existence, the UMW was quite successful in organizing the miners of Illinois, Indiana, Ohio, and to a lesser extent, Pennsylvania—the central competitive field—and the small southwestern area, composed of Arkansas, Kansas, and Oklahoma. Attempting to forestall unionism, the coal companies of these areas frequently staffed their mines with "judicial mixtures" of native whites, recent immigrants, and Negroes. As early as 1880, and as late as 1927, southern Negroes, fresh from the cotton fields and totally ignorant of industrial conflict, were imported as strike-breakers. Although this resulted in serious racial outbreaks on several occasions, the UMW officials did not attempt to fight the operators by drawing the color line. Had they done so, they would undoubtedly have encouraged the importation of more colored strikebreakers. Instead, they encouraged the Negroes to join the union and guaranteed them full privileges of membership. Racial friction and discrimination in the central competitive and south-western fields did not vanish, to be sure. But the methods used by the UMW to combat the importation of Negro strikebreakers kept it at a minimum.[11]

In the Southern Appalachian region, where Negro labor was used from the beginning of mining operations, the UMW found the going much rougher, as its experiences in Alabama and West Virginia illustrate.

Labor organization among Alabama coal miners dates as far back as 1883; and a decade later the United Mine Workers first entered the region. Progress was at first slow, but by 1902 the union had entered into compacts with most of the operators in the region. Two years later, however, some of the larger producers denounced the agreement and, despite a series of strikes, the Alabama miners' unions were completely destroyed by 1908.[12]

The next attempt at organization of Alabama came some ten years later. Aided by the federal government's World War I labor policy, which officially approved of collective bargaining, the UMW succeeded in organizing several thousand miners—again, as previously, mainly Negroes. Although the operators refused to recognize the union, they did accept successive arbitration awards by federal officials, and thus stoppages during the war were prevented. In the fall and winter of 1920-21, however, the UMW was defeated after a bitter strike, and coal unionism disappeared from Alabama till 1933.

In both the 1908 and the 1920-21 strike, the employers and their supporters found the race issue a valuable ally. In the former year, the tent colony, in which the strikers lived after they had been evicted from the company-owned houses, was burned to the ground in order to prevent the "mobilization of Negroes in union camps." In addition a committee of citizens threatened a race riot unless the president of the UMW ordered the miners to return to work. The UMW executive was informed that "no matter how meritorious the union cause, the people of Alabama would never tolerate the organization and striking of Negroes along with white men." The union officials then proposed to transfer all of the Negroes out of the state and make the strike a "white man's affair." But the governor of Alabama stated that he "would not permit white men to live in camps under the jurisdiction" of the UMW. The apparent hopelessness of the struggle, plus the fact that there had occurred no little violence and bloodshed, undoubtedly induced the miners' president to terminate the strike.

In the 1920-21 struggle, the race issue was given no less prominence. Over 76 per cent of the strikers were Negroes. To this the operators declared the success of the strike to be due, because "southern Negroes . . . are easily misled, especially when given a prominent and official place in an organization in which both races are members." A citizens' committee stressed the fact that *northern* Negro and white organizers spoke from the same platform. And the strike was featured by violence as primitive and brutal as in any of the earlier coal mining tragedies of the North and West, with Negroes being especially singled out for savage treatment.

While there is every likelihood that racial friction would not have been absent in an atmosphere so tense as that of an Alabama coal strike, it is clear that the coal operators and their friends were responsible for bringing the question of color to the forefront and making it a central issue of the industrial conflicts of both 1908 and 1920-21. The attempts of the UMW to organize the coal fields of West Virginia further demonstrate the difficulties encountered by unions which attempt to build effective organizations where the labor force is represented by large numbers of both races.

The UMW first entered West Virginia a few months after it was founded in 1890, but its efforts were for the most part unsuccessful until the period during and immediately following World War I. Then the heads of the miners' union realized that the very existence of their organization was threatened by the low wage and price schedules of the non-union southern fields. After a strenuous campaign, the UMW secured contracts with about 80 per cent of the producers in northern West Virginia, and with the operators in the southern counties of Fayette, Kanawha, and Raleigh, but failed to secure even a foothold in Logan, Mingo, Mercer, and MacDowell, the counties along the southeastern rim of the state. Within a few years after the war, the UMW was driven entirely from southern West Virginia, and from most of the northern part of the state as well.[13]

Likewise, the miners' union obtained a precarious footing in eastern Kentucky during the war, but was driven out soon thereafter.[14]

The failure of the miners' union to organize the workers in the southernmost counties of West Virginia is not difficult to understand. The operators in this section of the state employed practically every device known to anti-unionists, including race-hatred propaganda, to defeat the union, which often also resorted to extreme measures.[15]

In their attempts to organize the miners of West Virginia, as in Alabama, the leaders of the UMW adhered to the policy of organizing both white and colored workers into the same local bodies. Although the union was successful in bringing large numbers of both white and colored miners into the fold, the presence of a large number of workers of both races played into the hands of the operators. The white miners, themselves divided between native "mountaineers" and recent immigrants from southeastern Europe, were loath to make common cause with the Negroes. The employers were quick to capitalize upon this situation by spreading rumors that, should the United Mine Workers be successful, the black miners would lose their jobs. In addition, the West Virginia operators, as in past labor disputes, imported large numbers of Negro agricultural workers from neighboring states farther South. The effect was both to supply a labor force with which strikes were defeated and to add to the antagonism between the races.

The failure of the United Mine Workers to organize the Southern Appalachian fields put it on the defensive during the remainder of the twenties. Unable either to compete with the low-wage South or to induce the UMW to make wage concessions, company after company broke with the union in order to cut wages, until in 1927, after the wholesale shift of production from North to South, the entire collective bargaining machinery in the central competitive field collapsed. The next five years were featured by vicious price and wage slashes, and by internal dissension within the shattered UMW.[16]

The organizing opportunity afforded by the NRA was taken advantage of by the UMW as by no other union. When the law went into effect, organizers were already in the field. Within three months, 90 per cent of the nation's coal miners had been enrolled by the UMW. The desperate conditions in which the miners found themselves as a result of the depression caused them to embrace unionism with such unanimity as to make opposition on the part of even the most bitter anti-union operator largely futile. Besides, after the experience of the preceding five years, many of the operators questioned the desirability of unrestricted wage and price competition in the industry.[17]

That is not to say that the majority of the southern coal mine owners welcomed the UMW. Company unionism, some violence, and race prejudice were used in an endeavor to stem the tide. This time, however, even the last-named failed. The terrible privations of the depression imbued both races with mutual understanding and tolerance. The arguments of the UMW organizers, both white and colored, that no union could succeed unless it had the support of both white and black miners, were heeded. When, in Alabama, the Ku-Klux Klan was revived to fight the union, white miners joined it, won control of it, and destroyed its effectiveness.[18]

With the assistance of President Roosevelt and the NRA machinery, the UMW won an agreement covering the entire Appalachian area in September 1933. Bolstered by federal regulation of competition in the industry, the UMW has steadily raised wages and extended its control until in 1941 it established a $7 basic wage rate for both North and South, and secured the union shop for almost the whole working force in the industry.[19] Since then more wage concessions have been obtained.

The Alabama mining field has never been included in the Appalachian agreements because of unique local conditions.[20] At present the basic wage in Alabama is approximately $1.50 below that of the Appalachian agreement.

AN APPRAISAL OF THE MINERS' FORMULA OF EQUALITARIAN UNIONISM

The revival of unionism in the bituminous coal industry and the subsequent establishment of industry-wide collective bargaining have, then, meant a substantial increase in the standard of living of the Negro, as well as of the white, miners in the South. But the consequences of organization to the thousands of colored miners in the South cannot be judged solely on the basis of immediate gain. What unionism has meant to them in other respects and whether they stand to gain from it in the long run are equally important questions.

It must be re-emphasized at this point that the UMW has an enviable record of practicing, as well as preaching, racial equality in its organization ever since it began to function. It is true that there have been instances of discrimination against Negroes in particular locals, both in the North and in the South. But the officials of the national union have never, to the writer's knowledge, condoned such action, and have not hesitated to chastise individual locals for failing to live up to the letter of the nondiscrimination policy.[21] Moreover, the UMW has always conducted both its organizing campaigns and its day-to-day union affairs without prejudice to any race.

When the 1933 organizing campaign was initiated in the South, the UMW did not deviate from its equalitarian policies. The success of the campaign was indeed a tribute to the forthright manner in which its representatives faced the race issue and preached the necessity of interracial co-operation.

More important than the success of the organizing campaign, however, has been the ability of the UMW district leaders in the South to devise a workable system whereby the two races could co-operate effectively and yet not antagonize the public by encroaching too sharply upon the customs of the communities. In West Virginia, where rigid separation is not the rule, and where race patterns are relatively fluid, the problem was not so serious; but in Alabama a good deal of both tact and courage was required.

For example, when the time came for the election of local officers, the Alabama district leaders advocated the selection of whites as presidents and Negroes as vice-presidents, and this procedure was followed in locals even where the Negroes were in a majority. "This device was designed to facilitate good employer-employee relations, for the local president usually heads the 'pit' committee which meets with representatives of management for the joint settlement of grievances arising from working conditions in the mines." It was felt that the employers should be accustomed to the novelty of joint grievance committees before being subject to the still more novel experience of having to deal with Negroes as equals. At the same time, the election of Negro vice-presidents and of other Negro officers provided the colored miners with representation in the policy-making decisions of the locals.

The results of this policy of gradualism are already discernible. According to a number of informants of both races, "Negro members of grievance committees, who a few years ago would have risked physical violence had they raised their voices in joint union-management meetings, now argue their cases quite as freely as their fellow white members." Local meetings are no longer featured by such "formal" relationships between the races as, according to Dr. G. S. Mitchell, was the case in 1934-35. White members no longer hesitate to call a Negro unionist "brother," or to shake hands with Negro delegates without displaying embarrassment. And, now, Negro delegates contribute rather freely to discussions.[22]

In West Virginia, it was not found necessary to adhere to a policy of strict gradualism. Negroes are usually well-represented among the local and district officers and in some cases have been elected local union presidents even though white miners are in the majority. In many mines where there are a large number of foreign-born workmen, it is the custom to elect on a three-man pit committee one from this group, one native white, and one Negro. By such means, the UMW has been able to weld into a united front that conglomerate mixture of races and nationalities which many coal operators once thought was an insurmountable bar to unionism.

The machinery for the settlement of grievances constitutes one of the major gains which unionism has brought to southern miners. Undoubtedly, Negroes have benefited more from it than whites. "Colored miners are more heavily concentrated in the hand loading jobs, where payment is computed on a tonnage basis. Output on these jobs is frequently seriously interfered with by unusual mining conditions and other unavoidable circumstances." It was not until the advent of unionism and its grievance machinery that equitable adjustments were made in such instances. In addition, the power of mine foremen to discharge without cause or to assign to the poorer workplaces—treatment which these petty officials have been more inclined to inflict upon Negroes than upon whites —is now subject to joint union-management review, where the aggrieved can seek, and find, redress. The results of grievance machinery have been material, as well as psychological.[23]

By far the most difficult problem which confronts the equalitarian program of the United Mine Workers involves the disposal of employment problems incident to the introduction of labor-saving machinery, nowadays principally loading machines. Coal loading machines were introduced into the mines on a large scale soon after World War I, but before 1933 their use was largely confined to the high-wage areas of the North. Since then, under the impetus of unionism and high wages, mechanical loading machinery has made rapid strides in the Southern Appalachian region. In West Virginia, for example, less than 1 per cent of the total production was loaded by machines in 1933; by 1940, however, the proportion had jumped to 70.2 per cent. Likewise in the other Southern Appalachian states, less than 1 per cent of the total ouput was mechanically loaded in 1933; but in 1940, the relevant figures were, for Alabama, 32 per cent; for Kentucky, 76.8 per cent; for Tennessee, 13.1 per cent; and for Virginia, 64.2 per cent.[24] Since then, the percentage of coal loaded by machinery has continued to increase in the Southern Appalachian region.[25]

It has been estimated by competent experts that 46 men working with mobile loaders can do the work of 100 hand loaders.[26] Along with unemployment attributable to declining markets, this technological displacement has meant a real hardship to the miners. Moreover, there is no doubt but that Negroes have borne the brunt of the unemployment, for it is to the introduction of these loading machines that the already noted sharp drop in the proportion of Negroes in the industry since 1930 is primarily ascribable.[27] Indeed, this was to be expected since Negroes are more heavily concentrated in the hand loading jobs than are whites. In addition, however, Negroes have not received a proportionate share of jobs as machine operators. There are several reasons for this.

The introduction of machinery, or the substitution of a new technique for an old, has often meant in the South the displacement of Negro handworkers by white machine operators. Thus when undercutting machines and other mechanical devices were installed in southern coal mines earlier in the century, whites were assigned in disproportionately large numbers to operate them, and most black workers remained hand loaders. This was the pattern *before* the advent of UMW and collective bargaining. Hence, when loading machines were installed, the employers gave white workers preference as a matter of course.

This, of course, is in direct conflict with the equalitarian policies of the UMW, but until recently the district officials of the union have hesitated to take a firm stand on the question. For the very reason that machine jobs have been traditionally "white man's work," the UMW officials, pursuing a policy of gradualism, did not attempt a quick break with the past. More important, it is at least questionable whether, before 1939, the heads of the UMW had given the question of technological unemployment the serious attention that it deserved.

The UMW has not opposed the introduction of machinery; it has merely insisted that the benefits therefrom be shared with its members.[28] But before 1939 few of the district agreements in the South contained clauses providing that workers who had been displaced by machines should be rehired, if possible, before newcomers could be employed.[29] Indeed, it was not until 1941 that such provision was written into the basic Appalachian agreements.* But since the qualifications for machine loading jobs are not possessed by all hand loaders, strict seniority cannot be observed in the transfer from handwork to machine operation, and so the way is still open for discrimination unless the national and district officials of the UMW are vigilant and the employers co-operative.

* The 1941 Appalachian agreement reads in part: "Seniority affecting return to employment of idle employees on a basis of length of service and qualification for the respective positions brought about by different mining methods or installation of mechanical equipment is recognized. Men displaced by new mining methods or installation of new mechanical equipment so long as they remain unemployed shall constitute a panel from which new employees shall be selected." (*United Mine Workers Journal*, July 15, 1941.)

A further point should be brought out. Because the white workers had performed the bulk of the machine jobs before the introduction of mechanical loaders, they often have been in a better position to learn how to operate the mobile loading machines. This, of course, has counted in their favor, and against Negroes.

THE FUTURE

In sum, then, because, for various reasons, the UMW has not obtained equal treatment for Negroes in the allocation of job opportunities, white miners may be said to have benefited from unionism to a somewhat greater extent than Negroes, although the advantages to the latter in the form of increased wages, better working conditions, and protection from arbitrary treatment on the job have been substantial. To what extent this will hold true in the future, depends upon the outcome of postwar adjustments.

Because of the war boom, current demands for coal exceed those in any previous period since World War I. In addition, the draft and the migration of miners to more lucrative jobs have depleted the industry's working force. Consequently, miners displaced by machinery at the present time have little difficulty in finding employment.

When the war is over, however, the abnormally large demand for coal may be expected to subside and, as a result, employment in the industry will decline. Moreover, the employment problem is likely to be aggravated by mechanization, by the use of more efficient methods of fuel utilization, and by the competition of substitute fuels, all of which adversely affected employment in the industry between the two World Wars. Especially are these three economic forces likely to threaten the stability of the industry if the UMW officials continue to use their great bargaining power to gain ever higher wages and shorter hours, for such a policy will probably accelerate the substitution of machines for men and the introduction of improved methods of fuel utilization, as well as worsen the competitive position of coal in relation to other fuels.[30]

If, as predicted, employment in the bituminous coal industry declines when peace returns, and if past experience is any guide, Negroes will suffer disproportionately heavy losses in jobs. This is particularly likely to occur in instances where machines replace men. These postwar adjustments will put the equalitarian policies of the UMW to their severest tests. If Negroes continue to bear the brunt of technological unemployment, the UMW will no longer be able to claim that it adheres to a policy of racial equality as steadfastly as any other American labor union.

CHAPTER VIII

IRON AND STEEL*

The present labor movement in the iron and steel industry was created by the leaders of the CIO, who were principally officers of the United Mine Workers. After an analysis of the position of the Negro in the industry and an account of the part played by colored workers in early attempts at unionization, the efforts of the leaders of the United Steelworkers of America, CIO, to apply the "miners' formula" of equalitarian unionism to the steel industry is discussed in this chapter.

THE NEGRO IN THE INDUSTRY

The iron and steel industry depended upon an ever-increasing supply of cheap labor during the early years of its expansion. In the great steel centers of the North, this need was met by the steady influx of European immigrants prior to World War I. A few Negroes did enter northern steel mills before that time, some via the strikebreaking route, but for the most part the Negroes in the industry were concentrated in the South, notably in the Birmingham, Ala., region.

Table VI shows the total laborers and operatives, and the number and proportion of Negroes in basic iron and steel production (i.e., blast furnaces, steel works, and rolling mills), for the United States and for the principal steel manufacturing states, 1910-1930. The proportion of Negroes in the "other iron and steel products" industry, which employs approximately 650,000 additional workers, is somewhat smaller, but the racial employment trend is similar.

The reader is cautioned to interpret the figures in Table VI with care. The term "operative," as used by the census, includes all direct production workers except the most highly skilled and highly paid categories. A large majority of these top-flight workers

* The sections of this chapter which deal with the Negro's position in the industry and the racial-occupational setup owe much to an unpublished manuscript by Dr. P. H. Norgren, assisted by the present writer.

TABLE VI

Total Laborers and Operatives, Number and Proportion of Negroes, in Basic Steel Production, for the United States, and for Selected States, 1910-1930

	1910			1920			1930		
	Total Laborers and Operatives	Negroes	% Negro	Total Laborers and Operatives	Negroes	% Negro	Total Laborers and Operatives	Negroes	% Negro
Total United States	269,430¹	15,060	5.0	352,457	47,898	13.6	342,390	45,472	13.3
Alabama	7,408	5,365	72.4	12,897	9,981	77.3	8,619	5,805	67.4
Illinois	21,439	446	2.1	22,910	2,618	11.4	27,625	3,073	11.1
Indiana	12,432	272	2.2	18,320	2,605	14.2	26,002	4,974	19.1
Maryland	3,020	1,231	40.8	4,034	1,733	43.0	8,870	4,519	50.9
Michigan	2,507	7	0.3	4,619	420	9.1	6,518	629	9.7
Ohio	42,252	921	2.2	63,722	5,632	8.8	6,518	629	9.7
Pennsylvania	121,432	3,322	2.7	150,142	16,317	10.9	66,498	8,206	12.3
West Virginia	4,724	25	0.5	9,673	467	4.9	126,631	11,851	9.4
							7,666	337	4.4

Source: U. S. Census of Occupations, 1910-1930.
¹ Approximate. National totals available for Illinois only. Figures included for operatives are totals for 17 states, containing approximately 98 per cent of the country's blast furnaces, steel works, and rolling mills.

not included as operatives are white. In addition, skilled maintenance and indirect production workers, less than 2 per cent of
whom are Negroes, are not classified as operatives. Hence the
figures in Table VI considerably overstate the proportion of Negroes
in the industry. Since, however, the sum of laborers and operatives comprise approximately two-thirds of the industry's total labor
force, an examination of the data in Table VI will show the racial
distribution of labor for the two decades before 1930.

The most striking feature revealed by these data is the near
tripling of the number of Negroes in the industry after 1910. This
occurred after the European immigrant labor supply was shut off
by World War I and restrictive immigration legislation. The steel
industry then turned to southern Negroes to fill its labor needs.
Thousands of Negroes were recruited for work in northern steel
mills; other thousands migrated to steel centers without urging by
steel management or its agents; a much smaller number was
brought in as strikebreakers, but most of those lost their places
when striking whites returned to work.[1]

During the twenties, Negro steel workers held their gains. A
decrease in their share of employment in Alabama, where they
suffered disproportionately from technological unemployment,[2] was
offset by gains elsewhere, particularly in Illinois, Ohio, and Maryland. More than 75 per cent of all Negro steel workers were found
in the North in 1930.

During the thirties the proportion of Negroes in the industry
declined in nearly all steel manufacturing centers. In 1930, the
census reported that 52,956, or 8.5 per cent, of the 620,894 workers in basic iron and steel production were Negroes; in 1940, the
same agency found that only 39,660, or 6.8 per cent of the 581,280
workers, there were colored. The trend of events in the "other iron
and steel products" industries was similar.[3]

Of special significance for this study is the fact that the decrease
in the proportion of Negro steel workers during the thirties seems
to have been the result primarily of employer personnel policies
which were adopted at a time when unionism was at most only a
future threat to unrestricted management control. After a comprehensive study of labor conditions in the industry during the NRA
period, Professor C. R. Daugherty stated that there was "general
agreement that Negro workers had been laid off in disproportionate

numbers. . . ." This was partly the consequence of the fact that Negroes are concentrated in the least skilled, and hence, least indispensable jobs, and partly of favoritism of white workers in layoffs. Many Negroes were so demoralized by these experiences that they were rendered unemployable. Others turned to unionism as a protection against unfair treatment. But since employers had hired Negroes to a considerable extent precisely because they were considered "bulwarks against outside labor organization," and since steel unionism remained weak throughout the NRA period, the net result was more, rather than less, loss of employment opportunities for Negro steel workers.[4]

In Alabama, another reason for the loss of ground of Negroes was the attitude of employers who, because they were forced to raise wages by the NRA codes, preferred to employ whites rather than to increase the wages of Negroes.[5]

Whether Negroes have recouped any of their losses of the previous decade since 1940 cannot be ascertained. The impressions of this writer, however, based upon his field investigations, are that there has been some increase in the proportion of Negroes in iron and steel production since this country entered the war. It is impossible to make an estimate of the extent of these supposed gains.

The Racial-Occupational Pattern

As in most other industries, Negroes were first employed in the most undesirable jobs in the iron and steel industry. Thus even today they are more heavily concentrated in blast furnaces and in coke ovens, where the hottest jobs are found, than in departments where working conditions are more pleasant.

The majority of Negroes in the steel industry also remain in unskilled jobs. A study, conducted by the U. S. Bureau of Labor Statistics in 1938, listed 49.2 per cent of the Negroes in the industry as unskilled, 38.3 per cent as semiskilled, and 12.5 per cent as skilled. The skill composition of the Negro steel workers was approximately the same for the North as for the South (the latter comprising in the Bureau's survey mainly the Birmingham area). Comparison of these percentages with the corresponding ratios for whites reveals the much less favorable position of colored workers. In the South, only 11.1 per cent of the whites were unskilled, whereas 43.9 per cent were semiskilled and 45.0 per cent, skilled. The skill composition of whites in the North was 23.6 per cent unskilled, 40.6 per cent, semiskilled, and 37.7 per cent, skilled.[6]

The fact that less than 2 per cent of the skilled maintenance and indirect production workers in the industry are Negroes has already been mentioned. This is, of course, as typical of American industry as is the concentration of Negroes in common labor jobs, for the majority of occupations in this skilled group—pipe fitting, electrical installation work, tool making, and most of the mechanical crafts—are closed to Negroes in most industries.

There is, however, a decidedly unusual feature of the racial-occupational pattern of the steel industry. That is the comparatively high proportion of Negroes among the skilled production workers. Probably there is only one other skilled category in American manufacturing industry where Negroes have been able to secure a percentage of the work anywhere near to their normal proportion of jobs—that is, the proportion which all Negroes comprise of all workers in the industry.* Thus whereas, in 1930, 8.5 per cent of the labor force in the entire steel industry were colored, so were 6.5 per cent of the skilled production workers.[7] Although the figures for later years are not available, the field work of the writer indicates that the data of 1930 may still be considered fairly representative.

The unusually high representation of Negroes in skilled production jobs is all the more remarkable when it is noted that the wages for this type of work usually exceed those paid for skilled maintenance and indirect production work, a classification in which few Negroes are found.[8] It is probably explainable, at least in part, by the fact that production workers learn their trade by serving as helpers to skilled men on the job. Despite considerable discrimination, Negroes so employed have been promoted, especially in time of labor shortages. On the other hand, maintenance men are recruited from the outside, and the training opportunities for Negroes in these crafts are quite limited. Also, excessive heat,

---

* The other skilled category is iron molding. Dr. Norgren notes (MS, *loc. cit.*) that this is "a trade which has three important points of similarity with steel mill work, namely, excessive heat, dirt, and noxious gases."

dirt, and noxious gases make some skilled production jobs quite unpleasant. This may influence white workers to prefer the more pleasant, if less remunerative, work.[9]

There is one other feature of the occupational pattern in steel industry to which attention should be directed. That is the unusually wide differential between common laborers' earnings and those of skilled production workers. According to the aforementioned Bureau of Labor Statistics survey, heaters and rollers in bar mills in the North earned an average of $1.07 and $1.71 per hour, respectively, and unskilled workers in the same branch of industry but $.63 per hour.[10] The writer knows of no other major manufacturing industry in which the gap between the best paid and poorest paid jobs is as great as it is in the iron and steel industry.[11]

THE NEGRO AND UNIONISM BEFORE 1936

Trade unionism in the iron and steel industry dates back to 1858, when a group of Pittsburgh iron puddlers founded the Sons of Vulcan. Other groups in the industry also organized unions of their crafts. In 1876, these joined forces as the Amalgamated Association of Iron, Steel, and Tin Workers, which later affiliated with the AFL.

The Amalgamated enjoyed a fair degree of success until the late 1880's. Then it suffered a number of defeats until by 1910 it was completely eliminated from the plants of the larger companies, including those of the United States Steel Corporation. For the ensuing quarter of a century, unionism was not an important factor in the industry outside of certain tin mills in the Middle West, where the bulk of the Amalgamated's membership was located after 1910. A significant exception occurred in 1919 when the Amalgamated somewhat halfheartedly joined with twenty other AFL unions to form a national council for the purpose of organizing the industry. Some 350,000 steel workers went out on strike in an effort to gain union recognition and to eliminate the twelve-hour day, but they were completely defeated.[12]

During these early years, the Amalgamated was quite hostile to the idea of organizing Negroes. Its policies were dominated by the highly skilled workers, especially former members of the Sons of Vulcan, a union which had barred Negroes by constitutional provision. Although the Amalgamated did not incorporate a like clause in its constitution, it refused to go on record as favoring the organization of Negroes till 1881, despite some experiences with Negro strikebreakers before that date. For some time thereafter, it favored placing Negroes into separate local unions. In several instances, white steel workers refused to work with Negro union members, but the Amalgamated's officers took no effective measures to protect their colored members from such discrimination.[13]

Negroes played a major role in defeating the steel strike of 1919. Birmingham was the only major center not closed down by the walkout. A strike under the leadership of the AFL Metal Trades Department unions[14] had been decisively defeated there the previous year. The Birmingham Negro steel workers were so intimidated by their experiences that they refused to heed the call to leave their jobs in 1919.[15]

Although in some northern centers, Negroes struck along with whites, other Negroes were brought in as strikebreakers by the thousands. Many had no idea that a strike was in progress until they arrived on the scene. Others acted with deliberation because of the failure of the Amalgamated and its associated unions to practice equality. As a result, many serious racial clashes occurred on the picket lines and within struck plants. But although Negroes performed yeomen service in helping the steel magnates break the strike, Spero and Harris reported that almost "all the Negro strikebreakers who came into the plants from outside lost their places when the walkout ended, while those already employed who had remained at work and had been advanced to the better jobs of the men who struck went back to their old places when the old employees returned." [16]

With the advent of the NRA in 1933, the Amalgamated again became active, but it had little permanent success. The steel companies sponsored company unions and discriminated against the Amalgamated's members, so that by mid-1934 the latter had lost most of its new recruits.

Although the failure of the 1919 strike had made it apparent that steel unionism could not succeed without the active co-operation of Negro labor, the top officials of the Amalgamated made no special effort to enroll them. They were still dominated by the limited craft outlook which considered the interest of the top production workers almost to the exclusion of all others. The slowness with which they comprehended the importance of technical changes, which were destroying skills and permitting the use of rapidly increasing numbers of unskilled immigrant and Negro laborers, alienated an ever-growing percentage of the nation's steel workers and materially assisted the steel interests in maintaining their non-union labor policy.

Despite the attitude of the top officials, the Amalgamated did have better success than ever before in enrolling Negroes. For one thing, Negroes were so obviously discriminated against in layoffs that a "stick with the company" philosophy had lost much of its appeal. Secondly, there arose among the Amalgamated's locals new leaders whose outlook was not limited by past tradition and who realized that unionism in the industry must be open to all workers, regardless of race or skill, if it was to succeed. Their NRA experience stood them in good stead when the CIO drive was inaugurated a few years later.[17]

Also during the NRA days, the Steel and Metal Workers Industrial Union, an affiliate of the Communist party, attempted the organization of steel workers. In accordance with party philosophy, special appeals were made to Negro workers, but this organization had almost no success in enrolling either Negroes or whites.[18]

Unionism Since 1936

In June 1936, the heads of the CIO succeeded in persuading the leaders of the then bankrupt and dissension-torn Amalgamated to sign an agreement which gave the Steel Workers Organizing Committee complete charge of a campaign to organize the steel industry, as well as exclusive jurisdiction over all newly organized workers. One month later the SWOC opened its drive.

The SWOC campaign was so carefully planned and so brilliantly executed that by January 1937 it became apparent that, if a strike was resorted to, the main plants of the United States Steel Corporation would be closed down. Fortunately, an agreement was reached by peaceful means between the corporation and the SWOC in February 1937, which recognized the latter as bargaining agent for its members in all steel plants of the corporation. Later the union won the right to bargain for all the corporation's steel mill workers by winning a series of National Labor Relations Board elections.

The SWOC also won bargaining rights in the plants of Jones & Laughlin, Crucible, and Wheeling in 1937. But that same year it was decisively defeated in a strike called to make Republic, Youngstown, and Inland sign agreements. It came back in 1941, however, and now has all these companies, as well as Bethlehem and several plants of National and American Rolling Mill, under contract. In addition, it has organized many railroad car manufacturing plants, pipe shops, fabricating concerns, etc. In May 1942, the SWOC held a constitutional convention at which its name was changed to the United Steelworkers of America (USA-CIO). Its membership in July 1943 exceeded 750,000.[19]

From the inception of their campaign, the leaders of the SWOC realized that "colored workers must be brought in to insure the success of their movement, and that if they were organized, special steps must be taken to insure them fair and equal treatment." [20] Accordingly, Negro organizers were used whenever a significant number of Negroes were involved, and special appeals were made stressing the union's nondiscriminating policy. Although there were exceptions in some localities, Negroes in general joined the union in almost the same degree as did whites both in the initial 1936-37 campaign and in the later "Little Steel" drives. Certainly, a far larger percentage of Negro steel workers embraced unionism than ever before.[21]

With the formation of local unions, care has usually been taken that Negroes are well-represented in the various union offices and committees. Besides being at least proportionately represented as shop stewards and on grievance committees, quite a number of Negroes hold positions in locals or district councils to which they have been elected because of their ability by the white majority.

In the deep South, steel union leaders followed the practice which the United Mine Workers had initiated in 1933. "Locals were encouraged to elect a white president and a Negro vice-president. This allowed Negro recognition on the executive councils of locals, but avoided unnecessary friction in union-management relations since the local president handles much of the negotiating." Such an arrangement was also in line with the policy of gradualism which steel union leaders have generally espoused when

organizing mixed unions or otherwise running counter to previously established customs in the South.[22]

One of the outstanding gains which unionism has brought to
steel workers is grievance machinery for appeal from the decisions
of foremen or other persons in supervising positions. "Traditionally the underdog, concentrated in unskilled jobs where his
place can easily be filled, and confronted by nominal superiors of
another race, Negro steel workers have found that the union has
provided them with the first real means of protection against
unfair and arbitrary treatment. Moreover, representation upon
grievance committees has taught the Negro worker how to stand
up for his rights and how to express himself." The importance
of this practical education cannot be overstressed, especially in
southern mills, where, by virtue of their disadvantaged social
status, Negroes have had to accept the treatment accorded to them
without protest. This has surely proved to be one of the most important and valuable aspects of unionism in steel in so far as
Negroes are concerned.[23]

RACIAL PROBLEMS OF UNIONISM IN STEEL

The national leaders of the United Steelworkers have, then,
adhered closely to a policy of racial equality based upon the experience of the United Mine Workers. The same results found
among the workers in the coal industry are now clearly discernible
in steel. White and Negro workers have become used to the idea
of working together within the union, as they have for many
years on the job, without embarrassment, reluctance, or hesitation on the part of either. Although Negroes do not as yet participate in union affairs to the same extent as whites, they are
gradually, if slowly, overcoming the psychology of "avoidance"
which so many Negroes have adopted to protect their feelings in
a white-dominated world. As might well be expected, active Negro
participation in union business or pleasure is much further advanced in such places as Pittsburgh and Chicago than in Birmingham.

The application of an equalitarian union policy to the steel
industry, however, has encountered problems which are different, and in many ways, more difficult than those found in the coal

industry. For one thing, successful unionism is newer in steel than in coal. Until quite recently, the leaders of the USA-CIO were compelled to devote the major portion of their time and efforts to purely organizational activities. It is not surprising, therefore, that the miners have been able to achieve a greater degree of solidarity in their local unions than have the steel workers.

In the second place, interracial co-operation in the steel union is complicated by the width of the wage differential between the unskilled and skilled work. In steel, skilled production men frequently earn upward of $25 per day while common laborers receive as little as $4 for a like period. In the coal mines, however, the top wages rarely rise far above $10, and the lowest rarely fall below $4 per day. This wide differential in steel has made it more difficult to build an effective union. The unusually high earnings of the skilled production workers tend to make them less solidarity conscious and less interested in being a part of a closely knit organization of all workers in the plant or the industry than would be the case if the wage gap were smaller. And, in areas where the skilled occupations are manned principally by whites and the unskilled occupations by Negroes, this tendency is usually more pronounced.

In addition, the highly paid workers quite naturally object to any attempts on the part of the numerically superior lower paid workers to decrease the wage differential by collective bargaining. For such a move decreases the proportion of the wages received by the skilled in favor of the unskilled. Again, because of the relative concentration of the Negroes in the unskilled brackets, the question of race introduces a complicating factor.

A third reason which makes mixed unionism more difficult in steel than in coal is the far greater importance of job segregation in the former industry. Whereas Negroes and whites generally work side by side and at the same occupations in coal mines where both races are employed, it is not exceptional to find steel mills with all-white sections. The leaders of the USA-CIO have been able to open jobs to qualified Negroes in various departments of many plants where formerly the working force has been all-white. Much more progress has been made in the North than in the South, but it would be too much to say that segregation has been completely broken down in the North, or that qualified Negroes are still not being kept from work in various departments of many plants. The fact that the USA-CIO leaders have opened up departments to Negroes for the first time has alienated some whites; the fact that the policy has not been followed without reservation has antagonized some Negroes. The result is a serious problem for the top USA-CIO leaders.

A closely allied question, which is also complicated by the race problem, involves the manner in which jobs should be allocated through collective action. The general principle adhered to by the USA-CIO, as by many other unions, is that seniority of tenure, with certain qualifications for ability, shall be the governing criterion.

The application of seniority without regard to race, to layoffs, and to rehirings has not caused too much difficulty. Although some white workers, especially in the South, have objected to being laid off while Negroes senior in service continue at work, the fairness of such action is so obvious that union leaders have not hesitated to take a firm stand on the matter.

On the other hand, the issue of the literal application of the equalitarian policy to seniority in promotion has encountered more serious difficulties. Although a sizable minority of Negroes do hold top production jobs, the overwhelming majority of these occupations are filled by white workers. Undoubtedly the latter have come to regard white priority on promotions as a part of the established order of things. With the advent of unionism, however, Negroes justly pointed out "that if the principle of equal treatment is to have any real meaning, it must be applied to this, as well as to other aspects of the collective agreement."[24]

The manner in which the seniority promotion problem has been met by the USA-CIO leaders has varied enormously from place to place. In the Birmingham region, the union accomplished so little in bettering the Negroes' position in the occupational hierarchy of two plants that the colored workers switched their allegiance to an AFL rival, which promised to press for a reclassification of jobs done by helpers, a general upgrading without regard to race, and the opening of the plants' apprentice training systems to Negroes. After the AFL union had won two NLRB elections with the Negroes' help, it fulfilled its promises.[25]

In the North, nondiscriminatory promotion seniority has been applied much more rigidly. The writer's field notes contain scores of incidents in which it has resulted in the upgrading of Negroes who might otherwise have been jumped over by whites whose seniority and/or ability made them less qualified for promotion. Again, however, it would be a mistake to assume that promotion has been purged of its discriminatory aspects since the advent of unionism. It has not, even in the North. Nevertheless, substantial progress has been made in obtaining equitable promotion opportunities for Negroes.

Whether seniority is applied on a departmental basis, on a plant basis, or on some combination of the two has a decided bearing on how it affects the welfare of Negro workers. Most companies prefer departmental seniority, for its operation interferes the least with the established order of things, and hence has not the adverse effect on the efficiency of operations which the application of plant seniority does. The fact that the former is more common in collective agreements than the latter accounts in large measure for the failure of the USA-CIO to open up some all-white departments to Negroes. On the other hand, in periods of depressed business, for example, 1937-1940, departmental seniority works to the advantage of Negroes in cases where they are heavily concentrated in a few departments, such as the coke oven, or the blast furnace. Then the bulk of the Negroes are secure from displacement by whites. The existence of seniority clauses in union contracts at the time of the 1937-38 recession prevented a recurrence of the discriminatory layoffs of the early thirties.

Many USA-CIO collective agreements do, however, provide for plant-wide seniority or some combination of it and the departmental type. In periods of expanding employment, some kind of plant-wide seniority offers Negroes their greatest opportunities for advancement. The failure of the USA-CIO to obtain promotion for Negroes under seniority clauses when, in certain instances, it was their just due has alienated some colored steel workers despite the improvements which the union has brought about. Yet the Negro workers themselves are not without blame. As a group, they have not been as active union members as white. If they had participated more in union affairs or, on occasions, stood up for their rights, they would have received more support from union leaders, or white workers, when it was needed most. Of course, it is not remarkable that many Negroes have hesitated to take an active part in union affairs. For the first time, they find themselves welcomed to an organization the majority of whose members are white. The natural reaction on the part of many Negroes in such a situation is to be cautious about taking a prominent role in the proceedings. But this they must do if they are to maintain the support of union officials and to win that of fair-minded white workers.

The 1942 USA-CIO convention unanimously endorsed a vigorous resolution pledging the union "to fight to secure equality of treatment for all workers, Negro and white, and all races and creeds *in industrial employment and promotion, in vocational training,* in union leadership and service, in government and in the armed forces."[26] In September of the same year, Philip Murray, president of the USA-CIO, appointed a Negro, Boyd Wilson, as his personal representative assigned "to look into, survey, and assist . . . in the solution of any problems which arise in connection with colored members and potential members . . ."[27]

The leaders of the USA-CIO thus have taken cognizance of the difficult questions of racial adjustment within their organization. They apparently realize that the seniority promotion problem is too complex to be ironed out satisfactorily within the local unions, and therefore, that it is up to them to assist in solving it. If, as a result, the day comes when race is no longer a factor of consequence in selecting candidates for promotion in industry, the USA-CIO will have performed a truly great service for Negro workers.

CHAPTER IX

AUTOMOBILES AND AIRCRAFT*

Since the rise of effective unionism in 1937, Negroes have played an important role in the turbulent industrial relations of the automobile industry. This chapter discusses Negro-union relations in that industry and includes a section on problems of Negroes in the conversion of the industry to war production. The final two sections deal with the attempts of Negroes to break down the color bar in the aircraft industry.

THE NEGRO'S SHARE OF WORK IN THE PREWAR AUTOMOBILE INDUSTRY

Perhaps if there had not been a shortage of labor during World War I, Negroes would never have found employment in the automobile industry. For in 1910, only 569 of the 105,759 automobile workers—exactly .006 per cent—were colored. During the war, however, thousands of southerners, white and colored, migrated to the Detroit area, the center of the industry. By 1930, the proportion of Negro automobile workers had risen to 4 per cent—25,895 of the industry's 640,474 workers. During the thirties, Negroes generally maintained their relative position despite a general decline in employment in the industry. In 1940, 20,720, or 3.8 per cent, of the 562,500 automobile workers were colored.[1] Since then both the number and the proportion of Negroes in the industry have increased substantially, but exact figures are not available.

Table VII shows the distribution of Negro workers in the ten leading Negro employing concerns of the automobile industry prior to America's entry into the war. Approximately one-half of the

* Considerably more field work would have been necessary before this chapter could have been written if Dr. Lloyd H. Bailer had not been kind enough to let the writer have prepublication copies of articles which he has written on the Negro in the automobile industry. For a more complete discussion of the Negro automobile worker, the reader is urged to consult Dr. Bailer's works, which are cited in the bibliography, and the notes.

Negroes in the industry were employed by the Ford Motor Company, and 99 per cent of these in the huge River Rouge plant. The Negro employees of General Motors and Chrysler were also concentrated in a few plants: Buick No. 70 in Flint, Pontiac Foundry in Pontiac, Chevrolet Forge in Detroit, and Chevrolet Grey-Iron Foundry in Saginaw—all of General Motors; and Main Dodge of Chrysler in a Detroit suburb. Few Negroes were employed in automobile plants outside of Michigan.[2]

TABLE VII

TEN LARGEST EMPLOYERS OF NEGRO AUTOMOBILE LABOR—PRECONVERSION PERIOD

Company	Employees		
	All	Negro	% Negro
Ford Motor Company[1]	90,000	11,000	12.2
General Motors Corporation[2]	100,000	2,500	2.5
Chrysler Corporation[1]	50,000	2,000	4.0
Briggs Manufacturing Corporation[1]	14,000	1,300	9.2
Midland Steel Products Company	4,100	1,250	30.5
Bohn Aluminum and Brass Corporation	2,798	668	23.9
Packard Motor Car Company	16,000	600	3.8
Kelsey-Hayes Corporation	3,050	365	12.0
Murray Corporation of America	7,000	350	5.0
Hudson Motor Car Company	12,200	225	1.8

SOURCE: Company personnel departments and Labor Division, Office of Production Management. Reprinted from L. H. Bailer, 51 *Journal of Political Economy* at 416, by permission of the University of Chicago Press.
[1] Michigan establishments only.
[2] Michigan and Indiana automobile plants only.

After an investigation of the automobile industry in the late twenties, Robert Dunn noted that "motor companies have employed [Negroes] primarily for processes involving chiefly unskilled manual work." He described one Chevrolet plant in which "Negroes were engaged in the dirtiest, roughest, and most disagreeable work, for example, in the painting of axles." He found similar conditions throughout the industry, concluding that "the Negro is given almost invariably the poorest paid jobs regardless of his ability . . . [and] almost always gets the rougher jobs and is usually not given a chance at the skilled operations unless he has already acquired some skill. It is more difficult for a Negro to get promoted. Opportunities for more skilled jobs are even fewer for him than for the white workers."[3]

After making an intensive field investigation more than a decade later, Dr. Lloyd H. Bailer found that Dunn's description was neither false nor exaggerated. According to the 1930 census data, which he found were still representative ten years later, nearly 75 per cent of the Negroes were unskilled, as compared with 25 per cent of the whites. Almost 50 per cent of the whites were white-collar workers, as compared with 12 per cent of the Negroes. The largest single class of white workers were semi-skilled operatives, but the largest group of Negroes were laborers and porters.[4]

Within skilled groups, Negroes were usually assigned to the most undesirable jobs. Thus, when they held skilled jobs, such work was usually of the hazardous and disagreeable sort. The largest number of Negro workers were found in the foundries, in which, in general, the most undesirable occupations in the industry are located. The few plants in which it was noted that General Motors' and Chrysler's Negro employees were concentrated, specialized in foundry work. Similarly, the high proportion of Negroes employed by Midland Steel and Bohn Aluminum and Brass were attributable to the fact that these concerns were engaged primarily in foundry operations. Negroes also were heavily concentrated in the heat-treat and paint departments, in which working conditions are of a nature similar to those in foundries. Briggs, a leading manufacturer of bodies, employed Negroes mostly as sanders and sprayers in its paint department. (Fisher Body of General Motors, however, maintained a "lily-white" policy.) A majority of the whites engaged in occupations in these sectors of the industry were foreign-born. Native whites preferred to seek employment elsewhere.[5]

In the Ford River Rouge factory, however, the pattern of Negro employment was somewhat different. Negroes were heavily concentrated in foundry work, in the heat-treat and paint departments, and in unskilled occupations there, as in other automobile factories. The proportion of Negroes was much higher than that for the industry as a whole, however, and in addition Negroes were found in all departments of the plant rather than only in the traditional occupations. Except for a few isolated instances, Ford employed the only Negroes who worked on automobile assembly lines. The River Rouge plant had the only Negroes employed on all the various types of machine and press operations. Negroes were employed as tool and die makers, the most skilled operation in the industry, virtually only at River Rouge. Although all the large companies maintained apprentice training schools, Negroes were admitted only to those operated by the Ford Company. And the number of Negro foremen at River Rouge was much greater than in all other automobile factories combined.[6]

There was not a large number of Negroes in skilled occupations at River Rouge. In 1938, for example, Negro tool and die makers comprised less than 1 per cent of this group. The significant fact was that only in this plant were Negroes actually employed in all occupations pertaining to automobile manufacturing.[7]

It was generally agreed among employers, workers, Negro and white, and union officials, whom Dr. Bailer interviewed, that the principal reason why Negroes were not employed in a wide range of occupations except at River Rouge was the attitude of white workers toward working with Negroes on the more desirable jobs. A large proportion of Detroit's white labor force is composed of migrants from the South; many of the remainder are either immigrants from Europe, particularly Poland, or their immediate offspring. Both types were found to be decidedly antagonistic toward Negroes. Employers, interested in a harmonious labor force, bowed to the prejudice of their white employees in their employment policy.

The Ford management was an exception, but not because its employees at River Rouge were any more broad-minded than the other white automobile workers. They had either to go along with the company's policy or to seek employment elsewhere. The Ford concern was the only major company that was willing to force its white employees to work with Negroes in all departments and occupations. Once Ford's white employees became used to the idea, however, there was little or no friction.[8]

Just why the Ford concern adopted the policy toward Negroes which it pursued at River Rouge is not known for certain. The story most frequently told is that at the beginning of the 1921 depression, a delegation, composed of Negroes employed at River Rouge and prominent members of the Detroit Negro community, approached Henry Ford and expressed their concern over discrimination in layoffs. Mr. Ford then adopted the policy of employing the same proportion of Negroes at River Rouge as the proportion of Negroes in the population of Greater Detroit, which is slightly less than 10 per cent. Actually, the proportion of Negroes at River Rouge usually exceeded that, and has risen above 12 per cent in recent years.

Mr. Ford also decided in 1921 to place Negroes in all departments and occupations in the plant. The proportional policy did not, however, extend to the individual departments. Nor was it extended beyond the River Rouge establishment. Ford assembly plants throughout the South employ no Negroes except a few janitors and porters.[9] After the Ford Company acquired the Lincoln Company, it made no attempt to alter the latter's employment policy. Only 31 of Lincoln's 2,332 employees were colored in April 1939.[10]

There is no evidence that Henry Ford originally decided to employ large numbers of Negroes at River Rouge for other than altruistic reasons. His move naturally won him great respect and admiration among Negroes, especially those in Detroit. At a later date, the support of Negroes proved to be a valuable ally for the propagation of Mr. Ford's ideas on politics and unionism, as he well realized.[11]

THE NEGRO AND THE RISE OF AUTOMOBILE UNIONISM

Collective bargaining made no headway in the automobile industry till 1933, and even three years later union recognition was still almost unknown. In 1937, after a series of spectacular sit-down strikes, unionism achieved recognition in most of the industry except the plants of the Ford Motor Company. In 1941, however, even this concern capitulated. Today the United Automobile, Aircraft, and Agricultural Implement Workers of America (UAW-CIO) boasts more than one million members and agreements covering the bulk of the workers in the converted automobile industry. The United Automobile Workers, AFL, founded after a split in the UAW-CIO ranks, has approximately 20,000 members, mostly in parts plants outside of the principal automobile manufacturing centers.[12] The ensuing discussion will be confined to the policies of the larger organization.

The UAW-CIO has always organized on an equalitarian basis, admitting to membership all workers, regardless of race. For the most part, Negro workers were accepted into local unions without incident, and several were soon elected as local officers and national organizers. In Atlanta, Ga., however, a General Motors local refused to admit the dozen Negro janitors employed in an assembly plant; nor was it forced to do so by the national union.[13]

Negro automobile workers appear to have been much slower to embrace unionism than fellow members of their race in the coal and steel industries. In the early days of organization, most Negroes refrained from playing a prominent role, and many of those that did join probably did so because most of the workers in the plant where they were employed were members.

On the other hand, Negroes did not play a prominent role on the employers' side in industrial disputes, such as the 1936-37 sit-down strikes, which occurred prior to the 1941 Ford strike. Most Negroes preferred a passive role, neither lending very active support to the strikers nor making any attempt to interfere with their activities.

A back-to-work movement, attempted at the Dodge plant in Highland Park, a Detroit suburb, during the last days of the Chrysler strike of October-November 1939, had its tense moments. A majority of the estimated 250 men who crossed the picket lines in the two days in which the plant was announced as open were Negroes, seeking employment in the foundry. R. J. Thomas, president of the UAW-CIO, publicly stated that the company was encouraging Negroes to return to work in the hope of creating a race riot. Some interpreted this announcement as a union threat to create a race riot if Negroes did return to work. But union leaders and a number of prominent Detroit Negroes made appeals to Negroes not to break the strike, and to the pickets not to use force. The presence of a few Negro pickets prevented any clashes on purely racial lines. The back-to-work movement failed, and the men who entered to work were sent home within a few hours. According to Dr. Bailer, none of the Negroes who crossed the picket lines were union members, and a number of them had never worked at the plant before.[14]

Negro workers who joined the UAW-CIO prior to the Ford strike were not usually very active in union business and social affairs. Their attendance at meetings was poor. In locals where

Negroes comprised a large segment of the membership, they were somewhat more active participants, however.

The fact that active Negro participation in union affairs was considerably less than that of whites when compared on a proportional basis is not surprising. Prior to the growth of unionism, Negro and white automobile workers had virtually no experience in interracial co-operation. Segregation of housing and recreational facilities and the concentration of Negroes in particular departments and occupations had kept them apart. The probably correct belief of Negroes that the principal reason why they were denied the right to work in the better jobs was the antagonism of the white workers contributed no little to their distrust of the union. And many white workers felt that because the Negroes were a small minority concentrated in a few jobs, their help was not needed to establish a strong union. Hence they made no effort to encourage the Negroes to join.[15]

The UAW-CIO thus had serious handicaps to overcome if it were to organize Negro workers. Realizing that Negroes must be organized if their union was to succeed, national leaders made serious efforts both to overcome suspicion of Negroes and to reduce the racial prejudice of whites.[16] Much publicity has always been given in the *United Automobile Worker* to the activities of Negroes and their contributions to the union. In the Dodge back-to-work movement, Negroes were virtually absolved from participation, and the entire blame was placed upon the company. Prominent Negro lecturers have been invited to speak before local unions. And Negro organizers have been used liberally to contact members of their race.[17]

As early as 1940, the UAW-CIO had been able to diminish considerably the racial animosity within its ranks. The union leaders realized, however, that they would not be able either to win over the majority of Negroes or to gain the support of the Detroit Negro community unless they organized the Ford Company.

FORD, THE NEGRO, AND UNIONISM

No analysis of Negro-union relations in the automobile industry could lay any claim to completeness without an examination of the unique personnel policies of the Ford Motor Company toward

Negroes employed at its River Rouge plant. The importance of the Ford policy, which affected about 50 per cent of the Negro employees in the industry, cannot be overestimated as a cause of the Negroes' attitude toward the UAW-CIO.

In order to ensure that Negroes would be employed in correct proportions, and that company policy toward Negroes would not be sabotaged by minor supervisory officials, two Negroes, Donald Marshall, a veteran Ford employee, and Willis Ward, former University of Michigan All-America football star, were attached to the Ford service department, which was a combination of personnel office and company police force. All Negro employees were hired through these men, and all issues in which Negroes were involved were referred to them.[18]

Most Negroes employed by Ford were recommended to Messrs. Marshall and Ward by particular individuals. Before 1938, certain Detroit Negro ministers were the most important group who gave job recommendations. These preachers had demonstrated complete agreement with Henry Ford in matters of politics and industrial relations. In other words, they were pro-Republican and anti-union. Prior to 1932, such qualifications invoked no hardships on the ministers, for the Detroit Negro community was overwhelmly in accord with Mr. Ford's views. Since that date, however, a majority of Negroes supported the Democratic party in the national elections, and a minority became pro-union. The result was a growing opposition to Ford employment policies among Detroit Negroes.

Negro leaders also expressed concern over Ford domination of the Negro church. Because Ford was by far the largest employer of Negroes in Detroit, and also because opportunities for occupational advancement were better at Ford than anywhere else, four times as many Negroes were usually seeking employment at River Rouge as were hired. Quite naturally, they flocked to the churches and Sunday schools of the ministers whose recommendations were known to carry weight with the Ford personnel office. This not only increased the power and prestige of the particular minister, but it made his church increasingly dependent on the Ford Company. Hence, every attempt was made by these Negro ministers and their church boards to avoid antagonizing the company. When, for example, such an outstanding Negro as Dr. Mordecai Johnson, president of Howard University, came to Detroit, he was denied the right to speak in a church because on a previous visit he had urged Negroes to join unions and had criticized the policies of the Ford Company. Such incidents occurred frequently.[19]

In 1938, the system of accepting recommendations from Negro ministers was largely discontinued after it had been publicly exposed in an article by Dr. Horace A. White, a liberal Detroit Negro minister.[20] Soon thereafter a Negro Republican political organization, the Wayne County Voters Districts Association, was formed. Allegedly Donald Marshall and Willis Ward of the Ford personnel office were its leading sponsors. Whether this was true or not, most Negroes *thought* it was. And because they thought it was, they hastened to join it. To precinct captains of the Association was alleged to have been bestowed the power of recommendation once reserved primarily for certain Negro ministers.[21]

Both Donald Marshall and Willis Ward were active in Detroit Republican politics. Usually they announced that they were speaking "as individuals"; sometimes they took "leave of absence" for a period of especially hard campaigning. They did not hesitate to point out, however, that "their employer . . . was disappointed when he saw the returns from the Negro districts—twenty to one Democratic!", and their universally known connection with the Ford Company had the result of making their statements appear as an expression of the company's official policy.[22]

Messrs. Marshall and Ward were always frank in advising Negroes that they had little to gain from joining labor unions. Contrasting the position of the Negro at River Rouge with that in plants of other companies which dealt with the UAW-CIO, they, by implication at least, blamed the union for the disadvantaged status of Negroes. As was well-recognized, any avowed union member, Negro or white, was subject to immediate dismissal from Ford plants, and sometimes to physical violence as well, almost up to the time of the unionization of the company in May 1941.[23]

That the Ford policies would create a severe obstacle for them was understood at an early date by the UAW-CIO officials. They realized that employment opportunities for Negroes were superior in River Rouge to those in any other automobile plant. Accordingly, the great UAW-CIO Ford organizational drive, which began in the autumn of 1940, stressed the union's determination not only to maintain the Negro's position at River Rouge, but to improve it. The UAW-CIO counted on the support of a minority of the colored workers at River Rouge who had become dissatisfied with unrestricted management control of wages and working conditions and with the lack of job security for which Ford plants were noted. These were problems facing all Ford workers, white and black.

The UAW-CIO Ford organization drive gained momentum early in 1941. A "traffic" ordinance in Dearborn, a Detroit suburb in which the River Rouge plant is located, which forbade the distribution of union literature, was declared unconstitutional, and soon thereafter the United States Supreme Court upheld the National Labor Relations Board's ruling that the company had been guilty of unfair labor practices. In March, the company was forced to recognize informal union grievance committees, and later a plant-wide committee. Ford officials terminated these negotiations on April 1, and discharged eight union committeemen, thus precipitating a strike. The strike was settled in less than a week by an agreement for a NLRB election. The brevity and success of the strike, plus a 10 cent per hour wage increase granted by the National Defense Mediation Board to General Motors workers in UAW-CIO organized plants about this time, greatly enhanced the prestige of the union. It won the NLRB election on May 21, polling approximately 70 per cent of the votes, to 20 per cent for the AFL, which had intervened in the struggle, and less than 4 per cent for "no union," and the remainder void. Soon thereafter, Ford amazed the world by signing a closed-shop, checkoff agreement with the UAW-CIO, covering all the company's plants.[24]

The fact that only 4 per cent of the workers voted for "no union" led some observers to believe that nearly all Ford workers wanted some union, CIO or AFL. After an intensive investigation, Dr. Bailer came to a different conclusion.[25] He noted that the rumor was widespread in the Detroit Negro districts ever since the union campaign began to make headway that any Negro could obtain a job at River Rouge. The proportion of Negroes in the plant increased before the strike, and after the strike commenced a sizable number of Negroes, as well as a few whites, remained within the plant. On the first day of the strike, serious clashes occurred between Negroes and white pickets. Further violence was averted when the governor of Michigan succeeded in inducing the company not to attempt to open the plant pending further efforts at a settlement.

Approximately 2,000 persons, mostly Negroes, still remained in the plant. The company charged that they were prevented from leaving by union pickets. But prominent Negro and white citizens urged them to leave and the union, as well as law enforcement officials, guaranteed them safe-conduct. A federal conciliator, who entered the plant to urge them to leave, declared that they were arming themselves with knives made from steel instruments. Allegedly the company was paying these men one dollar per hour, twenty-four hours per day, to remain in the plant.

The UAW-CIO charged that the AFL had made a deal with the Ford management whereby the former would receive company support. Between the strike settlement and the election, foremen and service department men apparently campaigned actively for the AFL. Just before the election Harry Bennett, Ford personnel chief, announced wage increases and attributed them to the AFL influence.

Negroes were especially prominent as AFL supporters within the plant. The AFL was commended for its excellent racial policies by a group of Detroit Negro ministers (probably the only time such a statement has ever been issued). On the other hand, one Detroit Negro newspaper was pro-UAW-CIO, as it had been for a number of years; the other avoided any opinion, as did the Detroit Urban League, which has sedulously refrained from taking the pro-union line of its national office. Undoubtedly, a large portion of River Rouge's colored workers voted for the AFL in the belief that they were supporting Ford policies. And that was the reason why the "no union" vote was so low.[26]

Nevertheless, the UAW-CIO did win by a comfortable margin. Surprisingly little bitterness followed the strike. The UAW-CIO leaders had done their utmost to play down the racial angle in their campaign, and they appear to have succeeded fairly well. There was no attempt at retaliation, and no effort was made to secure the dismissal of Donald Marshall and Willis Ward. Moreover, the bulk of the Negroes soon took kindly to the changed regime. The union contract gave them job security and increased wages instead of harming their position in the occupational hierarchy as many feared it would. Consequently, Negro participation in the River Rouge local (No. 600) was soon much better than that in most other UAW-CIO local unions. After No. 600 was granted local autonomy, Sheldon Tappes, a Negro, was elected recording secretary by the biggest margin given any of the candidates for office.[27]

The organization of Ford has also contributed to a marked increase in the activities of Negroes within all UAW-CIO locals, although Negro participation continues to lag in many places. The fact that the Ford contract brought more than 10,000 members of their race into the UAW-CIO has naturally strengthened the position of the Negro unionists and thus enables them to be more aggressive in demanding equal treatment.

THE SENIORITY QUESTION BEFORE CONVERSION

No question has proved a more difficult barrier to interracial co-operation within the UAW-CIO than that of seniority. Several types of seniority are used in the industry, departmental, occupational and plant-wide, or some combination of the three. Usually other factors, particularly ability, are also taken into account.

Most of the larger plants operate under either departmental or occupational seniority, or some combination thereof, although a not inconsiderable number of UAW-CIO contracts call for the plant-wide type. As a rule, managements prefer narrow limitations upon seniority because plant-wide seniority interferes more with production by shifting many workers about each time a job is eliminated or production curtailed. Although most union leaders prefer the broader forms of seniority, some officials have come to regard departmental and/or occupational lists as the more practical in larger plants.[28]

Generally Negroes have not been unfairly dealt with in layoffs, rehirings, and even promotions in the application of *departmental* or *occupational* seniority. The reason for their fair treatment in these instances is not difficult to understand. Negroes are heavily concentrated in a few departments and occupations. So long as seniority is applied within these narrow limits, it results in no substantial change in the racial-occupational pattern, and therefore does not invoke serious protest from white workers.

On the other hand, a majority of Negroes have been quite unsatisfied with the operation of departmental and occupational seniority. They regard it as a thinly disguised ruse to keep them concentrated in the poorer and more undesirable departments and occupations. This feeling has been increased by the failure of Negroes to profit when some form of plant-wide seniority has been in effect. In such instances, Negroes have frequently been discriminated against when their seniority entitled them to promotion to some occupation or department in which no colored workers were employed. The reason generally given for the failure to apply promotion seniority equitably to Negroes has been that they did not possess the ability to perform the job. The real reason, however, has undoubtedly been the opposition of white workers to working with Negroes on the better jobs and the reluctance of both union and management to force a showdown.[29]

This has, of course, aroused considerable resentment on the part of the Negroes and has contributed to their poor participation in union affairs. Yet they are, to some extent, to blame. For their very failure to participate more actively in the union has prevented them from receiving the support of the white workers who have been desirous of granting them the equal rights prescribed by the UAW-CIO constitution.

Thus, by mid-1941, the advent of unionism had not made any substantial changes in the racial-occupational distribution in the industry. There were, to be sure, some exceptions by then, and it would be a mistake to conclude that the UAW-CIO had not improved the standings of Negroes in the occupational hierarchy. But the improvements were the exception rather than the rule.[30]

Prior to conversion, a sizable minority of Negro automobile workers were not dissatisfied with departmental or occupational seniority, and some actually preferred it. They regarded it as a protection in layoffs and rehirings, for whites with greater seniority in other departments or occupations could not displace them. This stress on maintaining the *status quo* was accentuated by the fact that the years 1938-1940 were ones in which automobile production was relatively depressed. With the advent of improved business in 1941, however, many Negro automobile workers, who had favored a seniority limited in scope, now questioned its advisability.[31]

THE CONVERSION OF THE AUTOMOBILE INDUSTRY TO WAR PRODUCTION

Following this country's entrance into war, the production of automobiles was stopped and the industry converted to the manufacture of aircraft and arsenal products, especially tanks. Conversion involved a change in production which threatened dire consequences for Negro automobile workers. The majority of the automobile foundries were either closed down entirely, or used on a limited basis. Since more than one-half of the Negroes in the industry were employed in foundries, it became apparent that colored, as well as white, foundry workers would have to be absorbed in general production jobs or else be thrown out of work at a time when a shortage of labor was developing. Moreover, it was obvious that the labor shortage would be felt first in jobs either requiring skilled training, or in others, for example, those on the assembly line, where the opposition to the use of Negroes had been the most uncompromising.[32]

For the most part, management was disinclined to experiment with training and employing Negroes for jobs other than those for which they were customarily hired. Past experience had taught them that white workers would not work with Negroes, and they did not believe they could be compelled to. As usual, Ford was an exception, and plans were made to train and upgrade colored foundry workers at River Rouge.[33]

Management's policy was first dramatically questioned in August 1941 when a series of stoppages were initiated by Negro laborers and foundry workers employed at a Dodge plant as a protest against the refusal of their employer to assign Negroes to production jobs at the Chrysler Tank Arsenal, although whites with less seniority were being transferred there. The local union then appointed a committee to deal with management on the question, but the latter declined to alter its policy. After the federal government, through the Office of Production Management, and later the Fair Employment Practice Committee, had entered the picture, the company admitted discrimination in transfers to war work, but placed most of the blame on the local union. The top UAW-CIO officials then assumed responsibility, and established an International Interracial Committee to assist in solving such problems. Similar committees were later organized on a local basis.[34]

Meanwhile, the transfer of two Negro metal polishers from civilian to defense production had precipitated a walkout of 250 white polishers at the Packard plant, with the result that the Negroes were temporarily removed. At Hudson, the opening up of defense training to Negroes soon resulted in some stoppages. Both situations were complicated by agitation on the part of the Ku-Klux Klan.

After some hesitation, the UAW-CIO executive board wrote the management of Chrysler, Packard, and Hudson reiterating its position that there should be no discrimination in transfers. Management continued to hesitate to upgrade Negroes, however, although it was pressed to do so by both government and national union officials.[35]

Commencing in April 1942, however, the labor shortage became acute and the availability of Negroes could no longer be ignored. The local union at Packard requested the management to transfer Negro metal polishers to war jobs, which it did. A slight disturbance resulted, but it was soon quelled. Packard has, however, been the scene of several disturbances since then. UAW-CIO officials claim the Klan has fomented trouble there.[36]

In February 1942, two Negroes were named to the executive board of the Hudson local. Two months later, this board for the first time went on record as favoring the upgrading of Negroes. A committee was appointed to meet with management, after which notice was posted throughout the plant informing the white workers that the War Production Board had requested the union to "take appropriate action to facilitate equitable employment of Negro workers," that the company had promised to co-operate, and that the local "solemnly warns any members who feel disposed to violate the principles of no discrimination . . . cannot expect to get the support of Hudson Local 154, UAW-CIO, in any discipline they may suffer as a result of defying the President of the United States, their own Union Constitution, International and local officers." [37]

Nevertheless, work stoppages did occur on June 17, 1942, when Negroes were placed on production work. As the company was working on Navy war contracts, Frank Knox, Secretary of the

Navy, intervened. He not only ordered the strikers back to work, but threatened to bar them from employment in war industries for the duration of the conflict. R. J. Thomas, president of the UAW-CIO, also issued a strong statement threatening to revoke the local's charter and reorganize it if the stoppage continued. Most of the strikers complied that day. A few persistent agitators were dismissed. The upgrading of Negroes has continued.

A few days before, white workers demonstrated against the employment of Negroes at the Dodge Main Plant. Both management and the union stood firm, and the ringleaders were discharged.[38]

Such spectacular incidents have overshadowed much of the real progress which has been made in integrating Negroes into the war industries which formerly manufactured automobiles and automobile parts and accessories. No serious trouble has occurred in most of the plants, although both the proportion of Negroes employed and the number working in jobs in which they were previously denied employment has increased substantially since the summer of 1942. Most notable has been the progress in the plants of the Briggs Manufacturing Corporation. Approximately 10 per cent of this company's 14,000 workers were colored in 1940. For the most part they were confined to the paint department or to unskilled jobs. In 1942, a comprehensive union-management program was begun for the purpose of integrating Negro men and women throughout Briggs plants. Foremen were instructed by the company that they would be discharged if outbreaks occurred. The local union directed its stewards to see that none of its members precipitated trouble. The necessity for introducing Negroes into previously all-white departments was explained to the white workers. Newly trained and upgraded Negroes were carefully educated to the importance of their jobs.[39]

Today approximately 20 per cent of Briggs employees are Negroes. They are fully integrated throughout the plant. No disturbances have interfered with their improved status.

Since the beginning of 1943, some progress has been made toward the use of Negro women in war jobs. Except for the Briggs Corporation, however, employers have been slow to utilize this source of labor. Even Ford has not employed many Negro women. The Willow Run bomber plant hired white women in the early months of 1942, but excluded colored women till December of that year, and even now employs the latter only in small numbers. The UAW-CIO has been attempting for some time to break down the barriers to the employment of Negro women, but its success has not been great.

The leaders of the UAW-CIO have thus made a substantial contribution to the welfare of Negroes since the conversion of the automobile industry to war production. Upgrading, reclassifying, and retraining has not proceeded without discrimination even since the summer of 1943, but the UAW-CIO leaders have done much to remove it. The war emergency has enabled them to obtain the backing of the government and of management, to be sure. But it has been because of the union that Negroes have been able to press for promotions, and it has been the union that has done the most important job of selling the right and, now, the necessity of promoting Negroes without discrimination.

Undoubtedly, a substantial number of white members of the UAW-CIO are still opposed to the union's fight for more equitable opportunities for Negroes. Yet the 1942 convention of the UAW-CIO passed a most emphatic resolution upholding the actions of its officers. In almost all previous conventions, the question of equality of treatment, especially with reference to promotions, has been discussed and the union's nondiscriminatory policy reaffirmed, but little material gains had resulted.[40] The question was brought to the floor of the 1942 conclave, when Negro delegates, and also a few whites, bitterly condemned the resolution dealing with discrimination which the resolutions committee reported. They demanded something that could be enforced. President R. J. Thomas noted that previous conventions had been unanimous on the subject, but that some locals continued to discriminate against Negroes quite openly. Moreover, his stand on the matter had brought anonymous threats of removal from office. Therefore, he challenged any delegates who opposed the union's antidiscrimination policy to "have guts enough to stand on this convention floor and say so."

The resolution was then remanded to the committee, which produced a revised edition, commending the officers for their fight against discrimination, admitting that discrimination existed within their ranks and condemning it, urging that each local establish a committee with "power to act" to eliminate discrimination, and ordering the union to take necessary steps to introduce Negroes, men and women, into plants where they were not employed. The resolution also recommended the establishment of a federal agency along the lines of the NLRB to prosecute discriminatory practices, and urged the establishment of racially mixed regiments in the armed forces. After some debate, it was adopted unanimously.[41]

Thus, for the first time, the UAW-CIO admitted publicly that discrimination existed within its ranks and announced its intention of curbing it. Also, for the first time, the union asserted its intention of opposing discriminatory hiring policies on the part of management. Previously, hiring had been left exclusively to management, so long as workers were returned to work in order of their seniority. The union's stronger stand in recent months on such questions as transferring Negroes to new war factories and opening up others to Negro women, indicates that the 1942 resolution has not been ignored.

UAW-CIO leaders continue to be hindered in their attempts to secure equality of opportunity for Negroes by the failure of Negroes in some plants to give the union their full support. Rather typical is the case at the Buick plant in Flint, Mich., where a strong stand by the union leaders resulted in the upgrading to production jobs of the more than 500 Negro foundry workers, who are now well-integrated on all types of work throughout the plant. Yet in July 1942, less than 50 per cent of the Negroes were union members, as compared with 90 per cent of the white workers.[42] If Negroes hope to maintain the unqualified support of union officials, they must recognize their responsibility to join and take an active part in union affairs.

THE FUTURE OF NEGROES IN THE AUTOMOBILE INDUSTRY

Some of the gains which Negroes have made in the converted automobile industry may be lost to them when the industry returns to peacetime production. As the last group to be upgraded, colored workers do not have the seniority which many whites possess; in addition, union members in the armed forces are guaranteed no loss of seniority while serving their country. Since employment in the industry will probably decline somewhat after the war, some layoffs and downgradings appear inevitable and seniority will adversely affect the Negroes. Moreover, the relations between the Ford officials and the Negro community do not appear too cordial at the moment. Ford's new Williow Run bomber plant has been repeatedly accused of discriminating against Negro women in its employment policy. River Rouge Local No. 600 has publicly condemned the company for its discrimination there, as have several Negro organizations. Ford officials appear particularly perturbed over the aggressive attitude displayed by Negroes in demanding their share of work, rather than merely accepting the company's paternalism.[43]

In recent months, Donald Marshall and Willis Ward, Negro members of the River Rouge personnel office, have departed from the scene. The former has been confined by illness; the latter has entered the army. Their places were taken by Jesse Owens, former Olympic track star, and a less-known personage. In May 1943, however, the Negro division of the personnel office was abolished and Mr. Owens transferred elsewhere. In August 1943, Local No. 600 charged that Ford ceased employing Negroes soon thereafter. Ford officials were reported as being dissatisfied with the caliber of Negroes who had recently been hired. This is not surprising. Before the conversion of the industry, there were four Negroes available to every one employed at River Rouge, and the company could take its pick. Later this condition no longer prevailed, and many of the Negroes hired were recent migrants from the South who had no previous experience in industry or sense of responsibility for it. Whether Ford officials will want to discontinue employing Negroes in large numbers after the war remains to be seen. If they do, it is clearly the responsibility of the UAW-CIO officials to maintain the employment opportunities of Negroes at River Rouge. Before the 1941 strike, they promised not only to do that, but to better them as well. If they fail to fulfill their promise in case Ford's hiring policy changes, it would not only be a crushing blow to Negroes, but it would also destroy the confidence of colored workers everywhere in the whole CIO movement.

Even if Negroes lose some of their present gains in the automobile industry, the postwar period should find them in a better position than they held before the outbreak of hostilities. For now they have broken the barriers to employment in the higher bracket jobs. Many will continue to hold top jobs after the war and that should ease the seniority promotion problem for others. Moreover, there is no reason to believe that UAW-CIO leaders will not continue to attempt to make their organization genuinely equalitarian.

Nevertheless, one must be cautious about being too optimistic. For no organization is the race question a more difficult problem than for the UAW-CIO. Detroit has been the scene of two serious race riots. The city and its environs are crowded with recent migrants from the South. Not only has this sharpened people's tempers by overcrowding, housing, recreational, and transportation facilities, but it has brought together white and black southerners in a different environment. The former want to retain the superior socio-economic status which they enjoyed at home; the latter are anxious to exercise their newly found freedom. Both are affected by such infamous demagogues as Father Coughlin, Gerald L. K. Smith, and agents of the Ku-Klux Klan. Detroit, which has twice spilled blood in race conflicts, is still tense, and little has been accomplished to ease the situation.

It is safe to say that no group wanted to prevent the race riots, or deplored their results more, than the leaders of the UAW-CIO. They realize that nothing can weaken their organization more than racial strife. Thus they have been actively attempting to eliminate friction and to see justice done. The firm backing given by the UAW-CIO to Negroes, who had been barred from entering the Sojourner Truth homes by white rioters, was an important factor in preventing any yielding to mob action. They also were active in preventing rioting from reaching the plants in the horrible June 1943 outbreak. But their task is difficult indeed. The liberal white majority in the organization needs the full backing of Negroes. For the latter to remain outside the union fold is an invitation to the advocates of discrimination and exclusion to assume command of union policies.

THE AIRCRAFT INDUSTRY EXCLUSIVE OF CONVERTED AUTOMOBILE PLANTS

Like the automobile industry, the aircraft industry had to experience a war before it employed Negroes in any number. The 1940 census reported that only 240, or 0.2 per cent, of the 102,740 employees in the "aircraft and parts" industry were Negroes.[44] Most of them were janitors and outside laborers. These data confirm the findings of the editors of *Fortune,* who reported seven months before America entered the present war, that the aircraft industry had "an almost universal prejudice against Negroes. . . . This statement," they added, "stands the test of observation: you almost never see Negroes in aircraft factories. . . . There is little concealment about the anti-Negro policy—the National Negro Congress did indeed receive a letter from Gerard Tuttle of Vultee [Aircraft Corporation] stating that 'it is not the policy of this company to employ people other than of the Caucasian race,' a frank statement that undoubtedly bespeaks the industry's belief that white workers have prejudices." [45]

Whether or not the white aircraft workers did "have prejudices" is not known. Most likely they did, and presumably still do. But the responsibility for excluding Negroes from the industry clearly rested upon management. No attempt was made to introduce Negroes into airplane factories, and since most of the companies operated non-union prior to 1940, union restrictions were not an important factor.

Employment in aircraft factories has expanded at a tremendous rate. In November 1942, 1,400,000 were employed in the industry (including, presumably, converted automobile plants), and before the end of 1943 employment is expected to reach 2,000,000.[46] The industry began to feel an acute labor shortage in the early summer of 1942, and this, together with some prodding from federal government agencies, induced many of its plants to employ Negroes for the first time. Only a few companies, however, notably the Curtiss-Wright Corporation, Bell Aircraft, North American Aviation at Kansas City, and Lockheed Vega have made any real effort to tap the Negro labor reserve. Exclusive of converted automobile factories, it is not likely the Negroes comprise more than 3 or 4 per cent of the aircraft industry's labor force.[47]

Since 1940, a considerable number of the aircraft industry's workers have been unionized by the International Association of Machinists and the UAW-CIO, which have been given exclusive jurisdiction in the industry by the AFL and the CIO, respectively. The Machinists' union excludes Negroes by a provision in its ritual.

In plants where it has won bargaining rights, it has strengthened management's reluctance to employ Negroes. At the Boeing plant, Seattle, Wash., for example, officials of the Machinists' local declared the introduction of Negroes would be "too great a sacrifice" for them to make. The attitude of the Vultee Company's management has already been noted. The UAW-CIO has bargaining rights in its southern California plant, and there, following an order by the Fair Employment Practice Committee, a few Negroes have been employed. In Vultee's Nashville, Tenn., factory, the Machinists has a closed-shop contract, and Negroes have had difficulty obtaining employment even as janitors.[48]

The Machinists' union also has an agreement with the Lockheed Vega plant, which is the only California aircraft factory employing large numbers of Negroes. The local in this plant has actually defied the union ritual and admitted Negroes to membership. The Negro press has hailed this action as an encouraging sign.[49] So it is. It should not be forgotten, however, that the national union could, and according to its bylaws should, order the Lockheed Vega local to dismiss its Negro members. Probably the only reason the national officials have not already acted is their reluctance to invite censure by the Fair Employment Practice Committee. Until the "white only" provision is removed from its ritual, the Machinists' union will continue to hinder the employment of Negro workers.

Negroes have been much more fortunate in their experiences with the UAW-CIO in aircraft factories. In several instances, such as in the case of Bell Aircraft in Buffalo, officials of this union assisted materially in obtaining employment for Negroes, and in seeing that they were upgraded and integrated throughout the plant. In the metropolitan New York area, UAW-CIO officials have displayed a more passive attitude. They co-operated with the management of the various plants when Negroes finally began to be employed during the early summer of 1942, but they did not take the lead in the matter. In one case, which occurred at a Curtiss-Wright plant in Cleveland, Ohio, a UAW-CIO local went out on strike over a number of grievances, including a protest against the continued employment and upgrading of Negroes. Both the company and the top UAW-CIO leaders acted vigorously. The former made it clear that it intended to employ whomsoever it wished, a right given it by the collective agreement. The latter dismissed the organizer in charge of the plant and ordered the workers to return. Operations were resumed in less than twenty-four hours.[50]

In May 1943, 950, or 5.6 per cent, of the 17,000 employees at the North American plant in Kansas City were Negroes. Colored workers were found in nearly all the departments and occupations in the plant. During the early part of 1941, the president of this company, which was then constructing the plant, announced that Negroes would be employed only as janitors. The apparently well-organized Kansas City Negro community raised a tremendous protest and put such pressure on the company and on various state and federal governmental agencies that the company was forced to employ Negroes, without discrimination. It has since found its Negro employees very satisfactory. Early in 1943, the UAW-CIO won bargaining rights at the plant. The Negro employees overwhelmingly supported it against the Machinists and now play an active role in the union local as shop stewards, committeemen, and officers.[51]

The Glenn Martin Company of Baltimore, where the UAW-CIO won bargaining rights in September 1943, employed no Negroes prior to America's entrance into the war.* Since then it has taken on more than 2,500 Negroes, who are employed in many skilled, as well as unskilled, occupations. But Negroes work only in the company's small plant which is within the city of Baltimore. The main factories, which are located fifteen miles out of the city, employ 40,000 workers, all of whom are white except for a few Negro porters. On the other hand, the new Glenn Martin plant in Omaha, Nebr., employs a considerable number of Negroes. It is as yet unorganized.[52]

Douglas Aircraft employs only a few Negroes in its many factories. Some Negroes have recently been employed in the southern California plants and a larger number in those located in Tulsa and Oklahoma City, Okla. In the latter two, however, Negroes are generally confined to unskilled work. Most Douglas plants operate non-union.[53]

---

* Leaflets distributed before the election said: "If you want a Negro for your foreman, vote for the UAW-CIO."

The Future of Negroes in the Aircraft Industry

The manufacturers of aircraft generally excluded Negroes from their industry until forced to employ them because of the acute labor shortage engendered by World War II. Consequently, Negroes have the least seniority and will presumably be the first discharged when operations are curtailed after the war.

In plants where the Machinists has won bargaining rights, Negroes can expect little opportunity for employment. This organization will undoubtedly strive to preserve as many of the employment opportunities as possible for its members. Since Negroes are not eligible to membership, it is likely to press for their early dismissal when employment contracts. Once they are laid off, it will probably oppose their employment.

On the other hand, the UAW-CIO may be expected to continue its sympathetic policies toward Negroes. It is fortunate for them that this union has had about as much success in organizing aircraft plants as has the Machinists. Even in plants in which the UAW-CIO has bargaining rights, however, Negroes were frequently not employed before the summer of 1942 in any numbers. They have not been able to accumulate much seniority and, therefore, are threatened with early layoffs in a period of contraction. Yet they can at least count upon a union which will strive to prevent discrimination.

Two plants which have barely begun to operate may prove an important factor in the future of the Negro in the aircraft industry. They are the Bell factory in Atlanta and the Higgins plant in New Orleans. Both expect to employ more than 25,000 persons, and both intend to use Negro labor. If they adhere to their plans, and if they remain in operation in the postwar period, the prospects of Negroes in the aircraft industry will be somewhat brighter. This assumes, of course, that if these plants are unionized, the UAW-CIO, and not the Machinists, will win bargaining rights. Otherwise Negroes may find that management's desire to employ them may be overridden by the objections of the white workers' union.

CHAPTER X

SHIPBUILDING: THE CASE OF A WAR INDUSTRY

Approximately 228,000 workers were employed in the shipbuilding industry in December 1940. By September 1942, employment in this industry had risen to 1,200,000, and before the end of 1943, it is expected to reach 1,500,000. Because the demand for shipyard labor is necessarily concentrated in a relatively few areas, most of the needed manpower has to be imported from other regions. The resultant congestion creates problems of transportation, housing, school, sanitation, and medical care. These, in turn, lead to turnover and absenteeism, which seriously interfere with production.[1]

Despite the tremendous additions to its working force, the shipbuilding industry continues to suffer from acute labor shortages in many areas. One method of ameliorating these shortages is for shipyards to make full use of labor, regardless of race or sex. This chapter discusses the manner in which the shipbuilding industry has availed itself of Negro labor, and compares its performance with the similar situation in World War I. Special attention is devoted to the effects of trade unionism in determining racial employment policies.

Negroes in the Industry, 1910-1943

The decennial census of 1910 listed 67,066 workers in the "ship and boat building" industry. Of these 4,347, or 6.5 per cent, were colored. Approximately 65 per cent of the Negroes were unskilled laborers, and most of the remainder were semiskilled "operatives," despite the fact that almost two-thirds of all shipyard workers were classified as skilled.[2]

During World War I, the industry expanded rapidly, so that, by the end of 1918, some 381,500 workers were employed in yards constructing ships for the Emergency Fleet Corporation.[3] Approximately 10 per cent, or 38,723, of these workers were Negroes. The

210

majority of the Negroes were found in unskilled jobs, but nearly 20 per cent were listed as skilled. Approximately 80 per cent of the Negroes were employed in shipyards in the South and in the Middle Atlantic states, but some also found work in New England, on the Great Lakes, and on the Pacific coast.[4]

Organized labor received its first important recognition in the shipbuilding industry during World War I. An agreement was reached between the Emergency Fleet Corporation and the Metal Trades Department of the American Federation of Labor, which established the Shipbuilding Labor Adjustment Board for the purpose of handling questions of wages and industrial relations in the industry. By 1919, the Metal Trades Department had obtained collective agreements with most of the nation's shipyards, but in only a few on the Pacific coast were closed-shop provisions included in them.[5]

The Metal Trades Department is a federation of several AFL unions, the largest of which are the Machinists, the Boilermakers and Iron Shipbuilders, the Electrical Workers, and the Plumbers and Steamfitters.[6] None of these unions has ever been eager to accept Negro workers. The Machinists specifically exclude Negroes from membership by a provision in the ritual, and before 1937 the Boilermakers did likewise. While neither the Electrical Workers nor the Plumbers have any such stipulation in their bylaws, their local unions generally practice exclusion by tacit consent.[7]

Three building trades unions, the Carpenters, the Painters and the Hod Carriers and Laborers, are also important members of the Metal Trades Department. Their racial policies in shipyards are the same as in the building industry. All admit Negroes, but in the South, during both the last war and this one, colored painters and carpenters who have been members of separate Negro locals, have been frequently discriminated against.

In shipyards where large numbers of Negroes were employed during World War I they were sometimes organized into local unions directly affiliated with the AFL. More often than not, however, they had no organization. As a result they had no representative on the Adjustment Board and were discriminated against by it. For example, when the board set wages for yards in the South, it fixed, "in conformity with established local custom," separate rates for "laborers" (white) and "common laborers" (Negro).

awarding the former 10 cents more per hour than the latter, although both performed the same work. Because the Newport News (Va.) Shipbuilding and Dry Dock Company "was unique in that it employed a large number of colored men and boys, not only as unskilled workers but for some of the most highly skilled work," and because "relations between the employing company and the majority of the employees were satisfactory," it was permitted to pay rates below those established for other yards on the east coast.[8]

During the 1920's, the shipbuilding industry slumped severely as the federal government largely abandoned both warship and merchant marine construction. In 1930, the census listed but 93,437 gainful workers in the "ship and boat building" industry. Only 7,628, or approximately 8 per cent, were colored. Sixty per cent of the Negroes were unskilled, 25 per cent semiskilled, and 15 per cent skilled. The corresponding figures for whites were 58 per cent skilled, 25 per cent semiskilled, and 16 per cent unskilled.[9] Thus the Negroes had lost some of their World War I gains by this date.

During the twenties, also, organized labor virtually disappeared from the industry. The slump in shipbuilding, the falling away of union membership, intra-union strife, and the employers' anti-union offensive, all combined to eliminate the Metal Trades Department from the shipyards. By 1930, employee representation plans, such as those instituted by the Bethlehem and Newport News companies, were the only formal organizations of labor recognized in shipyards.[10]

After 1933, government orders for war and merchant ships revived the industry. The 1940 census found 147,920 workers employed in shipyards, only 6.7 per cent of whom were colored.[11] Hence Negroes continued to lose ground although employment in the industry increased. Until recently, this trend was not reversed despite the tremendous war expansion program. In September 1942, for example, when 1,200,000 workers were employed in shipyards, only 5.5 per cent were Negroes. On March 1, 1943, however, 8.4 per cent of all shipbuilding workers and 9.2 per cent of those employed in yards hiring 5,000 or more were colored.[12] The latter figures indicate a tendency for shipyards to increase the employment of Negroes as the manpower shortage becomes more acute.

If this trend continues, the proportion of Negroes in the industry may reach the 10 per cent figure achieved in World War I, which is also the approximate proportion of Negroes to the total population.

On the other hand, Negroes have not been afforded the same training and upgrading opportunities that they were during World War I. Data from a large sample made in 1942, revealed that only 3.1 per cent of the Negroes in shipyards were skilled, whereas 20 per cent were semiskilled, 75.2 per cent unskilled, and 1.7 per cent classified as "other.[13] When one recalls that approximately 20 per cent of the Negroes in the industry in 1918 and 15 per cent of those in 1930 were skilled, it becomes apparent that the shipbuilding industry has utilized Negroes to relieve the manpower shortage mainly in unskilled occupations.

Why the use of Negroes in shipyards has been retarded and what, if any, counteracting influences are in operation can best be understood by an examination of the racial employment pattern in several representative yards. We shall examine the position of Negroes, first in yards which have been organized by AFL affiliates, then in those which deal with a CIO union, and finally in those where independent unions are recognized.

The AFL Metal Trades Department

Once again the AFL Metal Trades Department has organized large numbers of shipbuilding workers. It now has agreements with nearly all Pacific coast yards north of Los Angeles, and with a majority of those on the Gulf, the South Atlantic, and the Great Lakes, but it has had little success in east coast yards north of Charleston, S. C.

The racial policies of three large Metal Trades unions, the Machinists, the Electrical Workers, and the Plumbers, have not been altered since the World War I. The first still excludes Negroes by a provision in its ritual; the latter two do likewise by tacit consent, although on the west coast locals of the Electrical Workers now admit Negroes to equal membership. The Boilermakers and Shipbuilders, which has 65 per cent of the AFL shipyard workers under its jurisdiction, has altered its rules. The exclusionist clause remains in its ritual, but its 1937 convention authorized the union executive council to establish Negro auxiliary locals. Members of Negro auxiliaries pay the same dues as do white members, but in every other conceivable manner they are discriminated against. Negro auxiliaries are established by fiat of the executive council, and may be peremptorily disestablished by it; they can only be organized where a white local exists, and they are under the supervision of the nearest white local. Negroes can transfer only to other auxiliaries; they have no voice in union conventions or other union policy making bodies; Negro auxiliaries are not permitted a business agent, but must depend upon the business agent of the supervising white local for jobs; they are not permitted a grievance committee, and are allowed only inadequate and ineffective representation on the supervising white local's committee; they receive only one-half as much in death and disability benefits as do white members, and Negroes are not eligible to participate in the union's voluntary insurance plans; only Negro auxiliary members may be fined for "intoxication or creating a disturbance" in a union meeting; whereas whites between the ages of 16 and 70 are eligible to membership, only Negroes between the ages of 16 and 60 may join the auxiliary; and worst of all, *Negroes may not be employed as apprentices, and no Negro may be promoted to a higher classification unless he receives first, the approval of his auxiliary local, second, the approval of the supervising white local, and third, the approval of the international union president!* It is surely a serious question whether an auxiliary with such bylaws constitutes an improvement over complete exclusion.[14] The discussion at the 1937 convention makes it clear that this change was effected for three reasons: (1) the desire to control the competition of Negroes without granting them full privileges of membership; (2) the realization that it would be impossible to organize certain yards, especially the Newport News Company, where large numbers of Negroes are employed, unless some provisions were made for colored workers; and (3) the desire to offset the activities of a new CIO union which was organizing workers of all races into the same locals with considerable success.[15]

The first opportunity which the Boilermakers' union had to put its new racial policy into practice came in the summer of 1938. The Metal Trades Department negotiated an agreement with the Tampa (Fla.) Shipbuilding and Engineering Corporation, which was about to receive a contract to build ships for the Maritime Commission. In return for a closed shop and wage concessions, the unions agreed to supply the company with the necessary additional labor.[16]

The Tampa Corporation had employed Negroes at skilled jobs for many years. At the time of the signing of the contract, about 600 of its 1,200 employees were colored. Instead of establishing an auxiliary, the Boilermakers, along with the Machinists, used the closed-shop contract to secure the dismissal of about 500 Negroes and the demotion of all but two of the remainder to unskilled jobs. One Negro hoisting engineer with twenty years' experience was assigned the job of picking up paper in the yard! When the Negroes protested, the Ku-Klux Klan demonstrated in front of their homes, indicating that the Klan and the Tampa Metal Trades Council were in collusion.[17]

At present, the Tampa Corporation employs more than 8,000 persons, all of whom, except a few hundred unskilled laborers, are white. The company president has repeatedly expressed himself as willing to employ Negroes in skilled positions, but the "unions positively refuse" to accept Negroes, or to grant them use of the training facilities which they control.[18]

In the shipyards in the Texas and Mississippi ports, and in the South Atlantic region, the Negroes who are hired are, with few exceptions, confined to unskilled occupations. Most of these yards deal with the Metal Trades unions, which have been unyielding in their opposition to the use of Negroes in skilled occupations. Moreover, management in these areas has made little effort to use qualified Negroes except as laborers.[19]

The Metal Trades Department has a preferential hiring contract with the Gulf Shipbuilding Corporation, Mobile, Ala. During World War I, Negroes were employed in this yard in both skilled and unskilled categories. In June 1942, exactly 22 Negroes, all porters, were included among the company's 10,000 employees. Although the Mobile Metal Trades Council had passed a resolution condemning racial discrimination, and although its leaders expressed much concern over the fact that Negroes employed in a neighboring yard, which is under contract to a CIO union, were excluded from skilled jobs, they denied that discrimination existed at the Gulf Corporation's yard. Quaintly they argued that, since almost no Negroes were employed there, there could be no discrimination! They also admitted, however, that they wanted no Negroes employed there. This is one of the major reasons why Mobile has become one of the nation's most overcrowded cities while thousands of local Negroes remain unemployed.

On November 19, 1942, the Fair Employment Practice Committee ordered the Gulf Company to cease its discriminatory hiring policies. Since then more Negroes have been employed, but only in unskilled capacities.[20]

In New Orleans, the situation is similar, although there are indications of a change for the better. Both the Delta Shipbuilding Corporation and Higgins Industries, Inc., the two largest shipyards there, have closed-shop agreements with the Metal Trades unions. In June 1942, the Delta Corporation employed about 7,000 workers, only 5 per cent of whom, all common laborers, were Negroes. In February 1942, the vice-chairman of the Maritime Commission was quoted as saying that this yard was "making the slowest progress of any shipyard in the country." Delta's defense was that skilled labor was not available locally: "700 or 800 additional workers would have made all the difference. But about 7,000 local Negroes had registered for defense training—unsuccessfully."[21]

Although the Boilermakers established a Negro auxiliary in New Orleans, its members are not permitted to work at Delta. A national union official ordered the head of the auxiliary to confine his efforts to obtain employment to the smaller local repair yards. When the latter persisted in his attempts to secure work at Delta for the auxiliary members, he was discharged.[22]

The Higgins yards likewise use only a few Negroes among their several thousand employees. When, however, in March 1942, this company received a contract for 200 "Liberty" cargo ships, its president, A. J. Higgins, announced that 50 per cent of his workers would be Negroes. Mr. Higgins obtained promises of "co-operation" from the local Metal Trades unions. The prospect that 20,000 Negroes would be trained and employed in all shipbuilding occupations aroused great enthusiasm among colored citizens.

The cancellation of the Higgins contract by the Maritime Commission on July 18, 1942, before any colored workers had been trained or hired, came as a terrific blow to Negroes. It is not surprising that many Negroes felt that the announced racial policies of Mr. Higgins had been a factor in the cancellation, something that scarcely seems likely, despite the hints to that effect by Mr. Higgins himself.*

On October 30, 1942, the hopes of New Orleans Negroes were again raised as Higgins received a contract for 200 Army cargo planes, and on April 23, 1943, a second contract calling for 200 small ships was announced. Mr. Higgins has declared that he will adhere to his plan to train and hire whites and Negroes on a fifty-fifty basis.[23] If and when his plans are brought to fruition, employment opportunities for Negroes in the war industries of New Orleans will be about as good as anywhere in the nation—something which is as yet far from being true.

Before February 1942, virtually no Negroes were employed in west coast shipyards principally because of the closed-shop agreements of the Metal Trades Department. When Negroes attempted to induce the Boilermakers' local in Portland, Ore., to alter its exclusionist policy, they were informed that "the available supply of Negro labor . . . could be absorbed as janitors."[24] Finally, after the personal intervention of President Roosevelt, a San Francisco local of the Machinists' union was compelled to give working permits to competent Negroes. Soon, thereafter, the Boilermakers established Negro auxiliaries on the west coast, and today several thousand Negroes are employed there, including 8,000 in the Richmond yard of the Kaiser Company in San Francisco, approximately that many in various Los Angeles yards, and about 5,000 in the Portland yards. The proportion of Negroes in these yards varies between 4 per cent in the Kaiser Portland yards to 10 per cent in Cal-Ship, Los Angeles, and as high as 40 per cent in some San Francisco yards, all indicative of the heavy migration of Negroes to the Pacific coast during the war years.[25]

Yet discrimination has not been eliminated from west coast yards. At the instigation of Tom Ray, business agent of the Boilermakers' local in Portland, the Negroes employed by the Kaiser Company in New York City for work in Pacific yards were ordered

* An Associated Press dispatch appearing in the *Cornell Daily Sun*, October 3, 1942, quoted Mr. Higgins as saying that, as a result of his plans to hire 50 per cent Negro labor, "Many people . . . prophesied dire results to the community. Many of the protestants were afraid they might lose their chauffeur, or have to pay their servants more. How much of this campaign by certain people had an effect . . . on the Maritime Commission . . . I can't say."

demoted to helper and laborer classifications regardless of their skill. The company refused to comply, but combined efforts of representatives of the War Manpower Commission, the Shipbuilding Stabilization Committee, and the War Production Board have not undone Ray's work at this writing. In San Francisco, an impartial committee, headed by Judge S. J. Lazarus of the California Superior Court, reported on February 2, 1943, that the failure of Local No. 513, of the Boilermakers, to clear qualified Negro applicants was causing to be withheld "a supply of labor which is desperately needed."[26] Besides preventing the employment of qualified Negroes, the racial policies of the Metal Trades unions has further aggravated the manpower shortage on the west coast by causing the discharge, pursuant to closed-shop agreements, of Negroes who have refused to enter auxiliaries of the Boilermakers. In July 1943, the Fair Employment Practice Committee ordered west coast shipyards to rehire 300 Negroes who had been discharged for this reason. The Committee then held extensive hearings in Portland and Los Angeles, during which the discriminatory policies of the Boilermakers' auxiliary setup was thoroughly exposed. It was clearly shown that Negroes joined the auxiliaries only because they could not otherwise obtain employment. On December 9, 1943, the Committee ordered the closed-shop provision of the west coast "master contract" inoperative and void until the Boilermakers afford Negroes equal status. It further ordered the various companies to employ and upgrade Negroes without regard to race. The companies are expected to comply, and the order may induce the Boilermakers to reconsider its racial policies at its January 1944 convention.

The racial pattern in Great Lakes shipyards, a majority of which are under contract to the Metal Trades Department, is similar to that on the west coast. There is active opposition to the employment of Negroes by the unions involved, and a general failure to use qualified Negroes in skilled capacities, but the situation has improved somewhat recently because of the activities of federal agencies and the acute labor shortage.[27]

In sum, the racial policies of the AFL Metal Trades Department unions have discouraged the use of large numbers of Negroes in shipyards with which they have agreements and have thus aggravated the manpower shortage. To be sure, managements in these yards are by no means blameless for the discriminatory personnel policies. Their willingness to sign agreements with the Metal Trades Department even before production has begun has been an important factor in establishing the discriminatory unions in many shipyards. Yet the prevalence of the closed shop and incidents such as those at the Tampa and Kaiser Portland yards show quite conclusively that these unions must bear the primary responsibility. Even when the Metal Trades unions relax their exclusionist rules, their use of such devices as working permits and auxiliaries is insurance that the jobs which remain in shipyards after the emergency will go to white workers exclusively.

The Industrial Union of Marine and Shipbuilding Workers of America—CIO

The racial policies of the Industrial Union of Marine and Shipbuilding Workers of America are quite different from those of the Metal Trades Department unions. The Industrial Union was founded in Camden, N. J., in October 1933. After a strike had won the first union contract signed by a shipbuilding concern in fifteen years, organization spread to other yards.[28] In 1936, the new union affiliated with the Congress of Industrial Organizations. Today, it has agreements with nearly all the yards in the metropolitan New York, Philadelphia-Camden, Wilmington (Dela.), and Baltimore areas, as well as several others in the South, southern California, New England, and on the Great Lakes.

The founders of the IUMSWA were convinced that "craft unionism . . . has been proved to be both ineffective and dangerous to the interests of the workers . . ." Therefore, they called for a "united front of all workers in the industry, regardless of creed, color, nationality, religion, sex, or political affiliation."[29] Accordingly, their union organizes all workers, white and black, into the same local unions. In areas where Negro labor is an important factor, colored organizers are used. Negro delegates have been present at the annual conventions, and at the 1942 conclave a Negro, W. Richard Carter, was elected alternate member of the national executive board.[30] In 1943, he was elected a full member.

The efforts of the IUMSWA officers to put their nondiscriminatory policy into practice has yielded varied results. They negotiated an agreement with the Federal Shipbuilding Corporation, Kearny,

N. J., which upgraded and reclassified Negro helpers, and for the
first time opened up many top-bracket jobs and the plant's apprentice training system to them. When, however, Negro welders were
put to work, missiles "fell" from above till the Negroes were removed. More recently, however, company and union officials co-
operated in integrating Negroes, including welders, in all departments of Federal's new yard at neary-by Port Newark where no
racial pattern had become institutionalized. Approximately 10 per
cent of Federal's employees at the two yards are colored, which is
roughly equivalent to the proportion of Negroes in the local population.[31]

At most of the other yards in the New York and the Philadelphia-
Camden areas, Negroes comprised, on the average, less than 5 per
cent of the total employment up to the time the United States
entered the war. Since then, the acute labor shortage has forced
most of these shipyards both to increase the employment of Negroes
and to upgrade some of those already employed. Both national and
local officers of the IUMSWA have co-operated with the efforts
of employees and government officials to increase the employment
of Negroes despite the opposition of a small minority of white
workers. In New York, however, Negroes continue to be under-
represented in the welding departments although most yards there
now use a few colored welders.[32]

The Sun Shipbuilding and Dry Dock Company, Chester, Pa.,
has employed a sizable portion of Negroes for many years. In April
1942, 10 per cent of its 20,000 employees were colored, but prior
to that date, these Negroes had only limited opportunities for
promotion. Since then, these inequalities have been corrected by
the company president "at the request of his employees."[33]

In May 1942, the Sun Company announced a plan to employ
Negroes exclusively in a new division and to transfer all colored
workers in its employ to this new yard. Because of opposition on
the part of Negro groups to the establishment of a completely
segregated pattern in the North, and later because of the labor
shortage, Negroes were also used in the other three yards of the
company after the all-Negro yard was opened on December 5,
1942, under a Negro personnel manager. In June 1943, approximately 15,000 Negroes were employed at Sun Ship, only about
6,500 of whom were in the all-Negro yard. Negroes thus comprised

approximately 43 per cent of the 35,000 Sun Ship employees, the highest proportion of Negroes in any shipyard in the country.

The Negro community has reacted to the Sun plan with mixed emotions. While extremely gratified by the employment opportunities made available, many prominent Negroes, as well as some whites, have questioned the wisdom of an exclusively Negro division in a northern community. The fact that Negroes and whites work together harmoniously in three of the company's yards indicates that they could do likewise in the fourth. Moreover, the separate Negro yard poses serious personnel problems. If, for example, the company finds it necessary to close the division manned by Negroes, should all the colored workers there be discharged, or should those with greater seniority and/or ability be permitted to displace workers in other divisions? The fact that large numbers of Negroes are already established in the other three divisions would ease the difficulty of transferring them from the all-colored yard. A more serious difficulty, however, exists if a division manned principally by white workers is forced to close and some whites must be transferred to the all-Negro yard. The question of whether to apply seniority on a plant or on a division basis caused considerable difficulty in the layoffs incident to the 1937-38 recession, and in this case, the race problem may complicate matters no little.

The Sun plan has also been criticized on the ground that it is an attempt to copy the Ford River Rouge experiment of employing large numbers of Negroes in order to ensure the co-operation of Negroes in politics and in industrial relations. Such allegations have been most emphatically denied by the Sun Ship management, and no proof can be found to verify them. Nevertheless, if only superficially, the Sun Ship plan bears a striking resemblance to the River Rouge setup before Ford signed a closed-shop contract with the CIO. Sun Ship is owned by the Pew family, leaders in the Republican party in Pennsylvania. The Negro personnel head of the all-colored yard is Dr. E. J. Scott, Negro representative on the Republican national committee. His chief assistant is Jerome ("Brud") Holland, like Willis Ward, former Negro member of the River Rouge personnel force, a former all-American football star. Whether these similarities are attributable solely to coincidence is not known.

The Sun management, like that of Ford, has long been opposed to the CIO. A strike called by the IUMSWA was broken in 1936, and shortly thereafter the IUMSWA was defeated by the newly formed Sun Ship Employees Association in a National Labor Relations Board consent election. Four years later, the NLRB ruled, on the basis of an extensive hearing and investigation, that the 1937 election was void because of company interference, and because the Association was a company-dominated union. The NLRB was, however, upset by a federal circuit court, and rather than await the outcome of an appeal to the Supreme Court, the IUMSWA agreed to another consent election, which was held on June 30, 1943. The CIO union won by the narrowest of margins, receiving 12,835 votes to 11,922 for the Association, and 895 for "no union," with 196 void and 15 challenged. The outcome was in doubt until 45 additional challenged ballots were examined by NLRB officials.

Sun Ship's Negro employees seem to have been only slightly better disposed toward the CIO than were those of Ford's River Rouge plant. The IUMSWA had fought for equal promotional rights for Negroes long before the Sun Company adopted this policy, and claimed much of the credit for the elimination of discrimination. This somewhat countered the agitation of the Association to the effect that Negroes would stick by the company which had done so much for them. Nevertheless, the investigations of the writer, made just prior to the 1943 election, gave him the impression that the Association support was especially strong in the all-Negro division. The *Pittsburgh Courier*, the Negro weekly with the largest circulation, claimed that "according to almost irrefutable facts and figures," the all-Negro division voted "approximately" 4,700 for the Association to 700 for the IUMSWA. CIO representatives, however, pointed out that the election was conducted by secret ballot and that the votes for all the yards were mixed up and counted together.

Although the *Pittsburgh Courier's* "almost irrefutable facts and figures" cannot be considered authoritative, it is probable that a majority of the workers in the all-colored yard voted for the Association. They were mostly new to industry and felt a debt of gratitude to the Pew family for their new employment opportunities. A vote for the IUMSWA was to them a vote against their benefactor.

In the other yards, the IUMSWA counted heavily upon the support of Negroes, but most of these Negroes did not vote. Rumors of impending race riots were current prior to the election. Fearing trouble, most Negroes in the mixed divisions stayed home on the election date.

Like Ford, the Pews had strong support for their labor policy in the Negro community. The *Pittsburgh Courier,* for example, while claiming to be neutral, gave the Association more space than the IUMSWA, and after the election editorialized to the effect that the latter had lost the Negro vote because it did nothing for them. Apparently, its editors assiduously avoided any attempt to obtain the facts, but merely took the Association's propaganda at face value.* The local affiliate of the Urban League took a similar line, despite the active support given the IUMSWA by the League's national secretary.

The Sun management showed no disposition to make a complete about-face as did Ford. It refused to deal with the IUMSWA immediately after the election. Instead, the Sun Ship Association sought an injunction in federal district court restraining the Board from designating the IUMSWA as bargaining agent. The case was dismissed, but not before the *Pittsburgh Courier* had headlined, "Claim CIO Used Unfair Methods." No IUMSWA rebuttal was reprinted till the following week. After the War Labor Board ordered the company to bargain, however, it did, and according to the IUMSWA, in good faith.

The task of the IUMSWA at Sun Ship is not easy. The heavy support given by Negroes to the Sun Ship Association has brought race friction to the fore. The fact that many Negroes in the all-colored division have continued to support the defeated organization has intensified the bad feeling. The Association actively solicited contributions for its court fight in the all-Negro division, but nowhere else. Negroes continued to support the Association so long as they believed it was management's choice, and the latter, by its almost undisguised opposition to dealing with the IUMSWA,

---

* Prior to the Sun Ship election, the *Pittsburgh Courier* was quite pro-CIO. Its change of heart may conceivably be attributable to its quite evident sympathy for the political affiliation of the Pew family. It has remained pro-CIO in other instances. The very issue which condemned the whole CIO for failing to win the Negro vote at Sun Ship—and did so most unfairly—praised the whole CIO for its promise to help Negroes obtain jobs on the Philadelphia urban transit lines. Since then, it has again praised and supported the CIO.

made it appear that the Association was, in fact, the company's choice as the union of its employees. By blindly following company policy in this matter, the Negroes in the all-colored yard have created a serious cleavage between white workers and themselves which cannot but react to their disadvantage in the long run. The fact that the IUMSWA has strong support among Negroes in the other divisions has prevented a break on purely racial lines. Even so, however, the advocates of racial equality within the IUMSWA have had the job of putting their policies into practice made more difficult by the support given an apparent company union by Sun's Negro employees.

In March 1943, approximately 10 per cent of the 6,000 workers employed at the Dravo Shipyard, Wilmington, Dela., were colored. For the most part, Dravo's Negro employees were denied upgrading beyond semiskilled levels. In May 1943, the Negroes took their complaints to the IUMSWA, which had held bargaining rights in the yard for more than one year. After a conference in which Negro, union, and company officials participated, the Dravo Company began upgrading Negroes and employing Negro women production workers, including welders. Since then, the IUMSWA local has taken the lead in an attempt to eliminate segregated toilets, eating places, and other vestiges of Jim Crow.[34]

During World War I, large numbers of Negroes were employed in Baltimore shipyards, but a survey made in July 1941 revealed that only 5 per cent of the city's 7,000 shipyard workers were colored. Since then the employment of Negroes has gone forward slowly, and especially slowly in skilled jobs at the Maryland Dry-dock and Bethlehem-Sparrows Point yards. The admission of Negroes to the riveting school of the latter yard precipitated a walk-out of white workers; then when the Negroes were removed from the school, they struck. A settlement was finally reached with the aid of national IUMSWA officials which definitely opened the school to colored employees. Although these difficulties resulted in a tense atmosphere, no racial clashes occurred.

On the other hand, the Bethlehem-Fairfield yard in Baltimore, which hired scarcely any Negroes before 1942, had employed approximately 8,000 colored workers by June 1943, about 20 per cent of its total working force. It is noteworthy, once again, that the Fairfield yard, in contrast to the others in Baltimore, is a relatively new one, where the racial pattern had little time to become institutionalized.

The industrial secretary of the Baltimore Urban League reported that Local No. 43 of the IUMSWA was "the most important factor" in obtaining employment for Negroes in the Fairfield yard. Moreover, the grievance committees of Local No. 42 have assisted newly employed Negroes to secure training for, and upgrading to, skilled positions. Despite the opposition of some union members, which once resulted in violence, and which necessitated the calling of Coast Guard reserves to prevent a threatened riot, both local and national IUMSWA leaders have remained firm. As a result, Negroes continue to be trained and upgraded.[35]

On the Gulf coast, the IUMSWA has agreements with the Alabama Dry Dock and Shipbuilding Company, Mobile, and the Todd-Johnson Dry Docks, Inc., New Orleans. The Alabama Company now employs approximately 30,000 persons. It has always hired Negroes, but rarely promoted them to skilled positions. Nor was this situation altered appreciably during the four years after the IUMSWA won bargaining rights in 1938. Moreover, as employment increased during those years, the proportion of Negroes in the yards declined from approximately 30 to 15 per cent.

The union officials realized from the first that their failure to open top-bracket jobs to Negroes violated their equalitarian policies, but they declared that, if they forced the issue, "disruption" would result. What they meant is that, if Negroes were accorded equality in promotion, most of the white workers would transfer to the rival AFL Metal Trades Department, which has made two unsuccessful attempts to wrest bargaining rights from the IUMSWA in Labor Board elections. In both election contests, nearly all the Negroes supported the IUMSWA, the second time in April 1942, despite the failure of that union to better their occupational status, and despite the promises of the Metal Trades unions to correct the discrimination. The fact that in the near-by Gulf Shipbuilding Corporation, which has a preferential hiring agreement with the Metal Trades unions, the only Negroes among the 10,000 employees were 22 porters, undoubtedly induced the Alabama Company's Negro employees to regard the IUMSWA as decidedly preferable, and not to take the promises of the Metal Trades unions seriously.[36]

On November 19, 1942, the Fair Employment Practice Committee ordered the Alabama Company to upgrade and train workers without regard to race. Following this order, the shipyard increased its porportion of Negroes to 23 per cent of its total working force. In March 1943, it upgraded some Negroes from laborers to chippers and calkers. No disturbance resulted, possibly because it has not been uncommon for Negroes to be employed in these two skilled capacities in southern shipyards. Then on May 3, 1943 a regional officer of the War Manpower Commission wrote the head of the Alabama Company approving a plan whereby a separate shipyard way would be manned entirely by Negroes. No reply was forthcoming, and so a second letter was dispatched on May 20. Two days later, the company informed the Manpower Commission that it intended to place crews of Negro welders on four ways on the third shift of May 24. The regional office of the Manpower Commission promptly notified the company that it could take no responsibility for any developments which might occur as a result of the latter's decision.

Twelve Negro welders worked on the night shift on May 24 without incident. After they went home, the racial-occupational set-up in the plant was no different from what it had been for the last forty years (except for a few Negroes working as calkers and chippers, and they were not involved in the ensuing riots). Yet at 9:30 A.M., May 25, anti-Negro rioting broke out. At least eighty people were hurt, nearly all Negroes. A few whites were injured, some by guards who resented their interfering with their beating of Negroes. No one, however, seems to have been killed. Undoubtedly more serious trouble would have occurred had it not been for the prompt appearance of troops and the courageous news reporting and editorial writing by Ralph B. Chandler, publisher of the *Mobile Register*.

D. R. Dunlap, president of the Alabama Company, blamed the policies of the Fair Employment Practice Committee for the riot, but all evidence points to the company as being at fault. Many of the new white employees in the yard are recent migrants from southern rural areas where opposition to equal opportunity for Negroes is powerful and unyielding. Observers generally agreed that this element led the rioting.* Some of the rural whites feared

---

* A prominent Mobile resident remarked to a friend of the writer during the riots: "Mobilians would never have been guilty of this outrage; the races have lived here in harmony for years. But Mobile surrendered to the hinterland without firing a shot."

that they would be displaced by the upgraded Negroes. The company did nothing to calm their fears or to ease the mounting tension in the yard. Instead it kept its plan secret from both its employees and their union.

Officers of Local No. 18, of the IUMSWA, condemned the participants in the riot without reservation. But the local union has not kept pace with the increased employment in the yard. At the time of the riot, it claimed only 6,000 of the 30,000 workers as dues-paying members. Company policy has always been to keep the union at arms' length even though co-operation with it might have enabled the management to explain the necessity of upgrading Negroes, thereby preventing any disturbances.

Several guards at the Alabama Company proved to be completely lacking in their sense of duty. Some took an active part in the riot. After declaring that the riot "can be laid at the door of the Alabama Dry Dock and Shipbuilding Company," the acting adjutant general of Alabama asked that the shipbuilding company "be informed that they [sic] must be responsible for the interior security of their plant and the discipline of their employes."

A plan for the settlement of the trouble was worked out in a meeting in which the company, the union, the Maritime Commission, the Manpower Commission, and the Fair Employment Practice Committee were represented. It provides that Negroes are to be used in all occupations for hull construction on four ways; then white outfitting crews will take over and the Negroes will begin work on new hulls. The plan is thus similar to the one agreed to by the Manpower Commission three weeks before the riot broke out.

The plan was publicly approved by the Fair Employment Practice Committee in Washington on June 4. Yet it was not released in Mobile until June 7, although that city was in constant danger of further outbreaks of violence. Allegedly the Alabama Company management, with the assistance of representatives of the Maritime Commission, kept the plan secret to keep rumors current that all segregation would be eliminated "by the New Deal Fair Employment Practice Committee." When the agreement was finally made public through the efforts of the *Mobile Register* and the Manpower Commission, the workers returned to their jobs in force for the first time since trouble began, and order was restored.

The lessons of the Mobile riot are clear. No company should

keep secret plans affecting the welfare of its employees without
good reason. Especially is this so in tense racial situations. If the
Alabama Company had made known the fact that it needed 2,500
welders, and that only Negroes were available, it is likely that the
riot would have been averted. The simplest manner in which the
company could have obtained co-operation from its workers was
through their union. That, however, would have necessitated building up the confidence of its employees in their union, instead of
doing the opposite by keeping the union at arms' length.[37] Fortunately, it appears as if the company now recognizes this. To
facilitate better relations, it granted the union a maintenance of
membership agreement, and a joint union-management committee
has been established to prevent further outbreaks.

At the Todd-Johnson yard in New Orleans, the situation is somewhat similar to that just described. In November 1942, approximately 500 of this company's 3,000 employees were colored. All
the Negroes were common laborers. Despite the failure of the
IUMSWA to improve the Negroes' occupational status, it has twice
received their support in NLRB elections contested by the AFL
Metal Trades Department, again because of the latter's discriminatory practices in near-by yards.[38]

Thus, in some instances the IUMSWA has been a positive aid in
opening up employment opportunities to Negroes and in improving their occupational status. In others, its attitude has been more
passive, but it has co-operated with employers and government
agencies intent on obtaining a full use of the available manpower.
In the deep South, it has organized Negroes on an equalitarian
basis, but it has not felt strong enough to run counter to southern
mores to such an extent as to demand equality of promotion regardless of race.

THE INDEPENDENT UNIONS

The final group of shipyards to be included in this discussion
are those on the Atlantic coast which deal with independent unions.
The largest of these are the Bethlehem plants in Quincy and Hing-
ham, Mass., the Electric Boat Company, Groton, Conn., the Newport News Shipbuilding and Dry Dock Company, Newport News,
Va., and the North Carolina Shipbuilding Company, Wilmington,

N. C. Most of these independent unions are descendants of employee representation plans and some have been under fire from the NLRB for alleged company domination. In January 1942, they formed a loosely knit organization, the East Coast Alliance of Independent Shipyard Unions.[39]

In the aforementioned New England yards, as in those in the same area which deal with the IUMSWA, there has been little evidence of discrimination. Competent Negroes are employed in accordance with their skills, but the proportion in the affected shipyards, as in the local population, is small.[40]

The Newport News Company has employed large numbers of Negroes since it commenced operations in 1886. In November 1942, its 8,200 Negro employees comprised 27.4 per cent of its total working force. Although Negroes are employed in many skilled capacities, they are, for the most part, denied employment as electricians, machinists, and welders. Moreover, Negroes are not admitted to the company's apprentice training school.[41]

The exclusion of Negroes from these skilled jobs is typical of the racial employment pattern in the industry, and especially in yards in the South. The introduction in recent years of welding into shipbuilding as a substitute for riveting has proved a serious blow to Negroes. Whereas more Negroes were employed as riveters or riveters' helpers than in any other occupations requiring skill, they have been virtually unable to obtain training for, and hence jobs as, welders. At the Newport News yard, for example, nearly all the riveters were colored, but now there are few, if any, colored welders.

Since the United States entered the war, training facilities have greatly expanded in most of the country so that Negroes, as well as whites, may become proficient in essential shipbuilding operations. In the South, however, where 70 per cent of the nation's Negroes dwell, training continues to be unavailable to a large portion of the Negro population. And that is true whether the cost of training is borne by the federal or by state governments, or whether the facilities which are used are located within or without the shipyards.[42]

The union recognized by the Newport News Company is the Peninsula Shipbuilders' Association. It was founded in 1939, after the Supreme Court upheld a NLRB decision directing the company to disestablish its employee representation plan. This plan, which had been in operation since 1927, provided for a certain number of committeemen to meet with an equal number of management officials to discuss grievances and personnel policies. Racial segregation was maintained, as each race elected its own committeemen. When the Peninsula Association replaced the representation plan, several Negroes were elected to the union's executive board.[43]

The occupational status of Negroes has not improved at the Newport News yards since the advent of the Peninsula Association, nor is it likely to so long as that union remains bargaining agent. For, since 72 per cent of the shipyard's workers are white, the majority of the Association's membership probably finds company policy in this respect quite satisfactory, and there are no strong national leaders to challenge this attitude. Besides, in view of the history of the Association, it is questionable whether it is so free of employer influence as to challenge a personnel practice which has existed for so many years.

The North Carolina Shipbuilding Company, which was established in the early part of 1941, is a wholly owned subsidiary of the Newport News concern. In November 1942, it employed 5,300 Negroes, who comprised 29.8 per cent of its working force. Its racial employment pattern is similar to that of its parent concern, and at least until recently it recognized the Cape Fear Shipbuilders' Association.[44]

For several years the IUMSWA has been conducting an organizational campaign at Newport News, but with little success. In July 1942, it began a drive among the employees of the North Carolina concern. Acting on its complaint, the NLRB found the Cape Fear Association to be company-dominated, ordered it disestablished, and ordered the company to cease interfering with employees who wished to join the IUMSWA, and to reinstate some IUMSWA members with back pay. Soon thereafter, the IUMSWA petitioned for a Labor Board election, claiming to represent a majority of the company's employees.[45] If the IUMSWA had won bargaining rights in the North Carolina yard, it would have been interesting to see if any new occupational opportunities were opened to Negroes; however, a majority of the workers voted for "no union." Of special interest is the fact that the IUMSWA's equalitarian program was a major factor in its defeat. For, whereas the North Carolina Company's Negro workers joined it in overwhelming numbers, the bulk of the white employees apparently chose to believe the propaganda of the IUMSWA's opponents to the effect that Negroes would displace whites "if the CIO took over the yard." Consequently, most of the whites voted for "no union."*

CONCLUSION

This survey of the shipbuilding industry has revealed that, with a few notable exceptions, serious attempts have not been made to utilize Negro labor, even when it is available locally, in order to mitigate the manpower shortage. Those employers and the AFL Metal Trades Department unions, who have hindered the use of Negroes in shipyards, must be charged with acting contrary to the national interest by creating artificial labor scarcities.

Negroes have found their best employment opportunities to be in east coast shipyards, located between New York City and Wilmington, N. C. The companies in this region deal either with the CIO Industrial Union of Marine and Shipbuilding Workers or with independent unions. The former has been a positive aid in opening up jobs to Negroes in some instances and has generally co-operated with employers desirous of increasing the employment of Negro workers. The latter have played a more passive role in so far as Negroes are concerned, and have not greatly interfered with employer racial policies. Two of these independent organizations are found in yards owned by the Newport News Shipbuilding and Dry Dock Company, which has the longest and most consistent record for hiring large numbers of Negroes. It is unfortunate that the Newport News Company's Negro employees continue to be barred from several important skilled occupations.

* Perhaps a more important reason for the IUMSWA's defeat was company opposition. The union claimed company interference in the election, and the NLRB trial examiner upheld the claim and recommended that the results of the election be voided. The Board had not taken action when this book went to press.

CHAPTER XI

CONCLUDING REMARKS

This study has revealed a variety of methods by which unions attempt to meet the problem of racial differences in the labor market. Some fundamental reasons for such variations in union policies are discussed in the first section of this chapter. The second section is devoted to questions of public policy raised by union racial policies; the third, to the prospects for constructive government action on a program designed to curb discrimination; and the fourth surveys in general terms the future prospects of Negro labor.

THE DETERMINANTS OF UNION RACIAL POLICIES

Why do some unions exclude Negroes while others not only admit them freely but also strive to give them equal treatment both in the union and on the job? Union racial policies are determined by a variety of factors, the most important of which appear to be: (1) the industrial environment; (2) the philosophy of the union and/or its leaders; (3) the availability of labor in terms of employment opportunities; (4) the degree of national union control over its local affiliates; and (5) the racial policies of rival unions.

Trade union action is, in large part, "the product of the market and the industry in which it is found." [1] The structure of an industry influences union policies both directly, by determining the racial employment pattern, and indirectly, by determining the form of union organization.

Many unions accept the racial employment pattern of an industry and make no attempt to alter it. They usually admit workers regardless of race, but permit employers almost complete freedom in job assignments. Unions which pursue this laissez-faire policy are found in the tobacco, textile, clothing, laundry, longshore, and perhaps to a somewhat less extent, bituminous coal industries.

232

These industries are featured by almost completely informal promotion schemes. One more or less "picks up" the trade. Moreover, proficiency in a particular occupation or department does not necessarily fit one for work in another sector of the industry. Consequently, the seniority promotion problem is generally absent. In the longshore industry there is the additional fact that the proportion of Negroes is so high that there is usually little question about their employment except in some northeastern and Pacific ports.

Within a particular industry, different racial employment patterns induce unions to pursue varying policies. The most striking example is found in building construction. White workers have been able to monopolize the electrical and plumbing crafts. Their very ability to keep Negroes out of these trades permits their unions to adopt exclusionist policies. The white carpenters and painters have been unable to exclude Negroes from their trades, but even in the South the latter have always been a minority. Hence white carpenters and painters have been able to segregate Negroes in their local organizations, and the Negroes, because of their numerical weakness, have been unable to secure better terms. In the trowel trades, however, Negroes in the South have been numerically strong enough to obtain reasonably equitable treatment from their unions. If the representation of Negroes in the bricklaying and plastering crafts continues its downward trend, one may expect that, within the unions of these crafts, the stress on equal treatment for all races also will diminish.

The tendency of union racial policies to be conditioned by their environment is also illustrated by the experience of Negroes in the shipbuilding industry. In yards where a formal racial employment pattern had become institutionalized, they have had great difficulty in obtaining employment in the skilled jobs, which had been reserved for whites prior to the present emergency. In newly opened yards, however, Negroes have broken into the top-bracket jobs with much less friction.

Unionism could not succeed in the automobile and iron and steel industries until the industrial form of organization was adopted. Since the bargaining strength of industrial unions depends upon their ability to enroll all workers in an industry, and not, like craft unions, upon the extent to which they can monopolize a certain skill, Negroes had to be admitted freely if the steel and automobile workers' unions were to succeed. In order to ensure the co-operation of Negroes, however, these organizations had not only to admit them, but they had also to strive to obtain equal treatment for them. This meant that they were forced to make an effort to open up occupations to Negroes which were formerly reserved for whites. We thus have the interesting case of the structure of the industries giving unions no choice but to adhere to an equalitarian program in organizing Negroes, which, in turn, led the unions to alter the structure of the industries by causing changes in their racial employment patterns.

The railroad industry presents a quite different case. The diversity of crafts in this industry, the fact that top-bracket workers, such as locomotive engineers, have little in common with the lower paid groups, for example, redcaps, trackmen, or dining car workers, and the early realization on the part of the operating crafts that they could enhance their material welfare more quickly if they ignored the less well-situated groups—all contributed to the adoption of the craft form of unionism. When the railroad unions were confronted with the problem of Negro workers who were being paid lower wages for the same work and were thus depressing their wage scales and weakening their organizations, they had two possible methods of remedying the situation. One was to admit Negroes to their unions and bring up their standards to those of the white workers. The other was to drive the Negroes from the industry, or at least to limit their employment by organizing them in Jim Crow auxiliaries under restrictive rules. They chose the latter.

It might be maintained that if the railroad industry had been conducive to industrial, rather than craft, unionism, the racial policies of the railway labor organizations would have been equalitarian rather than discriminatory. An industrial union would have had large numbers of Negroes under its jurisdiction, and perhaps could not have fought them group by group, as the craft unions have done. Thus it might have been compelled to offer them equal protection. One cannot be too sure, however. Eugene Debs' short-lived American Railway Union, which represented the most important attempt to bring industrial unionism to the railroad industry, excluded Negroes.[2] It is not likely that the racial policies of railroad unions would have been any different, whatever the form of organization, as long as the philosophy of the unions remained what it was. That brings us to our second point.

The railroad unions have always placed considerable stress on the fraternal and beneficial aspects of their organizations. Their exclusionist rules are similar to those adopted almost universally by purely social organizations. Initially, at least, they refused admission to Negroes on the ground that racially mixed unions would mean granting Negroes "social equality," something which a majority of their members have refused to countenance.

The philosophical outlook of the International Association of Machinists is similar to that of the unions whose jurisdiction is confined to the railroads. In addition, the Machinists' exclusionist policies reflect its southern origin. Other discriminatory unions which were organized largely by southerners are the Blacksmiths and Drop Forgers, the Railway and Steamship Clerks, the Boilermakers and Iron Shipbuilders, and the Maintenance of Way Employes. It should not be forgotten, however, that all these unions, as well as the Railway Brotherhoods, were organized by skilled craftsmen, and their policies reflect the "work scarcity consciousness" of craft unionists rather than just race prejudice.

A union's philosophy may vary from place to place. Although the national leaders may regard discrimination as morally wrong, they may find it necessary to yield to the prejudices of their members in the South. Most CIO unions are, to some extent, examples of this development.

The philosophy of a union, or of its leaders, may also make an organization a militant champion of the Negro's rights. Left-wing adherents fall into this class. This explains, to a considerable degree, the racial policies of the Fur & Leather Workers, the United Cannery and Agricultural Workers, and the west coast longshoremen. Very often "leftists," and particularly Communist party followers, concentrate their energies toward pushing a few Negroes to the forefront and making them union officials, rather than working for the general improvement of the colored membership. Not infrequently, however, they are the staunchest supporters of the Negro unionists' struggle for job equality. This sometimes brings them the support of the colored unionists, who are rarely impressed with the "party line," but who do appreciate aid for their legitimate aspirations. Dr. Bailer has found such to be the case in the automobile industry.[3]

The leaders of the Amalgamated Clothing Workers and the International Ladies' Garment Workers' union are certainly no adherents of the Communist party. But their policies reflect a broad social philosophy to which race discrimination is repugnant. The officers of the CIO steel and automobile workers' unions possess a similar outlook. To them, race discrimination is without justification and is morally wrong. They would undoubtedly oppose it even if the structure of the steel and automobile industries permitted their unions complete freedom in the matter.

Union racial policies are influenced to an important extent by the condition of the labor market. In the railroad industry, for example, Negroes suffered their greatest losses after employment began to decline. In the automobile industry, they made their greatest gains after a labor shortage developed. Such events are typical. In periods of declining employment, white workers generally strive to protect themselves at the expense of Negroes. Exclusionist unions find the greatest support for their programs, and equalitarian-minded organizations find it extremely difficult to enforce their principles. Race consciousness increases; class consciousness declines.

In periods of labor shortages, Negroes have made their greatest gains in industry. Exclusionist unions soft-pedal their program, and equalitarian-minded ones find less difficulty in enforcing their policies. Race consciousness diminishes in favor of class consciousness.

In a very real sense, the government of labor unions can be compared to the American federal system. Unions have their national, state, and local organizations as does the government of our country. In the administration of programs of relief, housing, industrial training, etc., Negroes receive the most equitable treatment, as a rule, when the federal government administers the program directly. In the South, it is particularly true that the greater the degree of local autonomy the less equitable the results are for Negroes.[4]

The same results are observable in matters of union policy. Negroes almost invariably fare better when national officers assume charge than they do when such questions as admissions or promotions are left for the local leaders to handle. The experience of Negroes in the automobile industry is a case in point. Examples may also be drawn from the bituminous coal and iron and steel industries, and from the building trades. Of course, if unions are committed to exclusionist policies, it makes little difference whether national or local leaders are in charge.

The fact that Negroes do profit from national control is easily understandable. Local leaders are usually less experienced than national ones and are more likely to take a narrow, short-run point of view. They frequently do not hold the respect of the membership which national officers command, and they are more likely to be voted out of office for displeasing the rank and file.[5] Hence the national officers can, and usually do, take a more detached view of the situation, to the resultant advantage of Negroes.*

Racial policies of unions affect their rivals in a variety of ways. Without question, the rise of the CIO has had a salutary effect on the older AFL organizations. Several of the latter made their first serious attempts to enroll Negroes after 1935. On the other hand, the fact that some usually equalitarian organizations must compete with exclusionist unions in organizing campaigns sometimes induces the former to relax their principles so as not to alienate the white majority. Examples of this development were noted in the shipbuilding industry.

We can sum up our findings as follows:

1. Union racial policies are to a large extent the product of their environment.

    (a) Unions frequently take the racial employment pattern of an industry as given and make no attempt to alter it. Such a laissez-faire policy is facilitated where promotion is informal and where experience in one occupation or department of an industry is not particularly valuable for work in another, so that the seniority promotion problem is absent.

    (b) The structure of an industry frequently determines the form

---

* This raises the interesting question of just what is meant by a democratic union. Most commentators have, by implication at least, assumed "democracy" and "local autonomy" to be synonymous. Yet a high degree of local autonomy can encourage all sorts of undemocratic practices, such as the exclusion of Negroes discussed here. It seems that those who sincerely want to encourage democratic labor organizations might well consider carefully the means of achieving their objectives, as well as the objectives themselves, before acting.

of union organization. Thus union racial policy is influenced by whether the industry is conducive to industrial unionism, with its all embracing membership policy or craft unionism, with its narrow, restrictive policy.

2. The philosophy of a union and its leadership exert an important influence on union racial policies.

(a) Unions which stress the social aspects of organization, and those which were developed under the influence of southern mores are likely to practice discrimination. In general, equalitarian policies are more difficult to practice in the South.

(b) Unions in which the radical element is strong, or whose leaders are imbued with a broad social or humanitarian outlook, are likely to oppose discrimination.

3. In times of labor shortages, union policies are likely to be more equalitarian than in times of labor surpluses.

4. National union control of such policies as admission and promotion is likely to prove of more benefit to Negroes than local control.

5. The policies of rival unions may induce a more liberal union racial policy, or a relaxation of an equalitarian policy, depending upon the attendant circumstances.

PUBLIC POLICY, THE NEGRO, AND UNIONS

In the preceding chapters, and especially in the one dealing with the railroad industry, some questions of public policy were raised. These, and related questions, may be summarized as follows:

1. Should unions which discriminate against any race be permitted to limit the employment opportunities of that race?

2. Should a union which discriminates against any race be permitted to sign closed-shop contracts?

3. Should a union which discriminates against any race be permitted to use public supported labor relations, mediation, or adjustment boards? This question, in turn raises two others: (a) What part should the race issue play in the determination of the bargaining unit? (b) Should a union which discriminates against Negroes be designated exclusive bargaining agent for a group of workers by a labor relations board?

4. If discriminatory practices by labor unions are regulated, should not similar practices by employers be subject to public supervision?

5. What should be the policy of the federal government toward the participation and compensation of workers in government agencies and public supported projects?

The answer to the first question will largely depend upon whether one regards labor unions as purely private organizations, such as churches, YMCA's or Elks' clubs, or whether one regards them as quasi-public institutions—that is, institutions in which the general public has a definite interest. The courts have generally adopted the former interpretation. They continue to regard union membership as a privilege rather than a right.[6] Consequently, they ordinarily will not interfere with restrictive union admission policies.

Any realistic analysis, however, will show that the latter interpretation is correct. Churches and Elks' clubs are concerned with man's *avocations*, not his *vocations*. They do not have the protection of public-supported administrative bodies which can obtain, through the courts, enforcing orders and assess damages in the form of back pay awards. The great power of unions to limit the employment opportunities of Negroes, or to open up new jobs to them, is additional proof of their public character. The claims of unions that they should be permitted to govern their own affairs, free from government interference of any sort, is a "sheer anachronism, out of keeping with their actual status in our present social organization."[7]

Once unions are admitted to be quasi-public institutions, it follows that their rules and practices should be subject to some public scrutiny, and those found contrary to the public interest should be forbidden. Since there can be little, if any, justification in a democracy for union laws or practices which have the effect of limiting the employment opportunities of a minority race, ways should be found of outlawing discriminatory union practices. Three states—Kansas, Nebraska, and New York—have attacked the problem directly. A fourth—Pennsylvania—has sought to meet it by amendments governing the conduct of the states' labor relations board. The Pennsylvania statute will be noted in connection with the problems of labor boards.

The Kansas statute (*Kansas Acts*, chapter 265), which was enacted in 1941, provides that any labor organization which discriminates or excludes from its membership any person because of his race or color may not be the representative unit for the purpose of collective bargaining. No test case involving this law has arisen, but the Kansas City Urban League has found it of some use as a club with which it can threaten unions who interfere with the

employment of Negroes.[8] The Kansas law, however, exempts railway labor organizations from its coverage, and so its usefulness is
seriously impaired; for two-thirds of the discriminatory unions are
found in that industry.

The Nebraska law (*Nebraska Acts,* chapter 96), which was also
passed in 1941, declares it to be against public policy for a representative of labor, in collective bargaining with employers, to discriminate against any person because of his race or color. The
state department of labor has been charged with the enforcement
of this policy, but the law does not specify what methods are to be
used to enforce it, and apparently no serious attempt has been made
to apply it.[9]

The New York law (*Laws of New York,* chapter 9), which was
enacted in 1940, forbids "any organization which exists and is constituted for the purpose . . . of collective bargaining . . . from
directly or indirectly, by ritualistic practice, constitutional or by-
law prescription, by tacit agreement among its members, or otherwise, [to] deny a person . . . membership in its organization by
reason of his race, color or creed, or by regulations, practice or
otherwise, deny to any of its members, by reason of race, color or
creed, equal treatment with all other members in any designation
of members to any employer for employment, promotion or dismissal by such employer."

Violators of the New York law are guilty of a misdemeanor and
subject to a fine of from $100 to $500 and/or imprisonment from
thirty days to one year. Virtually every union which habitually
discriminates against Negroes has a local union in New York. Yet
the state's carefully written law has only figured in one ruling, to
this writer's knowledge. In the autumn of 1942, a local of the Railway Mail Association removed the color bar from its constitution
and admitted seven Negroes to membership. The national union
ordered its local to dismiss the colored members and to reinsert
the color bar in its bylaws. The local then appealed to the state
labor commissioner, who, in turn, requested an opinion from the
state attorney general. He ruled that if the local obeyed the
national union, it would violate the laws of New York. Hence the
national union could not compel it to write the color bar in its
bylaws. The national officials of the Railway Mail Association challenged this opinion in the New York State courts. They contended

that the Railway Mail Association was not a union, but a mutual benefit society, and hence that it was outside the jurisdiction of this law. In one of the most amazing decisions in the annals of labor law, Judge William H. Murray of the State Supreme Court, Albany County, upheld this view.[10] He further stated that unions could not exist in the government service. He thus ignored the fact that unions have existed and have been recognized in the government services for many years; that it is no limitation on its sovereignty for a government to deal with a union—indeed it is difficult to see how a government can operate without entering into agreements of various types; that the Railway Mail Association has bargained with officials of the U. S. Post Office for many years and has boasted of the results that it has obtained; that the Association is an affiliate of the AFL, which permits only "bona fide labor unions" to affiliate; that because railway mail clerks are civil service employees does not obviate their need for unions; and that many unions were, like this Association, organized as beneficial societies and continue to stress these insurance features.[10] The New York State attorney general has appealed this decision. Unless it is overturned, civil liberties will receive a decided setback. For not only are the rights of Negroes concerned, but of all government employees, who could, by such a decision, be deprived of the right to organize. And then, the Railway Mail Association would be among the chief losers.

In order to prosecute unions which are ignoring state antidiscrimination laws, cases have to be instituted for each violation. The procedure involved is necessarily long and drawn-out. Although some reforms can be expected from court decisions, they would probably come too late to assist particular individuals who are being deprived of the right to earn a living by discriminatory union regulations. From a practical point of view, therefore, it seems preferable to attack the problem in other ways. This brings us to the activities of the Fair Employment Practice Committee.

The Committee was established by the President's Executive Order No. 8802 in June 1941. The Order provided that "there shall be no discrimination in the employment of any person in defense industries or in Government by reason of race, creed, color, or national origin . . .", and it placed the positive duty on government officials and employers to put this duty into effect. No special duty was placed on labor unions, but the Committee did not hesitate to declare a closed-shop contract void in so far as that contract operated, by reason of union exclusion, to bar Negroes from defense work.

After the original Committee had been rendered virtually defunct by the sudden postponement of the railroad hearings, a new Committee was established with a permanent chairman and a more vigorous membership. Moreover, Executive Order No. 9346, which created the new Committee, placed the positive duty on employers, government officials, and *labor organizations* "to eliminate discrimination in regard to hire, tenure, terms or conditions of employment, or *union membership* because of race, creed, color, or national origin" (Italics supplied).

The new Committee was not long in carrying out its mandate. It declared the closed-shop agreements between the Boilermakers' union and the west coast shipyards void in so far as Negroes are concerned until the Boilermakers abolishes its discriminatory auxiliary and affords Negroes equal status. In its findings in regard to the southern railways and the railway unions, it noted that the Brotherhood of Locomotive Firemen and Enginemen and the Brotherhood of Railroad Trainmen "while purporting to bargain for and represent" Negro firemen and trainmen "nevertheless discriminates against . . . [them] because of their race in that it denies them membership . . . refuses them any voice in the negotiations of agreements, or changes therein, affecting working conditions, policies, or practices." The Committee thereupon directed these unions and the railway companies involved to set aside their discriminatory agreements and to place no discriminatory provision in future agreements, and it further directed the unions to "cease and desist" from the above discriminatory practices, including all those "which deprive Negro employees of the same opportunities afforded their white fellow-workers in choosing and conferring with bargaining representatives in respect to the negotiation of any agreements concerning hiring, tenure, promotion, or other conditions of employment."

It is difficult to understand how these directives can be complied with unless the offending unions admit Negroes to membership. The Committee will find this difficult to accomplish. The Committee's authority is not based on statute, but derives from the vast and nebulous war powers of the President. It has fairly effective sanctions which it can use against some employers. For example, through the U. S. Employment Service, it can shut off a company's labor supply. It is conceivable that the President might take over a plant for non-compliance with the Committee's directives, or even withdraw war contracts from a company for non-compliance. But unless the employer cooperates—and the southern railways have refused to do so—it is very difficult to check union discrimination by similar methods, especially if such discrimination involves a more subtle policy than a bar to employment by means of a closed-shop contract. What is needed, therefore, is an agency with a statutory basis, which can take action that may clearly be enforced in the courts. Before discussing such possibilities of curbing trade union discrimination, the closed shop needs to be explored further.

Whether the closed shop ought to be permitted under any circumstances cannot be answered without running into a logical impasse. If one believes that under no conditions should a person be forced to join a labor organization against his will because such compulsion amounts to a denial of individual liberty, then it follows that the closed shop in any form is undesirable. If, on the other hand, one believes that the minority ought to be compelled to support a union which contributes to its welfare, then it follows that the closed shop is desirable under certain circumstances. A comparison of the two arguments involves, basically, a value judgment, and hence no objective analysis of their relative merits is possible.[11]

The closed shop is a powerful weapon, and as such it can be exerted either for desirable or for undesirable objectives. To take examples from our immediate subject, union officials can better afford to take what they believe to be correct, although perhaps an unpopular, step, if the collective agreement contains a provision which will prevent union membership from declining as a result of their action. Thus union officials are usually more courageous in applying nondiscriminatory policies despite the opposition of the white membership when the agreement has a closed-shop provision than they are otherwise. Conversely, however, a closed-shop contract permits the complete exclusion of Negroes if a discriminatory union is a party to the contract.

The Railway Labor Act forbids the closed shop in any form. Although it may be desirable, this study has not shown the need for adopting a similar provision to all industries. The approach initiated by the National Labor Relations Act does, however, appear sound. What this Act does is to permit the closed shop only if the union is free from company domination and if the union is representative of the majority of the employees in the appropriate bargaining unit. Thus it sets conditions which have to be met before a union can be a party to a closed-shop agreement. These limitations should be extended so that unions which in any way deny equal treatment to all races, creeds or colors should be forbidden to sign closed-shop agreements.* The Fair Employment Practice Committee has already made several such rulings, as have been already noted. In the Chicago Plumbers case, the Committee stated:[12]

Said agreement as to that part which in effect prevents the employment of Negro plumbers on Defense projects solely on account of their race or color is hereby declared illegal, inoperative, unenforceable, undemocratic, and contrary to the national policy expressed in the President's Executive Order 8802 [which created the FEPC].

No clearer statement of sound public policy in matters of racial discrimination has ever been enunciated. The language of the Committee's decision should serve as a declaration of policy; and that of the New York antidiscrimination law should be written into the Wagner Act, making it an unfair labor practice, rather than a misdemeanor, for unions to discriminate because of race, color or creed. Enforcement should be given to the National Labor Relations Board.

The National Labor Relations Board, the principal governmental agency dealing with labor relations, has been confronted with two general problems involving Negroes. The first involves employer unfair labor practices; the second, representation cases.[13]

In unfair labor practice cases in which the Board is concerned with activities of employers which discourage the right to self-organization, there have been several cases where Negroes have been especially singled out for intimidation and violence. Such coercion has been uniformly proscribed by the Board's orders,

---

* It seems quite sound, also, that unions which sign closed-shop contracts should also be subject to further regulation, e.g., periodical financial reports, free election of officers, arbitration of expulsions from the union (and hence from the job), etc.

which have ordered companies to afford all its employees adequate protection.[14] The Board has also found inapplicable a company rule which either forbade white employees (in this case, union representatives) from visiting company-owned houses occupied by Negroes, or required that they obtain a company pass to do so. In finding that such a rule violated the Wagner Act, the Board stated:[15]

The establishment or enforcement of any rule, such as that here under consideration, which makes it impossible for employees to have access in their homes to those who may advise and counsel them with reference to their rights of self-organization, or prevents those attempting self-organization from having access to their fellow employees in their homes, interferes with self-organization. When a company rule conflicts with the rights guaranteed by an Act of Congress, there can be no doubt as to which must give way.

Similarly, the Board has found that the extension and application of a company's customary rule of racial segregation in its company town, so that white persons may not attend meetings of Negro union members, constitute interference with rights guaranteed under the Wagner Act. And finally, the Board has indicated that an employer's discharge of workers because they engaged in strike activity designed to incite racial discrimination is not a discharge proscribed by the Wagner Act.[16]

The National Labor Relations Board has thus interpreted the Wagner Act, in cases involving unfair labor practices, in a manner designed to extend civil liberties to Negroes on a wide scale. More recently, it has shown definite indications of adopting a similar position in representation cases in which its principal problem is the determination of the appropriate bargaining unit.

The Board will not set up separate bargaining units for white and colored workers unless it can be shown that there is a definite differentiation of functions between the white and Negro employees.[17] Thus Negroes have been placed in the same bargaining units as whites even when the union involved does not admit them.[18] The Board has also ruled that a contract between a company and a union covering only Negro employees is no bar to a determination of bargaining representative for all employees.[19] The Board may, however, providing all parties agree, establish two units for separate plants of the same company, as it has done on at least two occasions in the tobacco industry, where stemmeries, which employ mainly Negroes, have been placed in different bargaining units from manufacturing plants, which employ mainly whites.[20]

In representation cases, the experience of Negroes under the Wagner Act has been somewhat similar to that under the Railway Labor Act.* It was found in Chapter III that if the National Mediation Board (which administers representation cases under the latter law) placed Negroes and whites in the same bargaining units, and the union which is designated as exclusive bargaining agent discriminates against Negroes, that union can use its power to limit the employment opportunities of the Negroes for which it bargains, and the latter have no redress. On the other hand, should a separate bargaining unit be established for Negroes, their bargaining strength is likely to be negligible. Besides, there is nothing to prevent the white union from demanding more of the work done by the "Negro craft."

The National Labor Relations Board has taken cognizance of this problem. In the U. S. Bedding decision (Case No. R-5792, September 4, 1943), the Board refused to establish a separate unit for skilled whites even though they would be outnumbered in an industrial unit by skilled Negroes. To set up such a discriminatory unit, the Board declared, "would be contrary to the spirit of the Executive Order [9346, amending 8802] and to the established principles of this Board." The NLRB further noted that the United Furniture Workers, CIO, to which the Negroes belonged, admitted whites without discrimination. Hence, there was "no occasion for passing upon the question whether a union which denies membership to employees on the basis of race may nevertheless represent a unit composed in part of members of the excluded race."

Perhaps taking their cue from the wording of this decision, the United Steelworkers, CIO, and the National Association for the Advancement of Colored People, as Amicus Curiae, asked the NLRB to dismiss a petition of the AFL Metal Trades Department for an election in the Bethlehem-Alameda shipyard, San Francisco, on the ground that the Department included unions, notably the Boilermakers, which denied non-whites equal membership.

* That is not to imply that the NLRB has ever, like the Mediation Board, engaged in questionable practices which assist discrimination. It has not, and has scrupulously avoided doing so.

The Board's decision (Cases Nos. R-5693-4) did not meet this request, but definitely moved in the right direction. Said the Board:

We entertain grave doubts whether a union which discriminatorily denies membership to employees on the basis of race may nevertheless bargain as the exclusive representative in an appropriate unit composed in part of members of the excluded race. Such bargaining might have consequences at variance with the purposes of the [Wagner] Act. If such a representative should enter into a contract requiring membership in the union as a condition of employment, the contract, if legal, might have the effect of subjecting those in the excluded group, who are properly part of the bargaining unit, to loss of employment solely on the basis of an arbitrary and discriminatory denial to them of the privilege of union membership. In these circumstances, the validity under the proviso of Section 8 (3) of the Act of such a contract would be open to serious question.

Unfortunately, the Board found no further need to go into either this question nor "to decide the broader question as to whether the discriminatory exclusion from membership on racial grounds of employees in the appropriate unit deprives such excluded employees of their full freedom of association, self-organization, and choice of representatives, which the Act was designed to protect." The reason adduced by the Board for failing to dismiss was that the Metal Trades Department had permitted a Negro Boilermarkers' auxiliary to become a party to the petition. This the Board construed as expressing the purpose of the Department "to accord to the Negro auxiliary locals the same rights of affiliation and representation as it accords other affiliated locals." Then after citing the President's Executive Order No. 9346 as a declaration of the national nondiscriminatory policy, the Board stated that it "expects that the Council [Department] and its affiliated organizations will comply with that policy."

Whether or not the NLRB declares bargaining units inappropriate because of union discrimination, there is an apparently satisfactory solution for this problem. It amounts to denying the use of public supported labor relations boards to discriminatory unions. The amended Pennsylvania State Labor Relations Act does this,[21] and there appears no logical basis for not extending a like provision to the Railway Labor and Wagner laws. Coupled with the proposed restriction on the closed shop, this provision would accomplish much to limit the activities of discriminatory unions without interfering with those of equalitarian labor organizations.*

The proposed ban on discriminatory unions making use of public-supported labor boards would have other salutary effects. The National Mediation Board, and also the United States Conciliation Service, would not be permitted to assist unions to reach agreements with management which limit the employment opportunities of Negroes or other minorities. It would also compel a decided change for the better in the policies of the National Railroad Adjustment Board, which has jurisdiction over disputes arising out of the interpretation of collective agreements on the railroads. It is doubtful, however, whether this Board will function in a really equitable manner unless two more changes are made in the Railway Labor Act. First, the bipartisan character of the Board must be altered to provide for public representation. As the Board is now constituted, no one represents either the broad viewpoint of the public or the non-union worker (or what amounts to almost the same thing, the union member who is opposed to the union's claims). And second, court appeal must be permitted to the losing, as well as to the winning, party. The ability of unions to enforce inequitable awards by direct action has made the Adjustment Board virtually a final labor court and has resulted in considerable injustice. Both these amendments would contribute materially to the welfare of the Negro railroad worker, and both are necessary supplements to the proposed restrictions on the closed shop and the use of public-supported labor boards by discriminatory unions.

Having advocated public control of certain labor union practices, should we now restrict management's freedom in the same manner? The logic of the situation compels an affirmative answer. Great business enterprises, like labor unions, have a public responsibility. The material presented in previous chapters showed the power of employers to inject the race issue into labor conflicts, as well as their ability to contribute toward the elimination of discrimination if they so desired. The value of outlawing discriminatory union practices would be greatly enhanced if similar practices by employers were forbidden.

The experience of the Fair Employment Practice Committee

* Here, again, other qualifications similar to those proposed for the closed shop might also be written into the law.

illustrates how such a program could be instituted. Its already noted sanctions are limited. Yet it has achieved some success in checking discrimination.

Several Negro organizations and some affiliates of the CIO, notably the United Automobile Workers, have urged that the Committee be given authority by Congress to enforce its orders. A detailed plan for such a project has been outlined by Mr. Carey McWilliams.[22] He advocates, first, a careful Congressional investigation of the problems of racial minorities, and then the creation of an administrative board, which would operate to curb race discrimination in the same manner as the National Labor Relations Board handles unfair labor practices. Mr. McWilliams' plan is not novel, but seems fundamentally sound. Its workability in practice does not appear to present insurmountable difficulties, provided the administrative body which he advocates co-ordinated its activities carefully with those of other federal agencies, particularly the National Labor Relations Board, in order to prevent dissimilar rulings on the same subject. Neither Mr. McWilliams nor sponsors of similar plans believe that federal fair practice legislation would eliminate race prejudice, but they do believe, and this writer agrees, that it would reduce discrimination.

If public policy demands conformance to nondiscriminatory rules on the part of labor unions and private businesses, there can be no excuse for the federal government to deviate from a like policy in the conduct of its affairs or in its administration of public-supported projects. This has not been the case in the past. It has not been uncommon for federal agencies either to employ no Negroes or to confine them to segregated units. Because of the labor shortage, and the stress on participation by minorities, Negro employment in federal agencies has increased rapidly during the last two years. Moreover, several federal agencies have made serious attempts to ensure to Negroes proportional participation in their activities by establishing race relations offices, and they have achieved some success. In relief, housing, training, and other federal programs, however, Negroes have rarely received even their proportional share, and almost never their share based on need.[23]

The attempt on the part of the housing administrations to ensure Negroes a proportional share of employment, which was described in Chapter II,[24] is a step in the right direction. However, this program merely institutionalizes a none too favorable *status quo*, because it bases its percentage of Negro participation on the last previous census of occupations. A federal nondiscriminatory program should include a program for increasing participation by minority groups if it is to achieve its purpose of better integrating them into the American social structure.

Equal pay for equal work, regardless of race, has now a well-accepted place in federal policy. During World War I, however, the Shipbuilding Labor Adjustment Board adopted the race differential wage. On the other hand, the United States Railroad Administration eliminated differential pay during the same period. And during this war, both the Fair Employment Practice Committee and the National War Labor Board have ordered equal pay for equal work in cases coming before them. The fact that the race wage differential does exist in some industries, notably the railroads, where it is usually disguised by separate occupational classifications for white and colored workers performing the same jobs, indicates the need for strong government action.

We can now summarize our antidiscrimination program as follows:

1. State laws forbidding union discrimination, if written in as unequivocal terms as the New York law, are likely to be of some value, but other measures should also be taken, specifically those advocated below.

2. Unions which practice race discrimination in any form should be forbidden to be parties to closed-shop agreements of any sort.

3. Unions which practice race discrimination in any form should not be permitted to use public-supported mediation, labor relations, or adjustment boards. The Railway Labor Act should be amended to provide for public representation on the National Railroad Adjustment Board and for court appeal from that Board's awards for the losing party.

4. A federal program designed to curb discrimination in industry should be adopted by Congress. Mr. Carey McWilliams' proposals for a Fair Racial Practice Act to be administered by a board similar in its functions to the National Labor Relations Board, appears the most workable method of achieving results. The administrators of this suggested act must co-ordinate their activities carefully with other federal agencies, particularly those dealing with labor relations.

5. The federal government should take steps to apply the nondiscriminatory program to its own agencies and to public-supported proj-

ects so as to insure the full participation of Negroes (and other racial minorities) wherever taxes (including those paid by the minorities) support payrolls. And of course, equal pay should be paid for equal work.

Possibilities for Adoption of Antidiscrimination Program

Having advocated a definite program to combat discrimination in industry, it is incumbent upon the writer to ascertain the possibilities for its early adoption. One cannot be optimistic. There is, first of all, almost no chance whatever that state laws forbidding discrimination will be adopted where they are needed most— namely, in the South. Nor are many northern states likely to pass effective legislation of that type. More important, however, is that after a start toward the policy advocated here, federal policy has recently veered in the opposite direction.

We have already noted that the National Labor Relations Act placed certain limits on the closed shop by stipulating that unions which are parties to such agreements must be free from company domination and must represent the majority of workers within the bargaining unit. We noted, also, that the Fair Employment Practice Committee went further by ruling that a closed shop was illegal on the grounds that it was used to exclude Negroes from employment, or that it forced Negroes to join a discriminatory auxiliary local in order to obtain work. Public policy in the United States, however, is formulated principally by Congress. In June 1943, that body attached a "rider" to an appropriation bill which prohibits the National Labor Relations Board from invalidating collective agreements which have been in effect ninety days without complaint. Hence an organization which represents only a minority of the workers now can sign a closed-shop contract so long as no official protest is made during the ensuing three months.

The origins of this curb on NLRB activities are of special interest. The Kaiser shipyards on the Pacific coast signed closed-shop contracts with the AFL Metal Trades Department unions when not more than 100 persons were in their employ. These yards now have more than 90,000 employees, who have been forced to pay initiation fees and dues to unions which they had no choice in selecting as their bargaining agents. Several hundred Kaiser employees have been discharged because of membership in rival unions at the same time the Kaiser concern was employing workers in New York and Chicago and transporting them to the west coast because of labor shortages there. The AFL Boilermakers and Iron Shipbuilders' local in Portland, Ore., grossed over $3,000,000 in one year, according to a statement issued by the NLRB, and its officers have built a magnificent marble union hall in which the rank and file is admitted only under certain restrictions.[25] Yet Congress saw fit to prevent the NLRB from giving the Kaiser employees an opportunity to select their own bargaining agent.*

This amendment was written by the AFL legislative committee at the direction of President William Green.[26] It was opposed by the CIO and by some AFL unions, notably the Ladies' Garment Workers. It should most certainly have been opposed by every Negro organization, for it vitally affects members of their race. It establishes, not only in the Kaiser yards, but in several others, including some in the South, the AFL Metal Trades Department unions. In Chapter X, numerous instances were cited in which these organizations had prevented the employment of Negroes in yards where they held agreements. The NLRB was acting on the complaint of the CIO Marine and Shipbuilding Workers, which has a good record for practicing equality. Thus even though an order of the Fair Employment Practice Committee does offset some of the ill effects of the rider, it still is a serious setback for Negroes, as well as for sound public policy.

There is perhaps some chance that discriminatory unions will be denied the right to use the National Labor Relations Board by the Board itself, but it does not seem probable that such a law will be enacted soon. The AFL is certain to oppose such a move. It is much less likely that constructive amendments to the Railway Labor Act will be passed. The AFL and the powerful railway labor union lobbies would both oppose any changes in the Act. Nor have the

* The passage of this rider by the House of Representatives raises the interesting question of whether the people's representatives are actually opposed to union abuses. The same House which passed the so-called Hobbs antiracketeering bill, gave its approval, by passage of the rider, to the very questionable practices described above. It was fully informed of the circumstances by the NLRB. Perhaps the paradox can be explained by the fact that the Hobbs bill, because of loose construction and omnibus clauses, probably forbids a host of perfectly legitimate activities, as well as several undesirable ones. It is anti-labor, not antiracketeering.

National Mediation Board nor the National Railroad Adjustment Board shown an indication of ceasing to interpret this Act so as to aid racial discrimination. Besides, Congress appears satisfied that labor peace on the rails has been maintained and shows no disposition to inquire into the costs of that peace.* Even though the Fair Employment Practice Committee's hearings on the railroads have revealed the inequities of the Act, no change can be expected.

The possibilities for the establishment of a fair racial practice law are slim. Recent Congresses have shown little sympathy for proposals aimed at the regulation of business, and it is likely that a majority of congressmen would not be sympathetic to this idea, constructive as it is. Moreover, most business groups would probably use their influence against it.

Finally, the prospects for increased participation by Negroes in federal agencies or federal-sponsored projects are none too bright. Agency after agency which has made an honest attempt to further Negro participation has been disbanded, has had its appropriations reduced, or has been forced to modify its policy to suit the working majority of recent Congresses, which have been composed of northern Republicans and southern Democrats. The United States Housing Authority, the Civilian Conservation Corps, the National Youth Administration, the Federal Works Agency, and the Domestic Branch, Office of War Information are all cases in point. Nathan Straus, former USHA Administrator, and John M. Carmody, former Federal Works Agency head, allegedly were both forced to resign to save their agencies from a Congress which they had displeased by their firm upholding of the rights of Negroes to a share of skilled jobs on building construction projects. The United States Employment Service was threatened by a House of Representatives committee with dismemberment if it abolished its Jim Crow setup in the nation's capital and consolidated white and colored offices.[27] One has only to read the *Congressional Record* or examine published hearings of the House of Representatives Appropriations Committee for many other examples.

Thus the opposition to a federal nondiscriminatory program is so strong that one must be pessimistic about its probable adoption.

* How different the situation in other industries! If peace in the coal industry means yielding to the demands of John L. Lewis, Congress is up in open revolt at once.

It should be noted, however, that the opposition will not be based on the actual merits of the program so much as upon its conflict with the self-interest of several powerful groups. If Negro organizations, and other minority groups, want discrimination curbed by governmental action, they must ally themselves with sympathetic groups, such as the CIO. In order to gain support for their objectives, they must, in turn, support the aspirations of their allies. Otherwise, their prospects for success are poor.

THE OUTLOOK FOR NEGRO LABOR

Assuming that nondiscriminatory legislation is not in the immediate offing, what are the future prospects of Negroes in American industry? This question can be answered only in general terms, but it is nonetheless worth considering. We shall, of course, assume that the United Nations will win the war; that the United States will remain firmly committed to democratic principles; and in addition, that unions will continue to play an important role in the national economy.

It seems likely that, following the war, employment will decline to some extent. Since Negroes were, as a group, the last employed, they will be the first dismissed in instances where seniority governs layoff procedure. Furthermore, both the Selective Service Act and most collective agreements have provisions guaranteeing the reemployment of men in the armed forces without loss of seniority rights for the time during which they have served their country. Again, Negroes will be hard hit.

Even though Negroes, as the last hired, may be expected to be affected disproportionately in postwar layoffs, many of their newly won employment opportunities will probably be retained. By accustoming both employers and white workers to their presence, this should facilitate the continued use of Negroes in occupations and industries from which they were once barred. Moreover, those who have learned new skills on war jobs, or in the armed forces, will be in a better position to compete for employment than previously.

A few labor organizations present grave dangers to the economic status of Negroes. Foremost among these is the International Association of Machinists, whose 600,000 members are found in the aircraft, shipbuilding, and railroad industries, as well as in machine shops in numerous others. The continued expansion of the International Brotherhood of Electrical Workers in the electrical products and electric power industries, as well as in the building trades, railway shops, and shipyards, is likewise a menace to the Negro's welfare. Since IBEW locals practice exclusion by tacit consent rather than by explicit rule, however, many of them in the first two industries and some in shipyards have begun to accept Negroes. The Brotherhood of Railroad Trainmen has invaded the motorbus industry, a fact which threatens to close more employment opportunities to Negroes. All these are discriminatory organizations which have extended their jurisdictions far beyond their original locale without altering their policies to conform to new environments.

In general, however, the trend of unionization appears favorable to Negroes. Prior to 1935, unionism was probably more of a hindrance than a help to Negroes. The most completely organized industries—railroads, building and printing trades—were those in which union policies are discriminatory and/or the proportion of Negroes small. Since 1936, the pendulum has swung the other way, and thousands of Negro workers have benefited from increased wages, improved working conditions, and job security as a result of collective agreements. It seems likely that unionism will continue to affect the welfare of Negroes favorably. Nineteen of the thirty-one unions which habitually practice discrimination are found in the railroad industry, where employment may be expected to continue to decline after the war, despite the current expansion. Most of the 500,000 members of Boilermakers and Iron Shipbuilders are found in the shipbuilding industry in which employment is certain to fall after the war. The remaining discriminatory unions are small and inconsequential. Thus with the exception of the Machinists,* and possibly of the Railroad Trainmen, the Electrical Workers, and the Plumbers and Steamfitters, the important unions in expanding industries are favorably disposed toward continued improvement in the economic status of the Negro. Trade unionism should thus continue its service of alleviating the American race problem.

* Both the Machinists and the Boilermakers and Shipbuilders will have conventions in 1944. In both organizations, strong movements are in progress to eliminate the exclusionist rules. Although the writer is not sanguine, there are better possibilities of improvement than ever before.

One cannot be too certain, however. A virulent racism has been sweeping the country, which threatens to undo much of the progress toward improved race relations that has been achieved during the last few years. Riots in Mobile, Beaumont, Detroit, Los Angeles, and New York are symptoms of the tense atmosphere. The unwarranted emphasis of the armed forces on Jim Crow and segregation have contributed no little to poorer interracial understanding. Soldiers, white and colored, returning from war may not be disposed to accept prewar social patterns. The possibilities for explosions in such cases are manifold. By bringing the races together, unions can contribute much to a better mutual understanding and overcome such threatened outbreaks. They must do just that, for their own self-interest, if for no other reason. Race riots, or other divisions on the basis of race within the working classes, threaten the very foundations of organized labor.

A small group of skilled white workers may profit from exclusionist practices by enhancing their monopoly power. The overwhelming bulk of organized labor, however, has everything to gain from continued improvements in the economic status of Negroes. A decline in the income of Negro workers imperils the wage standards of white workers and the strength of unions by creating a supply of cheap labor and, possibly, of strikebreakers. Already at a low ebb in popularity, organized labor cannot afford to alienate any race.

As for its part, the Negro community owes its friends in the labor movement greater support than has been forthcoming. The Negro community apparently realizes this. In a nation-wide poll conducted in July 1943 by the Negro weekly with the largest circulation, the *Pittsburgh Courier,* 96.4 per cent of the Negroes questioned thought "Negro workers should seek closer co-operation with organized labor."[28] In practice, however, neither the rank and file of Negroes nor their leaders (including the *Pittsburgh Courier*) have supported the liberal elements in the labor movement to a degree even distantly approaching a figure of 96.4 per cent. Yet it is difficult to understand how Negroes can improve their lot without the aid of organized labor. It is, therefore, obvious that Negro workers who want unions to continue their fight for equal opportunity must join and support the unions. Negroes might well hesitate more than they have in the past to suport unions of their employer's choice rather than avowedly equalitarian organizations. The possibilities of creating a cleavage in the working-class movement, which will react to their own disadvantage, are furthered by such opportunistic behavior as was exhibited by Negroes in the Ford River Rouge and Sun Ship elections, however understandable such actions were. Assuming that the country is able to avoid a drastic business depression which would reduce the living standards of all workers, and assuming that the majority of American trade unions can continue their present equalitarian policies in spite of the rising racism, Negroes may expect continued, if slow, improvement in their material well-being. Their responsibility is to support the organizations, and those within these organizations, who champion their rights.

NOTES

CHAPTER I

1. An unpublished manuscript by Dr. P. H. Norgren was of some benefit in writing this chapter.
2. The term "racial policies" as used here refers to policies directed at Negroes. No attempt has been made to investigate policies toward the other colored races. However, the evidence at hand indicates that unions generally treat Orientals, Indians, and often Mexicans in the same manner as they treat Negroes. An exception is the Journeymen Barbers' Union, AFL, which admits Negroes, but excludes Orientals.
3. "At least" is said advisedly. During the last few years many independent, quasi-independent, and company unions have been formed, mostly local in jurisdiction. No effort has been made to examine the racial policies of these organizations.
4. The Wire Weavers Association admits to membership only "white Christian males" and subjects aliens to an admission fee of $1,000. To the writer's knowledge, it is the only union in America which excludes non-Christians. Having a membership of less than 300, its influence is negligible.
5. During the last few years, two small exclusionist unions, the independent Dining Car Conductors, and the AFL Sleeping Car Conductors, merged with the Railroad Trainmen and the Railway Conductors, respectively.
6. Locals of the Electrical Workers in the electrical power and electric products industries, and a few in the shipyards have now begun to admit Negroes. Exclusion is still widespread, however, in the building and railway industries, and predominates in the shipyards.
7. S. D. Spero and A. L. Harris, *The Black Worker*, New York, 1931, p. 56. All quotations from this book by permission of the Columbia University Press.
8. This, of course, does not apply to the unaffiliated exclusionist unions. However, when one examines the official pronouncements of any of them on "brotherhood," "progressive unionism," etc., one can unearth a multitude of inconsistencies.
9. Spero and Harris, *op. cit.*, pp. 87-89.
10. U. S. Congress, *Report of the Industrial Commission*, Washington, 1901, 37.
11. AFL, *Proceedings of Convention*, 1920, pp. 307-10, 351-52; Spero and Harris, *op. cit.*, pp. 93-94, 101-02, 104-07.
12. In 1937, the Boilermakers amended its rules to give the Negroes auxiliary status, but the ritual remained unchanged.

13. Spero and Harris, *op. cit.*, pp. 89-91; Brotherhood Railway Carmen, *Proceedings*, 1921, pp. 5-6, 351-55, 383-85.
14. Brotherhood of Railway . . . Clerks, etc., *Proceedings*, 1922, p. 163. Later the Clerks granted Negroes auxiliary status.
15. Spero and Harris, *op. cit.*, pp. 107-12.
16. AFL *Proceedings*, 1934, pp. 330-32.
17. *Ibid.*, 1935, p. 809.
18. This was the convention which led to the formation of the CIO and to the split in labor's ranks.
19. AFL *op. cit.*, 1935, pp. 787, 807-08, 814.
20. *Ibid.*, 1936, pp. 235-38. The Act of the AFL Executive Council in suspending the CIO unions from membership was, of course, unconstitutional. Article IX, section 12, of the AFL constitution states that such action can be taken only by a two-thirds majority vote of an AFL convention.
21. AFL, *op. cit.*, 1941, pp. 475-92.
22. *Ibid.*, pp. 536-37.
23. *Ibid.*, 1942, pp. 574-80, 646-49.
24. Of course, today the CIO and the AFL can no longer be differentiated along craft vs. industrial lines. But it is fair to say that the policies of the former have been, and still are, made by industrial union-minded leaders, and those of the latter by craft union-minded leaders.
25. The Ladies' Garment Workers later returned to the AFL and the Mine Workers left the CIO.
26. Paul H. Norgren and Herbert R. Northrup, "Negroes in the Iron and Steel Industry," unpublished report made to the Carnegie Corporation of New York's Negro in America survey, 1940.

CHAPTER II

1. See, e.g., W.E.B. DuBois (ed.), *The Negro Artisan*, Atlanta, 1902, pp. 13-23; Yates Snowden, *Labor Organizations in South Carolina, 1742-1861*, Columbia, S. C., 1914, pp. 1-14; R. B. Pinchbeck, *The Virginia Negro Artisan and Tradesman*, Richmond, 1926, pp. 17-68; R. W. Shugg, *Origins of Class Struggle in Louisiana*, University, La., 1939, pp. 118-20, 302-03; C. H. Wesley, *Negro Labor in the United States*, New York, 1927, pp. 1-150; L. G. Greene and C. D. Woodson, *The Negro Wage Earner*, Washington, 1930, pp. 14-17; and Spero and Harris, *op. cit.*, pp. 5-10. Quotation from P. H. Norgren, "Displacement and Exclusion in the Skilled Trades" unpublished report made to the Carnegie Corporation of New York's Negro in America survey, 1940.
2. J. R. Brackett, *The Negro in Maryland*, Baltimore, 1889, pp. 104-106, 206-16; *idem.*, *Progress of the Colored People of Maryland*, Baltimore, 1890, pp. 26-33; and H. Schoen, "The Free Negro in

the Republic of Texas," *Southwestern Historical Quarterly*, XL (1936-37), 199; XLI (1937-38), 95-99.

3. Industrial education is very expensive, and few southern cities can afford an adequate plant. When one is built, it usually is for whites only. Sometimes this is in accord with the demands of white mechanics. See Greene and Woodson, *op. cit.*, pp. 322-23.

4. DuBois, *op. cit.*, pp. 106-49.

5. *Ibid.*; Brackett, *Progress of Colored People, loc cit.*; Lilian Brandt, "The Negroes of St. Louis," *American Statistical Association Publications*, VIII (1900), 237-39; W. A. Crossland, *Industrial Conditions among Negroes in St. Louis*, St. Louis, 1914, pp. 65-72; and Urban League of Kansas City, *The Negro Worker of Kansas City*, mimeo., 1940, pp. 9-14.

6. Mary W. Ovington, "The Negro in the Trade Unions of New York," *The Annals*, XXVI (1906), 551-58; *idem.*, *Half a Man*, New York, 1911, pp. 95-99; W.E.B. DuBois, *The Philadelphia Negro*, Philadelphia, 1899, pp. 126-31; R. R. Wright, Jr., *The Negro in Pennsylvania*, Philadelphia, 1911, pp. 94-95; F. U. Quillan, *The Color Line in Ohio*, Ann Arbor, Mich., 1913, pp. 130-31, 138-39, 141, 147-49, 155-56; and E. L. Bogart, "The Chicago Building Trades Dispute," *Political Science Quarterly*, XVI (1901), 240.

7. Fair Employment Practice Committee, "Summary of Hearings and Complaints of Negro Plumbers Against the Chicago Journeymen Plumbers' Union, Local 130," press release, June 1942; *Kansas City Call*, July 3, 1942.

8. J. H. Ashworth, *The Helper and American Trade Unions*, Baltimore, 1915, pp. 16-18, 27, 54-56, 92.

9. Spero and Harris, *op. cit.*, 59-60, 477-81; S. H. Slichter, *Union Policies and Industrial Management*, Washington, 1941, pp. 47-50. Professor Slichter notes that "no careful study has been made of the administration of these laws, of their value to the public, or of the abuses that may occur in their administration."

10. Spero and Harris, *op. cit.*, p. 121.

11. Copy in writer's possession, courtesy of Mr. Buchman.

12. M. A. Mulcaire, *The International Brotherhood of Electrical Workers*, Washington, 1923, pp. 37-39; Spero and Harris, *op. cit.*, pp. 58-59; IBEW, *Proceedings of Convention*, 1927, p. 146. The question was not discussed for the record of the last two conventions of the IBEW held in 1929 and 1941, respectively.

13. Fair Employment Practice Committee, "Hearings, Birmingham, Ala.," typed MS, 1942, p. 690.

14. *Ibid.*, and personal investigation. Unless otherwise stated, local conditions described in ensuing pages are based upon writer's field work.

15. Mr. Brown graciously supplied the writer with a copy of his letter. See also *Norfolk Journal and Guide*, January 17, 1942.

16. Correspondence, March 15, 1942.

17. Slichter, *op. cit.*, pp. 47-50; Spero and Harris, *op. cit.*, p. 121; IBEW, *Proceedings*, 1941, p. 46.
18. Spero and Harris, *op. cit.*, p. 66; DuBois, *Negro Artisan*, pp. 155, 158, 160.
19. F. E. Wolfe, *Admission to American Trade Unions*, Baltimore, 1911, p. 128.
20. Greene and Woodson, *op. cit.*, p. 323; R. C. Weaver, "Racial Employment Trends in National Defense," *Phylon*, II (1941), 345-46.
21. I. DeA. Reid, *Negro Membership in American Labor Unions*, New York, 1930, p. 40.
22. Spero and Harris, *op. cit.*, p. 120.
23. Reid, *loc. cit.*; C. A. Shorter, "Philadelphia's Employers, Unions and Negro Workers," *Opportunity*, XX (1942), 4; C. L. Franklin, *The Negro Labor Unionist of New York*, New York, 1936, pp. 71-72, 169, 218-19, 345-48.
24. R. C. Weaver, "Racial Policy in Public Housing," *Phylon*, I (1940), 153-54.
25. Federal Works Agency, *Report on Employment of Negro Workers in Construction of USHA-Aided Projects*, mimeo., 1941.
26. Weaver, "Racial Employment Trends . . .," pp. 338, 341, 352-54; E. S. Lewis, "We Tackled the Unions—and Won!" *Opportunity*, XVIII (1940), 138-40; idem., "Defense Problems of Baltimore Negroes," *Opportunity*, XIX (1941), 245-46; and T. A. Webster, "Employers, Unions, and Negro Workers," *Opportunity*, XIX (1941), 295.
27. AFL, *Proceedings*, 1941, p. 498; A. B. Walker, "St. Louis' Employers, Unions and Negro Workers," *Opportunity*, XIX (1941), 337.
28. AFL, *op. cit.*, p. 499; Fair Employment Practice Committee, "Hearings, Birmingham," pp. 664 *et seq.*, idem., "Findings and Directions in Case of McAvoy Shipbuilding Corporation and Savannah Buildings Trades Council," press release, December 8, 1942.
29. Reid, *op. cit.*, pp. 40-41; *Mobile Register*, July 24, 1941; FEPC, "Hearings," pp. 363 *et seq.*
30. *Richmond Times-Dispatch*, January 18, 19, 20, February 1, 5, 11, March 20, June 19, and September 10, 11, 1941.
31. Memorandum filed with USHA, copy courtesy Urban League of Greater Little Rock.
32. L. H. James, "Policies of Organized Labor in Relation to Negro Workers in Atlanta, 1869-1937," unpublished M. A. thesis, Atlanta University, 1937, pp. 52-54.
33. E. E. Johnson, "Public Houser No. I," *Opportunity*, XX (1941), 324-26, 344-45; *New York Times*, February 18, 1942.
34. William Haber and Robert Winters, "Building Construction," in H. A. Millis *et al.*, *How Collective Bargaining Works*, New York, 1942, p. 205.

35. Statistical verification of this is found in unpublished tabulations of the U. S. Bureau of Labor Statistics, summarized in the *Monthly Labor Review*, XLV (August 1937), 895-915.
36. Wolfe, *op. cit.*, p. 125; and James, *op. cit.*, p. 58.
37. Reid, *op. cit.*, p. 43.
38. Brotherhood of Painters, *Officers Reports*, 1941, pp. 51-52.
39. *Ibid.*, *Constitution* (ed. 1942), Sec. 105; *idem.* (ed. 1940), Sec. 150.
40. The business agent of the painters was elected vice-president of the Council with the help of colored delegates. He then prevailed upon his local to admit Negro members.
41. Brotherhood of Painters, *Constitution* (ed. 1940), Sec. 218 (a).
42. *Ibid.*, *Proceedings*, 1941, pp. 324-43; Walker, *op. cit.*, p. 336; and James, *op. cit.*, pp. 58-59.
43. Webster, *op. cit.*, p. 336; Chicago Commission on Race Relations, *The Negro in Chicago*, Chicago, 1922, pp. 417-418; AFL, *Proceedings*, pp. 481-482; New York State War Council, *How Management Can Integrate Negroes in War Industries*, New York, 1942, pp. 33-34; Brotherhood of Painters, *Constitution* (ed. 1942), Sec. 238 (a).
44. Federal Works Agency, *loc. cit.*
45. Brotherhood of Painters, *Officers Reports*, 1941, pp. 58-59, 62-68.
46. William Haber, *Industrial Relations in the Building Industry*, Cambridge, Mass., 1930, Chapter V. Professor Haber notes that employers frequently do not train as many apprentices as union rules permit.
47. Wolfe, *op. cit.*, pp. 125-27; Haber, *op. cit.*, pp. 285-91. Bricklayers, Masons, and Plasterers Union, *Constitution* (ed. 1936), Article XII, Sec. 1; Article XIII, Sec. 1; Article XVIII, Sec. 14.
48. N. R. Whitney, *Jurisdiction in American Building-Trades Unions*, Baltimore, 1914, p. 32; Wolfe, *op. cit.*, p. 127; Lewis, "We Tackled the Unions," p. 139; Walker, *op. cit.*, pp. 336-37; Ovington, *Half a Man*, pp. 95-99; Quillin, *op. cit.*, pp. 155-56; Bogart, *loc. cit.*; Crossland, *loc. cit.*; and Urban League of Kansas City, *op. cit.*, p. 40.
49. Weaver, "Racial Employment Trends. . . ," p. 338.
50. Reid, *op. cit.*, p. 40; James, *op. cit.*, pp. 41-45.
51. Federal Works Agency, *loc. cit.*
52. AFL, *Proceedings*, 1941, pp. 477, 490; letters from a member of Mobile local, November 21, 1941, and from Mr. Gray, March 12, 1943.
53. Wolfe, *op. cit.*, p. 123; Operative Plasterers, *Constitution* (ed. 1941), Sec. 64.
54. Federal Works Agency, *loc. cit.*
55. Reid, *op. cit.*, p. 44; Operative Plasterers, *Constitution*, Secs. 22, 25.
56. "Bi-Racial Cooperation in the Placement of Negroes," *Monthly Labor Review*, LV (1942), 231-34.

57. U. S. Bureau of Census, *Sixteenth Census of the United States: 1940*, Series P-16, 1942.
58. A comparison of registrants and placements at U. S. Employment Service offices is further proof of employers' preference for Negroes. The writer has examined a few samples and found that the proportion of Negro placements is greater than that of Negro registrants. For skilled jobs the reverse is true.
59. AFL, *Proceedings*, 1941, p. 492.

CHAPTER III

1. The Locomotive Engineers was founded in 1863; the Railway Conductors in 1868; the Locomotive Firemen in 1873; and the Railroad Trainmen in 1883. They are not affiliated with either the AFL or the CIO.
2. Unless otherwise stated, the material presented in this section is based on the excellent account in S. D. Spero and A. L. Harris, *The Black Worker*, New York, 1931, pp. 284-307.
3. Harry D. Wolf, "Railroads," in Harry A. Millis *et al.*, *How Collective Bargaining Works*, New York, 1942, p. 321.
4. Some railways, e.g., the St. Louis and San Francisco, reduced the wages of porter-brakemen to porters' levels after the war, but forced them to continue performing brakemen's work.
5. E.g., the contract in effect between the BRT and the Norfolk & Western Railway since 1908 provides that all vacancies as road brakemen shall be filled with promotable men.
6. S. H. Slichter, *Union Policies and Industrial Management*, Washington, 1941, pp. 187-89.
7. B.L.F. & E., *State Laws Relating to Full Crew, Qualification of Personnel, Train Lengths, Etc.*, Cleveland, 1939, pp. 2-42.
8. *Beal v. Missouri Pac. R. R. Corp.*, 312 U. S. 45 (1941).
9. Copies of agreements in writer's possession.
10. From Interstate Commerce Commission wage reports.
11. Wolf, *op. cit.*, p. 321.
12. During 1932-33, the average age of conductors was 50 years, with 25 years of service. From 75 to 90 per cent of the trainmen were demoted conductors. Trainmen of 15-25 years' experience were on furlough or discharged. A similar situation existed among engineers and firemen. See J. Douglas Brown *et al.*, *Railway Labor Survey*, New York, 1933, esp. p. 106.
13. H. R. Cayton and G. S. Mitchell, *Black Workers and the New Unions*, Chapel Hill, N. C., 1939, pp. 439-43; and "Proposed Report of the Federal Coordinator of Transportation on Alleged Discrimination Against Colored Railway Employees of the Illinois Central System," unpublished MS. in U. S. Archives.
14. *Brotherhood v. Texas and N. O. Railroad Co.*, 281 U. S. 557 (1930).

15. See below, pp. 81-86.
16. National Mediation Board, *Eighth Annual Report*, 1942, p. 31.
17. The experience of the NRA Labor Board is a case in point. For a view similar to that expressed here, see A. P. Randolph, "The Crisis of Negro Railroad Workers," *American Federationist*, XLVI (August 1939), 818-19.
18. See B.L.F. & E., *Officers Reports*, 1937, pp. 128-30, 144; 1941; pp. 212-29; *Locomotive Firemen's and Enginemen's Magazine*, XCVI (1934), 39; Special Agreement Between Scott M. Loftin and Edward M. Lane as trustees of the Florida East Coast Railway . . . and the Brotherhood of Locomotive Engineers, February 19, 1942.
19. See B.L.F. & E, *Officers Reports*, 1931, pp. 149-51; 1937, pp. 91-98; 1941, pp. 232-50.
20. Quoted in *ibid.*, 1937, pp. 142-49. Italics supplied.
21. See below, p. 89.
22. B.L.F. & E, *Officers Reports*, 1941, p. 157; and personal investigation. See also National Mediation Board, Case No. R-621, April 30, 1940. The Mediation Board is vested with wide powers and discretion, and in the absence of clear fraud or other gross impropriety, the courts will not interfere. Nevertheless, the courts have severely condemned the Board's procedure on a number of occasions. See e.g., *Brotherhood* v. *Board*, 88 F. (2d) 757; *Cole* v. *Atlanta Terminal*, 15 F. Supp. 131; and *McNulty* v. *Board*, 18 F. Supp. 494.
23. National Mediation Board, *Second Annual Report*, 1936, pp. 11-12. The National Labor Relations Board has adhered to a similar policy. See the discussion in the concluding chapter.
24. *National Federation of Railway Workers* v. *National Mediation Board*, 110 F. (2d) 529; certiorari denied, 310 U. S. 628 (1940).
25. National Mediation Board, *First Annual Report*, 1935, pp. 20-22.
26. See below, pp. 85, 95-96, 99. The courts have influenced the Board's procedure in relying upon history to determine the appropriate unit. *See Brotherhood of R. R. Trainmen* v. *National Board*, 88 F. (2d) 757 (1936).
27. *Locomotive Firemen's and Enginemen's Magazine*, XCI (1931), 221; B.L.F. & E., *Proceedings of the Thirty-Third Convention*, 1937, pp. 22, 584-85; and *idem., Officers Reports*, 1941, pp. 549-50.
28. *A. Johnson et al* v. *A.T. & S.F. Railway et al.* 225 ICC 519.
29. *Teague* v. *Brotherhood of Locomotive Firemen and Enginemen*, 127 F. (2d) 53.
30. Slichter, *op. cit.*, p. 190.
31. B.L.F. & E, *Officers Reports*, 1941, pp. 553-54.
32. Notice was served on March 28, 1940, to the following railroads: Frankfurt & Cincinnati, Atlantic Coast Line, Atlantic & West Point, Atlanta Terminals, Central of Georgia, Georgia, Jacksonville

Terminal, Louisville & Nashville, Norfolk Southern, Memphis Union Terminal, St. Louis & San Francisco, Seaboard Air Line, Southern, Cincinnati, New Orleans & Texas Pacific, Alabama Great Southern, New Orleans Terminal, New Orleans & Northeastern, Georgia Southern & Florida, St. John River Terminal, Harriman & Northeastern, Cincinnati, Burnside and Cumberland River, Tennessee Central, Gulf, Mobile, & Northern, Louisiana & Arkansas, Gulf, Mobile, & Ohio, Columbus & Greenville, and Norfolk & Western. The first-named accepted the B.L.F. & E. proposals in full; the last five refused to accept the proposals, or to participate in the concerted handling of the question; the remainder participated in the concerted movement.

33. B.L.F. & E., *Officers Reports,* 1941, pp. 549-52.

34. Whether a federal agency should assist parties to reach an agreement aimed at displacing a particular race from its jobs is a question that Congress might well consider.

35. *Agreement between the Southeastern Carriers' Conference Committee representing . . . [the railroads mentioned in note 32, above] and the Brotherhood of Locomotive Firemen & Enginemen,* February 18, 1942.

36. Material from files of Fair Employment Practice Committee and from personal investigation.

37. *Ibid.*

38. ICC Wage Statistics.

39. From reports issued by the Railroad Retirement Board in its monthly survey of employment.

40. Spero and Harris, *op. cit.,* p. 307.

41. B.R.T., *Proceedings of the Sixth Triennial Convention,* 1931, pp. 632-33.

42. The facts for the ensuing discussion of the Adjustment Board are taken from W. H. Spencer, *The National Railroad Adjustment Board,* Chicago, 1938; L. K. Garrison, "The National Railroad Adjustment Board: A Unique Administrative Agency," *Yale Law Journal,* XLVI (1937), 567-98; Attorney General's Committee on Administrative Procedure, *Administrative Procedure in Government Agencies,* Sen. Doc. No. 10, 77th Cong., 1st Sess., 1941, Part 4, pp. 1-20; and H. E. Jones (ed.), *Inquiry of the Attorney General's Committee Relating to the National Railroad Adjustment Board,* New York, 1941.

43. The First Division hears cases involving train, engine, and yard employees; the Second, those involving shop employees; the Third, those involving clerical, station, store, express, tower and telegraph, and dining car employees, signal men, train dispatchers, maintenance of way men, and sleeping car conductors, porters, and maids; the Fourth, railroad employees engaged in water transportation, and all others not covered in the first three. The first three divisions are each composed of five employer and five union

members; the Fourth, of three from each side. The First Division handles 80 per cent of the cases which come before the Board.

44. Only the Second Division members have been able to agree on a selection of referees. The Mediation Board now appoints them to the First and Third Divisions without waiting for the Divisions to request its aid. Employer members have protested against both this method of selection and the referees chosen by the Board.

45. National Mediation Board, *Eighth Annual Report,* 1942, p. 31.

46. Quotations follow Spencer, *loc. cit.,* by permission of the University of Chicago Press.

47. The First Division also refuses to hear cases brought by nonparticipating organizations, but the Third will hear those.

48. *Nord* v. *Griffen,* 86 F. (2d) 281; certiorari refused, 300 U. S. 673 (1937); and *Estes* v. *Union Terminal Co.,* 89 F. (2d) 768 (1937).

49. *Patterson* v. *Chicago & E. Ill. R. R. Co.,* U.S.D.C., N. Dis. Ill., May 3, 1943.

50. Slichter, *op. cit.,* pp. 195-96.

51. NRAB, First Division, Award No. 6640. The discussion of the case is presented entirely on the material in the published award.

52. Italics supplied.

53. *Ibid.*

54. This would seem to follow from *Nord* v. *Griffen,* note 48 above.

55. From monthly surveys of Railroad Retirement Board.

56. Spero and Harris, *op. cit.,* p. 315.

57. United Service Transport Employees, *Proceedings,* 1942, pp. 58, 61; interviews with officials of the Brotherhood of Sleeping Car Porters.

58. D. H. Mater, "Seniority Rights before the Courts," *Journal of Business,* XII (April 1939), 158.

59. *Idem.,* "Effects of Seniority upon the Welfare of the Employee, the Employer, and Society," *Journal of Business,* XIV (October 1941), 393-94. Quoted by permission of the University of Chicago Press.

60. *Harrison Bruce* v. *Atlantic Coast Line Railway et al.,* Virginia State Court, Richmond, Va., September 12, 1932; *Bester Williams Steele* v. *Brotherhood et al.,* Alabama Circuit Court, 10th Judicial Circuit, In Equity No. 52279 (1943).

61. *Teague* v. *Brotherhood of Locomotive Firemen and Enginemen,* 127 F. (2d) 53 (1942); *Tunstall* v. *Brotherhood et al.,* U. S. Dis. Ct., East. Dis. Va., Civil Action No. 210 (1943).

62. Spero and Harris, *op. cit.,* pp. 311-25.

63. Personal investigation.

64. See U. S. Board of Mediation, *Annual Report,* 1931, pp. 19-28; 1932, pp. 36-42; BRT, *Annual Report of the President,* 1936, pp. 179-85; B.L.F. & E., *Officers Reports,* 1937, pp. 432-42; and the files of the Association.

65. Complaint of the Association . . . Against the Louisiana & Arkan-

sas Railway, filed before the Fair Employment Practice Committee, June 3, 1942.

66. Interview with the general chairman of the Association, December 23, 1942.

67. Railroad Retirement Board, *Compensation and Service, Railroad Employees*, 1940, Washington, pp. 147, 164.

68. Unless otherwise indicated, the material in this section is based on B. R. Brazeal, "The Brotherhood of Sleeping Car Porters," an as yet unpublished Ph.D. thesis, Columbia University, 1942. Dr. Brazeal kindly placed a copy of his thesis at the writer's disposal.

69. For a history of this union, see *Sleeping Car Conductor*, XXI (July-December 1939); and *Railway Conductor*, LIX (July 1942), 192.

70. Brazeal, *loc. cit.*; and *Sleeping Car Conductor, op. cit.*, p. 4.

71. *Sleeping Car Conductor, op. cit.*, pp. 33-39; and A. P. Randolph, *The Case of the Porters Against the Conductors' Bill*, mimeo., 1940 (?).

72. NRAB, Third Division, Awards 779, 1461-65, and 1883. The Pullman Company has refused, at least till recently, to put these awards into effect. Now that the Sleeping Car Conductors has amalgamated with the Railway Conductors, it may have either the finances to initiate a court test or the economic strength to force compliance.

73. When the amendments were first proposed to the Railway Labor Act, no mention was made of porters. But Randolph pleaded his case at Congressional hearings and threatened to lobby against the bill among senators from northern states having a large Negro population unless "sleeping car porters, maids and dining car employees" were included among those empowered to select representatives to the Third Division.

74. See below, p. 86.

75. National Mediation Board, *Eighth Annual Report*, 1942, p. 32.

76. Interview with BSCP officials, December 26, 1942.

77. Spero and Harris, *op. cit.*, p. 308.

78. Ruth A. Allen, *The Great Southwest Strike*, Austin, Texas, 1942, p. 76.

79. Spero and Harris, *op. cit.*, p. 308.

80. *Ibid.*, pp. 308-09; personal investigation.

81. Data from U. S. Decennial Census.

82. Cayton and Mitchell, *op. cit.*, pp. 284-309; and material from writer's field notes, summers of 1940 and 1941.

83. D. H. Mater, "The Development and Operation of the Railroad Seniority System," *Journal of Business*, XIV (January 1941), 60, 64.

84. J. H. Ashworth, *The Helper and Amrican Trade Unions*, Baltimore, 1915, pp. 46, 92.

85. National Mediation Board, *Eighth Annual Report*, 1942, p. 31.

86. Brotherhood of Railway Carmen, *Subordinate Lodge Constitution,* ed. 1941, Sec. 6, clauses A and C; *idem., Proceedings of Conventions,* 1905, pp. 24-26, 34-37; 1909, p. 159; 1921, pp. 56, 351-55, 383-85; 1929, pp. 348, 350; 1935, p. 451; and 1941, pp. 522-23.

87. For specific instances, see Cayton and Mitchell, *op. cit.,* pp. 288-289, 295-309; and Ruth A. Allen, *Chapters in the History of Organized Labor in Texas,* Austin, Texas, 1941, p. 143.

88. Spero and Harris, *op. cit.,* pp. 310-11; data from files of the FEPC.

89. See below, pp. 85-92. Railroad car manufacturing plants are probably included in some of the census data used in this section, but they are not ordinarily included within the railway industry and are not covered by the Railway Labor Act. A few of these plants have been organized by the Railway Carmen, but most are under contract to the CIO United Steelworkers, the racial policies of which are discussed in Chapter VIII below.

90. A. M. McIssac, *The Order of Railroad Telegraphers,* Princeton, N. J., 1933, esp. pp. 3-18, 221-53; National Mediation Board, *op. cit.,* 1942, p. 31.

91. National Mediation Board, *loc. cit.;* E. M. Stewart, "Handbook of American Trade-Unions," *Bulletin No. 618,* U. S. Bureau of Labor Statistics, Washington, 1936, p. 271.

92. Harry Henig, *The Brotherhood of Railway Clerks,* New York, 1937, pp. 10-65. 175-213; Brotherhood of Railway and Steamship Clerks, *Constitution,* ed. 1939, Article 35, Sec. 1 (a).

93. Estimates based on ICC, *Wage Statistics,* October 1942; BR & SC, *Officers Reports,* 1943, p. 2; U. S. Department of Labor, Wage and Hour Division, *Redcaps in Railway Terminals under the Fair Labor Standards Act, 1938-1942,* mimeo., 1942, p. 32.

94. AFL, *Proceedings,* 1920, pp. 307-10; BR & SC, *Proceedings,* 1922, p. 163; 1925, 1928, 1931, *passim;* Spero and Harris, *op. cit.,* pp. 89-90, 93-99, 102-03.

95. BR & SC, *Officers Reports,* 1935, p. 5; 1939, p. 5; *idem., Proceedings,* 1935, pp. 282, 453.

96. Henig, *op. cit.,* pp. 208-09; BR & SC, *Officers Reports,* 1939, p. 5.

97. BR & SC, *Officers Reports,* 1939, p. 5; idem., *Proceedings,* 1939, pp. 135-36, 317, 440.

98. *Idem., General, Local and Protective Regulations for the Government of Lodges of the Auxiliary,* ed. 1940; *Railway Clerk,* XXIX (1940), 322.

99. AFL, *Proceedings,* 1940, pp. 644-49.

100. Mr. Green's letter is reprinted in BR & SC, *Grand President's Monthly Bulletin,* IV (1940), 339-40. See also U. S. Department of Labor, Wage and Hour Division, *Wages, Hours and Working Conditions of Red Caps in Western Railway Terminals,* mimeo., 1941, p. 17.

101. Henig, *op. cit.*, pp. 168-70; *Bags and Baggage,* November 1940, July 1941; National Mediation Board, *loc. cit.* In the one instance known to this writer in which the Board placed storehouse and station employees and clerks in separate groups, the Railway Clerks lost the election in one of the classes. Had both been put in one class, the Clerks would have won the combined election. See *Railway Clerk,* XLI (1942), 358.
102. *CIO News, Utility Worker Edition,* August 31, 1942.
103. *Railway Clerk,* XL (1941), 336; and BR & SC *Officers Reports,* 1943, p. 4.
104. Harry Weiss and Philip Arnow, "Recent Transition of Redcaps from Tip to Wage Status," *American Labor Legislation Review,* XXXII (September 1934), 134. The discussion of the "economics of redcapping" is based mainly upon this study, which effectively summarizes the results of an investigation ordered by the U. S. Senate, and conducted by the Wage and Hour Division, Department of Labor.
105. *Ibid.,* pp. 134-35.
106. On at least three occasions, Mr. Randolph had asked the AFL Executive Council to give the Sleeping Car Porters jurisdiction over the redcaps, but each time his request was blocked by the Clerks. Unalterably opposed to the Clerks' racial policies, he then helped the redcaps found a union of their own.
107. *In the Matter of Regulations Concerning Class of Employees and Subordinate Officials to be Included Within Term "Employee" Under the Railway Labor Act,* 229 ICC 410 (1938). The Railway Clerks have assumed full credit for obtaining employee status for redcaps. (See, e.g., *Officers Reports,* 1939, p. 103.) But these claims cannot be corroborated by the facts. Why, e.g., did the Clerks wait until *after* the formation of the IBRC before petitioning the ICC?
108. Weiss and Arnow, *op. cit.,* pp. 135-36.
109. *Williams* v. *Jacksonville Terminal Co.,* and *Pickett* v. *Union Terminal Co.,* 315 U. S., 386 (1942).
110. Weiss and Arnow, *op. cit.,* pp. 138-140.
111. *Ida M. Stopher* v. *Cincinnati Union Terminal Co., Inc.,* 246 ICC 41 (1941). The Commission did rule, however, that the rate was subject to its tariff regulations.
112. Weiss and Arnow, *op. cit.,* pp. 141-43.
113. National Mediation Board, *loc. cit.* The Board does not distinguish redcaps from the other workers covered by the Clerks' agreements. In March 1943, the Clerks represented redcaps on forty-four depot and railroad companies, including other than Class I roads. (See *Officers Reports,* 1943, p. 4.)
114. *United Service Transport Employees* v. *National Mediation Board,* U. S. Dis. Ct., D. C., July 1942.
115. *Brotherhood of Railway Clerks* v. *United Transport Service Em-

ployees, U. S. C. C. A., D. C. Circuit, August 2, 1943; U. S. Sup. Ct., December 6, 1943.

116. See below, pp. 95-96.
117. *Ibid.,* p. 99.
118. *Bags and Baggage,* December 1942, January, February, March, and April, 1943; *CIO News, UTSEA Edition,* May 5, 1943.
119. National Mediation Board, *Case No. R-1050,* May 21, 1943.
120. Efforts to bring the leaders of these organizations to an understanding have not been successful.
121. *Ibid.* One of the standard railway group, the Signalmen's union was founded in 1901, and was affiliated with the AFL between 1914 and 1928. Since then, it has functioned independently.
122. Railroad Retirement Board, *op. cit.,* pp. 60-61, 156-157. Because the census is usually taken in the late winter or early spring months when heavy repair, and hence, extra gangs, are kept at a minimum, the number of maintenance of way laborers reported is usually far less than the maximum employed. E.g., in 1940, the Retirement Board reported that 114,041 extra gang men were employed by Class I railways, but the average for the year, according to the ICC, was only 31,484, or less than one-fourth the maximum.
123. Data from U. S. Decennial Census.
124. Federal Co-ordinator of Transportation, *Extent of Low Wages and Long Hours in the Railroad Industry,* Washington, 1936, p. 3.
125. Railroad Retirement Board, *op. cit.,* pp. 60-62, 86-87, 156-57, 159-60, 165.
126. In 1940, the census reported that 31,608 or 74.4 per cent, of the 42,510 "railroad and railroad shop laborers" were colored.
127. U. S. Department of Labor, Wage and Hour Division, *A Memorandum on Recent Economic Developments in the Railroad Carrier Industry,* mimeo., 1941.
128. In addition to improvemnts in ties, rails, and ballast, which have decreased the amount of maintenance work, machines are now in use which wash ballast, lay rails, and dig ditches. See G. M. Rountree, *The Railway Worker,* Toronto, 1936, pp. 145-46; Charles S. Johnson, "Negroes in the Railway Industry," *Phylon,* III (1942), 5-14, 196-98; and J. Douglas Brown, "The History and Problems of Collective Bargaining by Railway Maintenance of Way Employees," unpublished Ph.D. thesis, Princeton University, 1927, pp. 203-04. Copy courtesy Professor Brown.
129. Brown, *op. cit.,* pp. 1-17.
130. *Ibid.,* pp. 3-5, 69. See BMWE, *Proceedings,* 1900, p. 18; 1917, pp. 2-7; 1919, pp. 89, 181-85; 1922, pp. 308-15, for a discussion of the race issue. Also *Constitution,* 1940, Article XIII, Sec. I.
131. BMWE, *Proceedings,* 1931, p. 132; 1934, p. 96; 1937, p. 59; 1940, p. 389.
132. National Mediation Board, *loc. cit.; Maintenance of Way Employes Journal,* XLI (March 1942), p. 29.

133. *Maintenance of Way Employes Journal,* XXXIX (August 1940), p. 38.
134. For a discussion of the foreman-union problem, see Herbert R. Northrup, "The Unionization of Foremen," *Harvard Business Review,* XXI (Summer 1943), 496-504.
135. See BMWE, *Proceedings,* 1931, pp. 82-83; *Maintenance of Way Employes Journal,* XL (December 1941), 21; National Mediation Board, *Case No. R-774,* November 12, 1941; UTSEA, *Protest of Conduct and Result of Election, Case No. R-774,* mimeo., 1941; and *United Transport Service Employees* v. *National Mediation Board,* U.S. Dis. Ct., D. C., Feb., 1943.
136. Railroad Retirement Board, *op. cit.,* pp. 108-109, 162, 166.
137. *Ibid.,* p. 107.
138. Ruth A. Allen, *Chapters in the History of Organized Labor in Texas,* Austin, Texas, 1941, pp. 196-97.
139. NRAB, Third Division, Award No. 493.
140. *Catering Industry Employee,* LII (May 1943), 33.
141. Spero and Harris, *op. cit.,* p. 125.
142. Hotel & Restaurant Workers, *Proceedings,* 1921, pp. 15, 53-54; 1923, p. 19; 1927, pp. 20, 46-52; 1929, pp. 13-14; 1934, pp. 20, 158-60; 1936, p. 138; 1938, pp. 213-14; and National Mediation Board, *loc. cit.*
143. *Ibid.,* 1938, pp. 211-16; 1941, pp. 230-32; and *Dining Car Worker,* March 1943. The Hotel Workers' vice-president representing dining car workers is also a Negro.
144. *Ibid.,* 1936, pp. 115-16; 1938, p. 179; *idem., Constitution,* ed. 1941, Sec. 3 (a); and Spero and Harris, *op. cit.,* pp. 75-76.
145. *Ibid.,* 1934, pp. 15-20; *Railroad Trainmen,* LV (1938), 3-5; and National Mediation Board, *loc. cit.*
146. National Mediation Board, *loc. cit.,* and *idem.,* Cases *R-21, R-46, R-475, R-511, R-527,* and *R-530.*
147. UTSEA, *Proceedings,* 1942, pp. 22, 62-64.
148. National Mediation Board, *First Annual Report,* 1935, p. 1.
149. Typical studies of industrial relations on the railroads which have ignored the racial policies of the unions and the federal agencies are those of Wolf, *loc. cit.,* and E. B. McNatt, "The Amended Railway Labor Act," *Southern Economic Journal,* V (April 1938), 179-96. A significant exception is, of course, the work of Spero and Harris.

CHAPTER IV

1. R. B. Pinchbeck, *The Virginia Negro Artisan and Tradesman,* Richmond, Va., 1926, pp. 54-59; Joseph C. Robert, *The Tobacco Kingdom,* Durham, N. C., 1938, pp. 170, 197, 208.
2. See below, pp. 119-120.
3. W. K. Boyd, *The Story of Durham,* Durham, N. C., pp. 71-73, 83;

U. S. Bureau of Corporations, *Report of the Commissioner of Corporations on the Tobacco Industry,* Washington, 1909 I, 63.

4. This description of the racial-occupational segregation pattern given here follows closely that by Charles S. Johnson, "The Tobacco Worker," unpublished study of the NRA, Industrial Studies Section, Division of Review, 1935, I, 13-16.

5. "Earnings and Hours in the Cigarette, Chewing and Smoking and Snuff Industry, 1940," *Monthly Labor Review,* LIV (January 1942), 184-208.

6. U. S. Bureau of Internal Revenue, *Production of Cigarettes, Cigars, Smoking and Chewing Tobacco and Snuff, 1880-1939,* mimeo. release No. 0-14, 1940. Production data hereafter cited are from this source.

7. H. Magdoff, I. H. Siegal, and M. E. Davis, *Production, Employment and Productivity in 59 Manufacturing Industries,* Philadelphia, WPA, National Research Project, 1939, II, 222.

8. Officials of two large companies which abandoned New York plants informed Professor J. P. Troxell, that "troubles with labor were responsible for their removal, and that the immigrant workers of Brooklyn and Manhattan were temperamentally unfitted for operating cigarette machinery," (J. P. Troxell, "Labor in the Tobacco Industry," unpublished Ph.D. thesis, University of Wisconsin, 1931, p. 55.) A company official explained to an investigator of the U. S. Women's Bureau that the cigarette industry had migrated "to localities where the tobacco leaf is grown, to good distributing points, and to a 'satisfactory' labor market." (C. Manning and H. A. Byrne, "The Effects on Women of Changing Conditions in the Cigar and Cigarette Industries," *Bulletin No. 100,* U. S. Women's Bureau, Washington, 1932, p. 20.

9. U. S. Dept. of Labor, Wage and Hour Division, *The Tobacco Industry,* mimeo. 1941, pp. 27, 90-91.

10. *Ibid.,* p. 222. Data extended from Magdoff, *loc. cit.*

11. Data from the census and from unpublished tabulations of the Bureau of Labor Statistics, courtesy of A. F. Henrichs, Acting Commissioner.

12. "Earnings in Cigarettes, Snuff, and Chewing—and Smoking—Tobacco Plants, 1933-35," *Monthly Labor Review* XLII (May 1936), 1331.

13. North Carolina Employment Service, "Survey of Tobacco Stemmeries," unpublished study, 1939, p. 12; personal investigation; and J. D. Rice, "The Negro Tobacco Worker and His Union in Durham, North Carolina," unpublished M. A. thesis, University of North Carolina, 1941, p. 49.

14. U. S. Dept. of Labor, *op. cit.,* p. 12.

15. *Ibid.,* p. 11.

16. Caroline Manning, "Hours and Earnings in Tobacco Stemmeries," *Bulletin No. 127,* U. S. Women's Bureau, Washington, 1934, p. 8;

Jacob Perlman, "Earnings and Hours of Negro Workers in Independent Tobacco Stemmeries in 1933 and 1935," *Monthly Labor Review,* XLIV (May 1937), 1153.

17. "Hours and Earnings of Employees of Independent Leaf-Tobacco Dealers," *Monthly Labor Review,* LIII (July 1941), 216.

18. *Ibid.,* p. 222; "Earnings in the Cigarette . . . Industry, 1933-35," p. 1331; "Earnings and Hours in the Cigarette . . . Industry, 1940," pp. 184-208.

19. Personal investigation in five most important tobacco manufacturing centers.

20. For a detailed history, together with a complete record of sources, see Herbert R. Northrup, "The Tobacco Workers International Union," *Quarterly Journal of Economics,* LVI (August 1942), 606-26.

21. *Ibid.*

22. See above, p. 40.

23. A. V. Jackson, "A New Deal for Tobacco Workers," *Crisis,* XIV (1938), 323.

24. *Matter of American Tobacco Company,* 9 NLRB 579; 10 NLRB 1171.

25. *Tobacco Worker,* November 1941; *UCAPAWA News,* December 1, 1941.

26. See *UCAPAWA News,* July, 1, 15, August 1, 15, 1943; *Pittsburgh Courier,* July 24, 1943; and personal investigation.

27. *Pittsburgh Courier,* July 24, 1943; *UCAPAWA News,* November 15, 1943, January 1, 1944.

CHAPTER V

1. Broadus Mitchell, *The Rise of the Cotton Mills of the South,* Baltimore, 1921, *passim;* Charles S. Johnson, *Patterns of Negro Segregation,* New York, 1943, pp. 83, 171-72; and data from U. S. Census.

2. Interview with Solomon Barkin, research director, Textile Workers Union, June 1943; *The Textile Worker,* December 1941, p. 9.

3. Data from U. S. Census; and S. D. Spero and A. L. Harris, *The Black Worker,* New York, 1931, pp. 337-40.

4. Personal investigation. Most of the subsequent material on the racial pattern in the industry is based upon the writer's field survey, conducted during June 1943.

5. C. L. Franklin, *The Negro Labor Unionist of New York,* New York, 1936, p. 162.

6. Letter from A. Plotkin, general organizer, ILGWU, Chicago, June 21, 1943.

7. Spero and Harris, *op. cit.,* p. 347.

8. *Ibid.,* p. 338.

9. Wilfred Carsel, *A History of the Chicago Ladies' Garment Work-*

ers' Union, Chicago, 1940, pp. 233-35; letter from M. Biulis, vice-president, ILGWU, Chicago, June 30, 1943.

10. Spero and Harris, *op. cit.*, pp. 339-40; personal investigation.

11. Urban League of Kansas City, *Negro Workers, Garment Industries and Employers*, mimeo., 1941; *Kansas City Call*, May 14, 1943; and letter from Thomas A. Webster, executive secretary, Kansas City Urban League, June 16, 1943.

12. Interview with officials of Baltimore ILGWU, June 23, 1943.

13. Personal Investigation.

14. Joel Seidman, *The Needle Trades*, New York, 1942, p. 281. Quoted by permission of Farrar & Rinehart.

15. *Ibid.*, p. 283.

16. *Ibid.*, pp. 284, 287-89.

17. Franklin, *op. cit.*, pp. 162, 305-07.

18. Spero and Harris, *op. cit.*, p. 346.

19. Personal investigation.

20. Seidman, *op. cit.*, pp. 284-85; Earl D. Strong, *The Amalgamated Clothing Workers of America*, Grinnell, Ia., 1940, pp. 201-46.

21. Franklin, *op. cit.*, pp. 319-21.

22. *Ibid.*, Spero and Harris, *op. cit.*, p. 347; Seidman, *op. cit.*, pp. 285-86.

23. Interview with George Kleinman, educational director of the International Fur & Leather Workers Union, June 18, 1943.

24. See International Fur Workers Union, *Proceedings*, 1939, pp. 95, 108-09, 113-14; International Fur & Leather Workers Union, Fur Division, *Proceedings*, 1942, p. 11; *idem.*, *Report of the Executive Board*, 1942, pp. 15-17, 66-69. See also Seidman, *op. cit.*, pp. 286, 289-90; and Spero and Harris, *op. cit.*, p. 347.

25. Cf. e.g., *Fur & Leather Worker*, June 1943.

26. Seidman, *op. cit.*, pp. 115-32.

27. Spero and Harris, *op. cit.*, p. 347; Franklin, *op. cit.*, pp. 318-19; Ira DeA. Reid, *Negro Membership in American Labor Unions*, New York, 1930, p. 74.

28. Bertha M. Neinburg and Bertha Blair, "Factors Affecting Wages in Power Laundries," *Bulletin No. 143*, U. S. Women's Bureau, Washington, 1936, p. 1; Amalgamated Clothing Workers, *Documentary History, 1936-38*, 1938, pp. 33-35.

29. Neinburg and Blair, *op. cit.*, p. 27.

30. Personal Investigation.

31. E. M. Stewart, "Handbook of American Trade-Unions," *Bulletin No. 618*, U. S. Bureau of Labor Statistics, Washington, 1936, pp. 327-28; Laundry Workers International Union, *Proceedings*, 1941, *passim*.

32. Interview with Mr. Frankel, president, Philadelphia local, Laundry Workers Union, June 1943.

33. Amalgamated Clothing Workers, *op. cit.*, pp. 35-37; Franklin, *op. cit.*, pp. 208-10; Laundry Workers Joint Board, *Facts About Your Union*, New York, n.d.

34. Interview with officials of Laundry Workers Joint Board, New York, June 1943.

CHAPTER VI

1. See above, p. 47.
2. See Boris Stern, "Cargo Handling and Longshore Labor Conditions," *Bulletin No. 550*, U. S. Bureau of Labor Statistics, Washington, 1932, pp. 70-73; and Maritime Labor Board, *Report to the President and to the Congress*, Washington, 1940, pp. 140-44.
3. *Ibid.*; Charles Barnes, *The Longshoremen*, New York, 1915; Mayor's Committee on Unemployment, *Report on Dock Employment in New York City and Recommendations for its Regularization*, New York, 1915; E. E. Swanstrom, *The Waterfront Labor Problem*, New York, 1938; and Elizabeth Ogg, *Longshoremen and Their Homes*, New York, 1939. For a concise statement of the avowed reasons why the ILA heads oppose decasualization, see the speech of President Joseph P. Ryan in ILA, *Proceedings*, 1935, pp. 201-03. The Texas and west coast decasualization plans are briefly described below, pp. 151-53.
4. Swanstrom, *op. cit.*, pp. 94-101; Ogg; *op. cit.*, pp. 22-24; and personal investigation.
5. ILA, *Proceedings*, 1939, p. 29.
6. The ILA was founded by longshoremen of the Great Lakes in 1892, and gradually expanded thereafter on the Atlantic and Pacific coasts. See John R. Commons, "The Longshoremen of the Great Lakes," in his *Labor and Administration*, New York, 1913, pp. 267-93.
7. Barnes, *op. cit.*, pp. 181-87; *Report of the Massachusetts Commission on the Employment Problems of Negroes*, Boston, 1942, p. 20.
8. Barnes, *op. cit.*, pp. 93-126; Stern, *op. cit.*, pp. 74-83; Maritime Labor Board, *op. cit.*, pp. 141-44; *New York Herald Tribune*, October 3, 1941; *New York Times*, October 16, 18, 1941, January 3, 6, 17, November 15, 22, 1942; *PM*, January 4, 1943.
9. S. D. Spero and A. L. Harris, *The Black Worker*, 1931, pp. 197-204; C. L. Franklin, *The Negro Labor Unionist of New York*, New York, 1936, pp. 25, 28, 61, 74, 165, 189-91, 325-27; and personal investigation.
10. Stern, *op. cit.*, pp. 83-84; Spero and Harris, *op. cit.*, pp. 204-05, 333-36; and personal investigation.
11. C. H. Wesley, *Negro Labor in the United States*, New York, 1927, pp. 184-85; J. R. Brackett, *The Progress of the Colored People of Maryland*, Baltimore, 1890, pp. 29-30; Stern, *op. cit.*, pp. 85-87; Spero and Harris, *op. cit.*, pp. 192-94; and personal investigation.
12. Spero and Harris, *op. cit.*, pp. 72-73; 194-97; personal investigation.
13. Spero and Harris, *op. cit.*, pp. 182-83; Mercer G. Evans, "The History of the Organized Labor Movement in Georgia," unpub-

lished Ph.D. thesis, University of Chicago, 1929, pp. 186-89; Ira DeA. Reid, *Negro Membership in American Labor Unions,* New York, 1930, p. 50; Samuel Harper, "Negro Labor in Jacksonville," *Crisis,* XLIX (January 1942), 13; and personal investigation.

14. *Matter of Mobile Steamship Association,* 8 NLRB 1297; 9 NLRB 60; and personal investigation.

15. For a full history of labor conditions in the port of New Orleans, together with detailed documentation, see Herbert R. Northrup, "The New Orleans Longshoremen," *Political Science Quarterly,* LVII (December 1942), 526-44.

16. Stern, *op. cit.,* pp. 87-89.

17. *Ibid.,* pp. 90-91; Ruth A. Allen, *Chapters in the History of Organized Labor in Texas,* Austin, Texas, 1941, pp. 193-94, 204; Samuel E. Warren, "The Negro in the American Labor Movement," unpublished Ph.D. thesis, University of Wisconsin, 1941, pp. 439-55; letter from Albert E. Anderson, secretary-treasurer, South Atlantic and Gulf Coast District, ILA, February 11, 1942.

18. Marvel Keller, *Decasualization of Longshore Work in San Francisco,* Philadelphia, WPA, National Research Project, 1939; Robert C. Francis, "A History of Labor in the San Francisco Waterfront," unpublished Ph.D. thesis, University of California, 1934, pp. 12, 103, 116, 149-55, 170, 172, 178-79, 182-83; Richard A. Liebes, "Longshore Labor Relations on the Pacific Coast, 1934-1942," unpublished Ph.D. thesis, University of California, 1942; *Norfolk Journal and Guide,* August 4, 1934; *Louisiana Weekly* (New Orleans), September 1, 1934; *Pittsburgh Courier,* March 30, 1940; and *Kansas City Call,* May 29, 1942.

CHAPTER VII

1. Only bituminous coal mining will be considered in this chapter. There never have been more than a few score Negroes in the anthracite mining region of Pennsylvania. The terms "coal mining" and "bituminous coal mining" will be used interchangeably hereafter.

2. See below, pp. 158-62.

3. For a more complete account of the North-South competition, see F. E. Berquist, *et al., Economic Survey of the Coal Industry under Free Competition and Code Regulation,* mimeo., NRA Work Materials Mo. 69, 1936, pp. 13-78. Quotations are from P. H. Norgren, "The Negro Coal Mine Worker," unpublished report made to the Carnegie Corporation of New York's Negro in America survey, 1940.

4. For an analysis of the effect of freight rate structure on coal production and mine location, see Glen L. Parker, *The Coal Industry,* Washington, 1940, pp. 43-50.

5. Spero and Harris, *op. cit.*, pp. 213-14, 217-25, 374-75.
6. J. T. Laing, "The Negro Miner in West Virginia," unpublished Ph.D. thesis, Ohio State University, 1933, pp. 189-249; Homer L. Morris, *The Plight of the Coal Miner*, Philadelphia, 1934, pp. 66-67; and Norgren, *loc. cit.*
7. The fact that in the past earnings of Negroes have been, on the average, below those of whites is attributable to the concentration of the former in the low wage, non-union areas of the South.
8. For an authoritative discussion of mechanization and its effects, see W. E. Hotchkiss, *et al.*, *Mechanization, Employment and Output Per Man in Bituminous-Coal Mining*, Philadelphia, WPA, National Research Project, 1939.
9. See below, pp. 168-70.
10. Herbert Harris, *American Labor*, New Haven, 1937, pp. 113-14.
11. Spero and Harris, *op. cit.*, pp. 210-13, 355-57; and F. L. Ryan, *The Rehabilitation of Oklahoma Coal Mining Communities*, Norman, Okla., 1935, pp. 39, 46-49, 64-68, 89, 98-99.
12. *Alabama News-Digest*, January 25, 1940. A special supplement of this issue of the Birmingham, Ala., CIO weekly, contains a complete history of the UMW in Alabama. See also, Spero and Harris, *op. cit.*, pp. 357-62.
13. C. P. Anson, "A History of the Labor Movement in West Virginia," unpublished Ph.D. thesis, University of North Carolina, 1940, pp. 98-100, 116-117, 122-23; and Spero and Harris, *op. cit.*, pp. 367-70.
14. U. S. Senate, 76th Congress, first session, *Report of the Committee on Education and Labor: Violation of Free Speech and the Rights of Labor*, No. 6, part 2, "Private Police Systems, Harlan County, Ky.," 1939, p. 1920.
15. See W. D. Lane, *Civil War in West Virginia*, New York, 1921; and A. F. Hinrichs, *The United Mine Workers of America and the Non-union Coal Fields*, New York, 1923.
16. For an account of the revolts and dual movements of the miners in this period, see Parker, *op. cit.*, pp. 77-81.
17. Waldo E. Fisher, "Bituminous Coal," in H. A. Millis, *et al.*, *How Collective Bargaining Works*, New York, 1942, pp. 268-69.
18. H. R. Cayton and G. S. Mitchell, *Black Workers and the New Unions*, Chapel Hill, N. C., 1939, pp. 321-23; 358-61; and Jonathan Daniels, *A Southerner Discovers the South*, New York, 1938, pp. 281ff.
19. Fisher, *op. cit.*, pp. 270-75.
20. The veins in which the coal is located in Alabama are generally thin, and the coal contains a high percentage of impurities. Both increase the cost of recovery.
21. See, e.g., Spero and Harris, *op. cit.*, p. 375.
22. Cayton and Mitchell, *op. cit.*, pp. 344-48; and G. S. Mitchell, "The Negro in Southern Trade Unionism," *Southern Economic Journal*,

II (September 1936), 30. Quotations from Norgren, *loc. cit.*, based upon material collected by the present writer.

23. Norgren, *loc. cit.*

24. Data from Hotchkiss, *op. cit.*, p. 210; and U. S. Department of the Interior, Bureau of Mines, Bituminous Coal Division, *Weekly Coal Report*, July 11, 1942, Table VIII. The machines under discussion here are primarily mobile loaders, which entirely eliminate hand loaders, but the figures also include "scrapers" and "duck-bills," for which the displacement rate is not so heavy. Conveyers and pit-car loaders are not included in these data. These last two types do not eliminate hand loaders, but affect mainly certain maintenance jobs and speed up operations. They do not affect Negroes disproportionately. For a description of the various machines, see Hotchkiss, *op. cit.*, pp. 113-42.

25. W. H. Young, *et al.*, "*Mechanical Mining*," reprinted from *Coal Age*, February 1942.

26. S. H. Slichter, *Union Policies and Industrial Management*, Washington, 1941, p. 271.

27. See above, Table V.

28. Slichter, *op. cit.*, pp. 271-72.

29. E.g., the agreement between the Alabama Coal Operators Association, and UMW, District 20, for 1937-39, makes no mention of the subject of seniority.

30. Slichter, *op. cit.*, pp. 362-63; Fisher, *op. cit.*, pp. 276-77.

CHAPTER VIII

1. Spero and Harris, *op. cit.*, pp. 262-63.

2. T. J. Woofter, Jr., *A Study of the Economic Status of the Negro*, mimeo., 1930, p. 38.

3. Data from U. S. Census. Data for 1940 include totals of "employed" and "experienced workers seeking employment" categories, which are roughly equivalent to the "gainful worker" designation of previous enumerations.

4. C. R. Daugherty, M. G. de Chazeau, and S. S. Stratton, *The Economics of the Iron and Steel Industry*, New York, 1937, pp. 885, 891, 902, 939.

5. *Ibid.*, p. 902.

6. "Earnings of Negro Workers in the Iron and Steel Industry, April 1938," *Monthly Labor Review*, LI (November 1940), 1144-46.

7. Data from U. S. Census. Skilled group includes rollers and roll hands, furnacemen, smeltermen, and heaters.

8. "Earnings and Hours in the Iron and Steel Industry, April 1938," *Monthly Labor Review*, LI (September 1940), 718, 725.

9. Paul H. Norgren and Herbert R. Northrup, "Negroes in the Iron and Steel Industry," unpublished MS presented to the Carnegie Corporation of New York's Negro in America survey, 1940.

10. "Earnings and Hours in the Steel Industry . . . ," p. 718.
11. Norgren and Northrup, *loc. cit.*
12. R. R. R. Brooks, *As Steel Goes* . . . , New Haven, 1940, pp. 22-45.
13. Spero and Harris, *op. cit.*, pp. 239, 252-53; Jesse S. Robinson, *The Amalgamated Association of Iron, Steel and Tin Workers,* Baltimore, 1920, pp. 46-47; Horace B. Davis, *Labor and Steel,* New York, 1933, pp. 231-33.
14. For a discussion of the Metal Trades Department, see below, pp. 211-19.
15. Spero and Harris, *op. cit.*, pp. 247-49.
16. *Ibid.*, pp. 255-63.
17. H. R. Cayton and G. S. Mitchell, *Black Workers and the New Unions,* Chapel Hill, N. C., 1939, pp. 104-10, 124-89.
18. *Ibid.*, pp. 111-22.
19. Frederick H. Harbison, "Steel," in H. A. Millis, *et al., How Collective Bargaining Works,* New York, 1942, pp. 510-25; *Steel Labor,* February and June 1943.
20. Norgren and Northrup, *loc. cit.*
21. Harbison, *op. cit.*, p. 518; Cayton and Mitchell, *op. cit.*, pp. 190-224; and personal investigation.
22. Norgren and Northrup, *loc. cit.*
23. *Ibid.*
24. This discussion in this section is based largely on personal investigation. See also Herbert R. Northrup, "The Negro and Unionism in the Birmingham, Ala., Iron and Steel Industry," *Southern Economic Journal,* X (July 1943), 27-40. Much of the material was originally written in Norgren and Northrup, *loc. cit.*, from which the quotations are taken.
25. Northrup, *loc. cit.*
26. *Steel Labor,* May 1942. Italics supplied.
27. *Ibid.*, September 1942.

CHAPTER IX

1. Data from U. S. Census. Data for 1940 are totals of "employed" and "experienced workers seeking work" categories, which are roughly equivalent to "gainful worker" designation of previous enumerations.
2. Lloyd H. Bailer, "The Negro Automobile Worker," *Journal of Political Economy,* LI (October 1943), 416-17. Hereafter cited as "*JPE* article." The writer is indebted to Dr. Bailer for lending this article in MS prior to publication and to the University of Chicago Press for permission to quote therefrom.
3. Robert W. Dunn, *Labor and Automobiles,* New York, 1929, pp. 68-69.
4. Bailer, *op. cit.*, pp. 417-18.
5. *Ibid.*

6. *Ibid.*, pp. 418-19.
7. *Ibid.*
8. *Ibid.*, pp. 421-24.
9. Personal investigation.
10. Data from company payroll.
11. See below, pp. 192-96.
12. W. H. McPherson and Anthony Luchek, "Automobiles," in H. A. Millis, *et al.*, *How Collective Bargaining Works*, New York, 1943, pp. 571, 578-89.
13. Personal investigation.
14. Lloyd H. Bailer, "The Automobile Unions and the Negro," an as yet unpublished article. Hereafter referred to as "MS." Copy courtesy Dr. Bailer.
15. *Ibid.*
16. *Ibid.*
17. *Ibid.*
18. *Ibid.*
19. *Ibid.* Thomas R. Solomon, "Participation of Negroes in Detroit Elections," unpublished Ph.D. thesis, University of Michigan, 1939, pp. 79-80; and Horace A. White, "Who Owns the Negro Churches?", *Christian Century*, LV (February 9, 1938), 176-77.
20. White, *loc. cit.*
21. Bailer, MS, *loc. cit.*
22. *Ibid.*
23. McPherson, *op. cit.*, p. 587.
24. *Ibid.*, pp. 587-89.
25. Bailer, MS, *loc. cit.* See also *United Automobile Worker*, March 15, April 1, 15, May 1, 15, June 1, 15, 1941; *New York Times*, April 2-June 1, 1941, *PM*, April 8, 1941; and *Detroit Free Press*, April 5, 8, 1941.
26. Bailer, MS.
27. *Ibid.*, *United Automobile Worker*, June 1, 1942, April 15, 1943.
28. McPherson, *op. cit.*, pp. 617-20.
29. Bailer, *JPE* article, pp. 421-24.
30. *Ibid.*
31. Robert C. Weaver, "Detroit and Negro Skill," *Phylon*, IV (1943), 133-34.
32. *Ibid.*, p. 136.
33. *Ibid.*, and *idem.*, "Racial Employment Trends in National Defense," *Phylon*, III (First Quarter 1942), 24-26.
34. *Ibid.*, "Detroit and Negro Skill," pp. 139-40.
35. *Ibid.*, pp. 137-38.
36. *Ibid.*, pp. 137-39; *New York Times*, June 7, 1943; *PM*, June 6-9, 1943.
37. Weaver, "Detroit and Negro Skill," pp. 139-40.
38. *Ibid.*, pp. 140-41.
39. Bailer, *JPE* article, p. 428.

40. See, e.g., UAW-CIO, *Proceedings*, 1940, pp. 667-68; 1941, p. 212.
41. *Ibid.*, 1942, pp. 182-87; 281-87.
42. Weaver, "Detroit and Negro Skill," pp. 141-42.
43. Bailer, MS, *loc. cit.*
44. Data from U. S. Census.
45. "Half a Million Workers," *Fortune*, XXIII (March 1943), 98, 163. A similar prejudice against Jews in west coast plants was also noted.
46. J. J. Joseph, "The Mobilization of Manpower," *Science and Society*, VII (Winter 1943), 3.
47. Robert C. Weaver, "With the Negro's Help," *Atlantic Monthly*, CLXIX (April 1942), 701; "Earnings in Aircraft-Parts Plants, November 1942," *Monthly Labor Review* LVI (June 1943), 1057; "Earnings in California Aircraft-Parts Plants, November 1942," *Monthly Labor Review*, LVI (April 1943), 760; and "Negro Employment in Airframe Plants," *Monthly Labor Review*, LVI (May 1943), 888-89.
48. Lester B. Granger, "Negroes and War Production," *Survey Graphic*, XXXI (November 1942), 471; Fair Employment Practice Committee, "Hearings, Birmingham, Ala.," typed MS, June 1942, I, 107 *et seq.*
49. See, e.g., the Associated Negro Press dispatch which appeared in the *Kansas City Call*, March 12, 1942.
50. Personal investigation; Granger, *op. cit.*, p. 544.
51. *Kansas City Call*, March 7, 21, 1941, March 20, April 10, 1942; letter to writer from Thomas A. Webster, executive secretary, Urban League of Kansas City, June 16, 1943.
52. Personal investigation.
53. *Ibid.*

CHAPTER X

1. J. J. Joseph, "The Mobilization of Manpower," *Science and Society*, VII (Winter 1943), 3; and Eleanor V. Kennedy, "Absenteeism in Commercial Shipyards, 1942," *Monthly Labor Review*, LVI (February 1943), 211-22.
2. Data from U. S. Census.
3. Charles Piez, *Report of the Director-General to the Board of Trustees of the United States Shipping Board, Emergency Fleet Corporation*, Washington, 1919, p. 86. These yards included all except approximately 6,000 of the industry's workers.
4. George E. Haynes, *The Negro at Work during the World War and during Reconstruction*, Washington, U. S. Department of Labor, 1921, pp. 58-61. Because of the definition of "skilled" used by Haynes is less exacting than that of the Bureau of Census, perfectly accurate comparisons cannot be made. It is quite clear, however, that Negroes made substantial gains in the industry during World War I.

5. W. E. Hotchkiss and H. R. Seager, "History of the Shipbuilding Labor Adjustment Board, 1917-1919," *Bulletin No. 283*, U. S. Bureau of Labor Statistics, Washington, 1921, pp. 7-14, 84-90.

6. See A. T. Helbing, *The Department of the American Federation of Labor*, Baltimore, 1931, pp. 40-67, for a discussion of the history and functions of the Metal Trades Department.

7. See above, pp. 23-26.

8. Hotchkiss and Seager, *op. cit.*, pp. 33, 35-36.

9. Data from U. S. Census.

10. Helbing, *op. cit.*, pp. 58-66.

11. Data from U. S. Census. The census was taken in March 1940, just before the war expansion program was inaugurated.

12. Data from study of the Bureau of Employment Security, Social Security Board, obtained through the courtesy of Dr. J. J. Joseph, Senior Administrative Officer, War Manpower Commission.

13. *Ibid.* The writer, of course, realizes that the data of the Bureau of Employment Security, the census, and the Haynes study are not strictly comparable. The differences revealed, however, are too large to be attributable solely to different methods of sampling.

14. Cf. Brotherhood of Boilermakers, *By-Laws Governing Auxiliary Lodges*, ed. 1942, with *idem.*, *Subordinate Lodge Constitution*, ed. 1938.

15. *Ibid.*, *Proceedings*, 1937, pp. 143, 332-34, 360-63.

16. *Boilermakers' Journal*, (1938), 145, 158.

17. *Crisis*, XLVI (September 1939), 273; AFL, *Proceedings*, 1940, p. 509; 1941, pp. 378-79; and personal investigation.

18. AFL, *Proceedings*, 1941, p. 479; Fair Employment Practice Committee, "Hearings, Birmingham, Ala.," typed MS, June 1942, I, 71.

19. FEPC, *op. cit.*, I, 54, 70, 73-75; III, 703 *et seq.*; Robert C. Weaver, "With the Negro's Help," *Atlantic Monthly*, CLXIX (June 1942), 800-01; personal investigation.

20. FEPC, *op. cit.*, II, 207 *et seq.*; *idem.*, "Findings and Directions Against Gulf Shipbuilding Corporation," press release, November 19, 1942. For more on Mobile, see below, pp. 225-28.

21. *Louisiana Weekly*, February 28, 1942; "The Negro's War," *Fortune*, XXV (June 1942), 160; and FEPC, *op. cit.*, III, 496 *et seq.*

22. FEPC, "Findings and Directions against Delta Shipbuilding Corporation and Local No. 37, International Boilermakers," press release, November, 1942.

23. *New York Times*, October 30, 31, 1942; *Louisiana Weekly*, November 21, 1943.

24. *Kansas City Call*, October 10, 1941.

25. *Ibid.*, March 21, July 24, 31, 1942; *Pittsburgh Courier*, May 8, 1943. The figures are from War Manpower Commission releases.

26. AFL, *Proceedings*, 1942, pp. 576-77; *Pittsburgh Courier*, October 31, November 7, 28, 1942; *PM*, January 31, 1943; and *New York*

Times, February 3, 1943. Also FEPC, *Summary, Findings, and Directions Relating to . . . Brotherhood of Boilermakers . . .* , December 9, 1943.

27. Personal investigation.

28. E. M. Stewart, "Handbook of American Trade Unions," *Bulletin No. 618*, U. S. Bureau of Labor Statistics, Washington, 1936, p. 184.

29. From the preamble of the IUMSWA constitution.

30. *Shipyard Worker*, September 10, 25, October 2, 1943; IUMSWA, *Proceedings*, 1941, pp. 124-25; 1942, pp. 4-5, 16-17, 22-23, 36-52, 237-39.

31. Personal investigation. Also Robert C. Weaver, "Racial Employment Trends in National Defense," *Phylon*, II (Fourth Quarter 1941), 357-58.

32. Personal investigation.

33. The story of Sun Ship is based primarily on personal investigation during June 1943, including interviews with Negro and white workers and company and union officials. See also, *Matter of Sun Shipbuilding*, 38 NLRB 234 NLRB press release, July 1943; *NLRB v. Sun Shipbuilding*, C.C.A., (Third Circuit), March 30, 1943; *Shipyard Worker*, August 16, September 13, 1940, April 17, October 9, 1942, April 2, and June-August issues, 1943; *Philadelphia Inquirer*, November 17, 1942; *Pittsburgh Courier*, July 10, 17, 31, 1943; and *Sun Ship Association v. National Labor Relations Board*, U. S. Dis. Ct., E. Dis. of Pa., August 3, 1943.

34. Personal investigation.

35. Edward S. Lewis, "Defense Problems of Baltimore Negroes," *Opportunity*, XIX (June 1941), 245; interview with industrial secretary, Baltimore Urban League, December 23, 1942; *Annual Report of the Baltimore Urban League for 1942*, pp. 11-12; *New York Times*, November 22, 1942; *Afro-American* (Baltimore), November 28, 1942; and *Shipyard Worker*, November 13, 17, 1942.

36. FEPC, "Hearings, Birmingham," pp. 300-45; *Matter of Alabama Dry Dock*, 5 NLRB 145, 7 NLRB 9, 39 NLRB 954, 40 NLRB 280; personal investigation; and above, pp. 216-17.

37. Most of the material on the Mobile riot is based upon personal investigation, verified by the following sources: FEPC, "Findings and Directions in the Case of the Alabama Dry Dock and Shipbuilding Corporation," press release, November 19, 1942; *New York Times*, May 26, June 12, 13, 1943; *PM*, June 1, 1943; *Mobile Register*, May 26-June 1, 1943; *Pittsburgh Courier*, June 5, 10, 1943; and *Shipyard Worker*, June 4, 1943.

38. Data contained in letter to writer from F. C. Pieper, CIO regional director, New Orleans, November 19, 1940; see also *Matter of Todd-Johnson*, 10 NLRB 629, 15 NLRB 973, 20 NLRB 615, 34 NLRB 736, 35 NLRB 1185.

39. *New York Times*, January 6, March 4, 1942.

40. Personal investigation; Weaver, "With the Negro's Help," p. 700.
41. Personal investigation, based, for the most part, on reports by former Hampton Institute students employed in the shipyard. See also *Richmond Times-Dispatch*, January 19, 1941; and *Pittsburgh Courier*, May 8, 1943. The writer has yet to see the picture of a Negro graduate of the Newport News apprentice school in its official publication, *Shipyard Bulletin*, in which pictures of the school's graduates are published.
42. Personal investigation. See also Weaver, "Racial Employment Trends . . . ," p. 350; and John Beecher, "Problems of Discrimination," *Science and Society* VII (Winter 1943), 37-44.
43. *National Labor Relations Board* v. *Newport News Shipbuilding Co.*, 308 U. S. 241 (1939); *Matter of Newport News Co.*, 8 NLRB 866, *Shipyard Bulletin*, June-July 1934, spring 1941; and personal investigation.
44. Data from War Manpower Commission, cited in *Pittsburgh Courier*, May 8, 1943; also *Shipyard Bulletin*, Spring 1941.
45. *Matter of North Carolina Shipbuilding Co.*, Case No. C-2500 NLRB, March 20, 1943; *Shipyard Worker*, March 26, April 30, 1943.

CHAPTER XI

1. C. L. Christenson, "Chicago Service Trades," in H. A. Millis, et al., *How Collective Bargaining Works*, New York, 1942, p. 868.
2. Almont Lindsey, *The Pullman Strike*, Chicago, 1942, p. 110.
3. Lloyd H. Bailer, "The Negro in the Automobile Industry," unpublished Ph.D. thesis, University of Michigan, 1943, pp. 318-25.
4. See Richard Sterner, *The Negro's Share*, New York, 1943, and John J. Carson, *Manpower for Victory*, New York, 1943, pp. 176-85.
5. Sumner H. Slichter, *Union Policies and Industrial Management*, Washington, 1941, pp. 374-77.
6. *Grovey* v. *Townsend*, 295 U. S. 45 (1934); *National Federation of Railway Workers* v. *National Mediation Board*, 110 F. (2d) 529; certiorari denied, 310 U. S. 628 (1940). See also the cases cited in Edward M. Dangel and Irene R. Shriber, *The Law of Labor Unions*, Boston, 1942, p. 169.
7. John V. Spielmans, "The Dilemma of the Closed Shop," *Journal of Political Economy*, LI (April 1943), 120. The writer is indebted to this article for clearing up some of the issues discussed in this section.
8. Reports of the Kansas City Urban League.
9. "Legislation on Labor Relations, 1941," *Monthly Labor Review*, LIV (January 1942), 80.
10. Letter from John J. Bennett, attorney-general of New York State, to Miss Freida Miller, Industrial Commissioner, New York State,

October 26, 1942; *Railway Mail Association* v. *Murphy*, N.Y. Sup. Ct., Albany Cy., November 4, 1943.

11. This statement of the case of the closed shop was suggested by my former colleague, Dr. Joseph Shister.

12. FEPC, "Summary and Findings in Matter of Chicago Plumbers' Union," press release, June 1942.

13. The writer is indebtd to Louis G. Silverberg, director of information, National Labor Relations Board, for a brief of the Board's cases discussed in the ensuing paragraphs.

14. *Matter of Alma Mills*, 24 NLRB 1; *Matter of Taylor-Colyuitt Co. and Mrs. Elma LaBoone*, 47 NLRB No. 22.

15. *Matter of Ozan Lumber Co.* 42 NLRB 1073.

16. *Matter of American Cyanamid Co.*, 37 NLRB 578; *Matter of Glomorgan Pipe & Foundry Co.*, Trial Examiner's report.

17. *Matter of Aetna Iron and Steel Co.*, 35 NLRB 36; *Matter of American Tobacco Co.*, 9 NLRB 579; *Matter of Union Envelope Co.*, 10 NLRB 1147; *Matter of Interstate Granite Corp.*, 11 NLRB 1046; *Matter of Utah Copper Co.*, 35 NLRB 1295; *Matter of Georgia Power Co.*, 32 NLRB 692.

18. *Matter of Sloss-Sheffield Steel & Iron Co.*, 14 NLRB 186; *Matter of Brashear Freight Lines, Inc.*, 13 NLRB 191.

19. *Matter of Crescent Bed Co., Inc.*, 29 NLRB 34.

20. See above, pp. 115-16.

21. *Laws of Pennsylvania*, Act No. 162, quoted in Spielmans, *op. cit.*, pp. 126, 133.

22. Carey McWilliams, *Brothers Under the Skin*, Boston, 1943.

23. Sterner, *loc, cit.*, L. G. W. Hayes, *The Negro Federal Government Worker*, Washington, 1941; "Employment of Negroes by the Federal Government," *Monthly Labor Review*, LVI (May 1943), 889-91; and Elmert W. Henderson, "Negroes in Government Employment," XXI (July 1943), 118-21, 142-43.

24. See above, pp. 29-33.

25. NLRB press release; personal investigation.

26. *AF of L Weekly News Service*, July 6, 1943.

27. See e.g., E. E. Johnson, "Public House No. I," *Opportunity* XX (November 1942), 324-26, 344-45; Lester B. Granger, "Negroes and War Production," *Survey Graphic*, XXI (November 1942), 543; *Pittsburgh Courier*, July 10, 1943.

28. *Pittsburgh Courier*, July 24, 1943.

SELECTED BIBLIOGRAPHY

BOOKS, PAMPHLETS, AND ARTICLES

ALLEN, RUTH A., *Chapters in the History of Organized Labor in Texas.* Austin, Texas, University of Texas Press, 1941. Publication No. 4143.

————, *The Great Southwest Strike.* Austin, Texas, University of Texas Press, 1942. Publication No. 4214.

American Federation of Labor, *Proceedings of Conventions,* 1881-1943.

ASHWORTH, JOHN H., *The Helper and American Trade Unions.* Baltimore, Johns Hopkins Press, 1915. Johns Hopkins University Studies in Historical and Political Science, XXXIII, No. 3.

Attorney General's Committee on Administrative Procedure, *Administrative Procedure in Government Agencies.* Senate Document No. 10, 77th Congress, 1st Session, 1941. Part 4, "Railway Labor: The National Railroad Adjustment Board and the National Mediation Board."

Automobile, Aircraft, and Agricultural Implement Workers, United, (UAW-CIO), *Proceedings of Annual Conventions,* 1938-42.

BAILER, LLOYD H., "The Negro Automobile Worker," *Journal of Political Economy,* LI (October, 1943), 415-28.

BARNES, CHARLES B., *The Longshoremen.* New York, Survey Associates, Inc., 1915.

BEECHER, JOHN, "Problems of Discrimination," *Science and Society,* VII (Winter 1943), 36-44.

BERQUIST, F. E., *et al., Economics Survey of the Coal Industry under Free Competition and Code Regulation,* mimeo., NRA, Division of Review, 1936. 2 vols.

"Bi-Racial Cooperation in the Placement of Negroes," *Monthly Labor Review,* LV (August 1942), 231-34.

BOGART, ERNEST L., "The Chicago Building Trades Dispute," *Political Science Quarterly,* XVI (March, June 1901), 114-92, 222-46.

Boilermakers, Iron Shipbuilders, Welders, and Helpers, Brotherhood of, *By-Laws Governing Auxiliary Lodges,* ed. 1942.

————, *Constitution,* ed. 1938.

————, *Proceedings of Sixteenth Consolidated Convention,* 1937.

BOYD, WILLIAM K., *The Story of Durham.* Durham, N. C., Duke University press, 1925.

BRACKETT, JEFFREY R., *The Negro in Maryland.* Baltimore, Johns Hopkins Press, 1888.

————, *Progress of the Colored People of Maryland.* Baltimore, Johns

Hopkins Press, 1890. Johns Hopkins University Studies in Historical and Political Science, VIII, Nos. 7-9.

BRANDT, LILIAN, "The Negroes in St. Louis," *Quarterly Publications of the American Statistical Association*, new series, VIII (March 1903), 203-68.

Bricklayers, Masons, and Plasterers' International Union, *Constitution*. ed. 1936.

BROOKS, ROBERT R. R., *As Steel Goes* . . . New Haven, Yale University Press, 1940.

BROWN, J. DOUGLAS, *et al.*, *Railway Labor Survey*. mimeo., Social Science Research Council, 1933.

CARSEL, WILFRED, *History of the Chicago Ladies' Garment Workers' Union*. Chicago, Normandie House, 1940.

CAYTON, H. R., and MITCHELL, G. S., *Black Workers and the New Unions*. Chapel Hill, N. C., University of North Carolina Press, 1939.

Chicago Commissoin on Race Relations, *The Negro in Chicago*. Chicago, University of Chicago Press, 1922.

Clothing Workers of America, Amalgamated, *Documentary History, 1936-1940*. 1940.

——, Laundry Workers Joint Board of Greater New York, *Facts About Your Union*. New York, The Joint Board, 1942 (?) Pamphlet No. 1.

COMMONS, JOHN R., "The Longshoremen of the Great Lakes," in the same author's *Labor and Administration*. New York, Macmillan Co., 1913, pp. 267-96.

Congress of Industrial Organizations, *Proceedings of Annual Constitutional Conventions, 1938-42*.

CORSON, JOHN J., *Manpower for Victory*. New York, Farrar & Rinehart, 1943.

CROSSLAND, W. A., *Industrial Conditions among Negroes in St. Louis*. St. Louis, Washington University press, 1915. Washington University Studies in Social Economics, I. No. 1.

DANIELS, JONATHAN, *A Southerner Discovers the South*. New York, Macmillan Co., 1938.

DAUGHERTY, C. R., DECHAZEAU, M. G., and STRATTON, S. S., *The Economics of the Iron and Steel Industry*. New York, McGraw-Hill Book Co., 1937. 2 vols.

DAVIS, HORACE B., *Labor and Steel*. New York, International Publishers, 1933.

DUBOIS, W. E. B. (ed.), *The Negro Artisan*. Atlanta, Atlanta University Press, 1902. Atlanta University Publications, No. 7.

——, *The Philadelphia Negro*. Philadelphia, University of Pennsylvania Press, 1899.

——, and DILL, A. G. (eds.), *The Negro American Artisan*. Atlanta, Atlanta University Press, 1912. Atlanta University Publications, No. 17.

DUNN, ROBERT W., *Labor and Automobiles*. New York, International Publishers, 1929.

"Earnings and Hours of Negro Workers in the Iron and Steel Industry, April 1938," *Monthly Labor Review*, LI (November 1940), 1139-49.

Electrical Workers, International Brotherhood of, *Proceedings of Conventions*, 1923, 1925, 1927, 1929, 1941.

"Employment of Negroes by the Federal Government," *Monthly Labor Review*, LVI (May 1943), 889-91.

Fair Employment Practice Committee, *Summary of Hearings, Findings and Directions in the Matter of the Alabama Shipbuilding and Dry Dock Corporation, Mobile, Alabama.* mimeo., 1942

————, *Summary of Hearings in Chicago.* mimeo., 1942.

————, *Summary of Hearings, Findings and Directions in the Matter of the Chicago Journeymen Plumbers' Union.* mimeo., 1942.

————, *Summary of Hearings, Findings and Directions in the Matter of the Delta Shipbuilding Corporation and Local #37, The International Boilermakers, Shipbuilders, Welders and Helpers of America.* mimeo., 1942.

————, *Summary of Hearings, Findings and Directions in the Matter of the Gulf Shipbuilding Corporation, Chickasaw, Alabama.* mimeo, 1942.

————, *Summary of Hearings, Findings and Directions in the Matter of the A. J. Honeycutt Company.* mimeo., 1942.

————, *Summary of Hearings in Los Angeles.* mimeo, 1941.

————, *Summary of Hearings, Findings and Directions in the Matter of the McAvoy Shipbuilding Corporation and the Savannah Building Trades Council.* mimeo., 1942.

————, *Summary of Hearings in New York.* mimeo., 1942.

————, *Summary of Hearings, Findings and Directions, in the Matter of the Vultee Aircraft, Inc., Nashville, Tennessee.* mimeo., 1942.

————, *Summary, Findings and Directions in re . . . [various railroads and railroad unions].* mimeo., 1943.

————, *Summary, Findings and Directions in re . . . [various west coast shipyards] and the International Brotherhood of Boilermakers. . . .* mimeo., 1943.

Federal Co-ordinator of Transportation, *Extent of Low Wages and Long Hours in the Railroad Industry.* Washington, 1936.

————, *Hours, Wages, and Working Conditions in Domestic Water Transportation.* Washington, 1936. 2 vols.

Federal Works Agency, United States Housing Authority, *Report on Employment of Negro Workers in Construction of USHA-Aided Projects.* mimeo., 1941.

FISHER, WALDO E., see Millis, Harry A., *et al.*

FRANCIS, ROBERT C., "Longshoremen in New Orleans," *Opportunity*, XIV (March 1936), 82-85, 93.

FRANKLIN, CHARLES L., *The Negro Labor Unionist of New York.* New York, Columbia University Press, 1936. Columbia University Studies in History, Economics, and Public Law, No. 420.

GARRISON, LLOYD K., "The National Railroad Adjustment Board: A

Unique Administrative Agency," *Yale Law Journal*, XLVI (February 1937), 567-98.

GRANGER, LESTER B., "Negroes and War Production," *Survey Graphic*, XXXI (November 1942), 469-71, 543-44.

GREEN, WILLIAM, *Labor and Democracy*. Princeton, N. J., Princeton University Press, 1939.

GREENE, L. J., and WOODSON, C. G., *The Negro Wage Earner*. Washington, Association for the Study of Negro Life and History, Inc., 1930.

HABER, WILLIAM, *Industrial Relations in the Building Industry*. Cambridge, Harvard University Press, 1930.

————, and WINTERS, ROBERT, see Millis, Harry A., *et al.*

"Half a Million Workers," *Fortune*, XXIII (March 1941), 96-98, 163-66.

HARBISON, FREDERICK H., see Millis, Harry A., *et al.*

HARPER, SAMUEL, "Negro Labor in Jacksonville," *Crisis*, XLIX (January 1942), 11, 13, 18.

HARRIS, HERBERT, *American Labor*. New Haven, Yale University Press, 1937.

HAYES, L. G. W., *The Negro Federal Government Worker*. Washington, The Graduate School, Howard University, 1941. Howard University Studies in the Social Sciences, III, No. 1.

HAYNES, GEORGE E., *The Negro at Work during the World War and the Reconstruction*. Washington, 1921. U. S. Department of Labor, Bureau of Negro Economics, Bulletin No. 2.

HELBING, ALBERT T., *The Departments of the American Federation of Labor*. Baltimore, Johns Hopkins Press, 1931. Johns Hopkins University Studies in Historical and Political Science, XLIX, No. 1.

HENDERSON, ELMER W., "Negroes in Government Employment," *Opportunity*, XXI (July 1943), 118-21, 142-43.

HENIG, HARRY, *The Brotherhood of Railway Clerks*. New York, Columbia University Press, 1937.

HINRICHS, A. F., *The United Mine Workers of America and the Non-union Coal Fields*. New York, Columbia University Press, 1923. Columbia University Studies in History, Economics, and Public Law, CX, No. 1.

HOLMES, S. J., *The Negro's Struggle for Survival*. Berkeley, Calif., University of California Press, 1937.

HOTCHKISS, W. E., and SEAGER, H. R., "History of the Shipbuilding Labor Adjustment Board, 1917-1919," *Bulletin No. 283*. U. S. Bureau of Labor Statistics, Washington, 1921.

HOTCHKISS, W. E., *et al.*, *Mechanization, Employment, and Output Per Man in Bituminous-Coal Mining*. Philadelphia, WPA, National Research Project, and U. S. Department of the Interior, Bureau of Mines, 1939. 2 vols.

Hotel & Restaurant Workers International Alliance, *Constitution*. ed. 1941.

————, *Proceedings of Conventions*, 1920, 1922, 1924, 1926, 1928, 1934, 1936, 1938, 1941.

"Hours and Earnings of Employees of Independent Leaf-Tobacco Dealers," *Monthly Labor Review*, LIII (July 1941), 215-20.

Interchurch World Movement, *Report on the Steel Strike of 1919*. New York, Harcourt, Brace, and Howe, 1920.

JACKSON, AUGUSTA V., "A New Deal for Tobacco Workers," *Crisis*, XLV (October 1938), 322-24, 330.

JOHNSON, CHARLES S., "Negroes in the Railway Industry," *Phylon*, (First and Second Quarters 1942), 5-14, 196-205.

———, "Negro Workers in Skilled Crafts and Construction," *Opportunity*, XI (October 1933), 296-300.

———, *Patterns of Negro Segregation*. New York, Harper & Brothers, 1943.

JOHNSON, E. E., "Public Houser No. 1," *Opportunity*, XX (November 1942), 324-26, 344-45.

JONES, H. E. (ed.), *Inquiry of the Attorney General's Committee on Administrative Procedure Relating to the National Railroad Adjustment Board: Historical Background and Growth of Machinery Set Up for the Handling of Railroad Labor Disputes. 1888-1940*. New York Eastern Committee for the National Railroad Adjustment Board, 1940.

JOSEPH, J. J., "The Mobilization of Manpower," *Science and Society*, VII (Winter 1943), 2-13.

KELLER, MARVEL, *Decasualization of Longshore Work in San Francisco*. Philadelphia, WPA, National Research Project, 1939.

KENNEDY, ELEANOR V., "Absenteeism in Commercial Shipyards, 1942," *Monthly Labor Review*, LVI (February 1943), 211-22.

KING, JOSEPH J., "The Durham Central Labor Union," *Southern Economic Journal*, V (July 1938), 55-70.

LANE, WINTHROP D., *Civil War in West Virginia*. New York, B. W. Huebsch, 1921.

Laundry Workers International Union, *Proceedings of Convention*, 1941.

"Legislation on Labor Relations, 1941," *Monthly Labor Review*, LIV (January 1942), 76-81.

LEWIS, EDWARD S., "Defense Problems of Baltimore Negroes," *Opportunity*, XIX (August 1941), 244-46, 253.

———, "We Tackled the Unions—and Won!" *Opportunity*, XVIII (May 1940), 138-40.

Locomotive Firemen and Enginemen, Brotherhood of, *Federal Legislation, Etc., Affecting Railway Employees*. Cleveland, The Brotherhood, 1940.

———, *Officers Reports to Conventions*, 1931, 1937, 1941.

———, *Proceedings of Conventions*, 1937, 1941.

———, *State Laws Relating to Full Crew, Qualification of Personnel, Train Lengths, Etc.* Cleveland, The Brotherhood, 1939.

Longshoremen's Association, International, *Constitution*. ed. 1940.

———, *Proceedings of Conventions*, 1935, 1939.

MAGDOFF, HARRY, SIEGAL, IRVING H., and DAVIS, MILTON B., *Production,*

Employment, and Productivity in 59 Manufacturing Industries. Philadelphia, WPA, National Research Project, 1939. 3 vols.

Maintenance of Way Employes, Brotherhood of, *Constitution.* ed. 1940.

———, *Proceedings of Conventions,* 1900, 1917, 1919, 1922, 1925, 1928, 1931, 1934, 1937, 1940, 1943.

MANNING, CAROLINE, "Hours and Earnings in Tobacco Stemmeries," *Bulletin No. 127,* U. S. Women's Bureau, Washington, 1934.

———, and Byrne, H. A., "The Effects on Women of Changing Conditions in the Cigar and Cigarette Industries," *Bulletin No. 100,* U. S. Women's Bureau, Washington, 1932.

Marine and Shipbuilding Workers, Industrial Union of, *Proceedings of Annual Conventions,* 1938-43.

Maritime Labor Board, *Report to the President and to the Congress.* Washington, 1940.

Massachusetts Commission on the Employment Problems of Negroes, Report of. Boston, 1942.

MATER, DAN H., "The Development and Operation of the Railroad Seniority System," *Journal of Business,* XIV (January 1941), 36-67.

———, "Effects of Seniority upon the Welfare of the Employee, the Employer, and the Public," *Journal of Business* XIV (October 1941), 384-418.

———, "Seniority Rights before the Courts," *Journal of Business,* XII (April 1939), 152-74.

Mayor's Committee on Unemployment, *Report on Dock Employment in New York City and Recommendations for its Regularization.* New York, 1916.

McISSAC, ARCHIBALD M., *The Order of Railroad Telegraphers.* Princeton, N. J., Princeton University Press, 1933.

McNATT, E. B., "The Amended Railway Labor Act," *Southern Economic Journal,* V (October 1938), 179-96.

McPHERSON, WILLIAM H., *Labor Relations in the Automobile Industry.* Washington, The Brookings Institution, 1940.

———, and LUCHEK, ANTHONY, see Millis, Harry A., *et al.*

McWILLIAMS, CAREY, *Brothers under the Skin,* Boston, Little, Brown & Co., 1943.

MILLIS, HARRY A., *et al., How Collective Bargaining Works.* New York, Twentieth Century Fund, 1942.

MITCHELL, BROADUS, *The Rise of the Cotton Mills of the South.* Baltimore, Johns Hopkins Press, 1920. Johns Hopkins University Studies in Historical and Political Science, XXXIX, No. 2.

MITCHELL, G. S., "The Negro in Southern Trade Unionism," *Southern Economic Journal,* II (January 1936), 26-33.

MORRIS, HOMER L., *The Plight of the Coal Miner,* Philadelphia, University of Pennsylvania Press, 1934.

MULCAIRE, MICHAEL A., *The International Brotherhood of Electrical Workers.* Washington, The University Press, 1923. Catholic University Studies in the Social Sciences, V.

National Labor Relations Board, *Annual Reports,* 1936-42.

National Mediation Board, *Annual Reports,* 1935-42.

"Negro Employment in Airframe Plants," *Monthly Labor Review,* LVI (May 1943), 888-89.

"The Negro's War," *Fortune,* XXV (June 1942), 77-80, 157-64.

NEINBURG, BERTHA, and BLAIR, B., "Factors Affecting Wages in Power Laundries," *Bulletin No. 143,* U. S. Women's Bureau, Washington, 1936.

New York State War Council, *How Management Can Integrate Negroes in War Industries.* New York, The Council, 1942.

NORTHRUP, HERBERT R., "The Negro and Unionism in the Birmingham, Ala., Iron and Steel Industry," *Southern Economic Journal,* X (July 1943), 27-40.

———, "The Negro and the United Mine Workers of America," *Southern Economic Journal,* IX (April 1943), 313-26.

———, "Negroes in a War Industry: the Case of Shipbuilding," *Journal of Business,* XVI (July 1943), 160-72.

———, "The New Orleans Longshoremen," *Political Science Quarterly,* LVII (December 1942), 526-44.

———, "Organized Labor and Negro Workers," *Journal of Political Economy,* LI (June 1943), 206-21.

———, "The Tobacco Workers International Union," *Quarterly Journal of Economics,* LVI (August 1942), 606-26.

———, "Unionization of Foremen," *Harvard Business Review,* XXI (summer 1943), 496-504.

———, "Unions, Restricted Clientele," *The Nation,* CLVII (August 14, 1943), 178-80.

OGG, ELIZABETH, *Longshoremen and their Homes.* New York, Greenwich House, 1939.

OVINGTON, MARY W., *Half a Man.* New York, Longmans Green & Co., 1911.

———, "The Negroes in the Trade Unions of New York," *The Annals,* XXVII (May 1906), 551-58.

Painters, Decorators, and Paperhangers, Brotherhood of, *Constitution.* ed. 1940, 1942.

———, *Proceedings of the Sixteenth General Assembly,* 1941.

———, *Reports of the General Officers to the Sixteenth General Assembly,* 1941.

PARKER, GLEN L., *The Coal Industry.* Washington, American Council on Public Affairs, 1940.

PERLMAN, JACOB, "Earnings of Negro Workers in Independent Tobacco Stemmeries in 1933 and 1935," *Monthly Labor Review,* XLIV (May 1937), 1153-72.

PHILLIPS, ULRICH B., *American Negro Slavery.* New York, D. Appleton-Century Co., 1918.

PINCHBECK, R. B., *The Virginia Negro Artisan and Tradesman.* Richmond, Va., William Byrd Press, 1926. University of Virginia Phelps-Stokes Fellowship Paper, No. 7.

Plasterers', Operative, and Cement Finishers' International Association, *Constitution*, ed. 1941.

———, *Proceedings of Convention*, 1941.

QUILLIN, F. U., *The Color Line in Ohio*. Ann Arbor, Mich., University of Michigan Press, 1913. University of Michigan Historical Studies, III.

Railroad Retirement Board, *Compensation and Service, Railroad Employees, 1940*. Washington, 1941.

Railroad Trainmen, Brotherhood of, *Annual Reports of the President*, 1935-41.

———, *Proceedings of Conventions*, 1931, 1935, 1939.

Railway Carmen of America, Brotherhood, *Constitution*. ed. 1941.

———, *Proceedings of Conventions*, 1905, 1909, 1921, 1929, 1935, 1941.

Railway and Steamship Clerks, Freight Handlers, Express and Station Employes, Brotherhood of, *Constitution*, ed. 1939.

———, *Officers Reports to Conventions*, 1935, 1939, 1943.

———, *Proceedings of Conventions*, 1922, 1925, 1928, 1931, 1935, 1939, 1943.

———, *Regulations for the Government of Lodges of the Auxiliary*, ed. 1940.

RANDOLPH, A. PHILIP, *The Case of the Porters Against the Conductors Bill*. mimeo., 1940 (?).

———, "The Crisis of the Negro Railroad Worker," *American Federationist*, XLVI (August 1939), 807-21.

REID, IRA DEA., *Negro Membership in American Labor Unions*. New York, National Urban League, 1930.

ROBERT, JOSEPH C., *The Tobacco Kingdom*. Durham, N. C., Duke University Press, 1938.

ROBINSON, JESSE, *The Amalgamated Association of Iron, Steel and Tin Workers*. Baltimore, Johns Hopkins Press, 1920. Johns Hopkins University Studies in Historical and Political Science, XXXVIII, No. 2.

ROSS, ARTHUR M., "The Negro Worker in the Depression," *Social Forces*, XVIII (May 1940), 550-59.

ROUNTREE, G. M., *The Railway Worker*. Toronto, Oxford University Press, 1936.

RYAN, FREDERICK, L., *The Rehabilitation of Oklahoma Coal Mining Communities*. Norman, Okla., University of Oklahoma Press, 1935.

SANFORD, EDWARD P., "Wage Rates and Hours of Labor in the Building Trades," *Monthly Labor Review*, XIV (August 1937), 281-300.

SCHOEN, HAROLD, "The Free Negro in the Republic of Texas," *Southwestern Historical Quarterly*, XXXIX (April 1936), 292-308; XL (July, October 1936, January, April 1937), 26-34, 85-113, 169-99, 267-89; XLI (July 1937), 83-108.

SEIDMAN, JOEL, *The Needle Trades*. New York, Farrar & Rinehart, 1942.

SHORTER, C. A., "Philadelphia's Employers, Unions, and Negro Workers," *Opportunity*, XX (January 1942), 4-7.

SHUGG, ROGER W., "The New Orleans General Strike of 1892," *Louisiana Historical Quarterly*, XXI (April 1938), 547-60.

————, *Origins of Class Struggle in Louisiana*. University, La., Louisiana State University Press, 1939.

Sleeping Car Porters, Brotherhood of, *Proceedings of Conference of Colored Locomotive Firemen*, 1941.

————, *Proceedings of Conference of Negro Railroad Workers*, 1939.

————, *Proceedings of Conventions*, 1938, 1940, 1942.

SLICHTER, SUMNER H., *Union Policies and Industrial Management*. Washington, The Brookings Institution, 1941.

SNOWDEN, YATES, *Notes on Labor Organizations in South Carolina, 1742-1861*. Columbia, S. C., The University Press, 1914. Bulletin of the University of South Carolina, XXXVIII, No. 4.

SPENCER, WILLIAM H., *The National Railroad Adjustment Board*. Chicago, University of Chicago Press, 1938.

SPERO, STERLING D., and HARRIS, ABRAM L., *The Black Worker*. New York, Columbia University Press, 1931.

SPIELMANS, JOHN V., "The Dilemma of the Closed Shop," *Journal of Political Economy*, LI (April 1943), 113-34.

STARNES, GEORGE T., and HAMM, J. E., *Some Phases of Labor Relations in Virginia*. New York, D. Appleton-Century Co., 1934.

Steelworkers of America, United, *Proceedings of First Constitutional Convention*, 1942.

Steel Workers Organizing Committee, *Proceedings of Wage and Policy Conventions*, 1937, 1940.

STERN, BORIS, "Cargo Handling and Longshore Labor Conditions," *Bulletin No. 550*, U. S. Bureau of Labor Statistics, Washington, 1932.

STERNER, RICHARD, *The Negro's Share*. New York, Harper & Brothers, 1943.

STEWART, ESTELLE M., "Handbook of American Trade-Unions," *Bulletin No. 618*, U. S. Bureau of Labor Statistics, Washington, 1936.

STRONG, EARL D., *The Amalgamated Clothing Workers of America*. Grinnell, Ia., Herald-Register Publishing Co., 1940.

SWANSTROM, EDWARD E., *The Waterfront Labor Problem*. New York, Fordham University Press, 1938.

Tobacco Workers International Union, *Constitution*. eds. 1932, 1941.

————, *Proceedings of Conventions*, 1939, 1940.

Transport Service Employees of America, United, *Proceedings of Conventions*, 1940, 1942.

————, *Protest of Conduct and Result of Election, Case No. R-774, Florida East Coast Maintenance of Way Workers*, mimeo., 1941.

United States Board of Mediation, *Annual Reports*, 1931-32.

United States Bureau of Census, *Decennial Census of the United States: Population*. 1890-1940. selected vols.

United States Bureau of Internal Revenue, "Production of Cigarettes, Cigars, Smoking and Chewing Tobacco, and Snuff, 1880-1939," press release No. 0-14, 1940.

United States Congress, *Report of the Industrial Commission.* Washington, 1901. 20 vols.

United States Department of Labor, Wage and Hour Division, *A Memorandum on Recent Economic Developments in the Railroad Carrier Industry.* mimeo., 1942.

———, *Redcaps in Railway Terminals under the Fair Labor Standards Act of 1938.* mimeo., 1942.

———, *The Tobacco Industry,* mimeo., 1941.

———, *Wages, Hours, and Working Conditions of Redcaps in Western Railway Terminals,* mimeo., 1941.

United States Senate, 76th Congress, 1st Session, *Report of the Committee on Education and Labor: Violation of Free Speech and the Rights of Labor,* No. 6, part 2, "Private Police Systems, Harlan County, Ky." Washington, 1939.

Urban League of Kansas City, *The Negro Worker of Kansas City,* mimeo., 1940.

———, *Negro Workers, Garment Industries and Employees,* mimeo., 1941.

VALIEN, PRESTON, "The Brotherhood of Sleeping Car Porters," *Phylon,* I (Third Quarter 1940), 224-38.

Virginia Writers' Project, *The Negro in Virginia.* New York, Hastings House, 1940.

WALKER, ARNOLD B., "St. Louis' Employers, Unions, and Negro Workers," *Opportunity,* XIX (November 1941), 336-38, 348.

WEAVER, ROBERT C., "Detroit and Negro Skill," *Phylon,* IV (Second Quarter 1943), 131-43.

———, "Racial Employment Trends in National Defense," *Phylon,* II (Fourth Quarter 1941), 337-58; III (First Quarter 1942), 22-30.

———, "Racial Policy in Public Housing," *Phylon,* I (Second Quarter 1940), 149-57.

———, "With the Negro's Help," *Atlantic Monthly,* CLXIX (June 1942), 696-707.

———, et al., *Urban Negro Worker in the United States, 1925-1936.* Washington, 1939. 2 vols. U. S. Department of the Interior, Office of the Advisor on Negro Affairs.

WEBSTER, THOMAS A., "Employers, Unions, and Negro Workers," *Opportunity,* XIX (October 1941), 295-97.

WEISS, HARRY, and ARNOW, PHILIP. "Recent Transition of Redcaps from Tip to Wage Status," *American Labor Legislation Review.* XXXII (September 1942), 134-43.

WESLEY, CHARLES H., *Negro Labor in the United States.* New York, Vanguard Press, 1927.

WHITE, HORACE A., "Who Owns the Negro Churches?" *Christian Century,* LV (February 9, 1938), 176-77.

WHITNEY, N. R., *Jurisdiction in American Building-Trades Unions*. Baltimore, Johns Hopkins Press, 1914. Johns Hopkins University Studies in Historical and Political Science, XXXII, No. 1.

WOLF, HARRY D., see Millis, Harry A., *et al.*

WOLFE, F. E., *Admission to American Trade Unions*. Baltimore, Johns Hopkins Press, 1912. Johns Hopkins University Studies in Historical and Political Science, XXX, No. 5.

WOLMAN, LEO, *Ebb and Flow in Trade Unionism*. New York, National Bureau of Economic Research, 1936. Publication No. 30.

WOOFTER, T. J., Jr., *A Study of the Economic Status of the Negro*, mimeo., Institute for Research in the Social Sciences, University of North Carolina, 1930.

WRIGHT, R. R., Jr., *The Negro in Pennsylvania*. Philadelphia. A.M.E. Book Concern, 1911.

YOUNG, W. H., *et al*, "Mechanical Mining," a reprint from *Coal Age*, February 1942.

COURT CASES

Batt Scott v. *J. Harvey Netter, et al.*, Civ. Dis. Ct., Parish of Orleans, Louisiana, March 2, 1942.

Beal v. *Missouri Pac. R. R. Corp.*, 312 U.S. 45 (1941).

Brotherhood of R. & S. Clerks v. *United Transport Service Employees*, U.S.C.C.A., D.C. Circuit, August 2, 1943; U.S. Sup. Ct., December 6, 1943.

Brotherhood of R. R. Trainmen v. *National Mediation Board*, 88 F. (2d) 757 (1936).

Bruce v. *Atlantic Coast Line Railway, et al.*, Virginia State Court, Richmond, Va., September 12, 1932.

Estes v. *Union Terminal Co.*, 89 F. (2d.) 768 (1937).

Grovey v. *Townsend*, 295 U.S. 45 (1934).

Local No. 231, International Longshoremen's Association v. *Ross*, 180 La. 293, 156 So. 357 (1934).

Loewe v. *Lawlor*, 208 U.S. 274 (1908).

National Federation of Railway Workers v. *National Mediation Board*, 110 F. (2d.) 529; certiorari denied, 310 U.S. 628 (1940).

National Labor Relations Board v. *Newport News Shipbuilding and Dry Dock Co.*, 308 U.S. 241 (1939).

National Labor Relations Board v. *Sun Shipbuilding and Dry Dock Co.*, U.S.C.C.A., (Third Circuit), March 30, 1943.

Nord v. *Griffen*, 86 F. (2d.) 281; certiorari denied, 300 U.S. 673 (1937).

Railway Mail Association v. *Murphy*, N.Y. Sup. Ct., Albany Cy., November 4, 1943.

Steele v. *Louisville & Nashville Railroad Co., et al.*, Cir. Ct., 10th Judicial Circuit, Alabama. In equity, No. 52,279 (1943).

Teague v. *Brotherhood of Locomotive Firemen*, 127 F. (2d.) 53 (1942).

Tunstall v. *Brotherhood of Locomotive Firemen,* U.S. Dis. Ct., E. Dis. Va., Civil Action No. 210 (1943).

Tobacco Workers International Union v. *Weyler, et al.,* 280 Ky. 365, 132 S.W. (2d.) 754 (1940).

Tobacco Workers International Union v. *E. Lewis Evans, et al.,* U.S. Dis. Ct., W. Dis. Ky. April 8, 1940; amended, May 2, 1940.

United Transport Service Employees of America v. *National Mediation Board,* U.S. Dis. Ct., D.C., July 1942. (St. Paul Union Terminal Co. case.)

United Transport Service Employees of America v. *National Mediation Board,* U.S. Dis. Ct., D.C., Feb., 1943. (Florida East Coast Railway case.)

Williams v. *Jacksonville Terminal Co.* and *Pickett* v. *Union Terminal Co.,* 315 U.S. 386 (1942)

INTERSTATE COMMERCE COMMISSION CASES

A. Johnson, et al., v. *A.T. & S.F. Railway, et al.,* 255 ICC 519.

Matter of Regulations Concerning Class of Employees and Subordinate Officials to be Included within Term "Employee" under the Railway Labor Act, 229 ICC 410.

Stopher v. *Cincinnati Union Terminal Co., Inc.,* 246 ICC 41.

NATIONAL LABOR RELATIONS BOARD CASES

Matter of Aetna Iron and Steel Co., 35 NLRB 36.

Matter of Alma Mills, 24 NLRB 1.

Matter of Aluminum Line, et al., 8 NLRB 1325; 9 NLRB 72.

Matter of American Cyanamid Co., 37 NLRB 578.

Matter of American Tobacco Co., Reidsville Branch, 2 NLRB 193.

Matter of American Tobacco Co., Richmond Smoking Branch, 9 NLRB 579; 10 NLRB 1171.

Matter of Bethlehem-Alameda Shipyard Inc., Cases Nos. R-5693-4.

Matter of Crescent Bed Co., Inc., 29 NLRB 34.

Matter of Glamorgan Pipe & Foundry Co., Trial Examiner's Report.

Matter of Georgia Power Co., 32 NLRB 692.

Matter of Interstate Granite Co., 11 NLRB 1046.

Matter of Mobile Steamship Association, et al., 8 NLRB 1297; 9 NLRB 60.

Matter of Newport News Shipbuilding and Dry Dock Co., 8 NLRB 866.

Matter of Ozan Lumber Co., 42 NLRB 1073.

Matter of R. J. Reynolds Co., December 11, 1943.

Matter of Sloss-Sheffield Steel & Iron Co., 14 NLRB 186.

Matter of Sun Shipbuilding and Dry Dock Co., 38 NLRB 234; Case No. 4-R-1085, June 30, 1943.

Matter of Taylor-Colquitt Co. and Mrs. Elma LaBoone, 47 NLRB No. 212.

Matter of Union Envelope Co., 10 NLRB 1147.
Matter of Utah Copper Co., 35 NLRB 1295.

NATIONAL MEDIATION BOARD CASES

Matter of A.T. & Sante Fe Railway Co., Dining Car Stewards, Etc., Case No. R-528.
Matter of Chicago and North Western Railway Co., Chefs and Cooks, Case No. R-475.
Matter of Florida East Coast Railway Co. Maintenance of Way Workers, Case No. R-774.
Matter of Louisville & Nashville Railroad Co., Train Porters, Case No. R-1050.
Matter of New York Central System, Lines West, Dining Car Employees, Case No. R-529.
Matter of Pullman Co., Laundry Employees, Case No. R-1044.
Matter of Union Pacific System, Chefs, Cooks, and Waiters, Case No. R-21; Case No. R-46.

NATIONAL RAILROAD ADJUSTMENT BOARD CASES

Brotherhood of Railroad Trainmen v. A.T. & Sante Fe Railway, First Division, Award No. 6640.
Brotherhood of Railroad Trainmen v. Southern Pacific Railroad, Third Division, Award No. 493.
Order of Sleeping Car Conductors v. Pullman Co., Third Division, Awards No. 779, 1461-65, 1883.

UNPUBLISHED WORKS

ANSON, CHARLES P., "A History of the Labor Movement in West Virginia." Ph.D. thesis, University of North Carolina, 1940.
BAILER, LLOYD H., "The Negro Automobile Worker." Report made to the Carnegie Corporation of New York's Negro in America survey, 1940.
———, "The Negro in the Automobile Industry." Ph.D. thesis, University of Michigan, 1943.
BRAZEAL, B. R., "The Brotherhood of Sleeping Car Porters." Ph.D. thesis, Columbia University, 1942.
BROWN, J. DOUGLAS, "The History and Problems of Collective Bargaining by Railway Maintenance of Way Employees." Ph.D. thesis, Princeton University, 1927.
"Complaint of the Association of Colored Railway Trainmen and Locomotive Firemen, Inc., Against the Louisiana & Arkansas Railway." Case filed before the Fair Employment Practice Committee, June 3, 1942.
EVANS, MERCER G., "The History of the Organized Labor Movement in Georgia." Ph.D. thesis, University of Chicago, 1929.

Fair Employment Practice Committee, "Hearings, Birmingham, Alabama." 1942. 3 vols. MS in Committee's Washington, D.C., office.
————, "Hearings in re . . . [discrimination against Negroes on certain railroads." 1943. 4 vols. MS in Committee's office.
————, "Hearings in re . . . [certain west coast shipyards] and the International Brotherhood of Boilermakers." 1943. 4 vols. MS in Committee's office.
Federal Co-ordinator of Transportation, "Proposed Report on Alleged Discrimination Against Colored Railway Employees of the Illinois Central System." 1934. MS in U.S. Archives, Washington, D.C.
FRANCIS, ROBERT C., "A History of Labor in the San Francisco Waterfront." Ph.D. thesis, University of California, 1934.
JAMES, L. H., "Policies of Organized Labor in Relation to Negro Workers in Atlanta, 1869-1937." M.A. thesis, Atlanta University, 1937.
JOHNSON, CHARLES S., "The Tobacco Worker." NRA, Division of Review, Industrial Studies Section, 1935. 2 vols. MS in U.S. Archives, Washington, D.C.
JONES, ALVIN H., "The Labor Situation on the New Orleans Waterfront." Report made to the Carnegie Corporation of New York's Negro in America survey, 1940.
LAING, J. T., "The Negro Miner in West Virginia." Ph.D. thesis, Ohio State University, 1933.
LIEBES, RICHARD A., "Longshore Labor Relations on the Pacific Coast, 1934-1942." Ph.D. thesis, University of California, 1942.
NORGREN, PAUL H., "Displacement and Exclusion in the Skilled Trades." Report to the Carnegie Corporation of New York's Negro in America survey, 1940.
————, "The Negro Coal Mine Worker." Report to the Carnegie Corporation of New York's Negro in America survey, 1940.
————, and NORTHRUP, HERBERT R., "Negroes in the Iron and Steel Industry." Report to the Carnegie Corporation of New York's Negro in America survey, 1940.
North Carolina Employment Service, "Survey of Tobacco Stemmeries." 1939. MS in writer's possession.
PEARCE, ARTHUR RAYMOND, "The Rise and Decline of Labor In New Orleans." M.A. thesis, Tulane University, 1938.
RICE, JOHN DONALD, "The Negro Tobacco Workers and His Union in Durham, North Carolina." M.A. thesis, University of North Carolina, 1941.
SOLOMON, THOMAS R., "Participation of Negroes in Detroit Elections." Ph.D. thesis, University of Michigan, 1939.
TROXELL, JOHN P., "Labor in the Tobacco Industry." Ph.D. thesis, University of Wisconsin, 1931.
————, "The TWIU under the NRA." 1935. MS in writer's possession.
WARREN, SAMUEL E., "The Negro in the American Labor Movement." Ph.D. thesis, University of Wisconsin, 1941.

INDEX